Excel® Data Analysis

Your visual blueprint™ for creating and analyzing data, charts, and PivotTables, 3rd Edition

by Denise Etheridge

WILEY

Wiley Publishing, Inc.

Excel® Data Analysis: Your visual blueprint™ for creating and analyzing data, charts, and PivotTables, 3rd Edition

Published by
Wiley Publishing, Inc.
10475 Crosspoint Boulevard
Indianapolis, IN 46256

www.wiley.com

Published simultaneously in Canada

Copyright © 2010 by Wiley Publishing, Inc., Indianapolis, Indiana

No part of this publication may be reproduced, stored in a retrieval system or transmitted in any form or by any means, electronic, mechanical, photocopying, recording, scanning or otherwise, except as permitted under Sections 107 or 108 of the 1976 United States Copyright Act, without either the prior written permission of the Publisher, or authorization through payment of the appropriate per-copy fee to the Copyright Clearance Center, 222 Rosewood Drive, Danvers, MA 01923, (978) 750-8400, fax (978) 646-8600. Requests to the Publisher for permission should be addressed to the Permissions Department, John Wiley & Sons, Inc., 111 River Street, Hoboken, NJ 07030, 201-748-6011, fax 201-748-6008, or online at www.wiley.com/go/permissions.

Library of Congress Control Number: 2010928469

ISBN: 978-0-470-59160-4

Manufactured in the United States of America

10 9 8 7 6 5 4 3 2 1

Trademark Acknowledgments

Wiley, the Wiley Publishing logo, Visual, the Visual logo, Visual Blueprint, Read Less - Learn More and related trade dress are trademarks or registered trademarks of John Wiley & Sons, Inc. and/or its affiliates. Excel is a registered trademark of Microsoft Corporation in the United States and/or other countries. All other trademarks are the property of their respective owners. Wiley Publishing, Inc. is not associated with any product or vendor mentioned in this book.

Contact Us

For general information on our other products and services please contact our Customer Care Department within the U.S. at 877-762-2974, outside the U.S. at 317-572-3993 or fax 317-572-4002.

For technical support please visit www.wiley.com/techsupport.

The Metropolitan Cathedral of Brasilia

A vision of architect Oscar Niemeyer, the breathtaking Metropolitan Cathedral of Brasilia reflects the innovative architecture and design that characterize this young and original city. Sweeping skyward, the Cathedral's sixteen gracefully curved columns symbolize hands lifted in prayer, while the unique bell tower replicates a candelabra. Begun in 1959, the Cathedral was designated a Historic Monument in 1967, thereby accessing public funds for its completion. It was dedicated in 1970.

Learn more about Brasilia's unusual history and architecture in *Frommer's Brazil, 5th Edition* (ISBN 978-0-470-59151-2), available wherever books are sold or at www.Frommers.com.

Disclaimer

In order to get this information to you in a timely manner, this book was based on a pre-release version of Microsoft Office 2010. There may be some minor changes between the screenshots in this book and what you see on your desktop. As always, Microsoft has the final word on how programs look and function; if you have any questions or see any discrepancies, consult the online help for further information about the software.

WILEY

Sales

Contact Wiley
at (877) 762-2974
or (317) 572-4002.

Credits

Executive Editor
Jody Lefevere

Project Editor
Jade L. Williams

Technical Editor
Namir Shammas

Copy Editor
Lauren Kennedy

Editorial Director
Robyn Siesky

Business Manager
Amy Knies

Senior Marketing Manager
Sandy Smith

Vice President and Executive Group Publisher
Richard Swadley

Vice President and Executive Publisher
Barry Pruett

Project Coordinator
Lynsey Stanford

Graphics and Production Specialists
Carrie Cesavice
Jennifer Mayberry

Quality Control Technician
Lauren Mandelbaum

Proofreading
Sossity R. Smith

Indexing
Johnna VanHoose Dinse

Media Development Project Manager
Laura Moss

Media Development Assistant Project Manager
Jenny Swisher

Media Development Associate Producer
Shawn Patrick

Screen Artist
Ana Carrillo
Jill A. Proll

Illustrator
Cheryl Grubbs

Special Help
Microsoft Corporation, Inc.

About the Author

Denise Etheridge is a certified public accountant as well as the president and founder of Baycon Group, Inc. She publishes Web sites and authors' computer related books. You can visit www.baycongroup.com to view her online tutorials.

Author's Acknowledgments

Writing this book was an absolute privilege. I would like to thank all of the people who assisted me. I give special thanks to Jody Lefevere, for allowing me this privilege; Jade Williams, for keeping things on track; Namir Shammas, for his technical review; and Lauren Kennedy, for her copy review.

Dedication

This book is dedicated to my brother, Erskine Etheridge.

How to Use This Visual Blueprint Book

Who This Book Is For

This book is for advanced computer users who want to take their knowledge of this particular technology or software application to the next level.

The Conventions in This Book

① Steps

This book uses a step-by-step format to guide you easily through each task. Numbered steps are actions you must do; bulleted steps clarify a point, step, or optional feature; and indented steps give you the result.

② Notes

Notes give additional information — special conditions that may occur during an operation, a situation that you want to avoid, or a cross reference to a related area of the book.

③ Icons and Buttons

Icons and buttons show you exactly what you need to click to perform a step.

④ Extra or Apply It

An Extra section provides additional information about the preceding task — insider information and tips for ease and efficiency. An Apply It section takes the code from the preceding task one step further and allows you to take full advantage of it.

⑤ Bold

Bold type shows text or numbers you must type.

⑥ Italics

Italic type introduces and defines a new term.

⑦ Courier Font

`Courier font` indicates the use of scripting language code such as statements, operators, or functions, and code such as objects, methods, or properties.

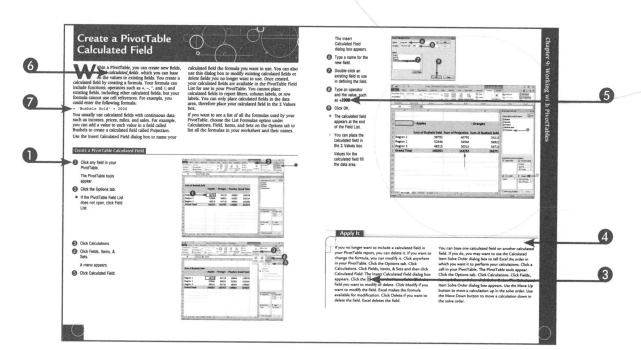

TABLE OF CONTENTS

TABLE OF CONTENTS

9 WORKING WITH PIVOTTABLES 168

10 CHARTING DATA. 186

TABLE OF CONTENTS

TABLE OF CONTENTS

Introducing Data Analysis with Excel

This book is about using Microsoft Excel to analyze your data. Microsoft Excel is an electronic worksheet you can use to perform mathematical, financial, and statistical calculations; create charts; analyze your data with a PivotTable; maintain lists; and much more. Excel can help you locate data, find trends in your data, and present your data to others.

Each Excel file is a workbook. Each workbook can have multiple worksheets. Worksheets are made up of rows and columns of cells you can use to enter information.

The most powerful feature in Excel is its ability to calculate. When you enter a formula into Excel, Excel can automatically calculate the result, and when you make changes to your worksheet, Excel can automatically recalculate.

You can also use Excel to create charts. A chart is a graphical representation of your data. When using Excel, you can choose from several types of charts, including Column, Line, Pie, Bar, Area, and Scatter. Charts can make your data easier to read, easier to understand, and easier to compare.

A *PivotTable* is an interactive table you can use to analyze data. A PivotTable gives you an easy way to summarize and view large amounts of data. Using a PivotTable, you can rotate rows and columns of data so you can see different views of your data easily. You can use Excel to create PivotTables.

Excel provides a way for you to create and maintain lists. A list is a series of rows and columns. Each column has a label — for example, name, address, telephone number. Each row under a column has information pertaining to the column label. You can sort, filter, and analyze your lists in Excel.

Introducing Data Analysis with Excel

Open a New Workbook

1 Click the File tab.

A menu appears.

2 Click New.

3 Double-click Blank workbook.

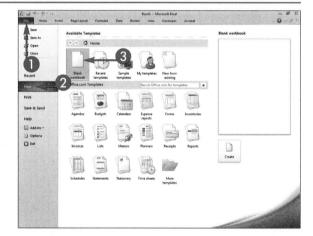

● Excel opens a new workbook.

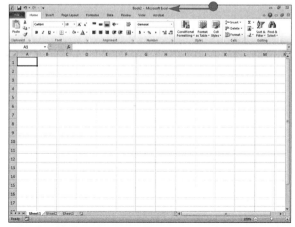

Tour the Excel Window

When you open an Excel workbook, Excel presents the Excel window. You use the window to create Excel documents. Your window should be similar to the one in the illustration.

It may not be exactly the same because Excel renders windows based on the size of your screen, the resolution to which your screen is set, and the other screen display options.

View of the Excel Window

Ⓐ FILE TAB

Click the File tab to open, save, print, prepare, send, publish, and close files.

Ⓑ QUICK ACCESS TOOLBAR

Place commands you use often on the Quick Access Toolbar.

Ⓒ TABS

Click a tab to view Ribbon options.

Ⓓ RIBBON

Click the buttons in the Ribbon to execute Excel commands.

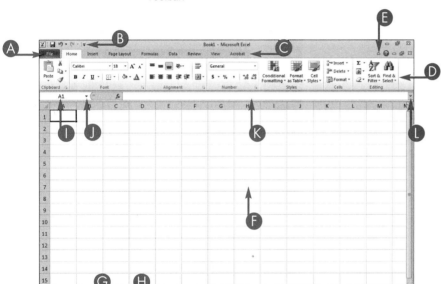

Ⓔ Minimize the Ribbon

Click the chevron to Hide the Ribbon so that only tabs show.

Ⓕ CELL

Enter data into cells.

Ⓖ SHEETS

Enter data into each sheet of a workbook.

Ⓗ INSERT SHEET

Click this button to insert a new sheet.

Ⓘ NAME BOX

Displays the name of the active cell.

Ⓙ DROP-DOWN LIST

Displays a list of defined range names.

Ⓚ FORMULA BAR

Use the formula bar to enter and edit data.

Ⓛ EXPAND FORMULA BAR

Click the chevron to make the formula bar larger.

Explore the Ribbon

You use commands to tell a program what you want it to do. In Excel, you use the Ribbon to issue commands. The Ribbon consists of several tabs. Tabs group related commands together. The most frequently used commands are on the Home tab, the commands you use to insert objects into a worksheet are on the Insert tab, the commands you use to layout your document are on the Page Layout tab and so on.

Within a tab, related commands are organized into groups. For example, on the Home tab, commands relating to cutting, copying, and pasting are in the Clipboard group. Commands, related changing the size, color, or style of a font, are in the Font group. Some groups have a launcher. When you click the launcher, a menu or dialog box appears. You can use the menu or dialog box to access additional commands.

Ribbon Commands

The Ribbon contains commands organized in three components: tabs, groups, and commands. Tabs appear across the top of the Ribbon and contain groups of related commands. Groups organize related commands with each group name appearing below the group on the Ribbon. Note some groups have a Dialog Box Launcher button in the lower-right corner. Commands appear within each group.

Ⓐ Tabs

Tabs appear across the top of the Ribbon and contain groups of related commands. The File tab provides access to the Backstage view in all Office programs. In Backstage view, you can open, save, and print worksheets.

Ⓑ Groups

Commands are arranged into groups with the group names shown at the bottom of the tab.

Ⓒ Dialog Box Launcher

This button appears in the lower-right corner of many groups on the Ribbon. Clicking this button opens a dialog box, menu or task pane that provides more options.

Contextual Tabs

Some tabs only appear when needed. These tabs are called contextual tabs. For example, the tabs that you use to edit a chart only appear when you are modifying a chart.

Galleries

Galleries provide you with a list of choices. As you hover over each gallery choice, Excel provides you with a live preview of how your document will appear if you choose that option. For example, in Excel you can apply a style to a table. When you hover over a style in the Table Styles gallery, Excel provides you with a live preview of how the style will appear if you choose it.

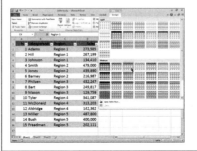

Using the Mini Toolbar and Context Menu

Excel makes some commands readily available via the Mini toolbar and the context menu. When you right-click in Excel, the Mini toolbar and a context menu appear. Most often, the Mini toolbar appears first and the context menu appears under it. What appears on the Mini toolbar and context menu depends upon what you are working on at the time you right-click. For example, if you right-click while you have a range of cells selected, options related to modifying cells appear. If you right-click while you are modifying a chart, options related to modifying a chart appear. In general, you can use the Mini toolbar to perform popular formatting commands. You can use the context menu to perform popular commands related to the object on which you are working.

Using the Mini Toolbar and Context Menu

① Right-click.

The Mini toolbar and context menu appear.

② Click a button or menu option to select a command.

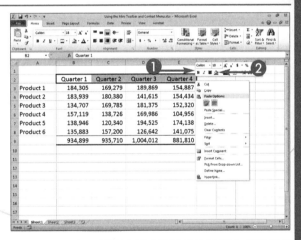

Excel executes the command.

● In this example, Excel applies a fill.

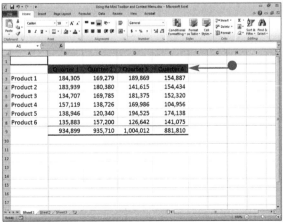

Select Options on the Status Bar

The status bar appears at the bottom of the Excel window. It displays the status of several options. For example, the Zoom button appears on the status bar. It displays the current zoom level. You can click the Zoom button to open the Zoom dialog box and manually set the zoom level. The Zoom slider also appears in the status bar. You can drag it to the right to zoom in, thereby making the contents of your worksheet larger, or drag it to the left to zoom out, thereby making the contents of your worksheet smaller. When you right-click the status bar, you can select which options appear on it. Several options, such as the Zoom slider, Zoom button, and Macro Recorder, appear by default.

Extra

You can automate the tasks you perform in Excel by recording a macro. By default, the Macro Recorder button ( ) appears on the status bar. Click the Macro Recorder button to begin recording a macro. The Record Macro dialog box appears. Fill in the fields and then perform the steps you want to automate. When you are finished performing the steps, click the Macro Recorder button again. See Chapter 14 for detailed information.

Select Options on the Status Bar

① Right-click the status bar.

A list of options appears. Selected options have a check mark. Deselected options do not have a check mark.

② Click options to select or deselect them (changes to ✔ or ✔ changes).

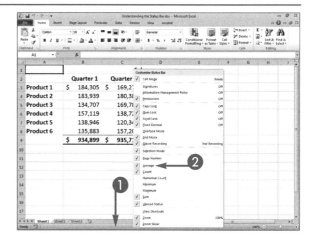

● Selected options appear on the status bar.

Some options only appear when appropriate.

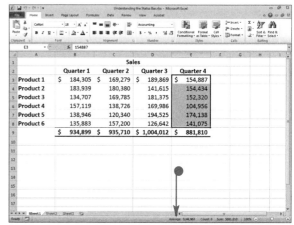

Take a Look at Backstage View

The File tab is located in the upper-left corner of the Excel window. When you click the tab, you are moved to an area Microsoft calls Backstage view. You can use this area to do such things as open a file, save a file, print a file, review a file, or set Excel options. In short, to create and edit your document you use the Ribbon; to work with your document you use Backstage view. The commands you need to open a new or existing document, to set document properties, or to share a file by printing, e-mailing, or faxing are all located in Backstage view.

Take a Look at Backstage View

① Click the File tab.

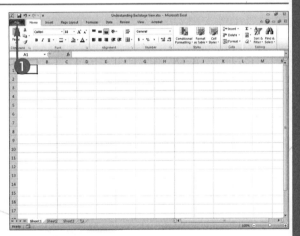

The Backstage view options appear.

② Click an option to select it.

● Excel opens the option's pane.

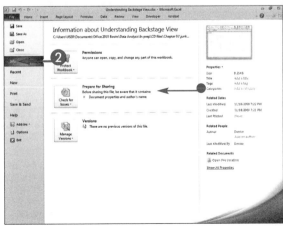

Upload a File to Excel's Web-based Application

With the Microsoft Excel Web App, you can create and edit an Excel workbook even if you are on a computer that does not have Excel installed. For example, if your office e-mails you an Excel document while you are staying in a hotel, you can update it. With the Microsoft Excel Web App, you can use the hotel's community computer to make the changes even if it does not have Excel on it. You can use the Web App in any supported browser — Internet Explorer, Firefox, or Safari.

The Microsoft Excel Web App is part of Windows Live, a collection of free services offered by Microsoft that include e-mail, photo sharing, personal Web pages, and more. The Web-based application is included in SkyDrive. You can use SkyDrive to store files online and share them

with others. To sign up for SkyDrive or to sign in to your SkyDrive account, go to http://skydrive.live.com. Signing up for a SkyDrive account is easy. Just click the Sign Up button and the Web site will prompt you through the process. If you have a Hotmail, Xbox LIVE, or any other type of Windows Live account, you already have a SkyDrive account.

You can use the Save to SkyDrive option in the Share section of BackOffice to save documents to SkyDrive. The Save to SkyDrive option lets you save any open file to a SkyDrive folder. By default, you have two SkyDrive folders: Public and My Documents. Documents you save to the Public folder are available to everyone. Documents you save to the My Documents folder are available only to you. You can also access an Excel file from a Share Point server that is running Web Apps.

Upload a File to Excel's Web-Based Application

1. Sign-up for a SkyDrive account.

2. Open the file you want to upload.

3. Click the File tab.

4. Click Save & Send.

5. Click Save to Web.

6. Click Sign In.

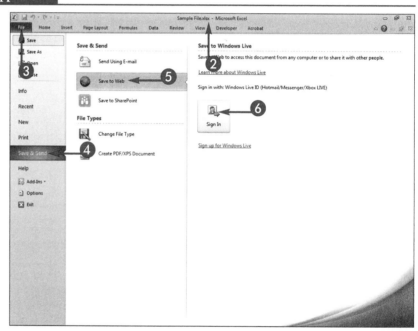

The Connecting to docs.live.net dialog box appears.

7. Type your e-mail address.

8. Type your password.

9. Click OK.

The Save to Windows Live pane appears.

⑩ Click a folder.

⑪ Click Save As.

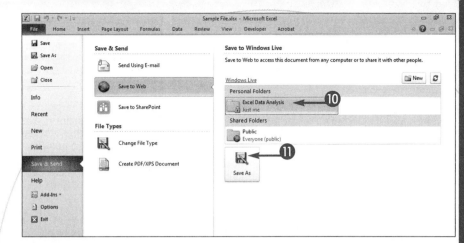

The Connect to doc.live.net dialog box appears.

⑫ Type your e-mail address

⑬ Type your password.

⑭ Click OK.

The Save As dialog box appears.

⑮ Click Save.

Excel saves your file to your SkyDrive account.

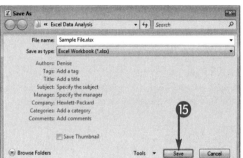

Create a File Using Excel's Web-based Application

Y ou can create Excel files with Excel's Web-based application. For example, if the computer you are using does not have Excel, you can sign in to SkyDrive and create an Excel worksheet.

The look a feel of the Excel Web-based application is the same as the desktop application. To issue commands, you use the Ribbon. For the most part, the commands work exactly as they do in the desktop application. Therefore, as you are learning Excel, you are also learning the Web-based application. You will find, however, that the commands available to you are limited and are not as sophisticated as they are in the desktop application.

If you upload a file to SkyDrive, you can view most features. For example, you can upload and view a PivotTable and the sort and filter buttons are available to

you. However, you cannot create a PivotTable in the Web-based application. You can view a chart, but you cannot create a chart. If you edit the data a chart is based on, the chart will update.

You cannot view comments, shapes, and a few other objects when using the Web-based application. If a workbook has any objects that you cannot view, the Web-based application will warn you when you attempt to view the workbook. You can view a workbook that has objects you cannot view in it, but you cannot edit it. If you need to edit the workbook, use the File menu to make a copy of the file and then edit the copy.

All the functions that are available to you in Excel are available to you in the Web-based application.

Create a File Using Excel's Web-Based Application

1 Sign in to SkyDrive.

2 Click the folder where you want to store the file.

You move to the folder.

3 Click New.

A menu appears.

4 Click Microsoft Excel workbook.

The New Microsoft Excel workbook page appears.

5 Type a name.

6 Click Create.

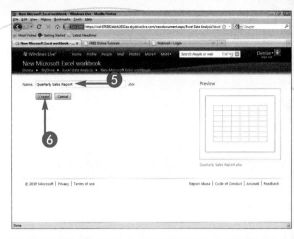

The Microsoft Excel Web App opens.

7 Create your document.

8 Click a path location.

Exit the file.

You do not need to save the file.

● Click here to sign out.

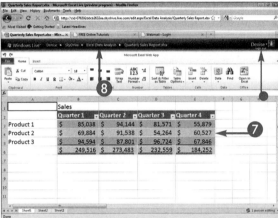

Apply It

You can view a workbook in SkyDrive. Sign in to Sky Drive. Click the folder where you saved the file. Click the file and then click View. The file opens in the Web-based application. If you want to edit the file, click Edit. The file opens in the Microsoft Excel Web App and you can edit the file.

You can edit a workbook in SkyDrive. Sign in to Sky Drive. Click the folder where you saved the file. Click the File. Click Edit. The file opens in the Microsoft Excel Web App. You can edit the file. Click a path location at the top of the page to exit the file.

In the Microsoft Excel Web App you can view a workbook that has objects in it that you cannot view, such as comments. However, if you want to edit the file, you must make a copy of the file and edit the copy. To make a copy of the file, click File. Click Save a Copy. Excel displays a message stating the unsupported features will not be saved. Click Yes. Enter a new filename and then click Save. Excel saves the file.

Enter
Data

Worksheets divide information into rows and columns of data. People often use worksheets to calculate financial, statistical, or engineering data. Microsoft Excel is an electronic worksheet. You can use it to enter, display, manipulate, analyze, and print the information you organize into rows and columns.

Each Excel worksheet has more than 1 million rows and more than 16,000 columns. Excel labels each row in numerical order, starting with 1. Excel labels each column in alphabetical order, starting with A. When Excel reaches the letter Z, it begins ordering with AA, AB, AC, and so on. You refer to the intersection of a row and column as a cell. The intersection of a row and column also forms the cell name. For example, you refer to the first row in column A as cell A1 and the seventh row in column C as cell C7. When using Excel, you enter your data into worksheet cells.

To move to a cell, move your mouse pointer to the cell and then click in it. The cell becomes the active cell and Excel surrounds it with a black border. Once in a cell, you can use the arrow keys on your keyboard to move up, down, left, and right. You can enter text, numbers, dates, and formulas into cells.

Alphabetic characters and numerical data you do not use in mathematical calculations are text. Excel considers any sequence of characters that contains a letter text. By default, Excel considers all numerical data numbers. If you wish to enter numerical data as text, precede your entry with an apostrophe.

As you type, the data you enter into a cell appears on the formula bar. You can click Enter — the check mark on the formula bar — or you can press the Enter key to enter your data into a cell.

Enter Text

1 Click in a cell.

2 Type the text.

3 Press Enter.

Excel enters the text and then moves down to the next cell.

Alternatively, you can click Enter (✔) — the check mark on the formula bar.

Enter Numbers

1 Click in a cell.

2 Type the number.

3 Press Enter.

Excel enters the number and then moves down to the next cell.

Alternatively, you can click ✔ on the formula bar.

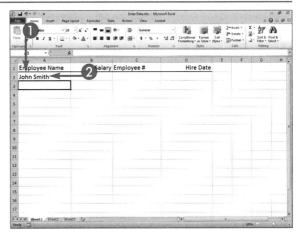

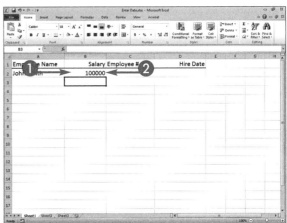

Enter Numbers as Text

1 Click in a cell.

2 Type an apostrophe followed by the number.

3 Click ✔ on the formula bar.

Excel enters the number as text.

Alternatively, press Enter.

If you receive an error, click the Error button (⬦) and then click Ignore Error.

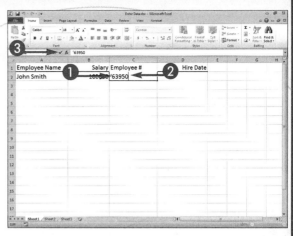

Enter Dates

1 Click in a cell.

2 Type the date.

3 Click ✔ on the formula bar.

Excel enters the date.

Alternatively, press Enter.

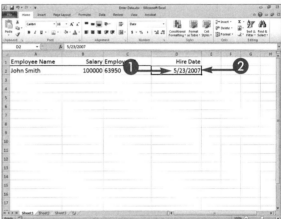

Extra

When you enter numbers as text, an Error button (⬦) may appear. Excel is checking to see if you entered the number as text by mistake. You should click the button and then click Ignore Error.

When you press Enter after typing an entry into a cell, by default, Excel moves down one cell. If you want Excel to move to the cell to the right, press the right-arrow key or the Tab key. If you want Excel to move up, press the up-arrow key. If you want Excel to move to the left, press Shift+Tab or the left-arrow key.

By default, when you press the Enter key after typing an entry, Excel moves down one cell. You can change the default location to which Excel moves. Click the File tab. A menu appears. Click Options. The Excel Options dialog box appears. Click Advanced. Make sure the After Pressing Enter, Move Selection check box is selected and then choose Right, Up, or Left in the Direction field to cause Excel to move right, up, or left when you press Enter. Click OK.

Select Cells

Before you can execute an Excel command, you must select the cells to which you want the command to apply. For example, if you want to bold several cells, you start the process by selecting the cells. The most common way to select cells is to click and drag. Excel highlights the selected cells. The range of cells you select does not have to be contiguous. You can hold down the Ctrl key as you click and drag to select multiple ranges of cells. If you select multiple ranges of cells, Excel highlights each selected range. If you do not hold down the Ctrl key, Excel deselects the first range of cells when you begin to select a new range of cells.

You can select a single cell or the entire worksheet. To select a single cell, click in the cell. To select every cell in a worksheet, click the Select All button or press Ctrl+A. To select an entire row or an entire column, simply click the row or column identifier. For example, to select all the cells in column C, click the C identifier for the column. To select multiple columns, click the first column and then continue holding down the mouse button as you drag to the other columns you want to select. To select entire rows, click the row identifiers on the left side of the rows.

You can quickly select a large range of cells by clicking in the first cell you want to select, holding down the Shift key, and then clicking in the last cell you want to select.

Select Cells

Select the Entire Worksheet

① Click the Select All button (⬜).

Alternatively, press Ctrl+A.

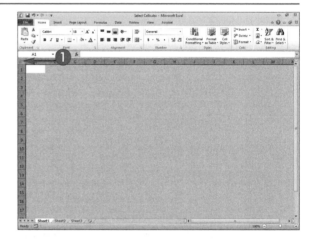

Select Contiguous Cells

① Click the first cell.

② Drag to the last cell.

Alternatively, click the first cell, hold down the Shift key, and then click the last cell.

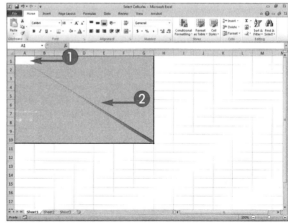

Select Noncontiguous Cells

1. Click the corner of the first block of cells.

2. Drag the mouse to highlight the desired cells.

3. Press Ctrl.

4. Repeat Steps 1 and 2 to select the next block of cells.

5. Repeat Steps 3 and 4 to select additional cell ranges.

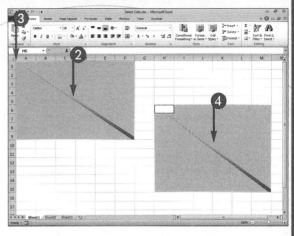

Select Columns or Rows

1. Click the label for the first column or row you want to select.

2. Drag to the last column or row you want to select.

● Excel selects the columns or rows.

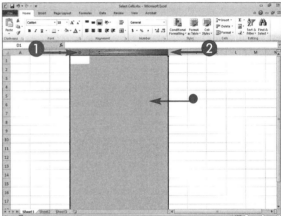

Apply It

You can easily select all cells with formulas, comments, conditional formatting, constants, or data validation. Click the Home tab. Click Find & Select in the Editing group. A menu appears. Click the option you want. Excel selects all the cells that contain the option you selected. For example, if you chose Formulas, Excel selects all the cells that contain formulas.

You can also use the arrow keys to select cells. Click in any cell, hold down the Shift key and then use the left, right, up, and down arrow keys to expand your selection.

You can press Ctrl+Shift+an arrow key to select everything from the active cell to the next blank cell that is to the right, to the left, above, or below the active cell.

You can press Ctrl+Shift+* to select a block of cells. You will find this option particularly useful with large tables. For a list of keyboard shortcuts, see the Appendix.

Using the Ribbon to Format Numbers

By applying formatting, you can change the way numbers display. For example, you can use Excel's formatting options to tell Excel you want to separate thousands or show decimal places. Formatting makes your data easier to read and helps you conform to company, country, or industry standards. Excel provides a variety of options for formatting numbers.

When you type numbers into a cell, in most instances they appear in the format you type them. However, if the number has decimal places and is too long to fit in the cell, Excel rounds the number. If the number is longer than 12 digits, Excel displays the number in scientific notation. If the number has leading or trailing zeros, Excel drops the zeros. For example, Excel displays both 0123 and 123.00 as 123.

The Number group on the Home tab has several buttons you can use to format numbers quickly. If you choose Comma Style, Excel separates the thousands with a comma, adds two decimal places, displays negative numbers in parentheses, and represents zeros with a dash (–).

The Accounting Number Format field has several currency formats you can choose from, including the United States currency format, the United Kingdom currency format, and the Euro currency format. For example, if you choose the United States currency format, Excel adds a dollar sign and aligns it with the left side of the cell, adds two decimal places, and displays negative numbers in parentheses. You can click the Increase Decimal or Decrease Decimal buttons to increase or decrease the number of decimal places that appear.

Using the Ribbon to Format Numbers

Comma Style Format

1. Select the cells you want to format.
2. Click the Home tab.
3. Click the Comma Style button (⑨).

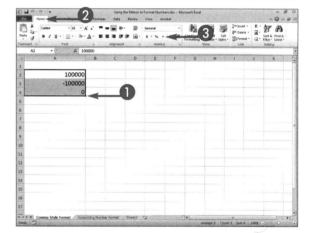

- Excel separates the thousands.
- Excel adds two decimal places.
- Negative numbers appear in parentheses.
- Zeros are represented by a dash.

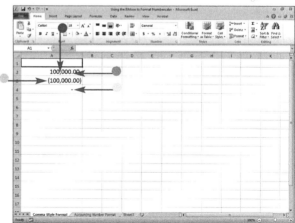

Accounting Number Format

1 Select the cells you want to format.

2 Click the Home tab.

3 Click the down arrow (▼) next to the Accounting Number Format field and then select an accounting number format.

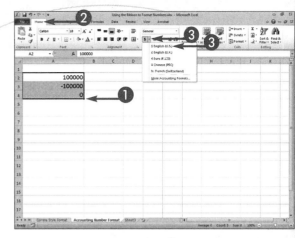

● Excel adds a currency symbol, aligned with the left side of the cell.

● Negative numbers appear in parentheses.

● If you click the Decrease Decimal button (⊞), each click removes a decimal place.

● If you click the Increase Decimal button (⊞), each click adds a decimal place.

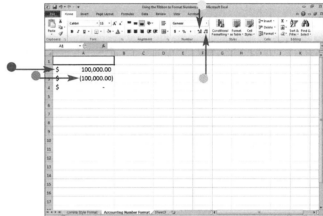

Apply It

You can use the Number Format field to apply a number format quickly. When you click the down arrow (▼) in the Number Format field a menu appears. Click General to apply the General format. The General format is the default format. Numbers appear as you type them.

Click Number to apply the Number format. The Number format does not display a currency symbol and does not separate thousands, but it does display two decimal places, zeros as 0.00, and negative numbers with a negative sign (–).

If you want to display a number as currency, choose either the Accounting number format or the Currency number format. The Accounting number format aligns the currency symbol with the left side of the cell, displays two decimal places, separates thousands, displays zeros as dashes, and display negative number in parentheses. The Currency format places the currency symbol immediately before the first digit, displays two decimal places, separates thousands, and displays negative numbers with a negative sign (–).

Using the Format Cells Dialog Box

A s an alternative to using the Ribbon, you can use the Format Cells dialog box to format cells. The Format Cells dialog box lets you specify how each number is formatted. The General format option is the default format. Generally, it displays numbers exactly as you type them. However, if the number has decimal places and is too long to fit in the cell, Excel rounds the number. If the number is longer than 12 digits, Excel displays the number in scientific notation. If the number has leading or trailing zeros, Excel drops the zeros. If you have changed a number's format and want to return to the original format, choose the General format.

In the Format Cell dialog box you can use Number Format options to set the number of decimal places, specify whether a number should display a thousands separator, and specify how to display negative numbers. You can

choose from four formats for negative numbers: preceded by a negative sign (–), in red, in parentheses, or in red and in parentheses.

The Currency format offers you the same options as the Number format except you can choose to display a currency symbol. The currency symbol you choose determines the options you have for displaying negative numbers. If you choose the dollar sign ($), thousands are separated by commas by default.

Excel designed the Accounting format to comply with accounting standards. When using the Accounting format, if you choose a currency symbol, the currency symbol aligns with the left side of the cell, decimal points are aligned, a dash (–) displays instead of a zero, and negative numbers display in parentheses.

Using the Format Cells Dialog Box

Apply a Number Format

1. Select the cells you want to format.

   By default, they are formatted in the General format.

2. Click the Home tab.

3. Click the Dialog Box Launcher in the Number group.

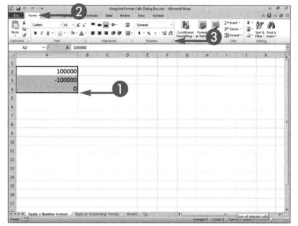

The Format Cells dialog box appears.

4. Click Number.

5. Type the number of decimal places you want.

6. Click the Use 1000 Separator option to select the thousands separator (☐ change ✔).

7. Click to select a format for negative numbers.

8. Click OK.

● Excel formats the numbers.

Note: *The options for the Currency format are the same, except you must select a currency symbol.*

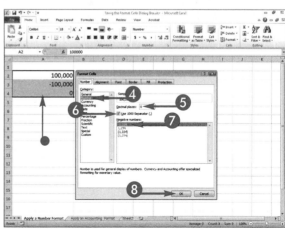

Apply an Accounting Format

1. Select the cells you want to format.

2. Click the Home tab.

3. Click the launcher in the Number group.

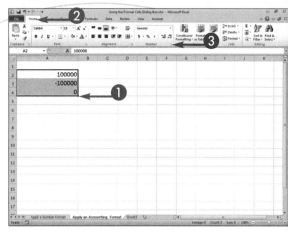

The Format Cells dialog box appears.

4. Click Accounting.

5. Type the number of decimal places you want.

6. Click the ▼ in the Symbol field and then select a currency option.

7. Click OK.

● Excel applies an accounting format.

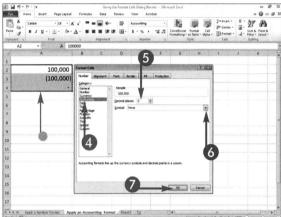

Apply It

Excel has several special formats you can use to format Social Security numbers, ZIP codes, and phone numbers. To apply a Special format, type numbers into a cell. Click in the cell. Click the launcher in the Number group. The Format Cells dialog box appears. Click Special in the Category box. Click the format you want in the Type box. Click OK. Excel formats the numbers you entered using the Special format you selected.

You can set the default number of decimal places Excel applies when you type a number into a worksheet. Click the File tab. A menu appears. Click Options. Click Advanced. Make sure the Automatically Insert Decimal Point check box is selected. Type the number of decimal places you want in the Places field. Click OK.

When you format a number, Excel changes the way a number displays, but does not change the number itself. For example, if you type 123.4567 in a cell and then apply an Accounting format, the number will display as $ 123.46. However, if you use the cell in a calculation, Excel will use 123.4567. The number as you originally typed it always appears on the Formula bar.

Understanding Dates and Times

In Excel, dates and times are numbers. All dates are whole numbers and all times are decimal fractions. By default, Excel for Windows uses a 1900 date system. January 1, 1900, is represented by the number 1; January 2, 1900, is represented by the number 2; January 3, 1900, is represented by the number 3; and every date thereafter is represented by the next sequential number. Times are represented by decimal fractions that range from .0 to .99999. The decimal fraction .0 represents 12:00:00 AM; the decimal fraction .5 represents 12:00:00 PM; and the decimal fraction .99999 represents 11:59:59 PM.

Formats turn these whole numbers and decimal fractions into recognizable dates and times. When you make a cell entry, if Excel recognizes it as a date or a time, it automatically assigns a format. To see the date's whole number or the time's decimal fraction, change the format to the General format. If you want to change the current format of a date or time to another format, you can choose one of the date or time options from the Number Format menu or you can use the Format Cells dialog box.

When using the Number Format menu to format Date and Times, the Short Date option formats October 15, 2011, as 10/15/2011; the Long Date option formats it as Saturday, October 15, 2011; and the Time option formats 3:15 p.m. as 3:15:00 PM.

Countries vary in the way they format dates and times. Hence, the Format Cells dialog box provides a variety of ways you can format dates and times based on locale. For example, if you choose English (U.S.) as the locale, Excel provides more then fifteen ways you can format a date.

Understanding Dates and Times

Using the Number Format Menu

① Select the cells you want to format.

② Click the ☑ in the Number Format and then select a format option.

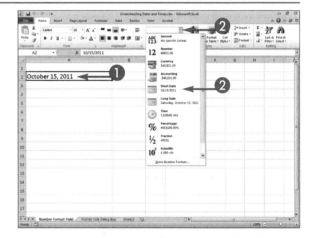

● Excel formats the cells.

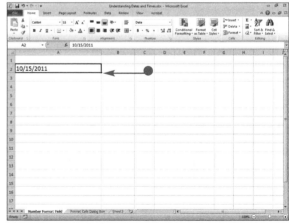

Using the Format Cells Dialog Box

1 Select the cells you want to format.

2 Click the Dialog Box Launcher in the Number group.

The Format Cells dialog box appears.

3 Click Date or Time.

4 Click the ⊡ in the Locale field and then select a location.

5 Click a format.

6 Click OK.

● Excel formats the cells.

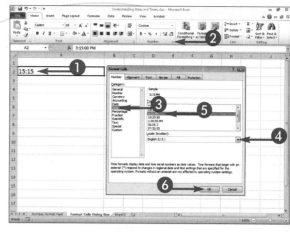

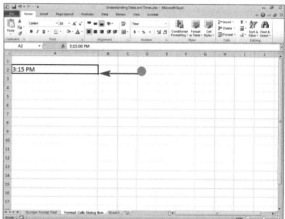

Extra

To have Excel recognize an entry as a date or time and automatically assign a format, follow these rules:

● Use a hyphen or a slash to separate the month, day, and/or year. For example, Excel recognizes the following as dates: 6/4/10, 4-Jun-10, 4-Jun, and Jun-10.

● Use a colon to separate the hour, minutes, and seconds. For example, Excel recognizes the following as times: 9:45 PM, 9:45:30 PM, 21:45 (military time), 21:45, and 21:45:30. You must include a space between the time and AM or PM.

● If you want to include both the date and the time in the same cell, separate them with a space. For example, Excel recognizes the following date and time entries: 6/4/10 21:45 or 9:45 PM 4-Jun-10.

● You can type in upper- or lowercase. Excel ignores case.

● If you do not include AM or PM, Excel uses military time. However, you can use an A or a P instead of AM or PM as long as you include a space between the time and the letter. For example, you can type 9:45 P.

Format Percentages

To format a number as a percent, apply the Percentage format. When you apply the Percentage format to an existing number, Excel takes the number, multiplies it by 100, and adds a percent sign. For example, if you apply a Percentage format to 50, you get 5000%. Use this formula to calculate a percentage: amount/total amount = percentage. For 50 out of 100 the calculation is 50/100 = .50; when you apply the Percentage format, you get 50%.

You can preformat a cell by applying a format to the cell before you make an entry. If you preformat, Excel handles percentages differently. If you enter a whole number, Excel converts the whole number to a percent. If you enter a decimal, Excel multiplies the decimal by 100. Both 50 and .50 are interpreted as 50%.

Extra

You can use the Format Cells dialog box to format a percentage. Select the cell range you want to format. Click the launcher in the Number group. The Format Cells dialog box appears with the Number tab activated. Click Percentage. Enter the number of decimal places you want to display. Click OK. Excel formats the range as a percentage.

Format Percentages

1. Select the cells you want to format.
2. Click the Home tab.
3. Click the Percent Style button (%).

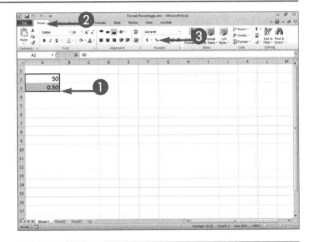

● Excel formats the cells as percents.

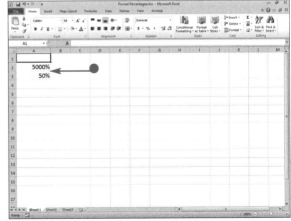

Format Fractions

You can format numbers as one-digit, two-digit, or three-digit fractions. When you format a number as a one-digit fraction, Excel rounds the number to the nearest single-digit fraction value; when you format a number as a two-digit fraction, Excel rounds the number to the nearest two-digit fraction value; and when you format a number as a three-digit fraction, Excel rounds the number to the nearest three-digit fraction value. For example, if you format the number 123.456 as a single-digit fraction, you get 123 1/2. If you format it as a two-digit value you get 123 26/57. And, if you format it as a three-digit value you get 123 57/125. You can also format number as halves, quarters, eighths, sixteenths, tenths, and hundredths.

Extra

You can use the Number Format menu to format a number as a one-digit fraction. Click the Home tab. Click the down arrow next (▼) to the Number Format field. A menu appears. Click Fraction. Excel formats your number as a one-digit fraction.

When you format a number as a fraction, the original number appears on the formula bar. Excel uses the original number when performing calculations.

Format Fractions

1 Select the numbers you want to format.

2 Click the Home tab.

3 Click the launcher in the Number group.

The Format Cells dialog box appears.

4 Click Fraction.

5 Click a Fraction type.

6 Click OK.

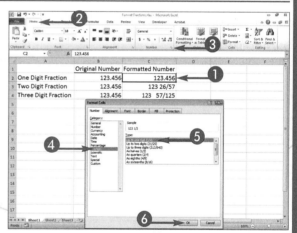

● Excel formats the number as a fraction.

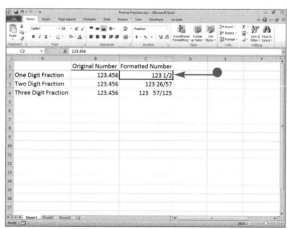

Format in Scientific Notation

In Excel, you can format numbers in scientific notation. When you are working with extremely large numbers, scientific notation saves space.

The number 1.23E+02 is scientific notation for 123. Scientific notation consists of a number followed by E+n. The E stands for exponent and n is the power to which you need to raise the number 10. To convert a number from scientific notation, multiply the number that precedes the E by 10 and then raise 10 to the power after the plus (+). For example, if you enter the formula =1.23*10^2 into Excel, you get 123. When you format a number in scientific notation, you can specify the number of decimal places you want to keep.

Extra

You can use the Number Format menu to format a number in scientific notation. Click the Home tab. Click the down arrow (▼) next to the Number Format field. A menu appears. Click Scientific. Excel formats your number in scientific notation.

When you format a number in scientific notation, the original number appears on the formula bar. Excel uses the original number when performing calculations.

Format in Scientific Notation

① Select the numbers you want to format.

② Click the Home tab.

③ Click the launcher in the Number group.

The Format Cells dialog box appears.

④ Click Scientific.

⑤ Type the number of decimal places.

⑥ Click OK.

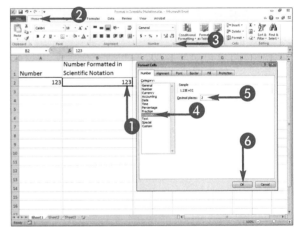

● Excel formats the number in scientific notation.

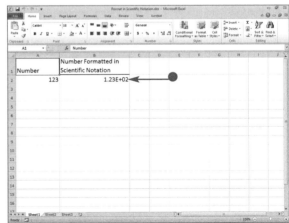

Format as Text

You can use the Text format in the Format Cells dialog box to convert a number to text. Numbers formatted as text are not used in mathematical calculations. Certain numbers — for example, employee numbers — are never used in mathematical calculations and should be formatted as text. If you want to format a number as text as you type it, precede the number with an apostrophe (').

When you enter numbers as text, an error indicator may appear. Excel is checking to see if you entered the number as text by mistake. You should click the Error Indicator button and then click Ignore Error.

By default, numbers are right aligned in the cell and text is left aligned. When you format a number as text, Excel left aligns the number.

Apply It

If you do not want an error indicator to display when you enter a number as text, you can deselect Numbers Formatted as Text or Preceded by an Apostrophe in the Excel Options dialog box. Click the File tab. Click Options. Click Formulas, which is located in the left column. Deselect the Numbers Formatted as Text or Preceded by an Apostrophe option (☑ changes to ☐), which is located under Error Checking Rules. Click OK.

Format as Text

① Select the numbers you want to format.

② Click the Home tab.

③ Click the launcher in the Number group.

The Format Cells dialog box appears.

④ Click Text.

⑤ Click OK.

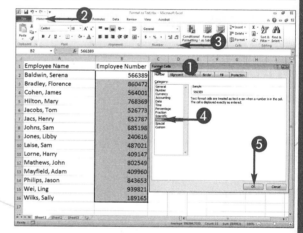

● Excel formats the numbers as text.

The numbers left align.

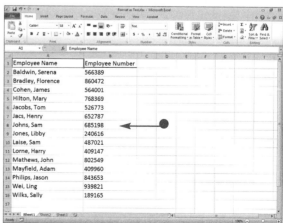

Add a Border

You can highlight important information by adding a border. A border is a set of lines that surround a cell or cell range. You can choose the style, color, and placement of border lines. Adjoining cells share borders. For example, placing a bottom border on cell A1 is the same as placing a top border on cell A2.

When creating a border, you can choose from the following styles: single line, double line, thick line, or a variety of dotted and dashed lines. You can also choose the color of the line from theme colors, standard colors, or other colors. The border lines can appear on the top of a cell, the bottom of a cell, the left side of a cell, the right side of a cell, diagonally from the top-left corner to the bottom-right corner, or diagonally from the top-right

corner to the bottom-left corner, or any combination thereof.

When you click the Border button, Excel provides you with a menu of preset border options. If any one of the border options meets your needs, you can click it to apply it to the selected cells. The Border button displays the last border you applied. If you want to apply that border to another group of cells, simply select the cells and then click the Border button.

You can use the Format Cells dialog box to customize borders. In the Format Cells dialog box, you can use presets to design a border, or you can select the placement of each border. The menu also has options that you can use to draw borders.

Add a Border

① Select the cells where you want to add a border.

② Click the Home tab.

③ Click the ▼ next to the Borders button (▦).

A menu appears.

If you see the style you want to apply, click it. Excel applies the style.

④ Click More Borders.

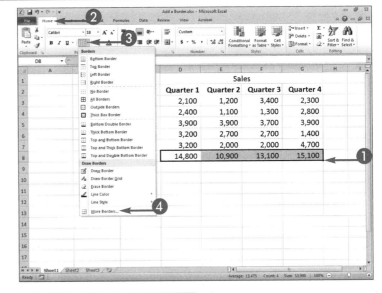

The Format Cells dialog box appears.

⑤ Click a Style option to select a border line style.

⑥ Click the ▼ in the Color field and then select a color.

⑦ Click in the Border box to select where you want to place the border.

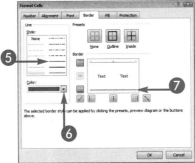

- Alternatively, click one of the presets.

8 Repeat Steps 5 to 7 until you have the border design you want.

9 Click OK.

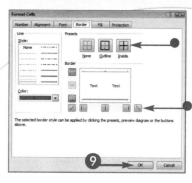

- Excel adds the border.

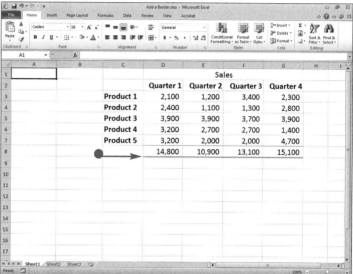

Apply It

You can draw a border around a cell or cell range by choosing Draw Border from the Border menu and then clicking and dragging to place the border around the cell or cell range. If you want to create a border on just one side of a cell, click the side but do not drag.

You can draw a grid around a cell range by choosing Draw Border Grid from the border menu and then clicking and dragging to create the grid.

You can erase a border or a grid by choosing Erase Border from the Border menu and then dragging over the border or grid you want to erase. If you want to erase the border on just one side of a cell, click the side but do not drag.

You can choose the color of the border you draw by choosing Line Color from the Border menu, selecting a color, and then clicking and dragging to draw. You can choose the style of the line by choosing Line Style from the Border menu, selecting a style, and then clicking and dragging to draw.

Change the Font or Font Size

A *font* is a collection of characters that all have the same basic style. When you open a workbook, if you do not make any changes, Excel uses the default font and font size. You may want to change the font or font size to conform to company standards or to make a portion of your worksheet standout. You can have a variety of fonts and font sizes in a single worksheet. If you select a range of cells, and then move your mouse pointer over each of the options on the Font or Font Size menu, Excel provides you with a preview of how that font or font size will appear if you select it.

In addition, in the Font group on the Home tab, Excel provides an Increase Font Size button and a Decrease Font Size button. You can click the Increase Font Size button to make the font in selected cells larger. You can

click the Decrease Font Size button to make the font in selected cells smaller. You can also enter a font size directly into the Font Size field.

Fonts are measured in points by measuring the longest character in a character set. There are 72 points to an inch. When choosing a font size, you are not limited to the options in the Font Size menu. For example, generally the largest font size in the menu is 72, but you can assign a font size larger than 72.

As you make a font larger, the text and numbers may no longer fit. Text spills over into the next cell and numbers display as pound signs (####). To view the data, make the cell larger or wrap the text.

Change the Font or Font Size

Change the Font

1. Select the cells you want to format.

2. Click the Home tab.

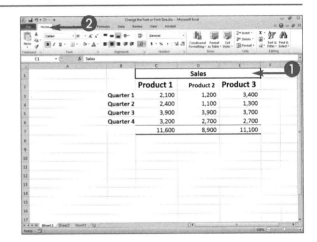

3. Click the ▼ in the Font field and then select an option.

● Excel changes the font.

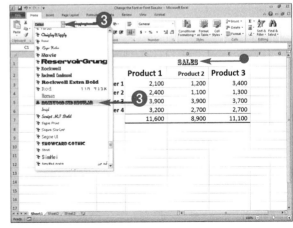

Change the Font size

1. Select the cells you want to format.

2. Click the Home tab.

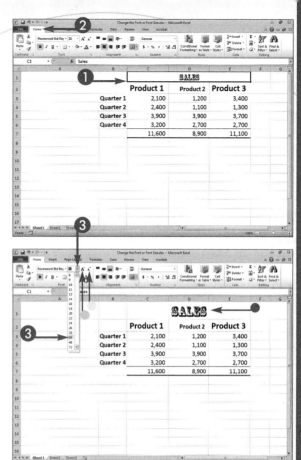

3. Click the ⏷ in the Font Size field and then select a font size.

● Excel changes the font size.

Alternatively:

● Click the Increase Font Size button (A).

● Click the Decrease Font Size button (A).

Apply It

You can change the default font and default font size used by workbooks. Click the File tab. A menu appears. Click Options. The Excel Options panel appears. Click General. In the Use this Font field, select the font you want to use. In the Font Size field, select the font size you want to use. Click OK. The next time you open a workbook, it will use the font and font size you selected as the default.

If text is too long to fit in a cell, you can use the Shrink to Fit option to automatically resize it. Select the text you want to resize. Click the launcher in the Alignment group. The Format Cells dialog box appears with the Alignment tab activated. Click Shrink to Fit in the Text Control section. Click OK. Excel resizes the text so that it fits in the cell.

You can use the Mini toolbar to change the font or increase or decrease font size.

Add a Background Color

You can make cells stand out by applying a background color, also known as a *fill*. The fill can be a theme color, a standard color, or any other color.

Theme colors are sets of colors for use throughout a document or document set. Theme colors change when you change the theme. Using theme colors gives documents a consistent look and feel. You can keep the look and feel of your documents consistent across products by using the same theme colors in Word, PowerPoint, and Excel.

You can also use a standard color or you can click More Colors to open the Colors dialog box where you can choose virtually any color. Standard colors and colors

from the Color dialog box do not change when you change themes.

Extra

With a gradient fill, one color blends into another. You can apply a gradient fill to cells. Click the Home tab. Click the launcher in the font group. Click the Fill tab, and then click Fill effects. Use the Color 1 and Color 2 fields to select the colors in your gradient. Click to select a Shading Style. Click to select a variant. Click OK to close the dialog boxes.

Add a Background Color

① Select the cells you want to format.

② Click the Home tab.

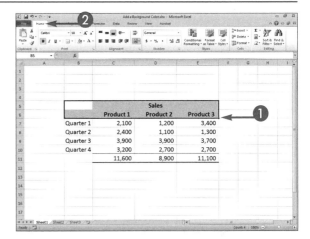

③ Click the ⏷ next to the Fill Color button (🖌) and then select a fill color.

● Excel applies a fill color to the cells you selected.

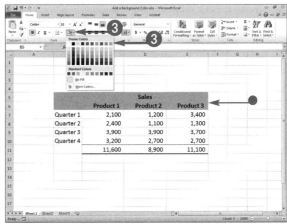

Change the Font Color

You can make cells stand out by changing the font color. The font color can be a theme color, a standard color, or any other color.

Theme Colors are sets of colors for use throughout a document or document set. If you change the theme, the theme color changes. Standard colors are popular colors. If you change the theme, standard colors do not change.

While you can use any color anywhere, if you have applied a fill, you should combine a light colored font with a dark colored fill or a dark colored font with a light colored fill, so that your text will always be visible in your fill. The first four columns of theme colors are designed for font and fill colors.

Apply It

When you choose a color, Theme Colors appear as an option. By default, Excel uses the Office Colors theme, but you can change the theme colors by choosing the Colors option in the Themes Group on the Page Layout tab. When you change theme colors, if you used a theme color as a fill or font color, the color of your fill or font changes to the color associated with the new theme.

Change the Font Color

① Select the cells you want to format.

② Click the Home tab.

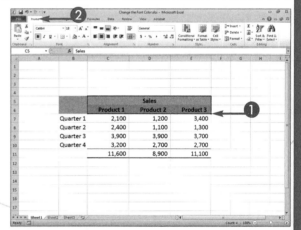

③ Click the ▼ next to the Font Color field and then select a font color.

● Excel applies a font color to the cells you selected.

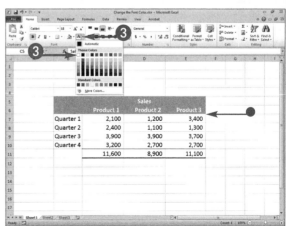

31

Bold, Underline, or Italicize

Bolding, underlining, and italicizing are all great ways to make data in your worksheet stand out. For example, you may want to bold your titles, italicize important information, put a single underline under subtotals, and/or put a double underline under totals. Applying these options is as simple as clicking the appropriate button.

If bold, italics, or underlines have been applied to a cell, when you click in the cell the option's button is highlighted on the Ribbon. You can remove the bold, italics, or underlines by clicking the button again. In other words, the Bold, Underline, and Italic buttons are toggle buttons. You click the button once to turn the option on; you click it again to turn the option off.

Extra

You can use the following shortcut keys to apply bold, italics, or underlines.

OPTION	KEY
Bold	Ctrl+B or Ctrl+2
Italic	Ctrl+I or Ctrl+3
Underline	Ctrl+U or Ctrl+4

Bold, Underline, or Italicize

① Select the cells you want to bold, italicize, or underline.

② Click the Home tab.

③ Click the Bold (**B**), Italicize (*I*), or click the ▾ next to the Underline button (U) and then select an underline type.

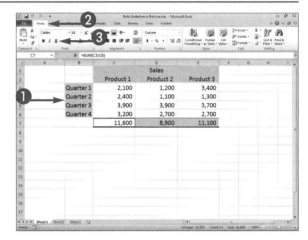

● Excel bolds, italicizes, or underlines the cells you selected.

In the example, Excel applies bold and italics.

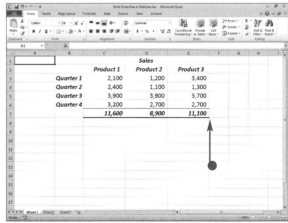

Align
Data

To make your data easier to read, Excel has several buttons you can use to align data in a cell. Click the Align Text Left button to align data with the left side of a cell, click the Align Text Right button to align data with the right side of a cell, or click the Center button to center data in a cell.

Excel also has buttons you can use to place data at the top, bottom, or middle of the cell. Click the Top Align button to align data with the top of the cell, click the Middle Align button to align data with the middle of the cell, and click the Bottom Align button to align data with the bottom of the cell.

Extra

By default, text is aligned with the left side of the cell, numbers are aligned with the right side of the cell, logical values are centered, and all data is aligned with the bottom of the cell.

You can press Ctrl+Alt+Tab or click the Increase Indent button (⯐) to indent data. You can press Ctrl+Alt+Shift+Tab or click the Decrease Indent button (⯐) to decrease an indent.

Align Data

① Select the cells you want to align.

② Click the Home tab.

③ Click an Alignment button.

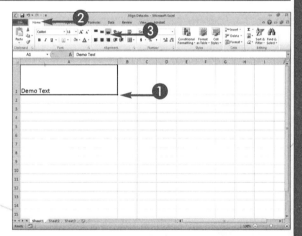

● Excel aligns the data.

Hover the mouse pointer over each button for a description of the button.

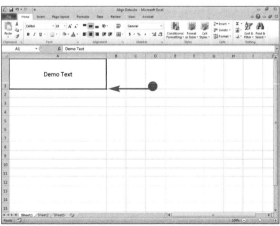

Rotate Data

By default, the data you enter is horizontal and reads from left to right. If you want to keep your columns narrow, you may want to rotate data so that you can display all of it without making the column wider.

You can use the Orientation menu to rotate data 45 degrees clockwise, 45 degrees counterclockwise, vertically, upward, or downward. You can use the Format Cells dialog box to enter the exact number of degrees you want to rotate data. Use the mouse pointer to tell Excel the angle you want or enter the exact number of degrees directly into the Degrees field. You can enter any number between –90 and 90. Enter a positive number to rotate upward. Enter a negative number to rotate downward.

Extra

In the Format Cells dialog box, clicking the Text box displays data vertically. The text box is a toggle button: Click the Text box once and the Text box turns black and your data displays vertically. Click the Text box again and the text box turns white and your data displays horizontally.

Rotate Data

1. Select the cells you want to rotate.

2. Click the Home tab.

3. Click the ▾ next to the Orientation button (▧) and select Format Cell Alignment.

   The Format cells dialog box appears.

4. Drag the pointer to the orientation you want.

- Alternatively, enter the degrees.

5. Click OK.

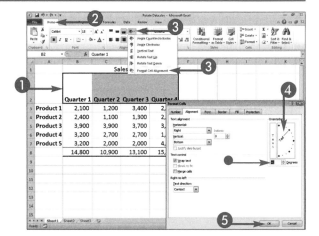

- Excel changes the orientation.

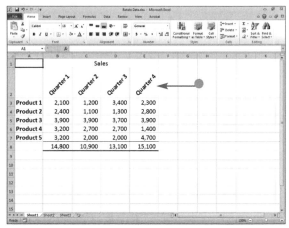

Wrap Text

I f the text you enter is too long to fit in a single cell, Excel allows the text to spill over into adjacent cells. At that point, the text takes up more that one cell. If you place data in an adjacent cell, Excel cuts off the text in the original cell and, as a result, you cannot see all of it. To rectify this problem, you can use the Excel Wrap Text feature to display the text on multiple lines. The Wrap Text feature increases the height of the cell and then wraps the text in the cell. If you cannot see all the text after performing the wrap text, try increasing the height of the cell manually or reset the row height by using the AutoFit Row Height feature.

Apply It

AutoFit Row Height automatically adjusts the height of a row so that all the data entered into cells are visible. To apply AutoFit Row Height, select the row numbers of the rows you want to adjust. Click the Home tab. Click Format in the Cells group. A menu appears. Click AutoFit Row Height.

Wrap Text

① Select the cells you want to wrap.

② Click the Home tab.

③ Click the Wrap Text button (⊞).

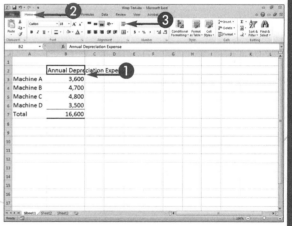

● Excel wraps the text.

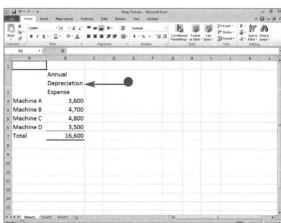

Merge and Center

Titles provide a brief summary of your data. You may want to center them over the data they summarize. You can center text within a cell by clicking the Center button. To center text across several cells, click the Merge & Center button. Merge & Center turns a cell range into a single cell and deletes all the data except the data located in the uppermost left corner cell.

When you click the down arrow next to the Merge & Center button, a menu with the following options appears: Merge & Center, Merge Across, Merge Cells, and Unmerge. You can click the Merge & Center option to merge and center rows or columns.

You can click the Merge Across option to merge columns without centering. In languages that read from left to

right, the data aligns with the left side of the cell. In languages that read from right to left, the data aligns with the right side of the cell.

You can click the Merge Cells option to merge rows or columns without centering. As with the Merge Across option, the column alignment depends on the language. In languages that read from left to right, the data aligns with the left side of the cell. In languages that read from right to left, the data aligns with the right side of the cell.

When you merge rows, the data aligns with the bottom of the cell. The Unmerge Cells option unmerges cells. You can change the alignment of merged cells. You can also rotate the data.

Merge and Center

① Select the cells you want to merge and center.

② Click the Home tab.

③ Click the ▼ next to the Merge & Center button (▦) and select the merge option you want to apply.

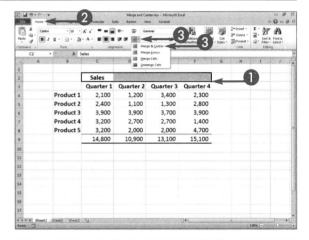

● Excel merges the cells and centers the data.

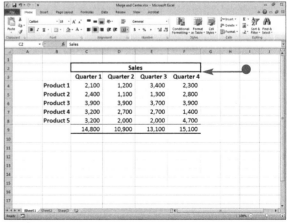

Apply a Style

By using Excel's many format options, you can format numbers, text, and cells. A *style* is a named collection of formats. Styles streamline the work of formatting so that you can apply a consistent set of formats to worksheet elements such as column heads and data values.

Excel divides styles into five categories: Good, Bad, and Neutral; Data and Model; Titles and Headings; Themed Cell Styles; and Number Format. The Good, Bad, and Neutral group and the Data and Model group make it easy for you to categorize cells; the Title and Headings group makes it easy for you to apply headings, the Themed Cell Styles group makes it easy for you to apply a theme color, and the

Number Format group makes it easy for you to format numbers.

Extra

To create a new style based on an existing one, right-click the style in the Cell Styles gallery and then click Duplicate. Type the name you want to give the style in the Style Name field and then click the Format button. The Format Cells dialog box appears. The formats for the style you duplicated are already selected. Use the dialog box to make changes. Click OK to close the dialog boxes.

Apply a Style

① Select the cells where you want to apply a style.

② Click the Home tab.

③ Click the ⊡ next to Cell Styles.

A gallery appears.

④ Click the style you want to apply.

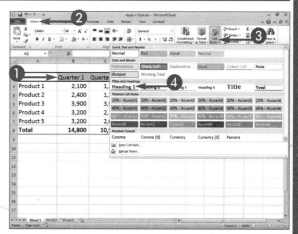

● Excel applies the style.

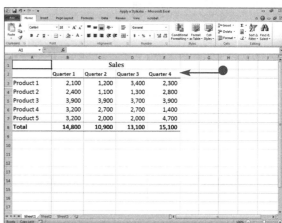

Using Format Painter

Format Painter can save you time when you need to reapply formats that already exist in your worksheet. You can use Format Painter to apply number, text, cell, shape, or object formats. For example, if you applied a number format to a number and you want another number to have the same format, you can use Format Painter; if you added a background color to a cell and changed the font color and you want another cell to have the same background color and font color, you can use Format Painter; or if you applied a border to a picture and you want another picture to have that same border, you can use Format Painter. Whether you are formatting numbers, text, cells, shapes, or objects, the process is the same.

Apply It

If you select the format you want to apply and then click the Format Painter once, you can apply the format once. If you select the format you want to apply and then double-click the Format Painter, you can apply the format multiple times. When you are finished applying a format, press the Esc key.

Using Format Painter

1. Select the cells or object with the format you want to copy.

2. Click the Home tab.

3. Click the Format Painter button (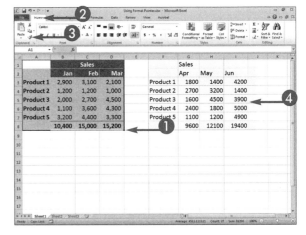).

4. Select the cells or click the object you want to format.

● Excel formats the cells or object.

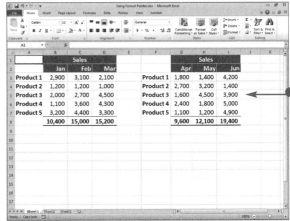

Clear Formats

A s you have learned by reading this chapter, you can apply a variety formats to Excel data. You can change the font; change the font size; change the font color; add a fill; add a border; apply bold, underlines, and italics; change the orientation of data; change the number format; and more. Once you have applied a format, you can remove the format or you can set the cells back to the default. For example, if you want to remove a border, click No Border on menu that appears when you click the down arrow next to the Border field. If you want to clear all the formats that have been applied to a cell range in a few clicks, use the clear formats option.

Apply It

To remove a Fill, click the Home tab. Click the down arrow next to the Fill Color button ( ) and then select No Fill.

To reset the Font Color back to the default, click the Home tab. Click the down arrow next to the Font Color button ( ) and then select Automatic.

To remove a word wrap, click the Home tab. Click the Word Wrap button ( ) to toggle word wrap off.

Clear Formats

1 Select the cells.

2 Click the Home tab.

3 Click the 🔽 next to the Clear button ( ) and then select Clear Formats.

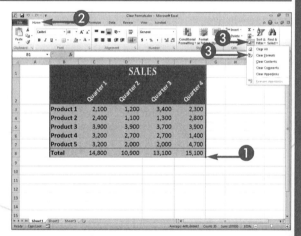

Excel clears the formats.

● Changes in orientation have been removed.

● Number formats have been removed.

● Borders have been removed.

Other formats have also been removed.

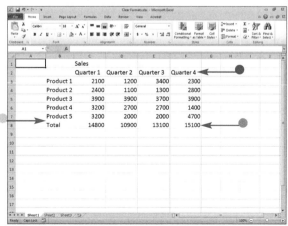

Cut, Copy, and Paste Cells

I f you want to use the same data in multiple locations, you can copy and paste the data instead of retyping it. For example, you can copy a list of data in one worksheet to another worksheet, or you can copy a formula to multiple other cells. When you copy and perform a standard paste to a cell or range of cells, Excel duplicates everything in the original cell — including the cell values, formulas, formatting, comments, and data validation — and leaves the original cell unchanged.

If you want to move information from one location to another, you can cut the information, and then paste it. Cutting and pasting removes data from its current location and places it in a new location. For example, you can move a list of data in one worksheet to another worksheet, or you can move a formula to another cell.

After you cut or copy a range of cells, you can paste the cell contents to any location within your current workbook, another Excel workbook, or any other Microsoft Windows program. When you paste to an Excel workbook, Excel replaces the content of the cells you paste into with the cut or copied values. For that reason, be careful when you paste, because you can overwrite other data.

You can copy and paste or cut and paste multiple cells only if the cells are adjacent. When you apply the Cut or Copy command to a range of cells, Excel surrounds the cells with a dotted line. The selected cells remain marked until you paste the cells or press the Esc key to deselect them.

If you do not want to paste all of the cell's contents, use Paste Special, explained in Chapter 12, or use a live preview, explained in this chapter.

Copy, Cut, and Paste Cells

Copy And Paste

1. Select the cells you want to copy.

2. Click the Home tab.

3. Click the Copy button (📋).

   A dotted line appears around the cells you selected.

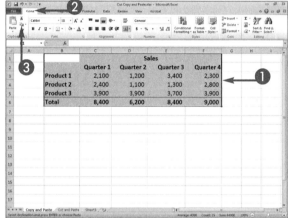

4. Click where you want to paste.

5. Click the Paste button (📋).

● Excel places a copy of the copied cells in the new location.

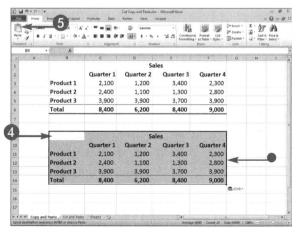

Cut And Paste

① Select the cells you want to move.

② Click the Home tab.

③ Click the Cut button (🔲).

A dotted line appears around the selected cells.

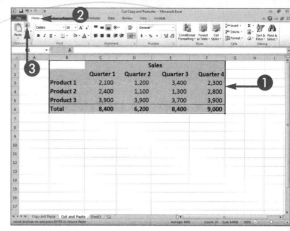

④ Click where you want to paste.

⑤ Click the Paste button.

● Excel places the data in the new location.

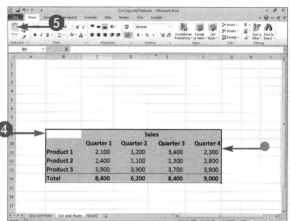

Apply It

To use your mouse to move a range of cells, select the cells you want to move and then point to the border of your selection. When your mouse pointer turns into a four-sided arrow (✥), drag your selection to a new location. To use your mouse to copy a range of cells, select the cells you want to copy and then press and hold down the Ctrl key while you point to the border of your selection. When your mouse pointer turns into an arrow (▷), drag your selection to a new location.

You can select cells and then press Ctrl+C to copy or Ctrl+X to cut. You can then press Ctrl+V to paste.

When you cut or copy a range of cells that have hidden rows or columns and then paste them, Excel includes the hidden rows and/or columns. If you want to copy only visible cells, select the cells you want to copy. Click the Home tab. Click Find & Select in the Editing group. A menu appears. Click Go To Special. The Go To Special dialog box appears. Click Visible Cells Only. Click OK. Press Ctrl+C. Move to the paste area. Press Ctrl+V.

Using Live Preview with Paste

S tarting with Office 2010, you can see a live preview of your paste by hovering over the choices in the Paste gallery. The Paste gallery provides you with a variety of paste options, such as Paste, Formulas, Values, and Formatting. If you choose Paste, Excel pastes everything. If you choose Formulas, Excel only pastes the formulas. If you choose Values, Excel does not paste the formulas, but instead pastes the results of the formulas. If you choose Formatting, Excel only pastes the formats.

You can view the Paste gallery by clicking the down arrow under the Paste button or by right-clicking and viewing the gallery on the context menu. The options that are available to you depend on what you have cut or

copied and where you are pasting. For example, the choices you see when you are pasting from one area of an Excel worksheet to another area of an Excel worksheet are different from the choices you see when you are pasting from an Excel worksheet to a Word document.

As you hover over each option, Excel displays a tooltip and an accelerator key. The tooltip explains the option. You can click the option or press the accelerator key to apply the option. After you paste, an Options button appears. To change the type of paste, you can click the Options button and then select a different paste method. If you paste by pressing Ctrl+V, press the Ctrl key after pressing Ctrl+V to view the gallery of paste options and then select the option you want.

Using Live Preview with Paste

① Select the cells you want to copy.

② Click the Home tab.

③ Click the Copy button.

④ Click in the cell in the upper-left corner of the paste area.

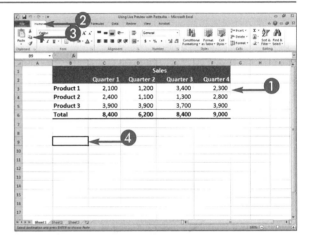

⑤ Click the Home tab.

⑥ Click the ⬇ under the Paste button.

The Paste gallery appears.

7 Hover your mouse pointer over an option.

Excel provides a live preview of the paste result.

8 Click the paste option you want or press the accelerator key.

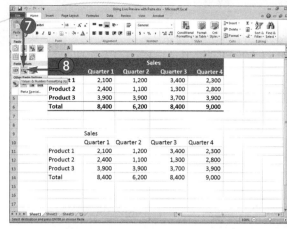

● Excel pastes using the option you selected.

● Click the Options button to change the paste option.

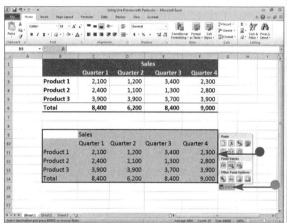

Apply It

When you copy and paste by clicking the Paste button on the Home tab, Excel pastes the values, formulas, and formats but does not adjust the column widths. If you select Keep Source Column Widths from the Paste gallery, Excel adjusts the column widths in addition to pasting the values, formulas, and formats.

If you select Paste Link in the Paste gallery, Excel links the copied cells to the pasted cells. When you change the value in the copied cell, the value in the pasted cell will change also. Excel uses a formula to make the pasted cell equal to the copied cell. You can view the formula on the formula bar.

If you select Picture in the Paste gallery, Excel pastes your selection as a picture and you can use all of the Picture tools on the pasted object. See Chapter 15 to learn more about Picture tools. If you select Linked Picture, Excel pastes your selection as a picture and links the picture to the original cells. Any change you make to the original cells will appear in the pasted picture.

Paste from the Office Clipboard

With Office, you can place data into a storage area called the Clipboard and then paste that data into Excel or another Office application. Cut and copied data stays on the Clipboard until you close all Office applications. The Office Clipboard can store up to 24 cut or copied items. When you add the 25th item, Office deletes the first item. You can store text and graphics on the Clipboard. As you add items to the Clipboard, they appear at the top of the Clipboard task pane. All the items on the Clipboard are available for you to paste to a new location in Excel or into another Office document.

The Clipboard is not visible until you access it. In Excel, you access the Clipboard by clicking the launcher in the Clipboard group on the Home tab. Each item on the

Clipboard appears with an icon that tells you the Office application the information originated from and shows a portion of the text or a thumbnail if the item is a graphic. You can use the Clipboard to store a range of cells. The Office Clipboard pastes the entire range, including all the values, but any formulas in the cells are not included when you paste.

You can paste everything on your Clipboard into your worksheet by clicking the Paste All button. You can clear the Clipboard by clicking the Clear All button.

After you paste an item from the Clipboard, Excel displays the Paste Options menu. You can use the menu to choose whether you want to use the source formatting or match the destination formatting.

Paste from the Office Clipboard

① Select the cells or object you want to copy.

② Click the Home tab.

③ Click the Copy button.

Excel places the cells or the object on the Office Clipboard.

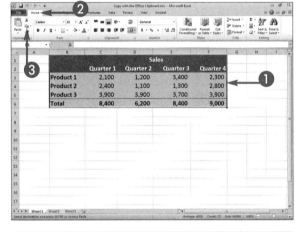

④ Click the launcher in the Clipboard group.

The Clipboard task pane appears.

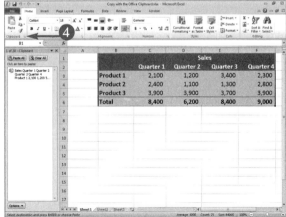

5 Click the destination cell.

6 Click the item you want to paste.

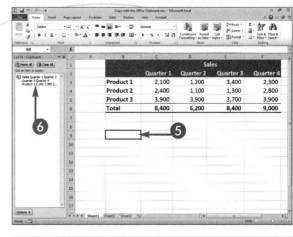

● Excel pastes the item you selected.

● In the Paste Options menu, choose a formatting option.

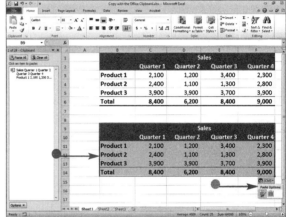

Extra

You can set the following options by clicking the Options button at the bottom of the Clipboard task pane.

OPTION	DESCRIPTION
Show Office Clipboard Automatically	Shows the Office Clipboard automatically when you copy.
Show Office Clipboard When Ctrl+C Pressed Twice	Shows the Office Clipboard when you press Ctrl+C twice.
Collect Without Showing Office Clipboard	Prevents the Clipboard task pane from appearing while you are copying.
Show Office Clipboard Icon on Taskbar	When the Office Clipboard is active, displays an icon on the Windows taskbar.
Show Status Near Taskbar When Copying	Shows the number of items collected out of 24 when you add an item to the Office Clipboard.

Insert or Delete

As you develop your worksheets, you will sometimes want to make changes to the layout. For example, as you modify your worksheet, you may find that you need to insert or delete cells or even insert or delete entire columns or rows of cells. In Excel, you can shift a cell or group of cells up, down, left, or right. You can also add or delete columns and rows.

When you insert cells, columns, or rows, Excel automatically adjusts any formulas that reference the cells, whether they are relative or absolute. For example, if your formula reads =SUM(C2:C4) and you insert three rows anywhere between C2 and C4, your formula will automatically change to =SUM(C2:C7) to accommodate the three new rows. See Chapter 4 to learn more about relative and absolute cell references. When you delete

cells, columns, and rows, Excel also automatically adjusts any formulas that reference the cells; however, if you delete a cell that you directly reference in a formula, Excel cannot adjust the formula and displays a #REF error instead.

If you want to insert columns, select columns to the right of where you want the new columns and then click Insert. For example, if you want to insert three columns, select three columns and then click Insert. If you want to insert rows, select the number of rows below where you want the new rows and then click Insert. For example, if you want to insert three rows, select three rows and then click Insert. If you want to insert nonadjacent columns or rows, hold down the Ctrl key as you select where you want to place the columns or rows.

Insert or Delete

Insert Cells

1. Select where you want to insert cells.

2. Click the Home tab.

3. Click the ⏷ next to Insert.

   A menu appears.

4. Click Insert Cells.

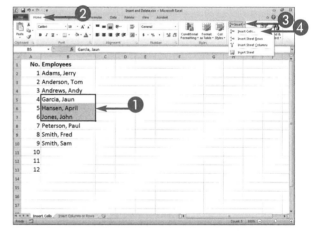

The Insert dialog box appears.

5. Click the direction to shift cells (◉ changes to ◉).

6. Click OK.

● Excel shifts the cells.

Note: If you want to delete cells, select the cells, click Home, click the ⏷ next to Delete, click Delete Cells, choose the direction in which you want to shift the cells, and then click OK.

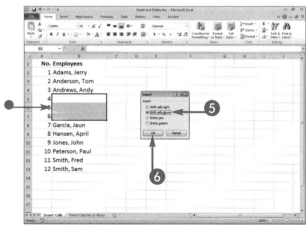

Insert Columns Or Rows

① Click and drag column or row labels.

This example uses rows.

② Click the Home tab.

③ Click Insert.

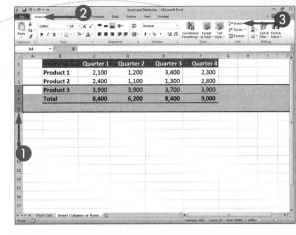

● Excel inserts the columns or rows.

Excel adjusts the formulas.

Note: *If you want to delete columns or rows,
click and drag to select the column or
row labels, click the Home tab, and
then click Delete.*

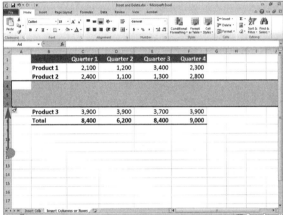

Extra

You can delete the contents of cells by selecting the cells
and then pressing the Delete key. You can also use
Excel's Clear options to remove everything or to delete
formats, contents, or comments from a cell. To remove
everything from a range of cells, select the cells, click the
Home tab, click Clear ( ) in the Editing group, and
then click Clear All. To remove formats while leaving the
contents intact, select the cells and then click the Home
tab. Click Clear in the Editing group, and then click
Clear Formats. To remove contents while leaving the
formatting intact, select the cells and then click the
Home tab. Click Clear in the Editing group, and then
click Clear Contents.

To insert a new worksheet, press Shift+F11 or click the
Insert Worksheet button ( ) next to the sheet name
tabs. To delete a worksheet, right-click the worksheet's
tab. A menu appears. Click Delete sheet. Excel deletes
the sheet. Or, you can click the Home tab, click the
down arrow next to Delete ( ), and then click Delete
sheet.

Find and Replace Information

As worksheets get larger, finding the information you want can be difficult. You can use Excel's Find feature to locate information. If you want to replace the found information with new information, use Excel's Find and Replace feature. Use the Find tab in the Find and Replace dialog box to find information. Use the Replace tab in the Find and Replace dialog box to find and replace information.

You can use substitutions in the Find and Replace dialog box. You can use the asterisk (*) as a substitute for any sequence of characters. You can use the question mark (?) as a substitute for any single character. For example, typing *ber finds September, October, November, and December. Typing J?ne finds Jane and June.

When you click the Find All button, by default Excel finds every instance of the value you are looking for in the active worksheet and lists the workbook, worksheet, cell name, cell address, value, and formula for each found value at the bottom of the Find and Replace dialog box. When you click Find Next, Excel moves to the first instance of the value. Excel moves to the next instance with every additional click of the Find Next button.

If you want to replace the values you find with a new value, click Replace All on the Replace tab to replace every instance of the value. Click Replace to replace the selected instance of the value and then move to the next instance. Click Find Next if you want to move to the next instance without replacing the selected instance.

In the Find and Replace dialog box, you can use the Options button to set additional options.

Find and Replace Information

Find Information

1. Click the Home tab.

2. Click the Find & Select button.

   A menu appears.

3. Click Find.

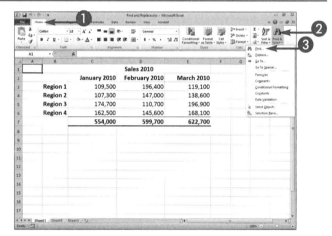

The Find and Replace dialog box appears.

4. Type what you want to find.

5. Click Find All to find all instances or click Find Next to find the first instance.

6. If you clicked Find All, click an instance.

   - Excel moves to the instance you clicked.

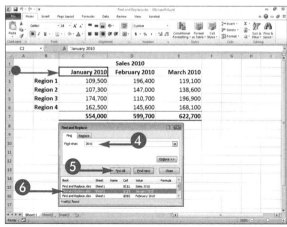

Replace Information

1 Repeat Steps 1 to 3 under Find Information.

2 Click the Replace tab.

3 Type what you want to find.

4 Type your replacement.

5 Click Replace All to replace all instances.

● You can click Find and then Replace to find and replace the first instance; then click Find Next to find the next instance.

● Excel replaces the data.

A message box appears telling you Excel made replacements.

6 Click OK.

Excel closes the message box

7 Click Close.

Excel closes the Find and Replace dialog box.

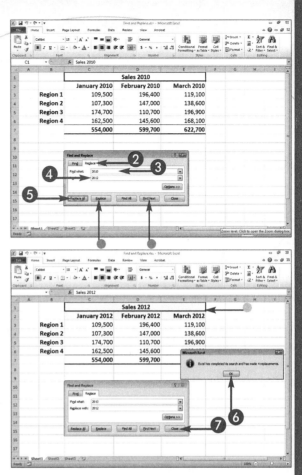

Extra

You can click the Options button on the Find and Replace tabs in the Find and Replace dialog box to set several options. In the Within field, select Sheet if you want to search only the active worksheet or select Workbook if you want to search the entire workbook.

In the Search field, select By Rows if you want to search left to right across the rows. Select Column if you want to search top to bottom down the columns.

Select the check box in the Match Case field (☐ changes to ✔) if you want your match to be case-sensitive. For example, if this option is not selected, abc is considered the same as ABC or aBc.

Select the check box in the Match Entire Cell Contents field (☐ changes to ✔), if you want what you type in the Find What field to match the cell contents and not contain any extraneous information. For example, one cell contains the value Jane Smith and another cell contains the value Smith. If you select Match Entire Cell Contents, Excel will find Smith but not Jane Smith.

Change the Name of a Worksheet

I f you have a number of worksheets in your workbook, naming your sheets enables users to determine easily which sheet they want to access. For example, if you keep sales figures for three regions and you keep each region on a separate worksheet, you can name those worksheets Region 1 Sales, Region 2 Sales, and Region 3 Sales. If you keep total sales on yet another worksheet, you can name that worksheet Total Sales.

By default, Excel names all worksheets Sheet#, replacing # with a number that represents the order in which the sheet was added. For example, a typical workbook contains three sheets: Sheet1, Sheet2, and Sheet3. If you add a worksheet, Excel names it Sheet4. Excel uses the name Chart# for chart sheets.

Apply It

The worksheet name appears on a tab at the bottom of the worksheet. You can change the color of the tab. Right-click the tab. A menu appears. Click Tab Color. A submenu appears. Click the color you want. Excel changes the color of the tab.

A quick way to rename a worksheet is to right-click the tab, click Rename Sheet, and then type the name you want to give the worksheet.

Change the Name of a Worksheet

1 Click the Home tab.

2 Click the ⬛ next to the Format field.

A menu appears.

3 Click Rename Sheet.

4 Type a new name for the worksheet.

5 Press Enter.

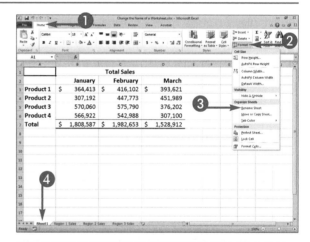

● Excel renames the worksheet.

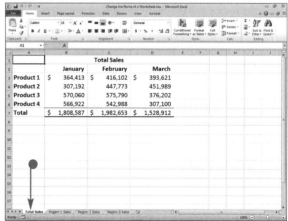

Change Column Widths or Row Heights

There are times when you may need to adjust a column width or row height. For example, text that is too long spills over into the next cell, numbers that are too long display as pound signs (####), and Excel cuts off fonts that are too large for the cell. To view the data, you can drag the right border of the column label to change the width of the cells or you can drag the bottom border of the row label to change the height of the cells.

Excel can automatically determine the proper height or width of a column or row. The AutoFit Row Height option automatically adjusts the height of rows. The AutoFit Column Width option automatically adjusts the width of columns.

Apply It

To change the width or height of a column or row, select it, click the Home tab; click the down arrow next to Format and then click Column Width or Row Height. Enter a column width or row height and then press OK.

To automatically adjust a column width or row height, click the Home tab; click the down arrow next to Format and then click AutoFit Column Width or AutoFit Row Height.

Change Column Widths or Row Heights

① Click the right border of the column to adjust the column width.

② Drag the border.

● Click the bottom border of the row to adjust the row height.

Double-click a border to automatically adjust the column width or row height.

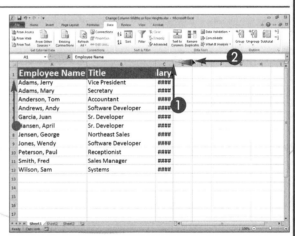

● Excel adjusts the column width or row height.

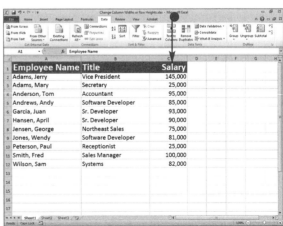

Hide Columns
or Rows

I n Excel, you can hide columns or rows. You usually hide portions of a worksheet so that you can focus on the visible data. For example, a worksheet may contain monthly data and quarterly summaries. You can hide the monthly data so that you can focus on the quarterly summaries.

When you hide a column or row, you can still access the values contained in the cells when you reference them in formulas and functions. Excel indicates the existence of hidden columns and rows by skipping over the hidden columns and rows in the column and row labels. For example if you hide columns B, C, and D, you will only see column labels for A, E, F and so on.

Apply It

To unhide columns or rows, select the column or row label before and after the hidden columns and rows. Click the Home tab. Click Format in the Cells group. A menu appears. Click Hide & Unhide. A submenu appears. Click Unhide Columns to unhide columns or click Unhide Rows to unhide rows. Excel displays the hidden columns or rows.

Hide Columns or Rows

① Select the column or row labels.

② Click the Home tab.

③ Click the ▼ next to Format.

   A menu appears.

④ Click Hide & Unhide.

⑤ Click Hide Columns or Hide Rows.

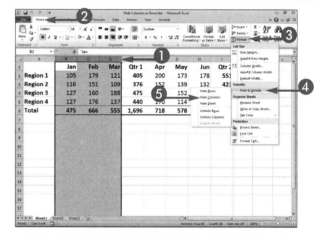

● Excel hides the columns or rows you selected.

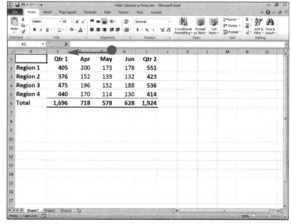

Hide a Worksheet

You can hide Excel worksheets. You may want to hide a worksheet to prevent users from viewing it. The worksheet might contain raw data that you use in calculations or to validate data entry. For example, in Chapter 4 you learn how to define constants. You may want to keep your constants in a hidden worksheet. In Chapter 13, you learn how to validate with a list. You may want to keep your validation lists in a hidden worksheet.

Hiding a worksheet does not always keep users from accessing it. Users can unhide sheets in Excel by using the Unhide option. If you want to prevent users from making changes to a hidden sheet, you must protect it. See Chapter 13 to learn how to protect a worksheet.

Apply It

To unhide a sheet, click the Home tab. Click Format in the Cells group. A menu appears. Click Hide & Unhide. A submenu appears. Click Unhide Sheet. The Unhide dialog box appears. Click the sheet you want to unhide. Click OK. Excel displays the hidden sheet.

You can also hide or unhide worksheets by right-clicking a sheet tab and then selecting Hide Sheet or Unhide Sheet from the menu that appears.

Hide a WorkSheet

1. Move to the worksheet you want to hide.

2. Click the Home tab.

3. Click the ▼ next to Format.

   A menu appears.

4. Click Hide & Unhide.

5. Click Hide Sheet.

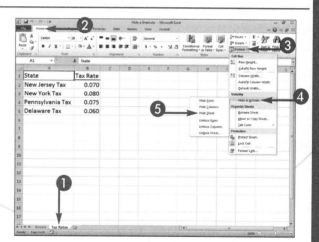

● Excel hides the worksheet.

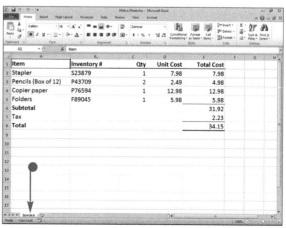

Move or Copy a Worksheet

You can copy a worksheet. You can place a copy of a worksheet in the same workbook or you can place a copy of a worksheet in another workbook. For example, if you collect sales data for three regions on three separate worksheets and you format each worksheet the same, you can format one worksheet and then make copies of the worksheet so that you can use the copies when working on the other two regions.

You can copy the worksheets to the same workbook or you can copy them to two separate additional workbooks — one for each region. When you copy a worksheet to the same workbook or if the workbook you are copying to already has a worksheet with the same name, Excel gives the worksheet the same name as the original worksheet and appends it with the copy number in parentheses.

You can rename the worksheet if you want. Before you can copy a worksheet to an existing workbook, the workbook must be open.

You can move a worksheet. For example, within a workbook, you can rearrange worksheets so that they appear alphabetically or in any other order you choose. You can also move a worksheet to another workbook. For example, if you keep sales data for three regions in a single workbook on three separate worksheets, you can move each worksheet to its own workbook. Be careful when you move a worksheet. If you have a formula that references the worksheet or if you have a chart that is based on the worksheet, moving the worksheet can cause errors.

Move or Copy a Worksheet

Copy a Worksheet

1. Press and hold down the Ctrl key.

2. Click the tab of the worksheet you want to copy.

3. Drag the tab until it is at the location you want to place it.

4. Release the mouse.

5. Release the Ctrl key.

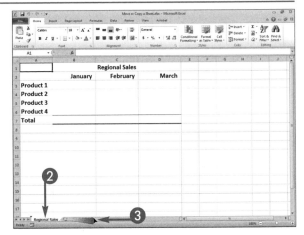

- Excel copies the worksheet.

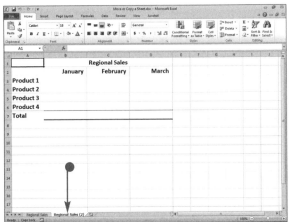

Move a Worksheet

① Click the tab of the worksheet you want to move.

② Drag the tab to the new location.

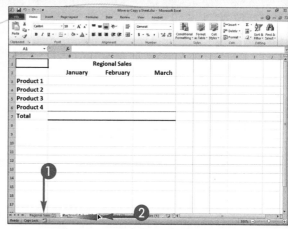

● Excel moves the worksheet.

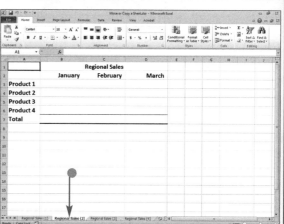

Apply It

To copy a worksheet to an existing workbook, open the workbook. Right-click the worksheet's tab. A menu appears. Click Move or Copy Sheet. The Move or Copy dialog box appears. Click the down arrow (▾) in the To Book field and then select the workbook to which you want to copy. The sheets in the selected workbook appear in the Before Sheet box. Click the sheet you want to place the copied sheet before or click Move to End to make the sheet the last sheet in the workbook. Click Create a Copy (☐ changes to ✔). Click OK. Excel copies the worksheet.

To move a worksheet to an existing workbook, open the workbook. Right-click the worksheet's tab. A menu appears. Click Move or Copy Sheet. The Move or Copy dialog box appears. Click the down arrow in the To Book field and then select the workbook to which you want to move the worksheet. The sheets in the selected workbook appear in the Before Sheet box. Click the sheet you want to place the copied sheet before or click Move to End to make the sheet the last sheet in the workbook. Click OK. Excel moves the worksheet.

Freeze Worksheet Titles

When you create a worksheet, you can create labels that identify the data in the columns and rows. For example, if you are collecting sales figures by sales person by month, you can place the month at the top of each column and the sales person's first and last name in the first two columns of each row. If you have more columns or rows than will fit on a screen, as you scroll down or across the window, the column and row labels you created disappear from view. You can freeze the column and row labels so that they remain in view as you scroll. You can freeze both the column and row labels. Or, you can freeze just column labels or just row labels.

Apply It

To just freeze column labels, click in the cell that is on the first row and to the left of the last column label you want to freeze. Click the View tab. Click Freeze Panes. Click Freeze Panes again.

To just freeze rows labels, click in the cell that is in the first column and under the last row you want to freeze. Click the View tab. Click Freeze Panes. Click Freeze Panes again.

Freeze Worksheet Titles

① Click where you want to freeze titles — below the column label and to the right of the row label.

② Click the View tab.

③ Click Freeze Panes.

A menu appears.

④ Click Freeze Panes.

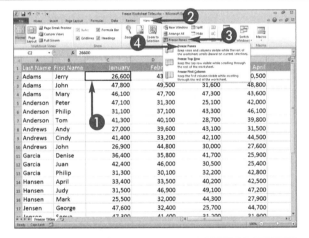

Excel freezes the column and row labels.

● As you scroll, the labels remain stationary.

Note: *After you freeze panes, you can choose Unfreeze Panes from the Freeze Panes menu to return to normal scrolling.*

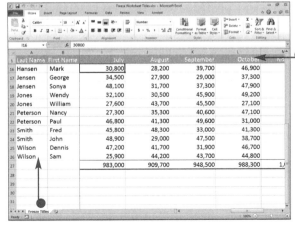

Hide Gridlines, Headings, or the Formula Bar

*G*ridlines are the faint lines that appear by default and separate the rows and columns in an Excel worksheet. Borders are a type of formatting that you can apply to cells to separate the rows and columns in a worksheet. To make borders stand out, you can hide gridlines.

Headings are the row and column labels that appear along the side and across the top of an Excel worksheet. If they are not relevant to the task you are preforming or if you want to make more room on your screen, you can remove them from view.

The *formula bar* appears below the Ribbon and displays the value or formula in the active cell. If you want to suppress the display of formulas, you can hide the formula bar.

Extra

You can change the color of gridlines. Select a worksheet. Click the File tab. Click Options. The Excel Options dialog box appears. In the bar on the left side, click Advanced. The Advanced Options for Working with Excel pane appears. In the Display Options for this Worksheet section, click Gridline Color. A color box appears. Click the color you want. Click OK. Excel changes the color of the gridlines.

Show or Hide Gridlines, Headings, or the Formula Bar

① Click the View tab.

② Click to deselect and hide gridlines, the formula bar, or headings (✔ changes to ☐).

● Gridlines

● Formula bar

● Headings

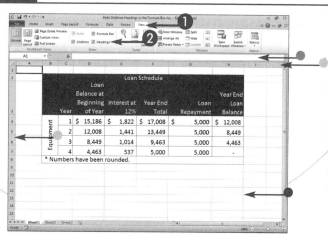

Excel hides the options you selected.

To display an option, select the option on the View tab.

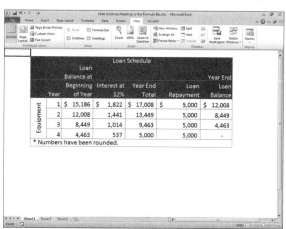

Understanding Formulas

I n Excel, you use formulas. A *formula* is an equation that performs a calculation. A formula can consist of operators, functions, numbers, text, and cell references. You place formulas in cells. You can click a cell and then type your formula into the formula bar or you can type your formula directly into a cell. You start most formulas by typing an equal sign (=).

Operators

You use operators to tell Excel the type of calculation you want to perform. There are four types of operators: arithmetic, comparison, text concatenation, and reference.

Arithmetic Operators

Use arithmetic operators to perform mathematical calculations such as addition (+), subtraction (–), multiplication (*), division (/), percent (%), and exponentiation (^). For example, the formula = 3 * 2 + 1 – A4 multiplies 3 times 2, adds 1, and then subtracts the contents of cell A4. If cell A4 is equal to 3, the equation returns 4.

OPERATOR	KEY	PURPOSE	EXAMPLE	ANSWER
+	Plus sign	Adds	=1+1	2
–	Minus sign	Subtracts	=3–2	1
–	Minus sign	Negates	–1	–1
*	Asterisk	Multiplies	=3*2	6
/	Forward slash	Divides	=6/2	3
%	Percent sign	Converts to a percent	.10	10%
^	Caret	Raises to a power	=3^2	9

Comparison Operators

Use comparison operators to compare values. The result of a comparison operation is either the logical value TRUE or the logical value FALSE. For example, the formula =A1=B1 compares the value in cell A1 to the value in cell B1 and returns the value TRUE if they are equal and FALSE if they are not equal.

OPERATOR	PURPOSE	EXAMPLE	ANSWER
=	Determines if values are equal	=1=1	TRUE
		=2=1	FALSE
<>	Determines if values are unequal	=1<>1	FALSE
		=2<>1	TRUE
>	Determines if one value is greater than another value	=1>2	FALSE
		=2>1	TRUE
<	Determines if one value is less than another value	=1<2	TRUE
		=2<1	FALSE
>=	Determines if one value is greater than or equal to another value	=1>=2	FALSE
		=2>=1	TRUE
<=	Determines if one value is less than or equal to another value	=1<=2	TRUE
		=2<=1	FALSE

Text Concatenation Operator

There is only one text concatenation operator — the ampersand (&). Use the ampersand to join values together to produce one continuous text value. For example, if the text "John" is in cell A1 and the text "Smith" is in cell B1, the formula = A1 & " " & B1 returns John Smith. A space within quotes returns a space " ". In a formula, place text within quotes. For example, ="John " & B1, returns John Smith, if "Smith" is in cell B1.

Reference Operators

Use reference operators to specify the range of cells you want to use in your formula. There are three reference operators: the colon (:), the comma (,), and the space. Excel refers to them as the range operator, the union operator, and the intersection operator, respectively. The colon references every cell included in and between the referenced cells. For example, A1:C3 includes cells A1, A2, A3, B1, B2, B3, C1, C2, and C3. The comma enables you to reference two or more cells or values. For example, A1, B2, 25 references cell A1, cell B2, and the number 25. The intersection operator references all the cells range operators have in common. For example, the reference B1:C3 C1:D3 references cells C1 to C3. You can use more than one reference operator in a single formula.

OPERATOR	PURPOSE	EXAMPLE
:	References every cell included in and between two cell references	A1:C3
,	References two or more values	A1, B3, C5, 15
space	References all the cells two range operators have in common	B1:C3 C1:D3

Operator Precedence

When you perform a mathematical calculation in Excel, you must be careful of precedence — the order in which Excel performs calculations. For example, Excel performs calculations from left to right, performing multiplication and division before addition and subtraction. The formula = 3 + 4 * 2 returns 11. Excel multiplies 4 times 2 and then adds 3. If you want to change the order of precedence, add parentheses. Excel calculates numbers in parentheses first. The formula = (3 + 4) * 2 returns 14. Excel adds 3 plus 4 and then multiplies the result by 2.

The following table shows the precedence order, from highest to lowest, that Excel uses to evaluate operators in formulas. If the operators in the formula have the same order of precedence, Excel evaluates the equation from left to right.

PRECEDENCE	OPERATORS	SYMBOL
1	Parentheses	( )
2	Reference operators	: (space) ,
3	Minus sign	– (negates a number)
4	Percent sign	%
5	Exponentiation	^
6	Multiplication and division	*, /
7	Addition and subtraction	+, –
8	Concatenation	&
9	Comparison operators	=, <, >, <=, >=, <>

Functions

A function is a formula that Excel has predefined. You can use a function to do such things as add numbers, find an average, or find the highest number in a list. Excel provides you with more than 300 functions that are divided into the following categories: Financial, Date and Time, Math and Trig, Statistical, Lookup and Reference, Database, Text, Logical, Information, Engineering, and Cube. You supply values — called *arguments* — to the function; Excel returns the result. Excel's Function Wizard steps you through the process of adding a function to your worksheet. See Chapter 5 for more information on the Function Wizard. You can also type functions directly into a worksheet. You start by typing an equal sign following by the function name. As you begin to type the function name, the formula AutoComplete list appears. Double-click the function you want to add to your formula. Excel adds the function and an open parenthesis. Type your arguments. A comma must separate each argument. End your function with a close parenthesis. The following is an example of a valid function: =SUM(25, B1, B5:D5).

You can nest a function within another function and arithmetic formulas can contain functions.

Calculate with an Operator

The real power of Excel comes from its ability to manipulate information and perform mathematical calculations. When calculating, you can use operators such as the plus (+), minus (–), multiplication (*), and division (/) signs. You start by typing an equal sign, followed by the values you want to add, subtract, multiply, or divide, each separated by an operator. For example, type =6*3/2-B1, and then press Enter. Excel does the math and displays the answer.

You can also include a value in a formula by clicking in the cell that contains the value. For example, if the value you want to include in your formula is in cell B1, type an equal sign (=) and then click in cell B1 type an operator and then continue creating your formula.

Extra

After you complete the entry of your formula, you can either click Enter (✔) on the formula bar or you can press the Enter key. Both will cause Excel to perform the calculation.

Expanding the formula bar enables you to enter longer formulas. You can click the chevron (⯆) on the right side of the formula bar or press Ctrl+Shift+U to expand and collapse the formula bar.

Calculate with an Operator

Calculate With An Operator

1 Type =.

2 Type the formula.

3 Click in the cell with the value you want to use in the formula.

4 Click Enter (✔) - the check mark on the formula bar to calculate your formula.

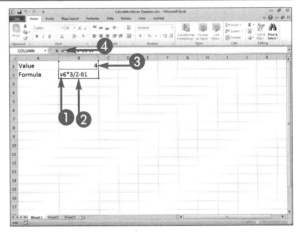

● The results appear in the cell where you typed the formula.

● The formula appears on the formula bar.

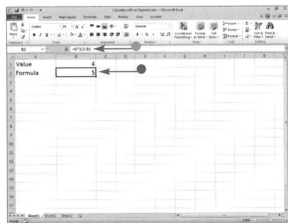

Calculate Using a Function and Cell Addresses

A function is a prewritten formula. You enter a value or values into a function; it performs the calculation and returns the result to you. Functions simplify and shorten long formulas. For example, instead of entering =B2+B3+ B4+B5+B6+B7, you can use the SUM function and enter =SUM(B2:B7). You can use a function alone, combine it with other functions, or embed it in a formula. All of the following formulas are valid: =2*SUM(B2:B7) multiplies the sum of cells B2 through B7 by 2; =ROUND(SUM(G2:G8),2) rounds the sum of G2 through G8 to 2 decimal places; and =SUM(B2:B8)+SUM(C2:C8) adds the sum of B2 through B8 to the sum of C2 through C8.

When a function begins a formula, it must be preceded by an equal sign. You type the equal sign followed by the function name and parentheses. As you begin to typing the formula name, the AutoComplete list appears. The AutoComplete list lists all functions. You double-click a function name to select it. You call the values that you enter into a function *arguments*. Place arguments inside the parentheses separated by commas. Arguments can be numbers, text, logical values, dates, arrays, error values, cells, or cell ranges.

Excel has a large number of functions from which you can choose. They are divided into categories, such as Statistical, Financial, and Date and Time. For a description of each function, click the Help button, and then click Function Reference. The functions are listed by category. The function description explains each function and describes each argument. Arguments can be constants or formulas. Some functions have arguments that are optional.

Calculate Using a Function and Cell Addresses

1. Type =.

2. Type the first letter or first few letters of the function name.

   The AutoComplete list appears.

3. Double-click the function you want.

4. Enter the arguments.

   ● The names of the arguments appear.

5. Click the check mark.

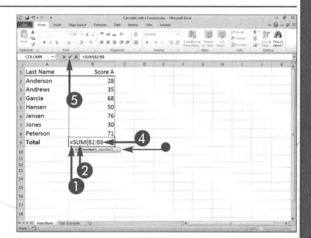

   ● The results appear in the cell where you typed the formula.

   ● The function appears on the formula bar.

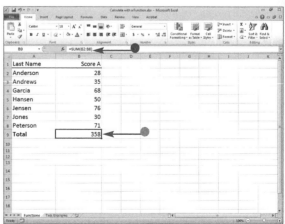

Create an Array Formula

If your find yourself repeatedly entering the same formula into adjacent cells and only changing the cell reference, you should consider using an array formula. With an array formula, you can enter a formula once and have it apply to multiple cells. In addition, array formulas use less memory.

Array formulas differ from regular formulas in that they can produce multiple results from a single formula. They are easy to recognize because curly braces always surround them. When you complete an array formula, you press Ctrl+Shift+Enter and Excel places the curly braces around the formula. You cannot create and array formula by typing curly braces. You must press Ctrl+Shift+Enter. Make sure you are holding down both the Ctrl and Shift keys when you press Enter. If you are only pressing the Shift key, Excel enters a regular formula in the active cell.

If you are only pressing the Ctrl key, Excel enters a regular formula in all the selected cells.

There are two types of array formulas: multi-cell formulas and single cell formulas. An array formula that places results in multiple cells is called a multi-cell formula. An array formula that places results in a single cell is called a single-cell formula. When you calculate a multi-cell formula, you place the results of the formula in multiple cells. When you calculate a single-cell formula, you place the results in a single cell.

The formula {=C2:E2*C3:E3} performs the following three calculation: C2*C3, D2*D3, and E2*E3 and places the results of each calculation in separate cell. The formula {=SUM(C2:E2*C3:E3)} performs the same three calculations, sums the results of the calculations and places that result in a single cell.

Create an Array Formula

Create a Multi-Cell Formula

1 Select the range where you want to the results to appear.

2 Enter the formula as you normally would.

3 Press Ctrl+Shift+Enter.

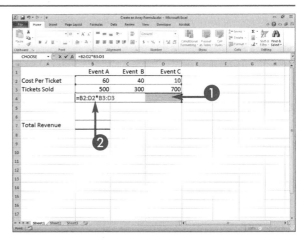

● Excel calculates the result.

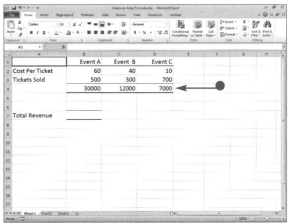

Calculate a Single Cell Formula

① Select the cell where you want the result to appear.

② Enter the formula as you normally would.

③ Press Ctrl+Shift+Enter.

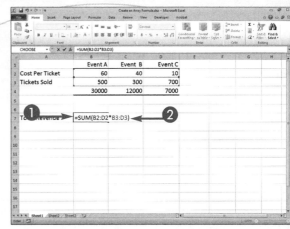

● Excel calculates the result.

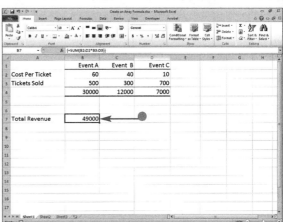

When working with array formulas, you cannot change the individual cells that contain the array formula; you cannot delete, clear, or move part of the array formula, and you cannot insert cells in the range of cells referenced by the array formula. If you attempt any of these operations, you will receive an error message.

To edit an array formula, select a cell in the formula range. Move to the formula bar. The curly braces disappear. Make your changes. Press Ctrl+Shift+Enter. Excel modifies the formula.

There are a few disadvantages to using an array formula. For example, the formula $\{=SUM(C2:E2*C3:E3)\}$ does not display interim calculations. If you want an audit trail, array formulas will not work for you. If others use your workbook, they may not be familiar with array formulas and therefore may have difficulty understanding your workbook. You may forget to press Ctrl+Shift+Enter.

Using the Sum, Average, Count, Min, and Max Functions

Excel's AutoSum feature offers instant access to the following functions: SUM, AVERAGE, MIN, MAX, and COUNT. The SUM function adds the numeric values in the selected range, the AVERAGE function finds the average of the numeric values in the selected range, the MIN function finds the lowest numeric value in the selected range, the MAX function finds the highest numeric value in the selected range, and the COUNT function counts the numeric values in the selected range. To use these functions, select a range and then select the AutoSum option you want. Excel places the result in the first available adjacent cell, generally to the right of a horizontal selection or below a vertical selection. Or, you can select a function and let Excel select the range. You can change Excel's selection.

Apply It

You can right-click on the status bar, which is located at the bottom of the Excel window, to display the Customize Status Bar menu. If you select Average, Count, Minimum, Maximum, and Sum from the menu, when you click and drag over two or more cells, Excel automatically places the average, a count, the lowest number, the highest number, and the sum of the values on the status bar.

Using the Sum, Average, Count, Min, and Max Functions

① Select the cell where you want the result.

② Click the Home tab.

③ Click the ⏷ next to AutoSum button (Σ) and then select a function.

   Excel selects a range.

● If necessary, adjust the selection.

④ Click the check mark.

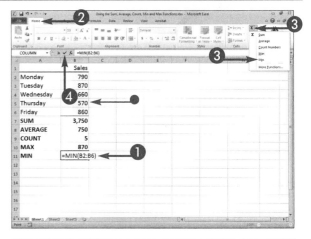

● Excel calculates the result.

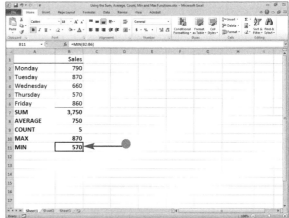

Create a Formula that Refers to Another Worksheet

ou can create formulas that reference other worksheets. For example, if you base your calculations on raw data, you can keep that data in a separate worksheet and reference it when needed. To reference cells in another worksheet, precede the cell address with the worksheet name followed by an exclamation point (!). For example, you can place the following formula in a cell in Sheet1 and use it to sum cells in Sheet2: =SUM(Sheet2!B2:B4). You can type the sheet reference, or you can select Sheet2 and then click and drag to reference cells B2 to B4. If you change the worksheet name, Excel automatically updates the formula. To learn how to change the worksheet name, see Chapter 3.

Apply It

When working with multiple worksheets, you may want the worksheets to appear side by side. Click the View tab and then click New Window. Excel opens a new window. To display the window, click Arrange All. The Arrange Windows dialog box appears. Click Tiled (○ changes to ◉). Click OK. In the new window, click the worksheet tab that has the data you want to reference.

Create a Formula that Refers to Another Worksheet

- Sheet1

- Sheet2

1 Type = to begin the formula or type the function name if you are using a function.

2 Select the cells you want to reference.

3 Click the check mark.

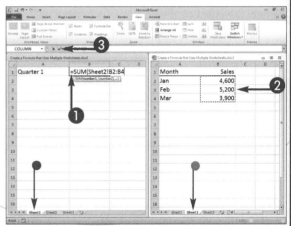

- Excel calculates the result.

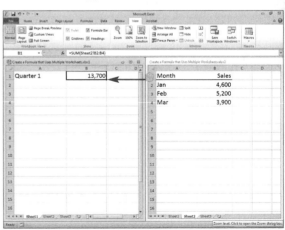

Understanding Relative and Absolute Cell Addresses

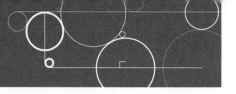

When you create a formula, you can refer to cells by using relative, absolute, or mixed cell addresses. The type of address you use is important when you copy the formula to another cell. When you use a relative cell address, the formula is based on the position of cells used in the formula relative to the cell where the formula is located. For example, if you enter the formula = B1+B2 in cell B3, Excel moves up two cells to cell B1 and gets that value and then moves up one cell to cell B2 and adds that value to the first value. If you copy the formula, Excel will always move up two cells to get the first value and up one cell to get the second value. So, if you copy the formula to cell B4, the formula automatically becomes =B2+B3. In most instances, by default, formulas use relative cell addresses.

When you use an absolute cell address, the formula is always based on the exact cell you enter into to the formula. For example, if you enter the formula =$D$1+$D$2 in cell D3, Excel adds cell D1 to cell D2. If you copy the formula, Excel will still add cell D1 to cell D2. You make a cell address absolute by placing a dollar sign in front of the column and row reference.

You can have a mixed cell address. With a mixed cell address, either the column stays the same and the row changes – an absolute column and a relative row – or the row stays the same and the column changes – an absolute row and a relative column. You can press the F4 key to cycle through absolute, relative, and mixed cell addresses.

Understanding Relative and Absolute Cell Addresses

Use a Relative Cell Address

1. Enter the formula.

2. Copy the formula and paste it where you want the results to appear.

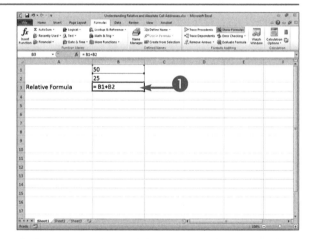

● Excel copies the formula in a relative fashion.

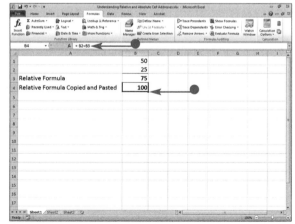

Use an Absolute Cell Address

1. Type =.

2. Click the cell address.

3. Press F4.

4. Type an operator.

5. Click the cell address.

6. Press F4.

7. Click the check mark.

8. Copy the formula and paste it where you want the results to appear.

- Excel copies the cell in an absolute fashion.

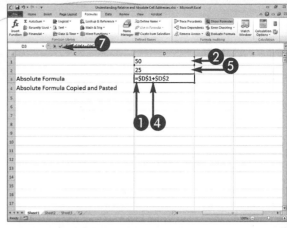

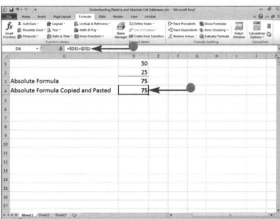

Extra

To use the same formula in multiple cells, you can use the Fill Handle to copy the formula to adjoining cells in the same row or column. This changes all relative cell references within the formula. For example, copying =SUM(A1:A5) from cell A6 to cell B6 results in =SUM(B1:B5). The Fill Handle is the black box on the bottom-right corner of a selected cell. You simply drag it to an adjacent range of cells. Excel copies the formula and any cell formatting to the new cells.

When you move a formula to a new cell on your worksheet, all cell references in the formula, whether absolute or relative, remain the same. For example, if you move the formula =SUM(A1:A5), which has a relative reference and is located in cell A6, into cell A7, the cell references in the formula do not change. You can move a formula simply by dragging it to a new cell. Hover your mouse pointer over the border of the cell; when you see a four-sided arrow (⁺⇧), drag the cell to a new location. Excel moves any formatting with the data.

Edit
Formulas

After creating a formula, you can update it to accommodate new data. You can change the cells your formula references or change the arguments in your function. For example, if the method of calculation changes, you can edit the formula. Or, if you need to make changes to a function, you can.

You can edit your formula directly, or, if your formula is a function, you can edit it using the Function Arguments dialog box. To edit a formula directly, double-click in the cell containing the formula and then type your changes or double-click in the cell containing the formula, and then use the formula bar to make your changes. When you double-click in a cell, Excel enters Edit mode — you can see the word Edit on the left side of the status bar. When

Excel is in Edit mode, it highlights the cells the formula references. The highlight for each value and range displays in a different color.

You can change function arguments by clicking in the cell that contains the function and then clicking the Insert Function (fx) button to open the Function Arguments dialog box. In the Function Arguments dialog box you can change the value or select new cell ranges for each argument. When you click OK to accept the changes, Excel updates the results.

You can use the same method you use to edit formulas to edit text. Just double-click in the cell you want to edit and then type your changes or use the formula bar to make your changes.

Edit Formulas

Edit a Formula

① Double-click in the cell that contains the formula you want to edit.

● Excel color-codes the referenced cells.

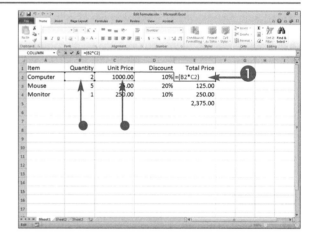

② Make your changes.

③ Click the check mark.

● Excel calculates the result.

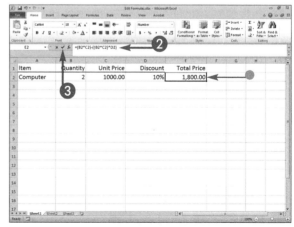

Edit a Function

1. Click in the cell that contains the function you want to edit.

2. Click the Insert Function button.

   The Function Arguments dialog box appears.

3. Type the desired changes to the formula arguments.

4. Click OK.

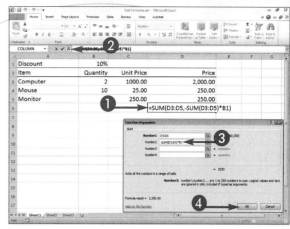

- Excel calculates the result.

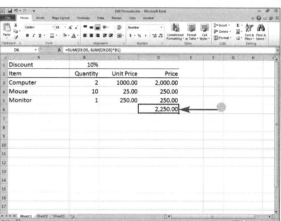

Extra

You can use cut, copy, and paste to move a formula from one location in your worksheet to another location. When you cut and paste a formula, the cell references do not change. This is true for formulas with relative cell addresses and for formulas with absolute cell addresses. When you copy and paste a formula, the cell references may change depending upon the type of cell reference. See Chapter 3 to learn how to cut, copy, and paste.

To delete a formula, click in the cell that contains the formula and then press the Delete key. Or click the Home tab. Click the 🖭 to the Clear button (🖉) in the Editing group. A menu appears. Click Clear Contents.

You can edit a formula by clicking in the cell that contains the formula, pressing F2, and then making your changes. Pressing F2 while you are in a cell, places you in Edit mode.

Name Cells and Ranges

In Excel, you can name individual cells, or groups of cells called *ranges*. A cell named Tax_Rate or a range named Region_1 is easier to remember than the corresponding cell address or range. You can use named cells and ranges in formulas to refer to the values contained in them. When you move a named range to a new location, Excel automatically updates any formulas that refer to it.

When you name a range, you determine the scope of the name by telling Excel whether it applies to a particular worksheet or the entire workbook. You can name several ranges at once by using Excel's Create from Selection option.

Excel range names must be fewer than 255 characters. The first character must be a letter, underscore (_), or

backslash (\). You cannot use spaces or symbols. You can use the period or underscore as a separator. It is best to create short, memorable names. Each range name must be unique within it scope. Range names are not case sensitive. Excel considers the name `cash` the same as the name `CASH`.

There is a down arrow located on the left side of the formula bar. When you click the down arrow, a list of named ranges appears. If you click a named range, you will move to the cells it defines. When you are creating a formula, if you click and drag to select a group of cells that have a range name, Excel automatically uses the range name instead of the cell address.

To learn how to use a named range, see the section "Create Formulas That Include Names" later in this chapter.

Name Cells and Ranges

Name a Range of Cells

1. Select the cells you want to name.

   Alternatively, click a cell with a value to create a named cell.

2. Click the Formulas tab.

3. Click Define Name.

   The New Name dialog box appears.

4. Type a name.

5. Click ▾ and then select the scope of the name.

● The range you selected in Step 1 appears here.

6. Click OK.

● Excel creates a named range.

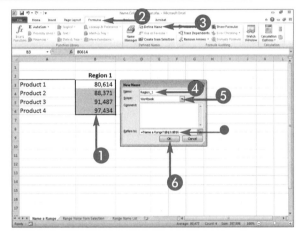

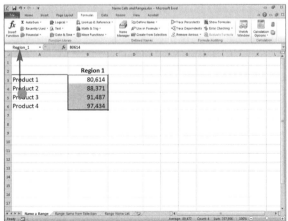

Create Named Ranges from a Selection

1. Select the range.

   Include the labels.

2. Click the Formulas tab.

3. Click Create from Selection.

   The Create Names from Selection dialog box appears.

4. Click the location of the range names (☐ changes to ☑).

5. Click OK.

   Excel names the ranges.

○ You can click 🔽 and then click a range name to move to a named range.

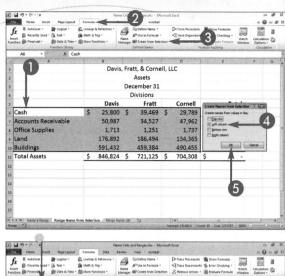

Apply It

You can use Excel's Name Manager to rename, edit, or delete named ranges and constant values. On the Formulas tab, click Name Manager. The Name Manager dialog box appears. Double-click the name you want to edit. The Edit Name dialog box appears. Make the changes you want and then click OK. To delete a range name or constant, click the name in the Name Manager dialog box and then click Delete. If you want to create a new range name or constant, click New in the Name Manager dialog box. The New Name dialog box appears. You can use it to make your entries.

If you have a worksheet that includes formulas that reference cells or ranges that are named, you can convert the cell or range references to range names. Select the cells containing the formulas and then click the down arrow next to Define Names on the Formulas tab. A menu appears. Click Apply Names. The Apply Names dialog box appears, displaying all the range names that exist within the workbook. Click OK. Excel updates the formulas in the selected cells to include the range names.

Define and Display Constants

U se a constant whenever you want to apply the same value in different contexts. With constants, you can refer to a value by simply using the constant's name.

You can use constants in many ways. For example, the sales tax rate is a familiar constant that, when multiplied by the subtotal on an invoice, results in the tax owed. Likewise, income tax rates are the constants used to calculate tax liabilities. Although tax rates change from time to time, they tend to remain constant within a tax period.

To create a constant in Excel, you need to type its value in the New Name dialog box, the same dialog box you use to name ranges, as shown in the previous section, "Name Cells and Ranges." When you define a constant,

you determine the scope of the constant by telling Excel whether it applies to the current worksheet or the entire workbook. To use the constant, simply use the name you defined.

The rules that apply to naming a range also apply to naming a constant. Excel constant names must be fewer than 255 characters. The first character must be a letter, underscore (_), or backslash (\). You cannot use spaces or symbols. You can use the period or underscore as a separator. It is best to create short, memorable names. Each name must be unique within its scope. Constant names are not case sensitive. Excel considers the name `tax` the same as the name `TAX`.

To learn how to use a constant, see the next section, "Create Formulas That Include Names."

Define and Display Constants

Define a Constant

1. Click the Formulas tab.

2. Click Define Name.

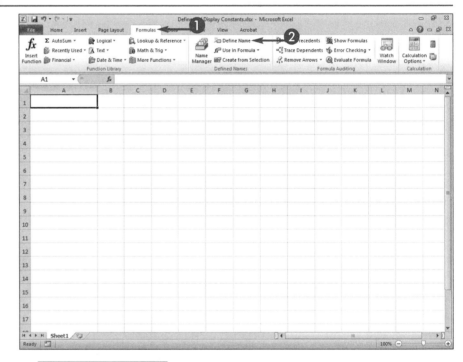

The New Name dialog box appears.

3. Type a name.

4. Click here and select the scope.

5. Type an equal sign (=) followed by the constant's value.

6. Click OK.

You can now use the constant.

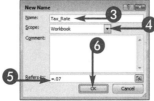

Display a Constant

1. Click in a cell.

2. Type an equal sign followed by the first letter or letters of the constant's name.

   The Autocomplete list appears.

Note: *If you do not know the constant's name, click the Formulas tab and then click Use in Formula. A menu appears. Click the name.*

3. Double-click the name of the constant.

4. Click the check mark.

● The constant's value appears in the cell.

Note: *To learn how to use named constants and named ranges in formulas, see the next section, "Create Formulas That Include Names."*

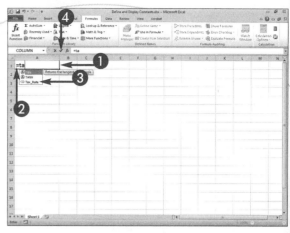

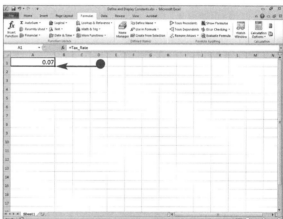

Extra

When you have a large number of named ranges and constants in your workbook, you may find it difficult to keep track of them all. Excel provides a feature that quickly creates a list of all names and the corresponding cell ranges. To create the list, press F3. The Paste Name dialog box appears. Click the Paste List button. Excel creates a list with the first column containing the range names, and the second column identifying the corresponding cell ranges. For example, if you have range names for accounts receivables, buildings, and cash, Excel pastes values similar to the following:

RANGE NAME	CELL RANGE
Accounts_Receivable	=Sheet2!$B$7:$D$7
Buildings	=Sheet2!$B$10:$D$10
Cash	=Sheet2!$B$6:$D$6

Excel places the list in your active worksheet, starting in the cell in which your cursor is located. Before creating your list, place your cursor in a blank cell with plenty of blank cells below it. Excel does not create a link to the list, so to keep your list up to date; you must re-create it whenever you make changes to the named ranges.

Create Formulas That Include Names

onstructing formulas can be complicated, especially when you use several functions in the same formula or when multiple arguments are required in a single function. Using named constants and named ranges can make creating formulas and using functions easier by enabling you to use terms you have created that clearly identify a value or range of values.

An argument is information you provide to the function so the function can do its work. A named constant is a name you create that refers to a single, frequently used value. See the previous section, "Define and Display Constants," for more information. A named range is a name you assign to a group of related cells. See the section "Name Cells and Ranges," earlier in this chapter, for more information. To insert a name into a function or use it in a

formula or as a function's argument, you must type it, access it by clicking Use in Formula on the Formulas tab, or select it from the Function AutoComplete list.

When you name a range, the name must be unique within its scope. When you define the same range name globally and/or for multiple worksheets, by default Excel uses the definition you created for the active worksheet. If you want to use the global definition, you must precede the name with the workbook name followed by an exclamation point (!); for example, `WorkBookName!RangeName`. If you want to use a definition created for another worksheet, you must precede the name with the worksheet name followed by an exclamation point (!); for example, `WorkSheetName!ConstantName`.

Create Formulas that Include Names

Use a Constant or Range Name in a Formula

1. Place the cursor in the formula.

2. Type the name of the constant or range.

   As you type, a list of possible values appears. Double-click a value to place it in the formula.

3. Click the check mark.

● Excel calculates the result.

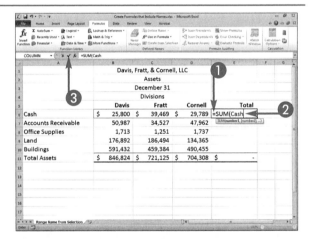

Use a Constant or Range Name in a Formula

Note: *Use this technique if you forget the name of a constant or range.*

1 Begin typing your formula.

2 Click the Formulas tab.

3 Click the ☑ next to Use in Formula.

A menu appears.

4 Click the constant or range name you want to use.

If necessary, continue typing your formula.

5 Click the check mark.

● Excel calculates the results.

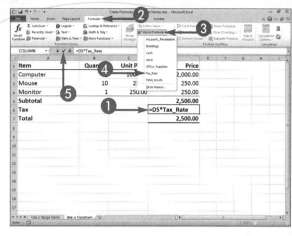

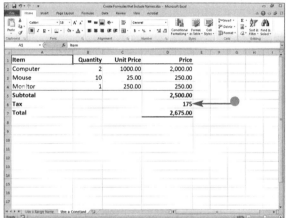

Extra

When working in one workbook, you may have information in another workbook that you refer to often. To simplify your work, you can define a range name in a source workbook and use that range name in a destination workbook. You start by opening both workbooks. Then, in the destination workbook on the Formulas tab, click Define Name. The New Name dialog box appears. In the Name field, type a name for your range. In the Scope field, define its scope and then delete the contents in the Refers to field. Click the Review tab. Click Switch Windows in the Window group. A menu appears. Click the name of the source file. Excel moves to the source workbook. Click and drag to select the range you want to define and then click OK. The range name is now in the destination workbook, ready for you to use.

Naming a formula enables you to reuse it by merely typing = followed by its name. To create a named formula, click in the cell that contains the formula, click the Formulas tab, and then click Define Name. The New Name dialog box appears. Type a name for the formula in the Names field, define the scope, and then click OK.

Check Formulas for Errors

When you create formulas, you can nest one formula within another formula. Because there are so many intermediate steps when you nest formulas, determining the accuracy of your results may be difficult. You can use the Evaluate Formula dialog box to check the result of intermediate calculations to determine if your result is correct.

When you open the Evaluate Formula dialog box, you see your formula. The Evaluate Formula dialog box steps you through the calculation one expression at a time so you can see how Excel evaluates each expression. Click the Evaluate button to begin the process. When your formula includes a function, Excels solves for each argument in the function, and then solves the rest of the formula. Excel underlines individual expressions. You can click the

Evaluate button to see the results of an expression. The results of expressions appear in italics.

If you based the reference on another formula, you can click the Step In button to display the formula. Click the Step Out button to return to the reference. When you have stepped through the entire formula, Excel displays the result and a Restart button. Click the Restart button to evaluate your expression again.

You cannot modify your formula while you are in the Evaluate Formula dialog box. If you find an error and you want to change to your formula, close the Evaluate Formula dialog box to make the change.

If you want to examine all the formulas in your worksheet, click the Show Formulas button in the Formula Auditing group of the Formulas tab. To return to displaying results, click the Show Formulas button again.

Check Formulas for Errors

① Click in the cell that contains the formula.

② Click the Formulas tab.

③ Click the Evaluate Formula button.

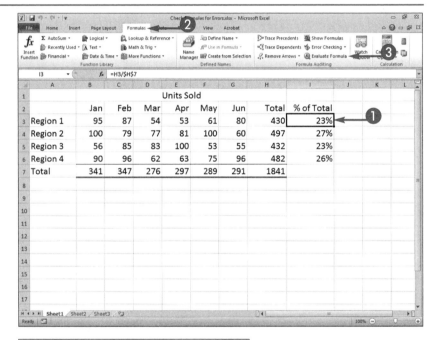

The Evaluate Formula dialog box appears.

④ Click Evaluate.

- Excels displays the results of the evaluation.

5 Continue clicking Evaluate to review each expression.

6 Click Step In to review the details of an expression.

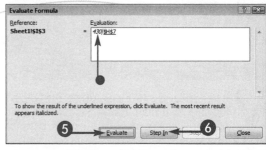

- Excels displays the details of an expression.

7 Click Step Out to return to the expression.

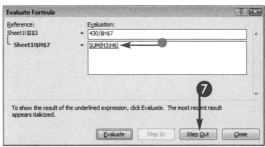

- When Excel reaches the end of the formula, it displays the results.

- You can click Restart to evaluate the formula again.

8 Click Close.

Excel closes the dialog box.

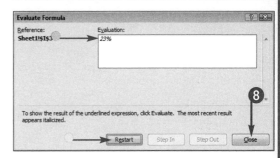

Extra

On the Formulas tab, if you click the Error Checking button in the Formula Auditing group, Excel checks your worksheet for errors. If Excel finds an error, the Error Checking dialog box appears. Click the Help on This Error button to obtain additional information on the error. Click Show Calculation Steps to open the Evaluate Formula dialog box. Click Ignore Error to leave the error unchanged. Click Edit in Formula Bar to edit your error. Click Previous or Next to move to the next or previous error in your worksheet. Click Option to open the Excel Options dialog box, where you can change the settings for error checking.

You can use the Watch Window to monitor the values in specified cells. To add a cell to the Watch Window, click Watch Window in the Formulas Auditing group on the Formulas tab. The Watch Window appears. Click the Add Watch button. The Add Watch dialog box appears. Select the cells you want to watch and then click Add. You can now monitor the values you have added to the Watch Window.

Trace Precedents and Dependents

When you create a formula, Excel evaluates all the values in the formula and returns a result. If Excel cannot calculate the formula, it displays an error message in the formula cell. You can use the Excel trace features to help you locate your error.

Typically, an error occurs when your formula refers to an invalid cell value. For example, if the cell contains the formula =B2/$B$8 and cell B8 contains the number 0 or is blank, Excel returns the error message #DIV/0!, which indicates that the formula attempted to divide by zero.

You can view a graphical representation of the cells a formula refers to by clicking in the cell and then clicking Trace Precedents in the Formula Auditing group on the Formulas tab. This option draws blue arrows to each cell

referenced in the formula, so you can identify the exact cells used in the formula.

If you want to find out which formulas use a specific cell, you can view a graphical representation by clicking in the cell and then clicking Trace Dependents in the Formula Auditing group on the Formulas tab. This option draws blue arrows to each cell that contains a formula that uses the active cell as an argument. By displaying the dependent cells for a formula, you can visually identify the cells that require the formula. If you perform this option before deleting a value, you can quickly determine if your deletion will affect any formulas on your worksheet.

You can remove arrows Excel draws to dependents or precedents by clicking Remove Arrows in the Formula Auditing group on the Formulas tab.

Trace Precedents and Dependents

Trace Precedents

1. Click in the cell containing the formula.

- If the cell has an error, an Error icon displays next to the formula.

2. Click the Formulas tab.

3. Click Trace Precedents.

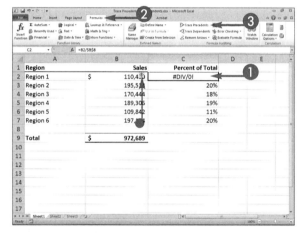

- Excel draws arrows between the cells on which the formula is based and the formula's cell.

4. Make the appropriate modifications to correct the error in the formula.

5. Click Remove Arrows.

  Excel removes the arrows.

Note: *Click the ▼ next to Remove Arrows to choose from Remove Arrows, Remove Precedent Arrows, or Remove Dependent Arrows.*

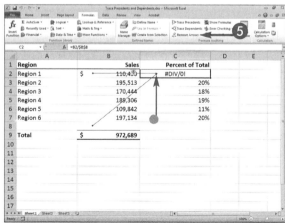

Trace Dependents

① Click the cell where you want to trace dependents.

② Click the Formulas tab.

③ Click Trace Dependents.

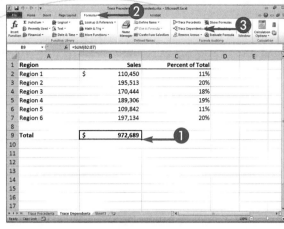

● Excel draws arrows between the formula's cell and the dependent cells.

④ Click Remove Arrows.

Excel removes the arrows.

Note: *Click the* 🔽 *next to Remove Arrows to choose from Remove Arrows, Remove Precedent Arrows, or Remove Dependent Arrows.*

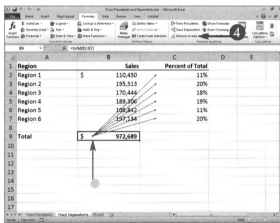

Understanding the Function Wizard

Excel's Function Wizard simplifies the use of functions. You can use the wizard with every one of Excel's functions, from the SUM function to complex statistical, mathematical, financial, or engineering functions.

There are two ways to access the Function Wizard. You can select the cell where the result is to appear, click the Insert Function button (fx), and then use the Insert Function dialog box to find the function you want. The Insert Function dialog box provides you with two ways to find a function. You can type a description of the function in the Search for a Function field and then click Go. Excel will retrieve all the relevant functions and list them in the Select a Function field. Or, you can use the Or Select a Category field to select the category in which your function falls. Excel will list all the functions in that category in the Select a Function field. To open the Function Wizard, double click a function listed in Select a Function field.

Another way to access the Function Wizard is to select the cell where you want the results to appear. Type an equal (=) sign and the beginning of the function name. In the list of functions that appears, double-click the function you want and then click the Insert Function button. This method is quicker and is the best choice when you know the name of the function you want.

Both methods bring up the Function Arguments dialog box, where you can type the values you want to use in your calculation, type the range that contains the values, or click the cells containing the values you want.

Understanding the Function Wizard

1 Type your data.

2 Click the cell where you want the results to appear.

3 Click the Insert Function button.

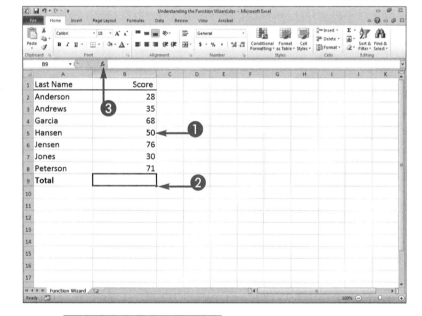

The Insert Function dialog box appears.

4 Click the ▼ and select All to list all functions.

● Alternatively, type a description of the function and then click Go.

● Or, click ▼ and select a function category.

5 Double-click the function you want to use.

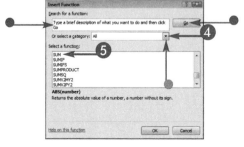

The Function Arguments dialog box appears.

6 Click the cell(s), type the range, or type the values requested in each field.

7 Click OK.

● The results appear in the cell you selected in Step 2.

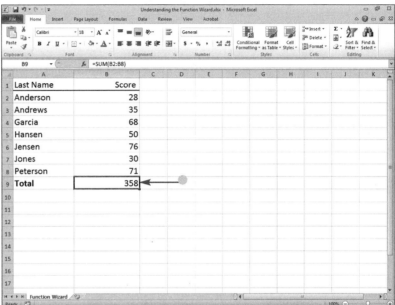

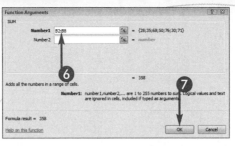

Extra

When you select a function in the Select a Function field of the Function Arguments dialog box, a brief explanation of the function appears below the field. If you need more information, click the Help on this function link. Excel will take you directly to a help screen with detailed information on how the function works. Excel also provides an example, which you can copy and paste into your worksheet.

The more than 300 functions built into Excel enable you to perform tasks of every kind, from adding numbers to calculating the internal rate of return for an investment. You can think of a function as a black box. You put your information into the box, and the results you want come out. You do not need to know any obscure algorithms to use functions. Excel calls each bit of information an argument, and the Function Wizard provides guidance on every argument and every function.

Round a Number

Frequently, when you are creating a worksheet you will need to round numbers. Excel has several functions to aid you. The most commonly used is the ROUND function. This function rounds to the number of digits you specify. It takes two arguments: Number, the number you want to round, and Num_digits, the number of digits to which you want to round your number. If Num_digits is 1 or higher, Excel rounds to the number of decimal places you specify. If Num_digits is 0, Excel rounds to the nearest integer. If Num_digits is −1 or lower, Excel rounds to the number of digits you specify that are to the left of the decimal point. The function =ROUND(1234.5678,2) rounds to 1234.57, the function =ROUND(1234.5678,0) rounds to 1235, and the function =ROUND(1234.5678,-2) rounds to 1200.

When you use the ROUND function, if the digit you are rounding to is 5 or higher, Excel rounds up. If the digit is 4 or lower, Excel rounds down. If you only want Excel to round up, use the ROUNDUP function. If you only want Excel to round down, use the ROUNDDOWN function. Both ROUNDUP and ROUNDDOWN take the same two arguments as ROUND: Number and Num_digits.

Do not confuse rounding with number formatting. Rounding works by evaluating a number in an argument and rounding it to the number of digits you specify. When you format numbers, you simplify the appearance of numbers in the worksheet, making them easier to read. The underlying numbers do not change.

Round a Number

1 Click the cell where you want the result to appear.

2 Click the Insert Function button.

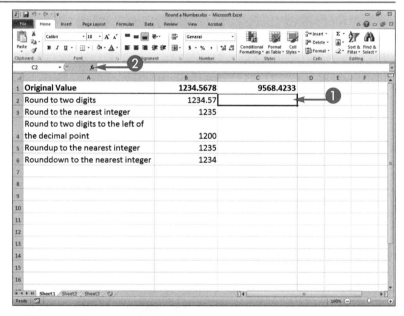

The Insert Function dialog box appears.

3 Click the ▼ and then select All to list all the functions.

4 Double-click ROUND.

The Function Arguments dialog box appears.

5 Enter the cell address of the number you want to round.

Alternatively, if the number is not in a cell, you can type the number into the Number field.

6 Type the number of decimal places to which you want to round.

A negative number rounds to the left of the decimal point. A 0 rounds to the integer. A positive number rounds to the number of decimal places specified.

7 Click OK.

● Excel rounds the number.

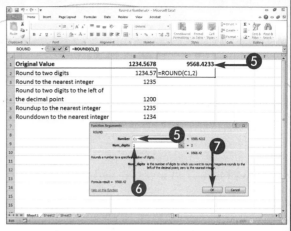

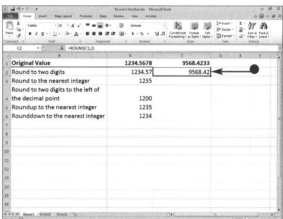

Extra

The following functions relate to the rounding.

FUNCTION	DESCRIPTION
INT	Rounds down to the nearest integer. The INT function takes one argument: the number you want to round. The formula =INT(7.9) rounds the number 7.9 down to 7. The formula =INT(-7.9) rounds the number -7.9 down to -8, the next lowest integer.
TRUNC	Truncates to the number of digits you specify. The TRUNC function takes two arguments: Number, the number you want to truncate, and Num_digits, the number of digits to which you want to truncate your number. The formula =TRUNC(7.9,0) truncates the number 7.9 to 7. The formula TRUNC (-7.9,0) truncates to number -7.9 to -7. The TRUNC function differs from the INT function in that when you are working with negative numbers, the TRUNC function does not round down.

Create a Conditional Formula

With a conditional formula, you can perform a calculation using values that meet a condition. For example, you can find the highest score for Team 1 from a list that consists of scores for Team 1 and Team 2.

A conditional formula often uses two functions. The first function, IF, defines the condition, or test, such as players on Team 1. To create the condition, you use a comparison operator, such as greater than (>), less than (<), greater than or equal to (>=), less than or equal to (<=), or equal to (=). If the condition evaluates to true, the second function is performed. The second function performs a calculation on numbers that meet the condition. Excel carries out the IF function first and then calculates the values that meet the condition defined in the IF function.

IF is an *array* function. It compares every number in a series to a condition and keeps track of the numbers that meet the condition. To create an array function, you press Ctrl+Shift+Enter instead of pressing the Enter key or clicking OK to complete your function. You must surround arrays with curly braces ({ }). Excel enters the curly braces automatically when you press Ctrl+Shift+Enter but not when you press Enter or click OK.

You can interpret the formula {=MAX(IF(B2:B13=1,C2:C13))} as follows: If the value in a cell between B2 and B13 is equal to 1, find the highest corresponding value in a cell between C2 and C13.

IF has an optional third argument. Use the third argument when you want to specify what happens when the condition is not met.

Create a Conditional Formula

① Click the cell where you want your results to appear.

② Click the Insert Function button.

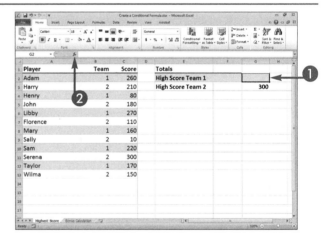

The Insert Function dialog box appears.

③ Click the ▾ and then select All.

④ Double-click the function on which you want to base your conditional function.

Note: *This example uses* MAX, *which finds the highest value in a list.*

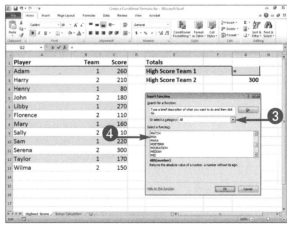

The Function Arguments dialog box appears.

5 Type **IF(**.

6 Type the range you want to evaluate.

7 Type a comparison operator, the condition, and then a comma.

8 Enter the series on which you want base the calculation.

9 Type **)**.

10 Press Ctrl+Shift+Enter.

● The result appears in the cell with the formula.

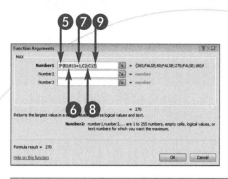

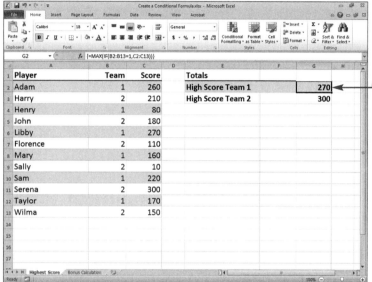

Apply It

You can use the `IF` function to execute one command if a condition is true and another command if a condition is false. For example, you can use the formula that follows to create a function that calculates bonuses. If a salesperson's sales are equal to or greater than $100,000, the formula calculates a bonus of 10 percent; otherwise, it calculates a bonus of 5 percent. The cell B2 contains the salesperson's sales.

```
=IF(B2>=100000,B2*.10,B2*.05)
```

In this case, the `IF` function takes three arguments: `Logical_test`, the condition for which you are testing; `Value_if_true`, the operation you want to perform if the cell being analyzed meets the condition; and `Value_if_false`, the operation you want to perform if the cell being analyzed does not meet the condition. The statement `B2>=100000` is the `Logical_test` argument. The statement `B2*.10` is the `Value_if_true` argument. It calculates a bonus of 10 percent. The statement `B2*.05` is the `Value_if_false` argument. It calculates a bonus of 5 percent.

Calculate a Conditional Sum

The SUMIF function combines the SUM and IF functions. SUMIF enables you to avoid complicated nesting and use the Function Wizard without making one function an argument of another.

SUMIF takes three arguments: Range, the range where you want to test a condition; Criteria, the condition you want to test; and Sum_range, the corresponding range you want to sum if the condition is met. For example, you can create a function that evaluates a list to determine if people are on Team 1, and if so, sum their scores. The third argument, the range to which the condition applies, is optional. If you exclude it, Excel sums the range you specify in the Range argument.

Extra

You can apply conditions to numbers or text. For example, you can sum all scores where the team is equal to 1, or you can sum all scores where the team is equal to "Team One". In the example, if the team names were text — "Team One" and "Team Two" — you would use the following formula to add the scores for all the players on Team One:
=SUMIF(B2:B13,"=Team One",C2:C13).

Calculate a Conditional Sum

① Enter the SUMIF function.

● The range where you want to test a condition.

● The condition.

Note: Enclose the Criteria in quotes.

● The range to sum.

② Click Enter (✔) - the check mark on the formula bar.

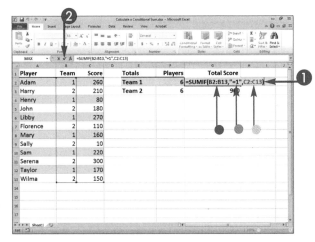

Excel calculates the result.

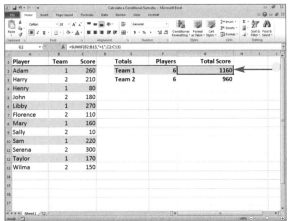

Calculate a Conditional Count

The COUNTIF function works like SUMIF. It combines two functions (COUNT and IF) and takes two arguments: Range, a series of values; and Criteria, the condition by which Excel tests the values. Whereas SUMIF sums the values, COUNTIF counts the number of items that passed the test. For example, you can create a function that evaluates a list to determine the team a person is on, and then counts all the people on Team One.

As with SUMIF, you can apply conditions to values and text. You can interpret the formula =COUNTIF(B2:B13,"=Team One") as count all the values in the cells between B2 and B13 that are equal to Team One.

Extra

You can use the question mark (?) and asterisk (*) wildcards when creating your condition. A ? will match a single character, and an * will match any series of characters. For example, 123?98 will match any value that starts with 123 and ends with 98, such as 123Y98, 123-98, or 123A98. *son will match any value that ends with son, such as Jackson or Johnson.

Calculate a Conditional Count

① Enter the COUNTIF function.

● The series of values.

● The Criteria, the condition used to test the values.

Note: Enclose the Criteria in quotes.

② Click the check mark.

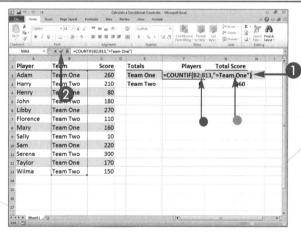

● Excel calculates the result.

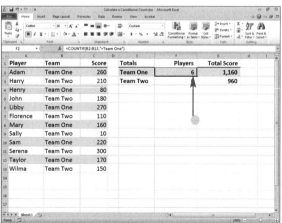

Y ou can use the SQRT function to find the square root of a number. You can find the square root by entering the number you want the square root of into your worksheet or, if you do not want the number to appear in your worksheet, you can enter the number directly into the formula.

Excel can only calculate the square roots of positive numbers. If a negative number is the argument, as in SQRT(-9) Excel returns the error #NUM. If you want to calculate the positive square root of a negative number, find the absolute value of the number first by using the ABS function. The ABS function returns a number without its sign. The following formula returns 3, =SQRT(ABS(-9)).

Extra

Related to SQRT is POWER. To find the power of any number, such as 3 to the second power, use the POWER function. The POWER function takes two arguments: the number you want to raise to a power and the power to which you want to raise it. The formula =POWER(3,2) raises the number 3 to the second power, yielding the number 9.

Find the Square Root

① Click the cell where you want the result to appear.

② Type **=SQRT(** in the formula bar or in the cell in which you want the result to appear.

As you begin to type, the Function AutoComplete list appears. Double-click SQRT to select it.

③ Type the value for which you want the square root.

Alternatively, you can click a cell containing the value.

④ Click the check mark.

● Excel calculates the square root.

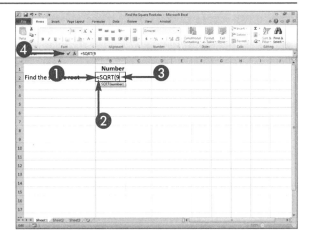

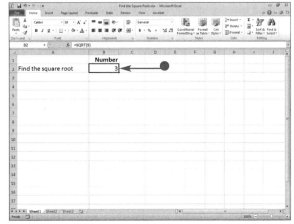

Retrieve Column or Row Numbers

When you use functions such as VLOOKUP or INDEX you enter a column number, a row number, or both. See the sections, "Using VLOOKUP" and "Using INDEX," to learn more. If you enter an actual number, when you copy the function to another cell, the column or row number does not change. If you want the number to change in the same way relative cell addresses change, use the COLUMN function or the ROW function.

Both the COLUMN and ROW functions take one optional argument, Reference, the cell or cell range for which you want to retrieve the row or column number. If you enter one of these functions without a cell reference, =COLUMN() or =ROW(), Excel returns the column or row number of the current cell.

Extra

When you enter =COLUMN(D1) in a cell, Excel returns the number 4, because D is the fourth column in a worksheet. When you enter =ROW(B7), Excel returns the number 7, because 7 is the seventh row in a worksheet.

If you enter a cell range into the COLUMN or ROW function, Excel returns the column or row number of the cell in the upper-left corner of the range.

Retrieve Column or Row Numbers

1 Enter the COLUMN function.

● The cell or cell range for which you want to obtain the column number.

  Alternatively, enter the ROW function.

2 Click the check mark.

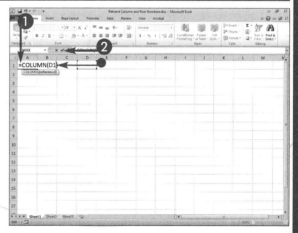

● Excel displays the column number.

3 Click and drag the Fill handle to copy the cell.

Note: See Chapter 12 to learn more about AutoFill.

● Excel copies in a fashion similar to copying a relative cell address.

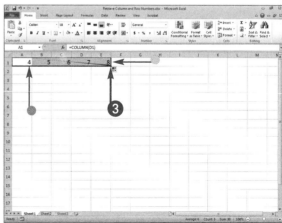

Using VLOOKUP

The VLOOKUP function searches the first column in your list, and when it finds the value that you are looking for, it returns another value in the same row. For example, you have a list, and in the first column there are names; in the second column there are regions; and in the third column there are sales numbers. If you have a name and you want to find the region, VLOOKUP can search for the name and return the region.

The first column of your list must contain the values you want to use to retrieve another value and you must sort the first column in ascending order. VLOOKUP has three required arguments: Lookup_value, the value or the cell address containing the value you want to use to retrieve another value; Table_array, the list's cell range; and Col_index_num, the column that contains the value you want to retrieve. The first column in the Table_array is column 1, the second column is column 2, and so on. If

you use the COLUMN function to obtain the column number, when you copy your formula the cell reference will change. See section "Retrieve Column or Row Numbers" to learn more.

The VLOOKUP function has an optional fourth argument called Range_lookup. If you enter TRUE or leave the argument blank, the function looks for the closest match to the value you seek. If you enter FALSE, the function returns exact matches only.

If you are searching text data, make sure the column you are searching does not contain any nonprinting characters, leading spaces, or trailing spaces, and that curly or straight quotation marks are used consistently. If you are searching for numbers or dates, make sure they are not formatted as text. These situations can cause VLOOKUP to bring back an unexpected result.

Using VLOOKUP

1. Type the value you want to use to retrieve another value.

2. Click the cell where you want the result to appear and start to type **=VLOOKUP(**.

   As you begin to type, the Function AutoComplete list appears.

3. Double-click VLOOKUP to select it.

4. Click the Insert Function button.

   The Function Arguments dialog box appears.

5. Enter an absolute cell reference to the value you entered in Step 1.

6. Enter the absolute cell range for the list.

7. Enter the COLUMN function for the column.

8. Enter TRUE to search for the closest match or FALSE to search for an exact match.

9. Click OK.

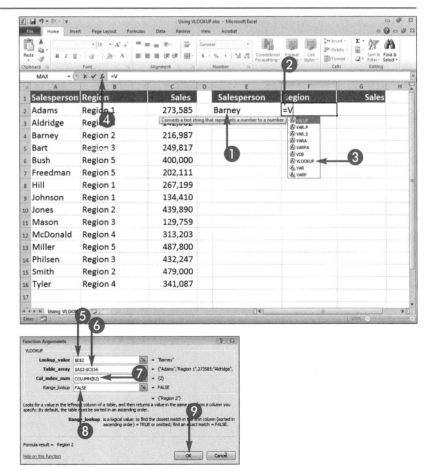

- The cell containing the formula displays the value corresponding to the lookup value.

⑩ Copy and paste the formula.

Note: See Chapter 3 to learn how to copy and paste.

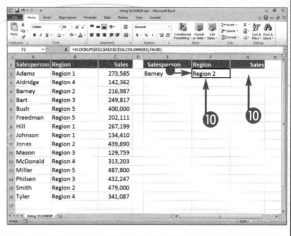

⑪ Type another lookup value.

- The cell containing the formula displays the value corresponding to the lookup value.

- The cell you copied and pasted retrieves the next column.

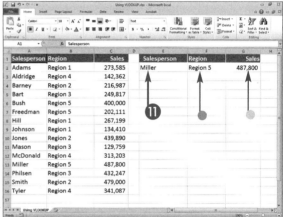

Apply It

HLOOKUP is the opposite of VLOOKUP. It searches for a value in a row and returns a value in the same column. For example, you may have names, addresses, and telephone numbers. Your names are listed across the first row, your addresses are listed across the second row, and your phone numbers are listed across the third row. HLOOKUP scans the first row to find the name. Then it returns the related phone number.

Like VLOOKUP, HLOOKUP takes four arguments: Lookup_value, the value or the cell address containing the value you want to use to retrieve another value; Table_array, the list's cell range; Row_index_num, the row that contains the value you want to retrieve; and the Range_lookup value. If the Range_lookup value is set to TRUE, the values in the first row of your table must be in ascending order. Setting the Range_lookup value to TRUE tells Excel you want to return approximate matches. With HLOOKUP, the first row of your table must contain the values you want to use to retrieve another value. When specifying the row that contains the value you want to retrieve, call the first row in your table row 1, the second row 2, and so on.

Determine the Location of a Value

To determine the relative location of a value within a row or column, you can use the MATCH function. For example, if you have a list and you want to find which row in the list the salesperson named Barney is located, you can use the MATCH function.

The MATCH function needs three pieces of information: Lookup_value, Lookup_array, and Match_type. The Lookup_value is the value you want to find. The Lookup_array is the range you want to search. The Match_type is a number that tells Excel how to match values from the Lookup_value argument to the Lookup_array argument.

The Match_type is optional. If you omit it, or you enter a value of 1, Excel finds the largest value that is less than or equal to the Lookup_value. If you enter 0, Excel finds

an exact match. If you enter –1, Excel returns the smallest value that is greater than or equal to the Lookup_value. If you omit the Match_type or enter a Match_type of 1, you must sort the Lookup_array in ascending order. If you enter a Match_type of 0, the Lookup_array can be in any order. If you enter a Match_type of –1, you must sort the Lookup_array in descending order. See Chapter 8 for more on sorting your data.

The MATCH function returns a number that identifies the relative location of the value within the specified range of cells. For example, if Excel returns the value 2 and the specified range of cells is B2 through B16, cell B3 contains the value, or the closest match. Excel interprets B2 to be the value 1, B3 to be value 2, B4 to be value 3, on so on.

Determine the Location of a Value

1 Enter the MATCH function.

- The value you want to find.
- The range you want to search.
- The match type.

2 Click the check mark.

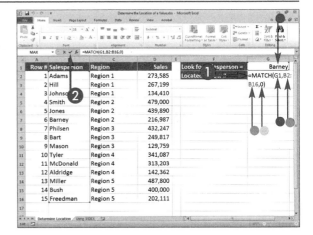

Excel calculates the result.

Type a new value to retrieve a new row location.

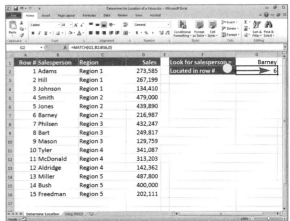

Using INDEX

The MATCH function retrieves the relative position of a value. See the section, "Determine the Location of a Value" for a detailed explanation of the MATCH function. If you want to retrieve the actual value, use the INDEX function in conjunction with the MATCH function. The INDEX function has two forms. This example uses the Array form. The Array form takes three arguments: Array, the range from which you want to retrieve a value; Row_num, the position of the row you want to retrieve; and Col_num, the position of the column you want to retrieve. If the Array argument only contains one column, you do not need to specify the Col_num. If the Array argument only contains one row, you do not need to specify the Row_num.

In the following formula, =INDEX(B2:B16,MATCH(G1,B2:B16,0)), B2:B16 is the column that contains the value you want. The MATCH function retrieves the row you want. The formula could also be written =INDEX(B2:B16, 6). Cell B2 is row 1, B3 is row 2, and so on. The formula returns the value in cell B7, because it is on row 6.

When using the INDEX function, if you include both the Row_num and the Col_num arguments, Excel returns the value of the cell that is at the intersection of the row and column. For example, if you enter the formula =INDEX(B2:D16,6,3), Excel looks at the range B2 to D16 and returns the sixth row and third column.

Using INDEX

1 Enter the INDEX function.

● The range from which you want to retrieve a value.

● The row number you want.

2 Click the check mark.

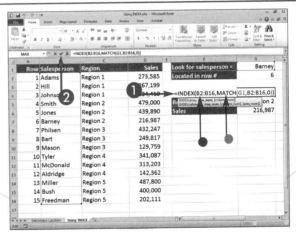

● Excel displays the value.

● You can use INDEX with the MATCH function to display additional columns.

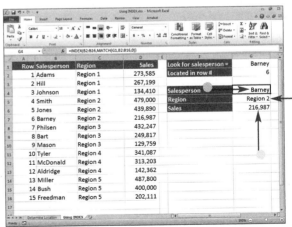

Perform Date and Time Calculations

You can perform date and time calculations. You can find, for example, the number of days that have elapsed between the start of a project and the end of a project or the number of hours worked from the start of the workday to the end of the workday. Excel bases every date and time on a serial value that it can use to add and subtract.

Excel calculates a date's serial value as the number of days after January 1, 1900, and represents each date with a whole number. Excel calculates a time's serial value in units of 1/60th of a second. Each time can be represented as a serial value between 0 and 1. A date and time consists of the date to the left of the decimal and a time to the right. Take the example April 1, 2012 6:00 p.m. The date and time serial value is 41000.75. See Chapter 2 to learn more about dates and times.

Subtracting one date or time from another involves subtracting one serial value from another. For example, the serial value for April 1, 2012 is 41000. The serial value for May 21, 2012 is 41050. To obtain the number of days between April 1, 2012 and May 21, 2012 Excel performs the following calculation: $= 41050 - 41000$, which equals 50. Showing a date or time in the General format displays its serial value. When performing a date or time calculation, you do not need to display the serial value. Instead use date and time formats to display recognizable dates or times.

If you are calculating the number of hours that have elapsed, use the Format Cells dialog box and set the results of the calculation to the hour and minutes (13:30) time format.

Perform Date and Time Calculations

Find the Number of Days Between Two Dates

1 Enter the formula.

2 Click the check mark.

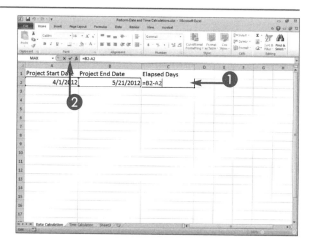

● Excel calculates the results.

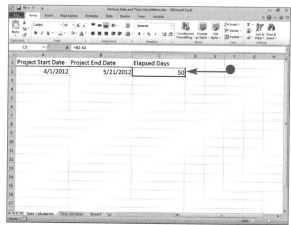

Find the Difference Between Two Times

1 Enter the formula.

2 Click the check mark.

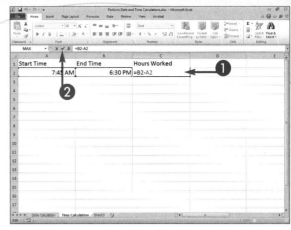

● Excel calculates the result.

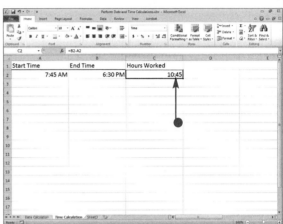

Extra

When calculating the difference between two times, you want to know the hours and minutes that have elapsed, so format your results as hours and minutes. Click the Home tab. Click the launcher in the Number Group. The Format Cells dialog box appears. Click the Number tab. Click Time. Click the format type 13:30. Click OK.

When subtracting times that cross midnight, such as 11 p.m. to 2 a.m., you need a function called modulus, or MOD. The formula is =MOD (later time - earlier time, 1).

In Windows, Excel can perform date arithmetic on any date after January 1, 1900. If you use dates before then, Excel treats them as text and does not perform a calculation on them. Instead, it gives you a #VALUE! error.

In Excel, you can enter the current date simply by clicking in the cell in which you want the date to appear and then pressing Ctrl+;. Typing =TODAY() also returns the current date. You can use the TODAY function to perform date arithmetic. Typing =TODAY() + 5 returns the date five days in the future. Typing =TODAY() - 5 returns the date five days in the past.

Calculate Future Value

I f you have $1,000 and you plan to invest it at 10 percent interest, compounded annually for ten years, the amount you will receive at the end of ten years is called the future value (FV) of $1,000. You can use Excel's FV function to calculate the amount you will receive.

An *annuity* is a series of payments where each payment is the same amount, the period between payments is the same, the interest rate for each period is constant, and the interest is compounded. If you deposit $1,000 per year for five years and receive 10 percent interest, compounded annually, the amount you receive at the end of five years is the future value of an annuity. You can also use Excel's FV function to compute the future value of an annuity.

When you are working with the FV function, negative numbers are *cash outflows* and positive numbers are

cash inflows. Enter a negative number when you are making a payment. Enter a positive number when you are receiving cash. Although the transaction is called a *payment*, note that there are two sides to the transaction. For example, when you make a payment to the bank, the bank considers the transaction a cash receipt.

Excel's FV function asks for five pieces of information: Rate, the interest rate; Nper, the number of payment periods; Pmt, the amount of each payment; PV, your investment — the value for which you are trying to find the future value; and Type, a number indicating when payments are due. If you make your payments at the beginning of the period, enter a 1 as the Type. If you make your payments at the end of the period, leave Type blank or enter 0.

Calculate Future Value

Calculate a Future Value

1 Type **=FV(**.

2 Click the Insert Function button.

The Function Arguments dialog box appears.

3 Enter the interest rate.

Note: *If you make payments more than once annually, divide the interest rate by the number of payments per year.*

4 Enter the number of payments.

Note: *If you make payments more than once annually, multiply the number of years by the number of payments per year.*

5 Enter the amount for which you want to find the future value.

6 Click OK.

● Excel calculates the future value.

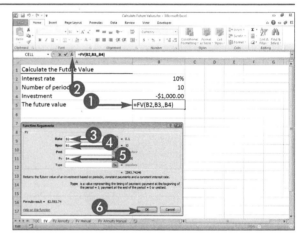

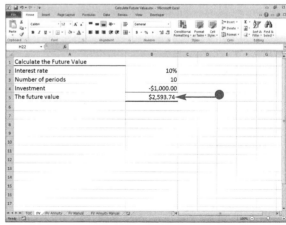

Calculate a Future Value of an Annuity

1 Type **=FV(**.

2 Click the Insert Function button.

The Function Arguments dialog box appears.

3 Enter the interest rate.

4 Enter the number of periods.

5 Enter the payment amount.

6 Enter the Type.

Note: *Enter **1** if you make payments at the beginning of the period. Leave the Type Field blank if you make payments at the end of the period.*

7 Click OK.

● Excel calculates the future value of the annuity.

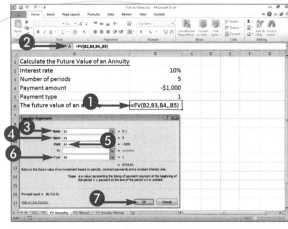

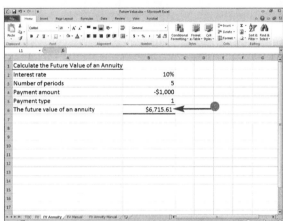

Extra

When you are calculating future value, be careful of the amount you enter in the `Rate` and `Nper` fields. You should divide the annual interest rate by the number of payments per year. If payments are monthly, you should divide the annual interest rate by 12. If your rate is 8 percent, enter **.08/12** in the Rate field. You should also multiply the number of payments in a year by the number of years of payments. If payments are monthly for five years, multiply 5 by 12 to get 60 and enter **60** in the Nper field.

You can use the following formula to calculate the future value of an investment: $fv = a*((1+i)^n)$ where `fv` equals the future value, `a` equals the amount for which you want to find the future value, `i` equals the annual interest rate, and `n` equals the number of periods. To find the future value of $1,000 at 10 percent for ten years, enter $=1000*((1+.10)^{10})$ or use Excel's FV function. For a detailed example of how to calculate future value, refer to the file Calculate Future Value.xlsx, which is on the Web site for this book.

Calculate Present Value

nvestors use the concept of present value (PV) to recognize the time value of money. Because an investor can receive interest, $1,000 today is worth less than $1,000 ten years from today. For example, if an investor invests $1,000 today at 10 percent interest per year, compounded annually, in ten years the investor will have $2,593.74. Therefore, the present value of $2,593.74 at 10 percent, compounded annually, for 10 years is $1,000. Or, worded differently, $1,000 today is worth $2,593.74 ten years from today.

You can use the following formula to calculate the present value of an investment: $pv = a/((1+i)^n)$ where pv equals the present value, a equals the amount you want to find the present value of, i equals the annual interest rate, and n equals the number of periods. To find the

present value of the $2,593.74, enter `=2593.74/((1+.10)^10)` or use Excel's PV function.

An *annuity* is a series of payments where each payment is the same amount, the period between payments is the same, the interest rate for each period is constant, and the interest is compounded. For example, a payment of $1,000 per year for five years at 10 percent interest compounded at the end of each year is an annuity. To find the present value of an annuity, you can add the present values of each payment or you can use Excel's PV function. Excel's PV function needs five pieces of information: Rate, the interest rate; Nper, the number of payment periods; Pmt, the amount of each payment; PV, the value you are trying to find the present value of; and Type, a number indicating when payments are due.

Calculate Present Value

Calculate the Present Value

① Type **=PV(**.

② Click the Insert Function button.

The Function Arguments dialog box appears.

③ Enter the interest rate.

Note: *If you make payments more than once annually, divide the interest rate by the number of payments per year.*

④ Enter the number of periods.

Note: *If you make payments more than once annually, multiply the number of years by the number of payments per year.*

⑤ Enter the value for which you want to find the present value.

⑥ Click OK.

● Excel calculates the present value.

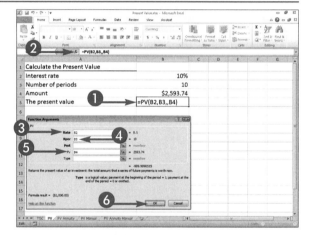

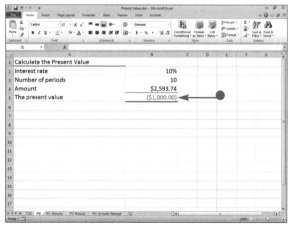

Calculate the Present Value of an Annuity

① Type **=PV(**.

② Click the Insert Function button.

The Function Arguments dialog box appears.

③ Enter the interest rate.

④ Enter the number of periods.

⑤ Enter the payment amount.

⑥ Click OK.

● Excel calculates the present value of an annuity.

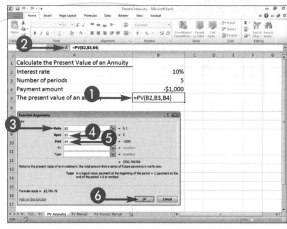

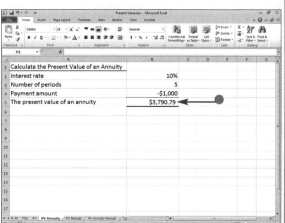

Extra

Car loans and mortgages are annuities. The money you receive when you take out the loan is the present value of the loan. When you are calculating present value, be careful of the amount you enter in the Rate and Nper fields. You should divide the annual interest rate by the number of payments per year. If payments are monthly, you should divide the annual interest rate by 12. If your rate is 8 percent, enter **.08/12** in the Rate field. You should also multiply the number of payments in a year by the number of years of payments. If payments are monthly for five years, multiply 5 by 12 to get 60 and enter **60** in the Nper field.

When you are working with the PV function, negative numbers are *cash outflows* and positive numbers are *cash inflows*. Enter a negative number when you are making a payment. Enter a positive number when you are receiving cash.

With an annuity, you can make payments at the end of the period or at the beginning of the period. When you are calculating present value, if you make payments at the beginning of the period, enter a **1** in the Type field; otherwise leave the field blank.

Calculate Loan Payments

You can use Excel's PMT function (PMT is short for payment) when buying a house or car. This function enables you to compare loan terms and make an objective decision based on factors such as the interest rate and the amount of the monthly payment.

You can calculate loan payments in many ways when using Excel, but the PMT function may be the simplest method because you simply enter information into the Function Wizard. You can create a loan calculator that shows how varying the elements affect the results. Place the labels Principal, Interest Rates, and Number of Months in your worksheet. Then type their respective values. For example, you can calculate the payment amount at 4.75 percent, 5 percent, and 5.25 percent to see the effect of changing the annual interest.

The PMT function requires three pieces of information. To calculate the periodic rate, you enter an annual interest rate such as 5 percent (.05) and then divide the interest rate by the number of payments you make per year. For example, if you pay monthly, enter **.05/12** as the Rate. Enter the number of loan periods for the loan you are seeking for the Nper. For example, if your loan is for 30 years and you will make payments monthly, multiply 30 years by 12 months to get 360 periods and then type **360** in the Nper field. For Pv, enter the amount of the loan. The PMT function calculates the amount of each payment. The payment amount appears surrounded by parentheses, signifying that the number is negative, and a cash outflow.

Calculate Loan Payments

① Type the principals, the amount of the loans; the interest rates; and the number of periods.

② Type **=PMT(**.

③ Click the Insert Function button.

The Function Arguments dialog box appears.

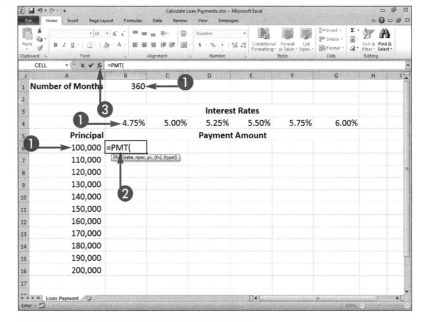

④ Enter the interest rate.

Make the row reference absolute.

Note: See Chapter 4 to learn more about absolute and relative cell references.

⑤ Divide the interest rate by the number of periods per year; for example, type **/12**.

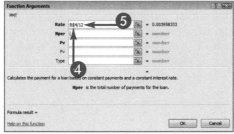

⑥ Enter the number of periods.

Make both the column and row reference absolute.

⑦ Enter the principal.

Make the column reference absolute.

⑧ Click OK.

● The result appears in the cell.

Note: *The result shows the amount of a single loan payment.*

⑨ Copy and paste the formula into the other cells.

Note: *See Chapter 3 to learn how to copy and paste.*

Excel calculates the loan payments.

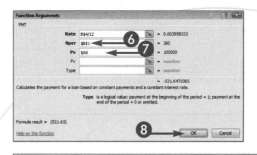

Principal	4.75%	5.00%	5.25%	5.50%	5.75%	6.00%
			Payment Amount			
100,000	(521.65)	(536.82)	(552.20)	(567.79)	(583.57)	(599.55)
110,000	(573.81)	(590.50)	(607.42)	(624.57)	(641.93)	(659.51)
120,000	(625.98)	(644.19)	(662.64)	(681.35)	(700.29)	(719.46)
130,000	(678.14)	(697.87)	(717.86)	(738.13)	(758.64)	(779.42)
140,000	(730.31)	(751.55)	(773.09)	(794.90)	(817.00)	(839.37)
150,000	(782.47)	(805.23)	(828.31)	(851.68)	(875.36)	(899.33)
160,000	(834.64)	(858.91)	(883.53)	(908.46)	(933.72)	(959.28)
170,000	(886.80)	(912.60)	(938.75)	(965.24)	(992.07)	(1,019.24)
180,000	(938.97)	(966.28)	(993.97)	(1,022.02)	(1,050.43)	(1,079.19)
190,000	(991.13)	(1,019.96)	(1,049.19)	(1,078.80)	(1,108.79)	(1,139.15)
200,000	(1,043.29)	(1,073.64)	(1,104.41)	(1,135.58)	(1,167.15)	(1,199.10)

Extra

Use the `Type` field in the payment function to specify whether payments are due at the beginning of the period or the end of the period. For example, if payments are due at the beginning of the month, enter a **1** in the `Type` field. If payments are due at the end of the month, leave the field blank or enter a **0**.

The PMT function returns both principal and interest. If you want to calculate the amount of interest paid in a period, use the IPMT function. If you want to calculate the amount of principal paid in a period, use the PPMT function. See the next section, "Calculate Principal or Interest," to learn more.

Excel's Goal Seek feature enables you to calculate payments. With Goal Seek, you can specify a goal, such as payments less than $1,100 per month, and have Excel vary a single value to reach the goal. The limitation is that you can vary only one value at a time. See Chapter 12 for more information.

Calculate Principal or Interest

When you use the PMT function to calculate a monthly loan payment, Excel calculates the total of the principal and the interest. See the previous section, "Calculate Loan Payments," to learn more about using the PMT function. If you need to know the principal or the interest portion of a payment, you can use the PPMT function or the IPMT function.

An *annuity* is a series of payments where each payment is the same amount, the period between payments is the same, the interest rate for each period is constant, and the interest is compounded. The PPMT function finds the principal portion of a loan payment when the loan is an annuity. The amount of the principal portion of a loan changes after each payment. The PPMT function needs six pieces of information: Rate, the interest rate; Per, the number of the payment for which you want to obtain the principal; Nper, the total number of payments; Pv, the loan amount; Fv, the future value amount; and Type, a number that indicates if payments are due at the end of the period or the beginning of the period.

The IPMT function finds the interest portion of a loan payment when the loan is an annuity. The amount of the interest portion of a loan changes after each payment. The IPMT function also needs six piece of information: Rate, the interest rate; Per, the number of the loan payment for which you want to obtain the principal; Nper, the total number of payments; Pv, the loan amount; Fv, the future value amount; and Type, a number that indicates if payments are due at the end of the period or the beginning of the period. For each period, the principal plus the interest should equal the payment amount.

Calculate Principal or Interest

Calculate the Principal

1. Type **=PPMT(**.

2. Click the Insert Function button.

   The Function Arguments dialog box appears.

3. Enter the interest rate.

Note: *If you make payments more than once annually, divide the interest rate by the number of payments per year.*

4. Enter the period for which you want to obtain the principal.

5. Enter the number of periods for which you will make payments.

Note: *If you make payments more than once annually, multiply the number of years by the number of payments per year.*

6. Enter the loan amount.

7. Click OK.

   ● Excel calculates the principal.

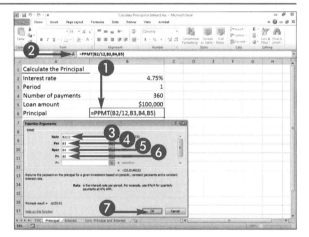

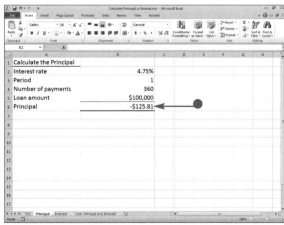

Calculate the Interest

1 Type **=IPMT(**.

2 Click the Insert Function button.

The Function Arguments dialog box appears.

3 Enter the interest rate.

4 Enter the period.

5 Enter the number of periods for which you will make payments.

6 Enter the loan amount.

7 Click OK.

● Excel calculates the interest.

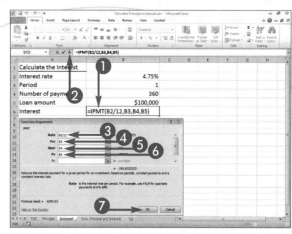

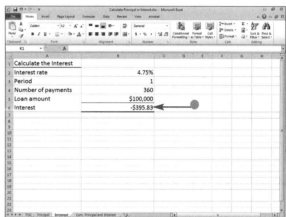

Apply It

If you need to find out how much principal or interest has accrued between two periods, you can use the CUMPRINC or the CUMIPMT function. Both of these functions ask for the same six pieces of information: Rate, the interest rate; Nper, the number of periods; Pv, the loan amount; Start_period, the first period in which you want to begin your calculation; End_period, the period in which you want to end your calculation; and Type, indicating when payments are due. Enter **0** as the Type argument if the payment is at the end of the period, or enter **1** if the payment is at the beginning of the period.

If you want to find the cumulative principal for periods 1 and 2 for a $100,000 loan at 4.75 percent per year for 360 periods, paid at the end of the period, you would enter the following formula: =CUMPRINC(.0475/12,360, 100000,1, 2,0). The formula returns −791.17. For an example of CUMPRINC and CUMIPMT, refer to the file Calculate Principal or Interest.xlsx, which you can find on the Web site for this book.

You can use Excel's RATE function to calculate the interest rate associated with an annuity. An *annuity* is a series of payments where each payment is the same amount, the period between payments is the same, the interest rate for each time period is constant, and the interest is compounded. Generally speaking, a bank loan is an annuity. If you receive a bank loan for $100,000 and you pay $521.65 monthly for 360 months, you can use the RATE function to calculate the interest rate.

When you are working with the RATE function, negative numbers are *cash outflows* and positive numbers are *cash inflows*. Your monthly payment of $521.65 is a cash outflow, so you enter it as a negative number. Your loan of $100,000 is a cash inflow, so you enter it as a positive number.

Excel's RATE function asks for six pieces of information: Nper, the number of payment periods; Pmt, the amount of each payment; Pv, the amount of the loan; Fv, the future value you want to attain; and Type, a number indicating when payments are due. If you make your payments at the beginning of the period, enter **1** as the Type argument.

Optionally, you can provide an additional argument, your best-guess estimate as to the rate of return. Calculating the rate is an iterative process where Excel starts with an initial guess for the rate and attempts to refine that guess to obtain the answer. The default value, if you do not provide an estimate is .10, representing a 10 percent rate of return. If after 20 tries Excel cannot return a value, it returns a #NUM! error. You should enter a value in the Guess field and try again.

Calculate the Interest Rate

1 Type **=RATE(**.

2 Click the Insert Function button.

   The Function Arguments dialog box appears.

3 Enter the number of periods.

4 Enter the payment amount.

5 Enter the loan amount.

Note: *Optionally, you can provide an estimated rate of return just to get Excel started.*

6 Click OK.

● The result appears in the cell.

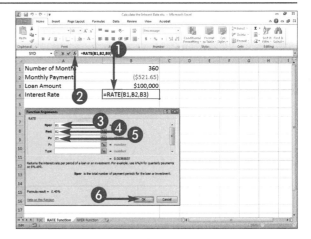

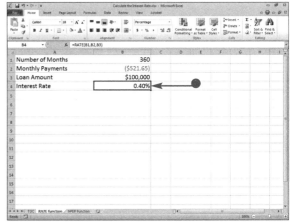

Note: In this example, payments are made monthly, so the monthly rate appears in the cell. To obtain the annual rate, you must multiply the monthly rate by 12.

7 Press F2.

8 Type *** 12**.

9 Press Enter.

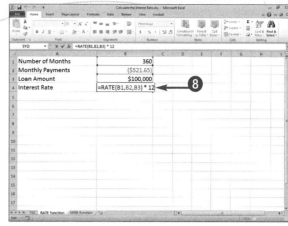

● The annual rate appears.

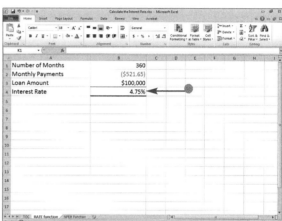

Apply It

If you know the amount of a loan, the interest rate associated with the loan, and the periodic payment, you can calculate the number of periods by using the NPER function. The NPER function asks for the following pieces of information: Rate, the interest rate; Pmt, the payment made each period; Pv, the loan amount; Fv, the future value; and Type, a number indicating when payments are due. Enter **0** or leave the Type argument blank if the payment is at the end of the period; enter **1** if the payment is at the beginning of the period.

If you want to find the number of periods for a $100,000 loan at 4.75 percent annually with monthly payments of $521.95, enter the following formula: =NPER(.0475/12,-521.95,100000). The function returns 360. To see an example of this function, refer to the file Calculate Interest Rate.xlsx, which you can find on the Web site for this book.

Calculate the Internal Rate of Return

You can use Excel's Internal Rate of Return (IRR function) to calculate the internal rate of return on an investment. When you are using the IRR function, the cash flows do not have to be equal, but they must occur at regular intervals. As an example, you make a loan of $6,607 on January 1, year 1. You receive payments every January 1 for four succeeding years. You can use the IRR function to determine the interest rate you receive on the loan.

Your loan of $6,607 is a cash outflow, so you enter it as a negative number. Each payment is a cash inflow, so you enter them as positive numbers. When using the IRR function, you must enter at least one positive and one negative number.

Optionally, you can provide an additional piece of information, your best-guess estimate as to the rate of return. Calculating the rate is an iterative process where Excel starts with an initial guess for the rate and attempts to refine that guess to obtain the answer. The default value, if you do not provide an estimate, is .10, representing a 10 percent rate of return. Your estimate gives Excel a starting point at which to calculate the RATE. If after 20 tries Excel cannot return a value, it returns a #NUM! error. You should enter a value in the Guess field and try again.

Excel's IRR function has strict assumptions. Cash flows must be regularly timed and take place at the same point within each payment period. IRR may perform less reliably for inconsistently timed payments and variable interest rates. Excel uses the order of the values to interpret the cash flows, so enter your values in the proper sequence.

Calculate the Internal Rate of Return

① Type the series of projected cash flows into a worksheet.

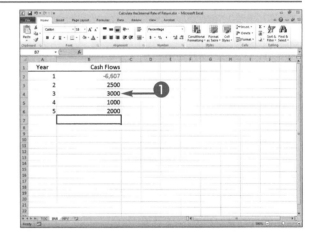

② Type **IRR(**.

③ Click the Insert Function button.

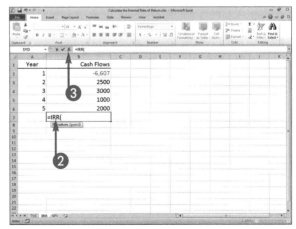

The Function Arguments dialog box appears.

④ Enter the cash-flow values you entered in Step 1 or type the range.

● Optionally, you can provide an estimated rate of return just to get Excel started.

⑤ Click OK.

● The cell with the formula displays the results of the calculations as a percent.

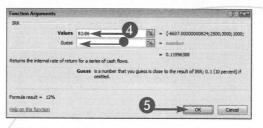

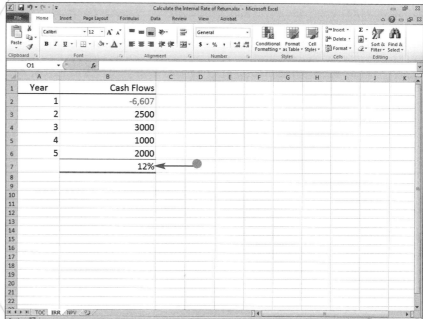

Apply It

The IRR function is related to the NPV function, which calculates the net present value of future cash flows. See the section "Calculate Present Value" to learn more about the concept of present value. The NPV function differs from the PV function in the following ways: when you are using the NPV function, the amount of each cash flow does not have to be the same and payments can only begin at the end of the period. Whereas IRR returns a percentage — the rate of return on the initial investment — NPV returns the amount that must be invested to achieve the specified rate of return.

The NPV function requires two pieces of information: Rate, which is the rate of return, and Values, which are the series of inflows and outflows. The NPV function can hold up to 254 value arguments. An *array* is a list of values enclosed in curly braces. You can enter an array into a Value field. Excel interprets the order of the cash flows as occurring in the order in which you enter them into the Value fields. To see an example of the NPV function, refer to the file Calculate the Internal Rate of Return.xls.

Calculate Straight-Line Depreciation

Buildings, cars, trucks, and equipment are all examples of depreciable assets. Accountants consider an asset depreciable if it has a useful life of more than one year but does not last indefinitely. Because accountants want to match the cost of an asset with the revenue produced from using the asset, they allocate the cost of a depreciable asset over the life of the asset. Accountants use several depreciation methods to allocate cost.

The straight-line method of depreciation allocates depreciation evenly over the useful life of the asset. Salvage value is the value of an asset once its useful life has expired. To calculate straight-line depreciation, you take the cost of the asset, subtract any salvage value, and then divide by the useful life of the asset. The result is

the amount of depreciation allocated to each period. For example, you purchase a piece of equipment on January 1 for $8,500, the equipment has a useful life of four years, and it can be sold for $500 at the end of four years. To calculate the annual depreciation, you use the formula = (8500–500)/4. The result, 2,000, is the annual depreciation.

You can use Excel's SLN function to calculate straight-line depreciation. The SLN function asks for three pieces of information: Cost, the initial cost of the asset; Salvage, the salvage value of the asset; and Life, the life of the asset in periods. If you purchase an asset mid-year, you may want to calculate depreciation in months. When calculating depreciation in months, enter the number of months that make up the useful life of the asset as the Life.

Calculate Straight-Line Depreciation

① Click in the cell in which you want the results to appear.

② Click the Insert Function button.

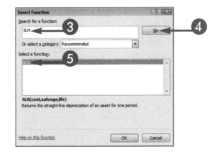

The Insert Function dialog box appears.

③ Type **SLN**.

④ Click Go.

⑤ Double-click SLN.

The Function Arguments
dialog box appears.

6 Enter the cost.

7 Enter the salvage value.

8 Enter the useful life.

9 Click OK.

● Excel calculates depreciation
for one period.

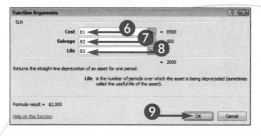

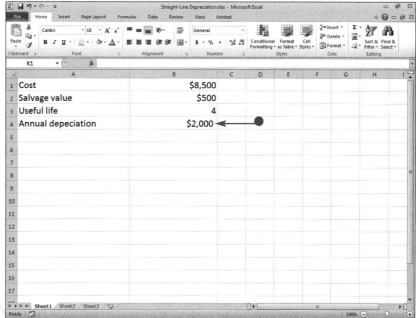

Extra

The carrying value is the cost of an asset minus the total depreciation taken to date. The depreciation for an asset
with a cost of $8,500, a salvage value of $500, and a useful life of four years would be allocated as follows:

YEAR	ANNUAL DEPRECIATION EXPENSE	ACCUMULATED DEPRECIATION	CARRYING VALUE
Beginning Year 1			$8,500
End Year 1	$2,000	$2,000	$6,500
End Year 2	$2,000	$4,000	$4,500
End Year 3	$2,000	$6,000	$2,500
End Year 4	$2,000	$8,000	$500

Calculate Declining Balance Depreciation

When calculating depreciation, accountants try to match the cost of an asset with the revenue it produces. Some assets produce more in earlier years than they do in later years. For those assets, accountants use accelerated methods of depreciation. Accelerated methods of depreciation take more depreciation in the earlier years than they do in the later years. Declining balance is an accelerated method of depreciation. You can use Excel's DB function to calculate declining balance depreciation.

The carrying value is the cost of an asset minus the total depreciation taken to date. When you use the declining balance depreciation method, you calculate a rate. The rate could be 50 percent, for example. You apply the rate to the carrying value to get the annual depreciation. Because the carrying value goes down each year, your depreciation

is higher in earlier years than it is in later years. Excel uses the following formula to calculate the rate: `rate = 1-((salvage/cost)^(1/life))`, rounded to three decimal places. After Excel calculates the rate, it uses the following formula to calculate depreciation: `depreciation =(cost-depreciation from prior periods)* rate`. The first and last periods are special. The formula for the first period is `cost*rate month/12`. The formula for the last period is `((cost-total depreciation for prior periods)*rate*12-month))/12`.

The DB function asks for five pieces of information: `Cost`, the cost of the asset; `Salvage`, the salvage value; `Life`, the useful life; `Period`, the period for which you are calculating depreciation; and `Month`, the number of months in the first year. If you leave the `Month` argument blank, Excel assumes the number of months in the first year to be 12.

Calculate Declining Balance Depreciation

① Click in the cell in which you want the results to appear.

② Click the Insert Function button.

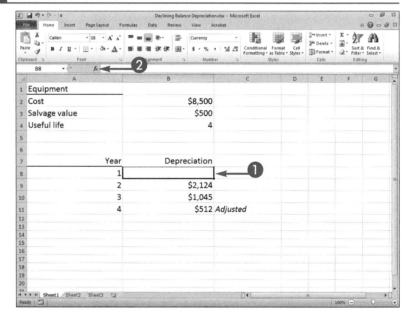

The Insert Function dialog box appears.

③ Type **DB**.

④ Click Go.

⑤ Double-click DB.

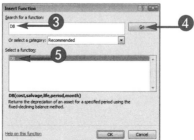

The Function Arguments dialog box appears.

6 Enter the cost.

7 Enter the salvage value.

8 Enter the useful life.

9 Enter the period.

10 Enter the month.

11 Click OK.

● Excel calculates the depreciation for one period.

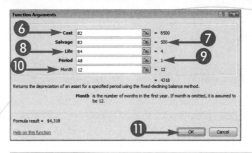

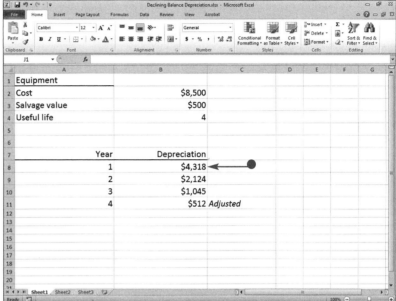

Extra

The declining balance method of depreciation depreciates an asset with a cost of $8,500, a salvage value of $500, and a useful life of four years as follows:

YEAR	ANNUAL DEPRECIATION EXPENSE	ACCUMULATED DEPRECIATION	CARRYING VALUE
Beginning of Year 1			$8,500
End Year 1	$4,318	$4,318	$4,182
End Year 2	$2,124	$6,442	$2,058
End Year 3	$1,045	$7,488	$1,012
End Year 4	$512*	$8,000	$500

*Amount adjusted for rounding error.

Calculate Double-Declining Balance Depreciation

ike the declining balance method discussed in the previous section, double-declining balance is an accelerated depreciation method. The carrying value is the cost of an asset minus the amount of depreciation taken to date. Salvage value is the amount you can sell an asset for after its useful life. Double-declining balance takes the rate you would apply by using straight-line depreciation, doubles it, and then applies the doubled rate to the carrying value of the asset. For example, under the straight-line method of depreciation, if you purchase an asset that has a useful life of four years, you would take depreciation at a rate of 1/4th per year or 25 percent. Under the double-declining balance method, you double the 25 percent and take 50 percent of the carrying value as the annual depreciation; however, you do not depreciate the asset below the salvage value. You can

use the DDB function to calculate double-declining balance depreciation. The DDB function uses the following formula to calculate double-declining balance depreciation:

```
=MIN((cost-depreciation taken to date)*
(rate),(cost-salvage value-depreciation taken
to date))
```

You must supply the DDB function with the following information: Cost, the cost of the asset; Salvage, the amount you can sell the asset for after its useful life; Life, the useful life in periods; Period, the period for which you are calculating depreciation; and Factor, the rate at which the balance declines. If you are doubling the straight-line rate, enter 2 as the Factor or leave the Factor argument blank. If you want to use a rate other than twice the straight-line rate, enter the factor you want to use. For example, enter **1.5** if you want to use a rate of 150 percent.

Calculate Double-Declining Balance Depreciation

① Click in the cell in which you want the results to appear.

② Click the Insert Function button.

The Insert Function dialog box appears.

③ Type **DDB**.

④ Click Go.

⑤ Double-click DDB.

The Function Arguments dialog box appears.

6 Enter the cost.

7 Enter the salvage value.

8 Enter the useful life.

9 Enter the period for which you want to calculate depreciation.

10 Enter the factor.

The factor is the rate at which the balance declines. For example, enter 1.5 for 150%, or 2 for double declining balance

11 Click OK.

● Excel calculates depreciation for one period.

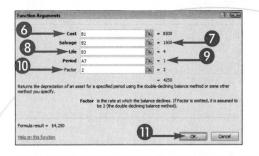

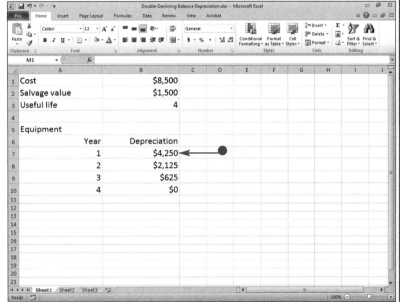

The declining balance method of depreciation depreciates an asset with a cost of $8,500, a salvage value of $1,500, and a useful life of four years as follows:

YEAR	ANNUAL DEPRECIATION EXPENSE	ACCUMULATED DEPRECIATION	CARRYING VALUE
Beginning of Year			$8,500
End Year 1	$4,250	$4,250	$4,250
End Year 2	$2,125	$6,375	$2,125
End Year 3	$625*	$7,000	$1,500
End Year 4	$0*	$7,500	$1,500

*The DDB function will not depreciate the asset below the salvage value.

Calculate Sum-of-the-Years-Digits Depreciation

When calculating depreciation, accountants try to match the cost of an asset with the revenue it produces. Some assets produce more in earlier years than they do in later years. For those assets, accountants use accelerated methods of depreciation. Sum-of-the-years-digits is an accelerated depreciation method. When you calculate sum-of-the-years-digits depreciation manually, you use a fraction to calculate annual depreciation. The numerator of the fraction is the remaining years of useful life. The denominator is the sum of the digits that make up the useful life. For example, if you want to calculate depreciation for the first year of an asset with a useful life of four years, cost of 8,500, and a salvage value of 500, the numerator is 4 and the denominator is 10, the sum of 1+2+3+4. You multiply the fraction by the cost

of the asset minus the salvage value. The calculation for the first year is `4/10*(8500–500)`, or 3,200; the calculation for the second year is `3/10*(8500–500)`, or 2,400; the calculation for the third year is `2/10*(8500–500)`, or 1,600; and the calculation for the fourth year is `1/10*(8500–500)`, or 800. You can use the SYD function to calculate sum-of-the-years-digits depreciation in Excel. The SYD function uses the following formula:

```
SYD=((cost-salvage)*(life-per+1)*2)/
     ((life)*(life+1))
```

You must supply the SYD function with the following information: `Cost`, the cost of the asset; `Salvage`, the amount you can sell the asset for after its useful life; `Life`, the useful life in periods; and `Per`, the period for which you are calculating depreciation.

Calculate Sum-of-the-Years-Digits Depreciation

① Click in the cell in which you want the results to appear.

② Click the Insert Function button.

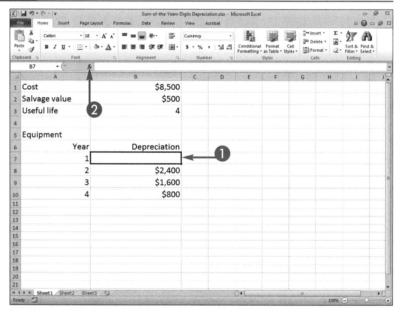

The Insert Function dialog box appears.

③ Type **SYD**.

④ Click Go.

⑤ Double-click SYD.

The Function Arguments dialog box appears.

6 Enter the cost.

7 Enter the salvage value.

8 Enter the useful life.

9 Enter the period.

10 Click OK.

- Excel calculates depreciation for one period.

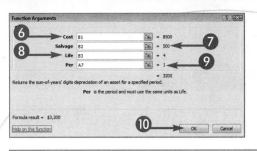

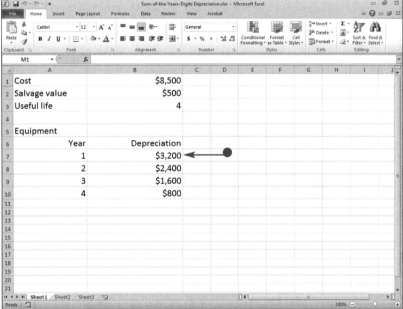

Extra

The sum-of-the-years-digits method of depreciation depreciates an asset with a cost of $8,500, a salvage value of $500, and a useful life of four years as follows:

YEAR	ANNUAL DEPRECIATION EXPENSE	ACCUMULATED DEPRECIATION	CARRYING VALUE
Beginning of Year 1			$8,500
End Year 1	$3,200	$3,200	$5,300
End Year 2	$2,400	$5,600	$2,900
End Year 3	$1,600	$7,200	$1,300
End Year 4	$800	$8,000	$500

Calculate an Average

An average is the sum of two or more values divided by the total number of values. You can use the AVERAGE function to calculate an average. The AVERAGE function takes one type of argument: Number1 through Number255. An *array* is a list of values enclosed in curly braces. For example {20, 25, 25, 30} is an array. In each Number argument, you can enter a number, a range that contains numbers, a range name, or an array. The AVERAGE function sums each value you enter and divides by the total number of values. If a cell contains a zero, Excel includes the value in the calculation. If a cell is blank, Excel does not include the cell in the calculation.

Calculate an Average

① Enter the average function.

● The range where the numbers are located.

You can enter a number, a range that contains numbers, a range name, or an array

② Click the check mark.

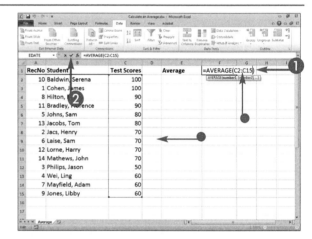

● Excel calculates the average.

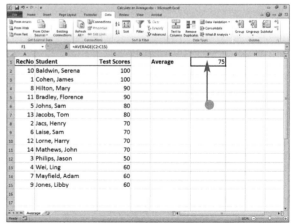

116

Calculate a Conditional Average

The AVERAGEIF function combines the AVERAGE function with the IF function. You can use the AVERAGEIF function to compute an average for data that meets the criteria you specify. For example, you can create a function that evaluates a list to determine the team a person is on, and then averages the scores of all the people on Team 1.

AVERAGEIF takes three arguments: Range, the range of values you want to evaluate by using the criteria you specify in the Criteria argument; Criteria, the criteria you want to apply to the range; and Average_range, the range of cells you want to average. The third argument, Average_range, is optional. If you do not include it, Excel averages the range you specify in the Range argument.

Extra

When using AVERAGEIF, you use a comparison operator to specify your criteria. For example, you can use 1 or "=1" to select all values that are equal to one, you can use ">50" to select all values greater than 50, or you can use "Jones" or "=Jones" to select all values equal to Jones.

Calculate a Conditional Average

1 Enter the averageIF function.

● The array or range you want to evaluate.

● The criteria.

● The range you want to average.

2 Click the check mark.

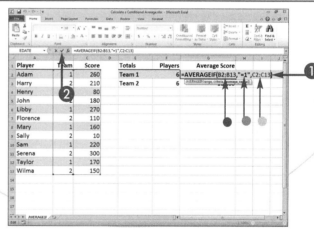

● Excel calculates the average.

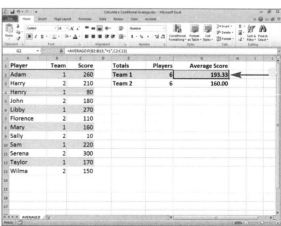

Calculate the Median or the Mode

When analyzing data, you may need to find the median. The *median* is the midpoint in a series of numbers, the point at which half the values are greater than the others and half the values are less than the others when you arrange the values in numerical order. If you are analyzing the scores students receive on a test and the median score is 75, half the students received a score greater than 75 and half the students received a score less than 75. When finding the median, if the number of items in the series is even, the median is the average of the two middle values. For example, in the series 100, 95, 90, 80, 60, 50, 40, the median is the number 80 because three numbers are greater than 80 and three numbers are less than 80. In the series 100, 95, 90, 80, 70, 60, 50, 40, the median is 75 — the average of 80 and 70. You can use Excel's MEDIAN function to calculate the median.

The *mode* is the most common value in a list of values. For example, if your list of values is 70, 65, 90, 70, 70, 90, 60, the mode is 70 because it is the value that occurs most often. You can use Excel's MODE function to find the mode.

Both the MEDIAN and MODE functions take one type of argument, Number1 through Number255. An *array* is a list of values enclosed in curly braces. For example {20, 25, 25, 30} is an array. In each Number argument, you can enter a number, a range that contains numbers, a range name, or an array.

Calculate the Median or the Mode

Calculate the Median

1 Enter the MEDIAN function.

● The numbers, range that contains numbers, range name, or array you want to evaluate.

2 Click the check mark.

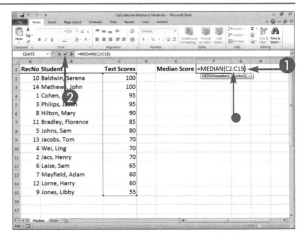

● Excel calculates the median.

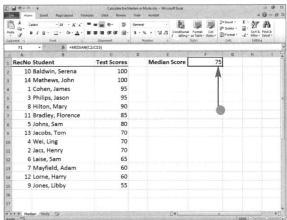

Calculate the Mode

1. Enter the MODE function.

● The numbers, range that contains numbers, range name, or array you want to evaluate.

2. Click the check mark.

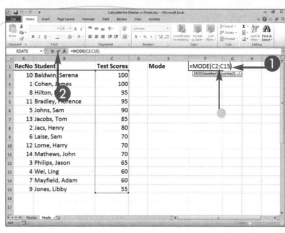

● Excel calculates the mode.

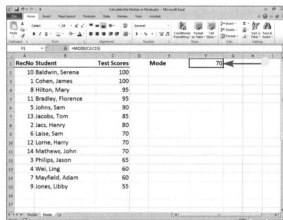

Extra

Excel interprets the logical value TRUE to be 1 and the logical value FALSE to be 0. You can enter logical values as arguments when calculating the median or mode. However, if an array or a range of cells contains a logical value, the MEDIAN and MODE functions do not include them in the calculation.

Statisticians refer to an average as the *mean*. *Central tendency* is defined as a typical value in a distribution or a value that represents the majority of cases. The most commonly used measures of central tendency are mean, mode, and median.

The Data Analysis Toolpak is an Excel add-in. Included in the Data Analysis Toolpak is a wizard you can use to calculate descriptive statistics. Among the statistics you can calculate are the mean, the mode, and the median. See the section "Calculate Descriptive Statistics" to learn more.

Calculate Rank

S ometimes you want to find how one thing ranks in relation to other thing. For example, you might want to find out how a particular student's test score ranks in relation to all other students: Did the student receive the highest score, the second highest score, and so on? The RANK.EQ function ranks a number relative to other numbers in a list. If you sort a list in numerical order, the rank is equal to the position where the number would fall in the list. You can tell the RANK. EQ function whether the list you want to base the rank on should be sorted in ascending order or descending order.

If two numbers have the same value, the RANK.EQ function gives them the same rank. For example, in the

list 100, 95, 90, 85, 85, 80, 70, the RANK.EQ function ranks the number 85 fourth. If two or more numbers have the same rank, subsequent numbers are affected. In the preceding list, the RANK.EQ function ranks 80 sixth.

The RANK.EQ function takes three arguments: Number, the number for which you want to find the rank in a list; Ref, the array or cell range with the list; and Order, the order in which you want to sort the list. Type a **0** or omit the Order argument if you want to sort the list in descending order. Type a nonzero value if you want to sort the list in ascending order. When using the RANK.EQ function, if you reference nonnumeric values, the RANK. EQ function ignores them.

Calculate Rank

① Enter the RANK.EQ function.

● The number you want to rank.

● The array or range you want to evaluate.

● The list order. Enter **0** for descending or **1** for ascending.

② Click the check mark.

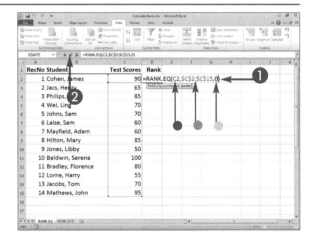

● Excel ranks the number.

③ Click and drag the Fill handle to copy the formula.

Note: See Chapter 12 to learn how to use the fill handle.

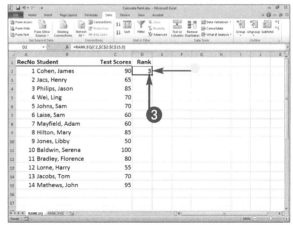

- Excel ranks every number in the list.

④ Sort the list.

Note: See Chapter 8 to learn how to sort a list.

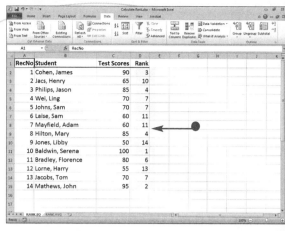

- If two or more numbers are the same, Excel gives them the same rank.

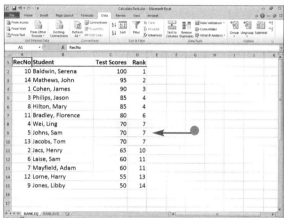

Extra

To better describe the function, Excel 2010 renamed the RANK function RANK.EQ. For backwards compatibility, the RANK function is still available.

You can also use the RANK.AVG function to calculate the rank. When using the RANK.AVG function, if two or more numbers have the same rank, Excel averages the rank. For example, in the list 100, 95, 90, 85, 85, 80, 70, the RANK.AVG function ranks the number 85 4.5, (4+5)/2. With RANK.AVG, if two or more numbers have the same rank, subsequent numbers are affected. In the preceding list, the RANK.AVG function ranks 80 sixth.

The RANK.AVG function takes three arguments: Number, a number for which you want to find its rank in a list; Ref, the array or cell range with the list; and Order, a number specifying whether you want to rank from highest to lowest or lowest to highest. Type the number **0** or leave the Order option blank if you want to rank from highest to lowest. Type the number **1** or any number greater than 1 if you want to rank from lowest to highest.

Determine the Nth Largest Value

ometimes you want to identify the top values in a series. For example, you might want to find the highest, second highest, and third highest score on a test.

The LARGE function evaluates a series of numbers and determines the highest value, second highest, or Nth highest value in the series, with N being a value's rank order. LARGE takes two arguments: Array, the array or range of cells you want to evaluate, and K, the rank order of the value you are seeking, with 1 being the highest, 2 the next highest, and so on. The result of the LARGE function is the value you requested.

Another way to determine the first, second, or Nth number in a series is to sort the numbers from largest to

smallest and then simply read the results. See Chapter 8 to learn how to sort. This technique is less useful when you have a long list or when you want to use the result in another function.

Another useful function that works in a fashion similar to the LARGE function is the SMALL function. The SMALL function evaluates a range of values and returns the smallest value, second smallest, or Nth smallest in a series. SMALL also takes two arguments: Array, the range of cells you want to evaluate, and K, the rank order of the value you are seeking, with 1 being the lowest, 2 the next lowest, and so on. For example, if you enter 1 as the K value, it returns the lowest number; if you enter 2, it returns the next lowest, and so on.

Determine the Nth Largest Value

Calculate the Nth Highest Value

① Enter the LARGE function.

● The array or range you want to evaluate.

● The rank order you want to find.

② Click the check mark.

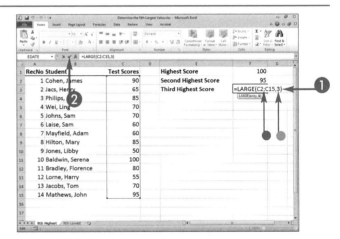

● Excel calculates the results.

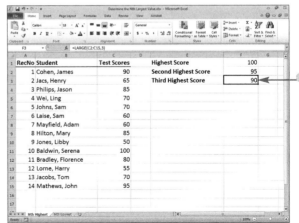

122

Calculate the Nth Lowest Value

1 Enter the SMALL function.

○ The array or range you want to evaluate.

● The rank order you want to find.

2 Click the check mark.

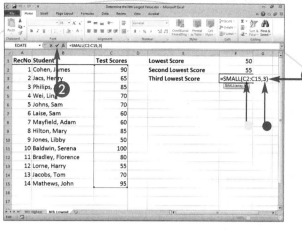

● Excel calculates the results.

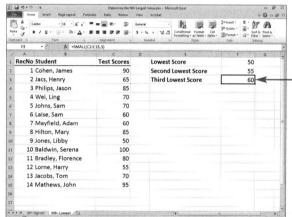

Extra

To better describe the function, Excel 2010 renamed the PERCENTRANK function PERCENTRANK.INC. For backwards compatibility, the PERCENTRANK function is still available.

You can use the PERCENTRANK.INC function to determine the rank of a value as a percentage of all the values in your data set. The PERCENTRANK.INC function takes three arguments: Array, the array or range you want to use to determine the percent rank; X, the value you want to rank; and Significance, the number of significant digits you want your results to return. The default is three digits. If you leave this argument blank, the PERCENTRANK. INC function uses the default.

The PERCENTRANK.INC function gives equal values the same rank. If you want to format the value returned as a percentage, select the cell, click the Home tab, and then click the Percent Style button (%).

Excel 2010 added PERCENTRANK.EXC to comply with industry standards for calculating the rank of a value as a percentage of all the values in a data set. The PERCENTRANK.EXC takes the same arguments as PERCENTRANK. INC. It excludes the ranks of 0 and 100.

Calculate Frequency

When you collect large amounts of data, organizing your data can help you see patterns. Usually, you start by sorting your data so you can see the range of values. The next step might be to do a simple frequency distribution so you can see how often each value occurs. To understand your data further, you might create a grouped frequency distribution. Grouping your data makes it easy for you to compare categories of data.

You can use Excel's FREQUENCY function to group your data into categories. For example, you can use the FREQUENCY function to display student test scores. The first group might be scores less than or equal to 50, representing scores 50 percent or lower; your second group might be 51 to 60; the next group 61 to 70, and so

on, up to scores of 90 percent or higher. Excel counts the number of occurrences in each group.

You must supply the FREQUENCY function with two arguments: the Data_array and the Bins_array. The Data_array is the list of values you want to group. The Bins_array is the list of groupings you want to use. To use the FREQUENCY function, you must select the cells into which you want to place your results. If you have five groups, select six cells — one more cell than the number of groups you have. Type the function or enter it into the Function Arguments dialog box. Frequency is an array function; curly braces must surround your function. Press Ctrl+Shift+Enter after you enter your arguments. Excel will place curly braces around your function. If curly braces do not surround your function, your function will not calculate.

Calculate Frequency

① Select the cells where you want the results to appear.

② Click the Insert Function button.

The Insert Function dialog box appears.

③ Click the ▼ and then select Statistical.

④ Double-click FREQUENCY.

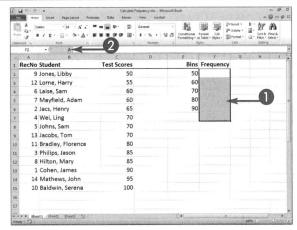

The Function Arguments dialog box appears.

⑤ Enter the range, or array, you want to evaluate.

⑥ Enter the grouping you want to use.

⑦ Press Ctrl+Shift+Enter.

Note: *Do not click OK. Clicking OK will not place curly braces around your formula.*

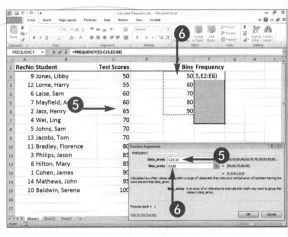

● The results appear in the cells you selected.

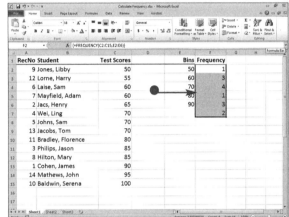

Extra

When you create your frequency distribution, keep the following rules in mind:

- Keep the number of groups reasonable: between five and ten is good. If you have too few or too many groups, you can lose your ability to convey information easily. Too few intervals can hide trends and too many intervals can mask details.

- Keep your intervals simple. Intervals of 5, 10, or 20 are good because they are easy to understand.

- Start your interval with a value that is divisible by the interval size. That will make your frequency distribution easy to read.

- All intervals should have the same number of values. Again, this makes your frequency distribution easy to understand.

You can use Excel's chart tools to chart your frequency distribution. Use a Column chart. Place your groupings on the horizontal axis and your frequencies on the vertical axis.

Calculate Variance and Standard Deviation

Statisticians refer to the average of a group of values as the *mean*. When you have a list of numbers, you can use the variance and standard deviation to show how much a group of numbers varies from the mean — the larger the variance, the more the values vary.

When manually calculating variance, you start by calculating the mean of all the values in your list, and then you subtract each value in the list from the mean value. This tells you how much each value deviates from the mean. You then square each deviation, sum the squared deviations, and then divide the sum by the number of values minus 1 to obtain the variance.

Instead of performing this complex calculation to calculate the variance, you can use the VAR function to obtain the

variance. The VAR function takes one type of argument, Number1 through Number255. An *array* is a list of values enclosed in curly braces. For example {20, 25, 25, 30} is an array. In each Number argument, you can enter a number, a range that contains numbers, a range name, or an array.

Finding the variance is often useful, but because the variance is a squared value, it is difficult to interpret the variance in relation to the mean. Therefore, statisticians often calculate the square root of the variance. They call the resulting value the *standard deviation*. You can use Excel's STDEV function to calculate the standard deviation. The STDEV function takes the same type of argument as the VAR function and works in much the same way.

Calculate Variance and Standard Deviation

Calculate Variance

1 Enter the VARIANCE function.

● The array or range you want to evaluate.

2 Click the check mark.

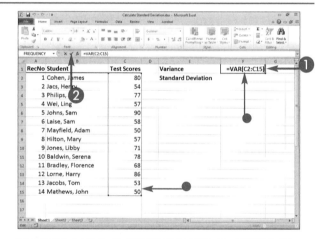

● Excel calculates the variance.

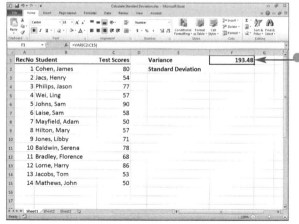

Calculate the Standard Deviation

① Enter the STDEV function.

● The array or range you want to evaluate.

② Click the check mark.

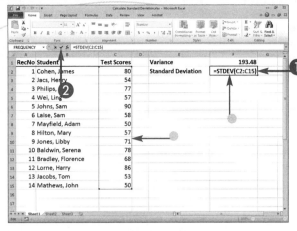

● Excel calculates the standard deviation.

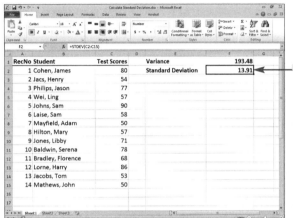

Extra

When calculating and using standard deviation, keep the following in mind:

● The standard deviation is always a positive number.

● A single outlier can distort the standard deviation.

● If every value in a data set is the same, the standard deviation is zero.

● If two sets of data have approximately the same mean, the higher the standard deviation the more variability there is in the data.

If your data is distributed normally, about 68 percent of your data lies between one standard deviation from both sides of the mean, approximately 95 percent of your data lies between two standard deviations from both sides of the mean, and approximately 99 percent of your data lies between three standard deviations from both sides of the mean.

Find the Correlation

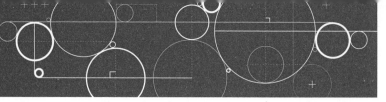

With the CORREL function, you can measure the relationship between two variables. You can explore questions such as whether there is a correlation between years employed and sales. A correlation does not prove one thing causes another. The most you can say is that one number varies with the other. Their variation may be the result of how you measured your numbers or the result of some factor underlying both variables. When you use correlations, you start with a theory that two things are related. If there is a correlation, you must then gather evidence and develop plausible reasons for the correlation.

Use the CORREL function to determine a correlation. CORREL takes two arguments: array1 and array2 — the two lists of numbers. The result of the function is a number, r, between –1 and 1. The closer r gets to –1 or 1, the stronger the relationship. If r is close to or equal to 0, that means that there is little to no correlation between the variables. If r is negative, the relationship is an inverse relationship — for example, as years employed increases, sales decrease. A positive result suggests that as one variable increases, so does the other. For example, as years employed increases, sales increase.

When using CORREL, if a reference cell contains text, logical values, or empty cells, Excel ignores those values. However, reference cells that contain a value of 0 are included in the calculation. If the number of data points in array1 and array2 are not equal, Excel returns the error message #N/A.

Find the Correlation

1 Type **=CORREL(**.

Alternatively, select CORREL from the AutoComplete list that appears after you begin typing.

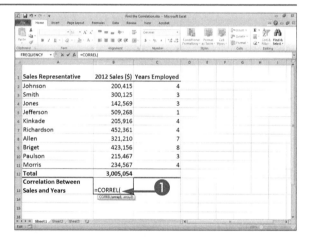

2 Click the Insert Function button.

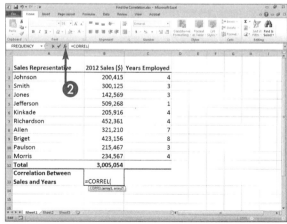

The Function Arguments dialog box appears.

③ Enter the cell range of the first series of number.

④ Enter the cell range of the second series of number.

Note: *You can select a subset of a list, but make sure the same subset is selected for each list.*

⑤ Click OK.

● Excel calculates the correlation.

Note: *The sign suggests whether the relationship is positive (+) or negative (−).*

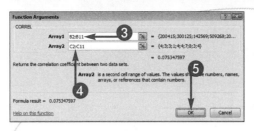

Sales Representative	2012 Sales ($)	Years Employed
Johnson	200,415	4
Smith	300,125	3
Jones	142,569	3
Jefferson	509,268	1
Kinkade	205,916	4
Richardson	452,361	4
Allen	321,210	7
Briget	423,156	8
Paulson	215,467	3
Morris	234,567	4
Total	3,005,054	
Correlation Between Sales and Years	0.075347597	

Extra

An *add-in* is software that adds one or more features to Excel. To learn how to install add-ins, see the next section, "Install Excel Add-Ins." The Analysis Toolpak is an add-in that contains a number of statistical tools, including the Correlation tool, which you can use to calculate correlations. The correlations you calculate by using the Correlation tool do not automatically update as you update your worksheet.

Squaring the value of r makes the value easier to understand. The square of r tells you how the percent of the variation in one value relates to the other value. To find the percent of variation, you square r and then drop the decimal point. For example, if r is equal to .5, the square of r is 25 percent. The 25 percent value tells you that 25 percent of the variation is related.

Install Excel Add-Ins

I nstalling add-ins gives you additional Excel features not available in the Ribbon by default. An *add-in* is software that adds one or more features to Excel. Bundled add-in software is included with Excel but is not automatically installed when you install Excel. There are several add-ins that come standard with Excel, including Solver, which enables you to solve optimization problems easily; the Euro Currency Tools, which enable you to calculate exchange rates between the Euro and other currencies; and the Data Analysis Toolpak, which provides you with a number of tools you can use for statistical analysis. The remainder of this chapter introduces a few of the statistical add-ins in the Data Analysis Toolpak.

You install the bundled add-ins by using the Excel Options dialog box. You can find them in the Add-Ins

section. Once installed, add-ins are available right away. They usually appear on a tab related to their function. The Data Analysis Toolpak appears on the Data tab.

You can also take advantage of third-party add-ins to gain functionality in support of advanced work in chemistry, risk analysis, modeling, project management, statistics, and other fields. Third-party add-ins usually have their own installation and usage procedures. Consult the vendors of these programs for documentation.

To learn about special-purpose Excel add-ins in your field, you can perform a Google search by going to www.google. com. Your search terms should include Excel, the field of knowledge — for example, chemistry — and other relevant information, such as a vendor's name. Third-party vendors are responsible for supporting their own products.

Install Excel Add-Ins

① Click the File tab.

A menu appears.

② Click Options.

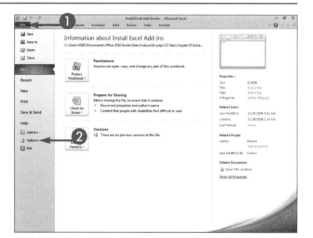

The Excel Options dialog box appears.

③ Click Add-Ins.

● The View and manage Microsoft Office Add-Ins dialog box appears.

④ Click an add-in.

This example uses the Analysis Toolpak.

⑤ Click Go.

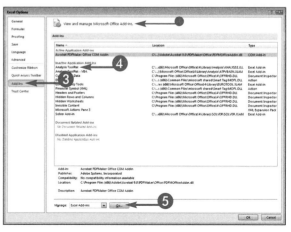

The Add-Ins dialog box appears.

6 Click an option in the Add-Ins available list to select an add-in (☐ changes to ☑).

7 Click OK.

● Excel places the Add-in in the Ribbon.

● The Analysis Toolpak is on the Data tab.

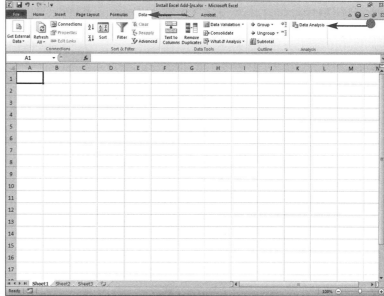

Extra

Removing an add-in is easy. Click the File tab, click Options, click Add-ins, click the add-in you want to remove, and then click Go. The Add-Ins dialog box appears. Deselect the add-in you want to remove and then click OK. Excel removes the add-in.

You can download additional add-ins from the Microsoft download site. For example, in Excel 2003, you could click a data point in a column point twice and you would then be able to resize the columns. This feature was deprecated in Excel 2007. However, Microsoft received a lot of feedback indicating that people like the feature, so they developed an add-in that can be used with Excel 2007 and Excel 2010. The add-in is called Manipulate Point on Chart.

For Excel 2010, you can download and use the Microsoft SQL Server PowerPivot add-in to work with large amounts of data from multiple data sources. You can then use PivotTables to analyze the data. This add-in produces a fast response time even if you are working with millions of rows of data.

Calculate a Moving Average

The Moving Average tool projects values based on the average value over a specified period. Using a moving average can reveal trends that are masked when you use a simple average because a simple average gives equal weight to each value. A moving average weighs recent values equally and ignores older values, thereby enabling you to spot trends. You can use a moving average to forecast sales, stock prices, or other trends.

You specify the number of values, or *intervals*, Excel should use to calculate the moving average. If you do not supply an interval, Excel uses the default value of 3, which means that the moving average is calculated by averaging the last three values.

Unlike other tools available for Data Analysis, the Moving Average tool can only output the values to the current worksheet. You need to specify the first cell you want to use for the results. If the first row contains a label, your data should start in the second row. In addition to a forecast, you can elect to have Excel compute the standard error. If you select this option, Excel creates an additional column that contains the standard error.

You can also create a chart that shows the relationship between the actual values in the data set and the forecasted moving average. If you select this option, Excel places the chart on the same worksheet as the moving average values.

Excel provides the Moving Average tool as part of the Data Analysis Toolpak. See the previous section, "Install Excel Add-Ins," to learn how to install the Data Analysis Toolpak.

Calculate a Moving Average

① Click the Data tab.

② Click Data Analysis.

The Data Analysis dialog box appears.

③ Double-click Moving Average.

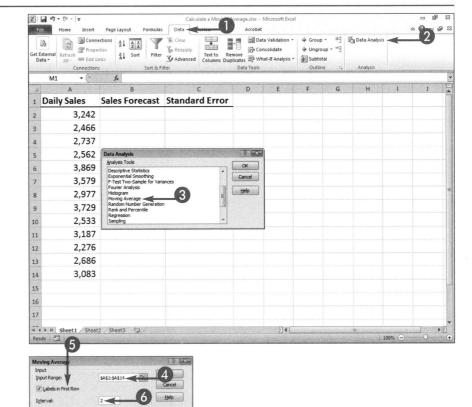

The Moving Average dialog box appears.

④ Enter the values you want to analyze.

⑤ If the first row contains labels, click Labels in First Row (☐ changes to ✔).

⑥ Enter the interval.

⑦ Specify the output range cell reference.

● Click Chart Output (☐ changes to ✔) to display a Chart.

⑧ Click Standard Errors (☐ changes to ✔) to create Standard Error values.

⑨ Click OK.

● Excel calculates the moving average and standard error.

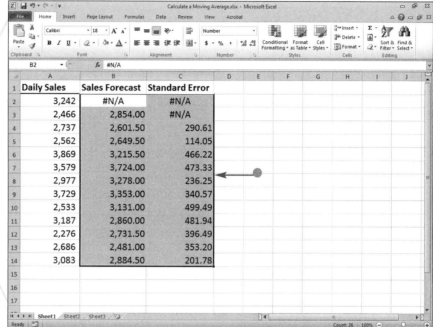

Extra

When you use the Moving Average tool, Excel calculates an average to determine each moving average value. The first few values in the column will contain the value #N/A. The number of cells that contain #N/A is one less than the integer value specified for the Interval value. For example, if the specified interval is 3, the first two cells in the Moving Average column contain the value #N/A because you do not have three values to average.

When you create a chart for the Moving Average, Excel automatically uses default labels for each data series, the axes, and the chart title. You can use the chart options to change the text of each label.

Compare Variances

You can use an F-test to determine whether two variances are equal. *Variance* is a measurement of how much a group of values varies from the group's mean value. For example, if you have two plants producing the same product, one in Indiana and one in Texas, and both have efficiency levels of 95 percent, but you want to know which plant remained consistently more efficient throughout the year; you can perform an F-test. If you find that the Indiana plant has a lower variance than the Texas plant, you know that the Indiana plant was consistently more efficient.

When you use an F-test analysis, Excel compares the ratio of the variance between the two groups of data. Excel calculates an F statistic (F) for the two sets of data, which is the ratio of the Mean Standard Square Error

(MS) between the groups to the MS within the groups. If the F statistic is less than the F critical value, you cannot reject the null hypothesis that the variances of the two groups are the same. An F statistic close to 1 indicates that two groups have equal variances.

To perform this test, you must provide Excel with the ranges of both data groups as well as an Alpha level, or the statistical confidence level you expect. The Alpha field is the probability of the null hypothesis being true. You specify a value between 0 and 1 for the confidence level. The default level of .05 is equivalent to a 95 percent confidence level. To make your table easily identifiable, you can let Excel know that you have labels in the first row of your worksheet.

Compare Variances

① Click the Data tab.

② Click Data Analysis.

   The Data Analysis dialog box appears.

③ Double-click F-Test Two-Sample for Variances.

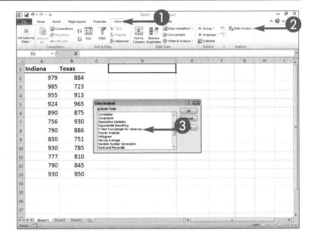

   The F-Test Two-Sample for Variances dialog box appears.

④ Enter the first range of cells to analyze.

⑤ Enter the second range of cells to analyze.

⑥ If your data range has labels, click Labels (☐ changes to ✔).

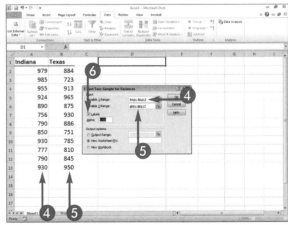

7 Type a value between 0 and 1 for the Alpha level.

8 Specify the output location (◎ changes to ◉).

9 Click OK.

● Excel compares the variances between the two groups.

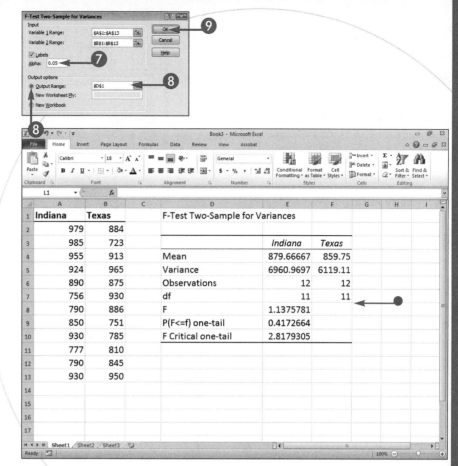

Extra

When you use the F-test analysis tool, Excel can calculate several values, as described in the following table.

STATISTIC	DESCRIPTION
Mean	The average value, or center of the distribution, of the data group.
Variance	A measurement of the spread or dispersion of the data. The average squared distance between each datum and the mean.
Observations	Indicates the number of values in each list.
Df	Indicates the Degrees of Freedom, or the number of values that are free to vary after a statistic has been computed from a set of data.
F	The ratio of the variance of the individual groups to the entire range of values. The F statistic is the ratio of the mean square between the data sets over the mean square within the data sets.

Using the Data Analysis Toolpak to Determine Rank and Percentile

I f you want to rank a series of values in a list, you can use the Rank and Percentile tool. With this tool, Excel takes a list of numeric values and ranks them from highest to lowest by both a numeric and a percentage value. It also calculates a percentile for your value. For example, you may want to rank the test scores of the students in a class to show not only which person had the highest score but also to determine the student's percentile when compared to the entire class. This feature is perfect for ranking the top-selling item, the most efficient facility within a company, or the machine or team that produces the highest level of output.

You can only rank one row or column of values at a time. Excel enables you to select multiple rows or columns as the input range, but only analyzes the first row or column. You can only have a label in the first row of a column. If the specified range contains any other text, an error message displays.

You can output the results of the Rank and Percentile tool to a specific range of cells within the current worksheet, a new worksheet, or a new workbook. If you select New Worksheet, you can specify the worksheet name or allow Excel to assign a default name.

Excel provides the Rank and Percentile tool as part of the Data Analysis Toolpak. See the section "Install Excel Add-Ins" to learn how to install the Data Analysis Toolpak.

Using the Data Analysis Toolpak to Determine Rank and Percentile

① Click the Data tab.

② Click Data Analysis.

The Data Analysis dialog box appears.

③ Double-click Rank and Percentile.

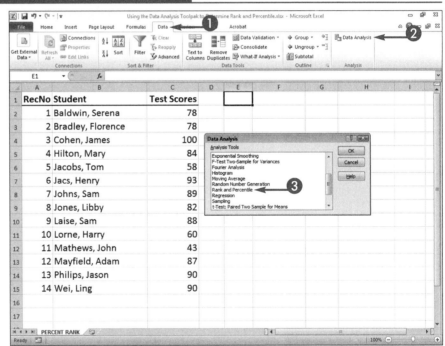

The Rank and Percentile dialog box appears.

④ Specify the range of cells to analyze.

⑤ Specify whether data values are in rows or columns (◯ changes to ◉).

⑥ If the first row contains labels, click Labels in First Row (☐ changes to ✔).

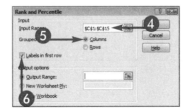

⑦ Specify the output location (◉ changes to ◉).

⑧ Click OK.

● Excel ranks the specified range of data.

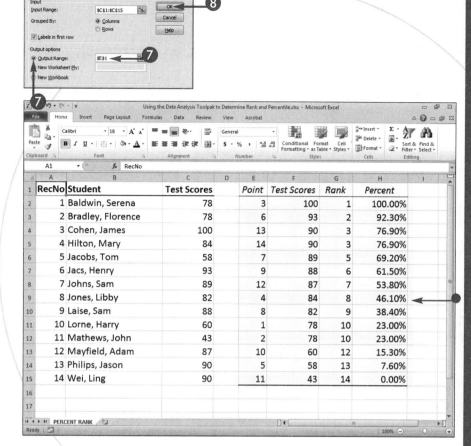

Excel creates a four-column table containing ranking information for the specified values, as outlined in the following table.

COLUMN	DESCRIPTION
Point	The location of the data value within the specified input range. For example, if the value was originally the third numeric value in the input data, the point value is 3.
Input	Contains the input values, sorted based upon the ranking.
Rank	The numeric ranking of each value with 1 being the highest ranking value in the list.
Percent	A percentage ranking for the input values. The percentage indicates the percentage of values that are below the specified value.

Calculate Descriptive Statistics

Y ou can have Excel quickly calculate 16 different statistical measurements and summarize them in a list using the Descriptive Statistics tool. For an analyst, this feature is perfect for calculating statistical information on large databases or worksheets. When you use this tool, Excel produces a table containing standard statistical calculations for each group of data values in your list, including the mean, standard error, median, mode, standard deviation, sample variance, kurtosis, skewness, range, minimum, maximum, sum, count, largest value, smallest value, and confidence level. For example, if you use it to compare a list containing sales amounts for different regions, Excel produces a table containing the statistical values related to each region.

With the Descriptive Statistics tool, you must specify the range of cells containing the sets of data. You also must indicate whether you have your data sets grouped in rows or in columns. Each row or column must contain a different set of data. You can make the output easier to identify by labeling your data.

You can use the last four options in the Descriptive Statistics dialog box to specify which descriptive statistic values Excel calculates. Use the Summary Statistics option to calculate all the common descriptive statistic values. Use the Confidence Level for Mean option to calculate the confidence level. Kth Largest and Kth Smallest enable you to find specific values in the group, such as the second smallest or third largest number. If you specify a value of 1, you receive the same values Excel gives you for the minimum and maximum values.

Calculate Descriptive Statistics

1. Click the Data tab.

2. Click Data Analysis.

   The Data Analysis dialog box appears.

3. Double-click Descriptive Statistics.

   The Descriptive Statistics dialog box appears.

4. Enter the range of cells to analyze.

5. Specify whether data values are in rows or columns (◎ changes to ◉).

6. Click Labels in first row if you have labels in your first row or column (☐ changes to ✔).

7. Specify the output location (◎ changes to ◉).

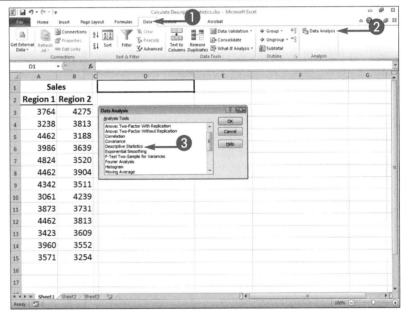

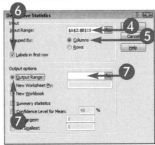

⑧ Click Summary Statistics (☐ changes to ✔) to produce a table with all 16 of Excel's statistical measurements.

⑨ Click Confidence Level for Mean (☐ changes to ✔) to show the confidence level.

⑩ Type a Confidence Level.

⑪ Click Kth Largest and Kth Smallest (☐ changes to ✔) to display the smallest and largest values.

⑫ Click OK.

● Excel produces descriptive statistics for each group of values.

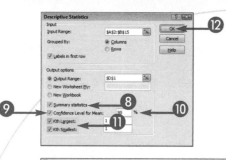

	Sales		Region 1		Region 2	
	Region 1	Region 2				
3	3764	4275	Mean	3956	Mean	3696
4	3238	3813	Standard Error	149.0151429	Standard Error	89.591
5	4462	3188	Median	3960	Median	3639
6	3986	3639	Mode	4462	Mode	3813
7	4824	3520	Standard Deviation	537.2817386	Standard Deviation	323.025
8	4462	3904	Sample Variance	288671.6667	Sample Variance	104345
9	4342	3511	Kurtosis	-0.952326355	Kurtosis	-0.01471
10	3061	4239	Skewness	-0.128917837	Skewness	0.38976
11	3873	3731	Range	1763	Range	1087
12	4462	3813	Minimum	3061	Minimum	3188
13	3423	3609	Maximum	4824	Maximum	4275
14	3960	3552	Sum	51428	Sum	48048
15	3571	3254	Count	13	Count	13
16			Largest(1)	4824	Largest(1)	4275
17			Smallest(1)	3061	Smallest(1)	3188
18			Confidence Level(95.0%)	324.6761052	Confidence Level(95.0%)	195.202

Extra

When you use the Descriptive Statistics tool, Excel can calculate several values:

STATISTIC	DESCRIPTION
Mean	The average value, or center of the distribution, of the data group.
Standard Error	The square root of the sample size (n) divided into the standard deviation over the square root of the sample size (n).
Median	The middle value in the group of data.
Mode	The most common value in the group of data.
Standard Deviation	The dispersion of the group of data values around the mean.
Sample Variance	The standard deviation squared, or the measure of the dispersion of the data.
Range	The difference between the largest and smallest values.
Minimum/Maximum	The smallest and largest values in the group.
Sum	The total when you add all the values in the group.
Count	The number of values in the group.
Largest(N)/Smallest(N)	The largest and smallest values in the group, where N is a specified integer.
Confidence Level for Mean	When using sample data, the percentage of samples that are expected to contain the true mean.

Enter Data with a Form

People often organize data into lists. You can use Excel to manage lists. In Excel, a *list* is a rectangular section of a worksheet structured as a set of columns and rows. You call each column a *field* and you give each field a *label*. Field labels appear on the first row of a list. Each row in a list is called a *record*. For example, you can have a list of sales people organized as follows: First Name, Last Name, Sales. You label the first column First Name, you label the second column Last Name, and you label the last column Sales. On each row of your list, in the First Name field, first names appear; in the Last Name field, last names appear; and in the Sales field, sales appear.

In Excel, you can use a form to simplify entering data into a list. A form speeds up your data entry by providing a blank field for each column in your list. A form uses field labels as field names. You can type your data into the form and use the Tab key to move from field to field. After you complete each set of fields, click the Next button to enter the record into a row in your list and then type in a new record. You can use the Find Prev (Previous) and Find Next buttons to move backward and forward through your list to view or modify your data.

You must add the Form button to the Ribbon or the Quick Access Toolbar before you can use forms. Refer to Chapter 17 to learn how to add items to the Ribbon and the Quick Access Toolbar.

Enter Data with a Form

① Click a single cell anywhere in the list.

② Click the Form button.

The data form appears.

③ Click the New button.

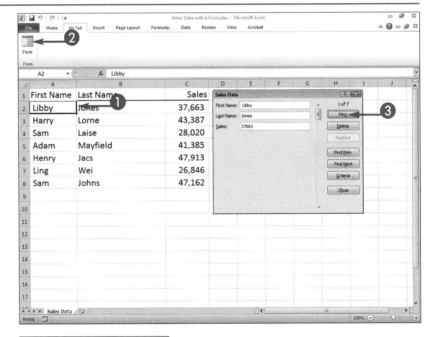

● Excel clears the form.

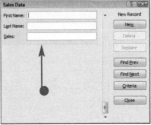

④ Type the requested information into the fields.

⑤ Press Tab to move to the next field.

⑥ Repeat Steps 4 and 5 to complete the remaining fields.

⑦ After completing the first set of fields, click New to start a new record.

● The data fills the worksheet and the form fields clear, ready for another record.

⑧ Repeat Steps 4 to 7 for each new record.

⑨ Click Close after entering all your data.

The entered records appear in the worksheet.

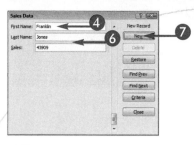

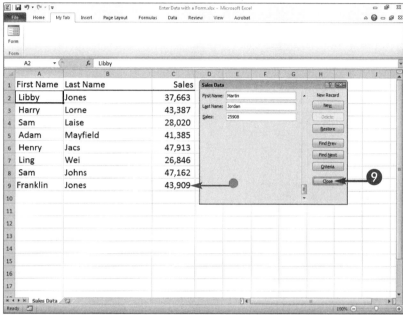

Apply It

Your form also doubles as a search box. You can use your form to search for and edit data. With the list and form displayed, click the Criteria button. In a blank field, type an operator, such as = or >, followed by a value in one or more fields. For example, if you are looking for the last name Jones type **=Jones** in the Last Name field. If you are looking for sales greater than 30,000, type **>30000** in the Sales field. After you enter your criteria, click Find Next. If several records match your criteria, you can display the additional records by clicking the Find Prev and Find Next buttons, as appropriate.

While you are editing a record through a form, you can click the Restore button at any time to bring back the original contents of the field. You can click the Delete button to delete a record. However, if you use the Delete button, Excel permanently deletes the record. You cannot bring back the record with the Undo command. You cannot use a form to edit values returned by a formula.

Perform Simple Sorts and Filters

Y ou can sort a list so that you can easily find and group data. You can use the Sort buttons on the Data tab to sort. When you sort, you rearrange your data in ascending or descending order. The meaning of these terms depends on the kind of data you are sorting. Dates sorted in ascending order show the earliest date first. Dates sorted in descending order show the latest date first. Text sorted in ascending order sorts A to Z. Text sorted in descending order sorts Z to A. Numeric data sorted in ascending order sorts from the lowest number to the highest. Numeric data sorted in descending order sorts from the highest number to the lowest.

With filtering, you can display only the data that you want to display. For example, if you have a list that

includes data for four quarters, you can choose to view data for the first quarter only.

When you click Filter on the Data tab, Excel places AutoFilter buttons next to each of the fields in your list. You can use the AutoFilter buttons to display a menu with options that enable you to sort and filter your data. You can click a sort option to sort a column or you can filter by deselecting the items that you do not want to appear in your list. You can apply filters to multiple columns in the same list. Each filter you apply narrows your selection further.

If after applying a sort or filter you make changes to your data, you can refresh you data by clicking Reapply.

Perform Simple Sorts and Filters

Sort a List

❶ Click a cell in the column you want to sort.

❷ Click the Data tab.

❸ Click a sort direction.

Click A to Z to sort from lowest to highest — ascending order.

Click Z to A to sort from highest to lowest — descending order.

● Excel sorts your list by the column you selected.

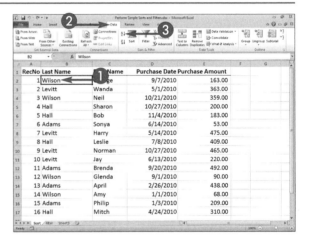

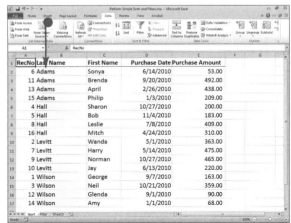

Filter a List

1 Click a cell in a list.

2 Click the Data tab.

3 Click Filter.

- AutoFilter buttons appear next to your field headers.

4 Click an AutoFilter button (▾).

The Sort & Filter menu appears.

5 Click items to deselect the ones you do not want (✔ changes to ▢).

6 Click OK.

- Excel filters your list.

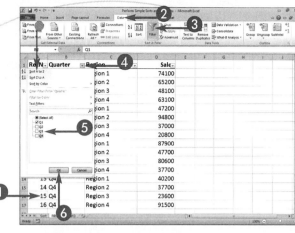

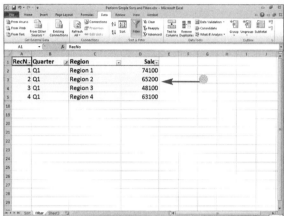

Extra

When you perform a filter, Excel places AutoFilter buttons (▾) next to your field labels. Fields you have filtered have a filter on the AutoFilter button (▾). Fields you have sorted in ascending order have an up arrow on the AutoFilter button (▾). Fields you have sorted in descending order have a down arrow on the AutoFilter button (▾).

To clear all filters, click Clear in the Sort & Filter group on the Data tab. To remove the AutoFilter buttons next to your field names, click Filter. To bring the AutoFilter buttons back, click Filter again. Filter toggles the Sort & Filter feature on and off.

Excel defines different sorts as follows: For numbers, ascending order goes from the smallest number to the largest. For text that includes numerals, as in U2 and K12, ascending order places numerals before symbols and symbols before letters. Case does not matter unless you click Options in the Sort dialog box and then click the Case Sensitive check box (▢ changes to ✔). To open the Sort dialog box, click Sort in the Sort & Filter group on the Data tab.

Perform Multilevel Sorts

When you perform a simple sort, you can only sort by one column in your list. If you need to sort multiple columns, you must perform a multilevel sort. With a multilevel sort, you can, for example, sort by quarter and within a quarter by region.

To perform a multilevel sort, you use the Sort dialog box. If your list has column labels, make sure the My data has headers check box is selected. You will select the first sort level, add a level, and then select the next sort level. For example, if you are sorting by quarter and then within quarter by region, the Quarter field is your first sort level and the Region field is your second sort level. You can have up to 64 sort levels.

In the Sort dialog box, use the Column drop-down list to choose the column you want to sort. Use the Sort On drop-down list to choose what you want to base your sort on. If you want to sort on text, dates, or numbers, choose Values. Use the Order drop-down list to choose a sort order. If you want to sort in ascending order, choose A to Z. If you want to sort in descending order, choose Z to A.

If you choose ascending order, Excel sorts values in the following order: numbers, text, logical values, error values blanks. If you choose descending order, Excel reverses that order for everything except blanks, which are sorted last. You can also sort by cell color, font color, or cell icon. See the section "Sort by Cell Color, Font Color, or Cell Icon" to learn more.

Perform MultiLevel Sorts

① Click a cell in the list.

② Click the Data tab.

③ Click Sort.

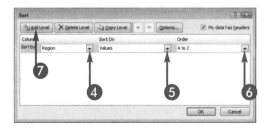

The Sort dialog box appears.

④ Click the ▾ and then select the column you want to sort.

⑤ Click the ▾ and then select Values.

⑥ Click the ▾ and then select a sort order.

⑦ Click the Add Level button.

---

8 Repeat Steps 4 to 7 to sort by additional criteria.

9 Click OK to close the Sort dialog box.

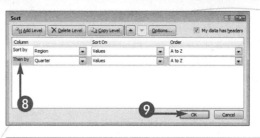

● Excel sorts the list.

RecNo	Region	Quarter	Sales
12	Region 1	Q1	74100
7	Region 1	Q2	47200
14	Region 1	Q3	87900
6	Region 1	Q4	40200
11	Region 2	Q1	65200
16	Region 2	Q2	94800
8	Region 2	Q3	47700
4	Region 2	Q4	37700
9	Region 3	Q1	48100
3	Region 3	Q2	37000
13	Region 3	Q3	80600
2	Region 3	Q4	23600
10	Region 4	Q1	63100
1	Region 4	Q2	20800
5	Region 4	Q3	37700
15	Region 4	Q4	91500

Extra

If you are sorting a list, click in any cell in the list and Excel will select the entire list when you open the Sort dialog box. If you are sorting a range of cells that are not a list, select the cells and then click Sort on the Data tab to open the Sort dialog box. If necessary, Deselect the My data has headers check box.

In the Sort dialog box, click the Delete Level button to delete a level of sort. Click the Copy Level button to copy a level of sort. Click (▲) to move a sort level up. Click (▼) to move a sort level down.

By default, Excel sorts from top to bottom. If you want to sort from left to right, click Sort on the Data tab. The Sort dialog box appears. Click the Options button. The Sort Options dialog box appears. Click Sort Left to Right (◎ changes to ◉).

By default, sorts are not case-sensitive. If you want to make them case-sensitive, click Case Sensitive (☐ changes to ✔) in the Sort Options dialog box. Excel orders lowercase letters before uppercase letters.

Perform a Custom Sort

You can use a custom sort to sort in an order other than ascending or descending. For example, if you have a list of sales data and you want to sort it by the months in a year — January through December — you can use a custom sort.

When you choose Custom List in the Order drop-down list in the Sort dialog box, the Custom Lists dialog box appears. There you can choose a custom sort order such as days of the week or months of the year. You can also add your own list to the Custom Lists dialog box and use it to sort. For example, if you often order your data North, South, East, West, you can add that list to the Custom Lists dialog box and use it to sort.

Apply It

If you have a data series you use often, you can create a custom list and use it to sort. To create a custom list, click the File tab. A menu appears. Click Options. The Excel Options dialog box appears. Click Advanced. Under General, click the Edit Custom Lists button. The Custom Lists dialog box appears. In the List Entries field, type your list and then click Add.

Perform a Custom Sort

1 Click a cell in the list.

2 Click the Data tab.

3 Click the Sort button.

   The Sort dialog box appears.

4 Click the ▾ and then select the sort column.

5 Click the ▾ and then select Values.

6 Click the ▾ and then select Custom List.

   The Custom Lists dialog box appears.

7 Click the months of the year.

8 Click OK.

9 Click OK.

● Excel sorts the column.

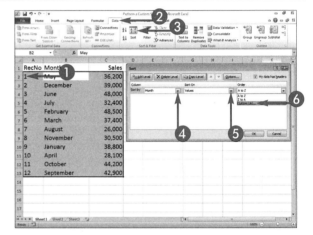

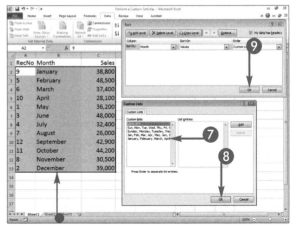

Sort by Cell Color, Font Color, or Cell Icon

Y ou can use conditional formatting to format your data. You can format your data with cell colors, font colors, or cell icons. You can then use the Sort dialog box to sort data based on the cell color, font color, or cell icon. For example, you can use an icon to mark the top one-third, the second one-third, and the lowest one-third of sales figures. You can then sort your data based on the icon assigned. You can also manually assign cells font and cell colors and then sort by the colors. Each level determines where the cell color, font color, or cell icon appears, either at the top of the list or at the bottom of the list.

Extra

To sort by cell color, font color, or cell icon, use the Sort dialog box. When you choose Cell Color, Font Color, or Cell Icon in the Sort On drop-down list, Excel places a list of cell colors, font colors, or cell icons in the Order field. You can then choose On Top to place the selection on the next highest level or On Bottom to place the selection on the next lowest level.

Sort by Cell Color, Font Color, or Cell Icon

1 Click a cell in the list.

2 Click the Data tab.

3 Click the Sort button.

The Sort dialog box appears.

4 Click the ▾ and then select the sort column.

5 Click the ▾ and then select Cell Color, Font Color, or Cell Icon.

6 Click the ▾ and then select a cell color, font color, or cell icon.

7 Click the ▾ and then select On Top or On Bottom.

8 Click Add Level.

9 Repeat Steps 4 to 7 until you are finished.

10 Click OK.

● Excel Sorts the column by cell color, font color, or cell Icon.

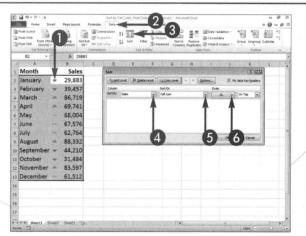

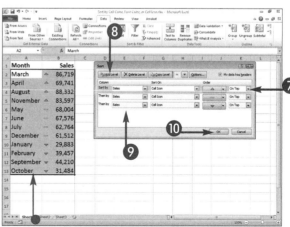

Perform Complex Filters

Y ou will find that there are times when you are not interested in all the data in your list. For example, you have a list of employee salaries but you only want to examine the salaries of people who earn between $50,000 and $100,000 per year. Excel's AutoFilter feature can aid you. By filtering, you can find every value in your list that falls between two values, equals a value, is greater than a value, or meets a number of other criteria you specify. Filtering hides data. When you remove the filter, Excel brings the data back.

When you click the Filter button on the Data tab, AutoFilter buttons appear to the right of every column label. You can click a column's AutoFilter button and then select Date Filters for date fields, Text Filters for text fields, and Number Filters for numeric fields. When you

select one of these options, a menu appears. From this menu, you can select the criteria you want to apply, such as between two values.

You can apply multiple filters. By applying multiple filters, you can quickly narrow a long list to the few records of interest to you. For example, if you want to examine the salaries of women who earn between $50,000 and $100,000 per year, you can filter your salary column for salaries between $50,000 and $100,000 and then filter your gender column for F (females).

In addition to choosing a filter type from the filter menu, you can choose to create a custom filter. By using a custom AutoFilter, you can create multiple filters in a single column by using the And or Or filter.

Perform Complex Filters

① Click a cell in your list.

② Click the Data tab.

③ Click Filter.

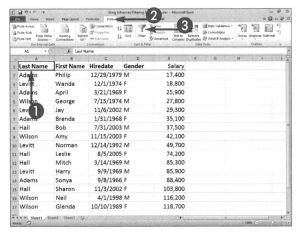

● AutoFilter buttons appear next to all your column labels.

④ Click the AutoFilter button (▼) next to the field you want to filter.

⑤ Click Number Filters if you chose a number field.

Alternatively, click Text Filters if you chose a text field or Date Filters if you chose a date field.

A menu appears.

⑥ Click an option.

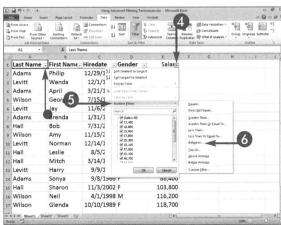

The Custom AutoFilter dialog box appears.

7 Enter the information requested.

8 Click OK.

● Excel filters the list.

You can filter additional columns.

Click the Data tab and then click Clear in the Sort & Filter group to clear your filter.

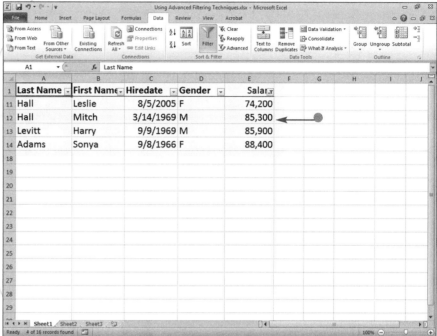

Extra

You can use a numeric filter to return all values that are above or below average. Click the AutoFilter button next to the numeric field you want to filter. A menu appears. Click Number Filters and then click either Above Average or Below Average, based on your preference. Excel filters your list and the appropriate values appear.

You can also use a numeric filter to view the top or bottom N values in a list, where N stands for the number of values you want to view. Click the AutoFilter button next to the numeric field you want to filter. A menu appears. Click Number Filters and then click Top Ten. The Top 10 AutoFilter dialog box appears. Select Top if you want to view the top N values. Click Bottom if you want to view the bottom N values. Type the number of values you want to view and then select whether you want Excel to return results based on a number or a percentage. Click OK. Excel returns the results you requested.

Enter Criteria to Find Records

Once you have created a list of data, you may want to retrieve specific information. Using Excel's Advanced Filter, you can set up complex filters and use them to limit the data you retrieve.

When using Excel's Advanced Filter, you must identify an area called the *criteria range*. In the criteria range, you tell Excel exactly what you are looking for. For example, you can tell Excel you want to retrieve all people with an income of $100,000 or more.

Types of Criteria

You can use two types of criteria to find records: comparison criteria and computed criteria. With comparison criteria, you enter your criteria underneath a field label. For example, if you want to find all people with an income greater than $100,000, you would enter **>100000** under the field labeled Income, as shown in the table.

Criteria

LAST_NAME	FIRST_NAME	PROPERTY_TAX	INCOME_TAX	INCOME
				>100000

List

LAST_NAME	FIRST_NAME	PROPERTY_TAX	INCOME_TAX	INCOME
Jones	Serena	4,143	23,487	75,436
Jacobs	Tom	4,230	14,537	146,621
Cohen	James	3,875	12,844	64,220
Jones	Libby	3,933	25,174	125,871

With computed criteria, you use a formula to find records. Use computed criteria when your list does not have a field with the information for which you are looking. For example, if you want to extract all records from the list in the illustration where the property tax plus the income tax is greater than $20,000, you could use the formula =Property_Tax+Income_Tax>20000 as your criteria.

When you use computed criteria, at least one variable in the formula must be a field in your list. However, the criteria label cannot be one of field labels used by your list. When using the example, you could create a new label called Total_Tax and place your formula under that label. Excel interprets all criteria that use field labels from your list as comparison criteria. Excel interprets all criteria that do not use field labels as computed criteria. The following is an example of computed criteria:

LAST_NAME	FIRST_NAME	PROPERTY_TAX	INCOME_TAX	INCOME	TOTAL_TAX
					=Property_Tax+Income_Tax>20000

Setting Up Your Criteria Range

You can place your criteria range anywhere in your workbook, but the best places are above your list or on a separate worksheet. You should create one row that lists your field labels. You do not have to include all your labels but you must include every label for which you are going to enter comparison criteria. You should also place the labels that you are going to use for computed criteria on this row. You need at least one additional row. You will place your criteria on the additional rows.

Entering Comparison Criteria

You can use comparison criteria to find text, numbers, dates, and logical values. If you want to match a series of characters, place the characters under the field label. For example, if you want to find all records for people with the last name Jones, type **Jones** under the field label Last_Name in the criteria range.

Wildcards are available for you to use. Use a question mark (?) to match any single character. For example, J?ne will find Jane and June. Use an asterisk (*) to match any series of characters. For example, *son will find Jackson and Johnson. If you need to find a question mark or an asterisk, place a tilde (~) in front of the asterisk or question mark. Excel assumes that there is an asterisk after every search entry. Therefore, if you type **John** under the Last_Name field label, Excel will find everyone whose last name

begins with John. If you want to find an exact match for a text value, enter your criteria in the format `="=text"`. For example, if you want to find John, but not Johnson, type `="=John"`.

You can also use comparison operators. To learn more about comparison operators, see Chapter 4. Type the comparison operator followed by the value you are trying to find. For example, to find all records where the income is equal to or greater than $100,000, type **>=100000** under the Income field label. To find all last names that are alphabetically greater than Cohen, you type **>Cohen** under the Last_Name field label. Comparison criteria are not case-sensitive. To find all blank fields, type an equal sign with nothing after it. To find all nonblank fields, type the unequal operator (<>) with nothing after it.

Entering Computed Criteria

When you enter computed criteria, you must use a formula that evaluates to the logical value TRUE or the logical value FALSE, based on whether your criteria match records in your list, and your formula must include a reference to at least one field label from your list. If you use computed criteria, your field labels must conform to the rules for naming a range. To learn more about naming ranges, see Chapter 4.

You create your formula by using a relative cell reference to the first data row in your list. For example, `=C8+D8>20000`

is a valid formula if the first data row in your formula is row 8. If you name the data fields in the first row of your data list, you can use range names in your formula. For example, if you name C8 Property_Tax and D8 Income_Tax, you can use the formula `=Property_Tax+Income_Tax>20000`.

You create a new label and place your formula under that label in the criteria range. The cell will display either the word TRUE or the word FALSE.

Using Multiple Criteria

You can use a criteria range to specify multiple criteria. For example, you can find all people with the last name Jones whose incomes are more than $50,000. You can also find all people whose property tax is more than $4,000 or

whose income tax is more than $20,000. If you want both criteria to be met, place your criteria on the same row. If you want either criterion to be met, place your criteria on separate rows.

Meet both criteria:

LAST_NAME	FIRST_NAME	PROPERTY_TAX	INCOME_TAX	INCOME
Jones				>50000

Meet either criteria:

LAST_NAME	FIRST_NAME	PROPERTY_TAX	INCOME_TAX	INCOME
		>4000		
			>20000	

Using Advanced Filtering Techniques

With advanced filtering, you can go beyond the limitations of the AutoFilter command. You can use advanced filtering to create two or more filters and easily coordinate a set of filters among columns. For example, you can filter a list to find all females with an income more than $100,000 and all males with an income less than $100,000.

Advanced filtering requires a bit of work, even when you are using the Advanced Filter menu command. You must find a block of cells on your worksheet and create a criteria range. Use one or more column heads from a list. In the cell below each label, type the criteria by which to filter each column, such as **>100000** to find people with an income greater than $100,000 and **M** to find all males. See the previous section, "Enter Criteria to Find Records," for detailed instructions.

You have two options when you create any type of filtered list. You can have your filtered list appear in place — under the column heads of your unfiltered list — thereby hiding the unfiltered list. Or, you can have your filtered list appear in another location, thereby enabling you to keep your original list in your worksheet. If you want to filter your list in place, in the Advanced Filter dialog box, click Filter the list, in-place. If you want to keep your unfiltered list in your worksheet, in the Advanced Filter dialog box, click Copy to another location and then enter the location where you want to place your filtered list in the Copy to field.

Make sure your Copy to range has enough room below it to include all the values that may return in the filtered list. If you place the Copy to range above your original list, the results may overwrite the list and disrupt the filtering. Placing the copy to the side of the list or on another worksheet protects your original list.

Using Advanced Filtering Techniques

① Type the labels for the columns you want to filter.

② Type the criteria by which you want to filter.

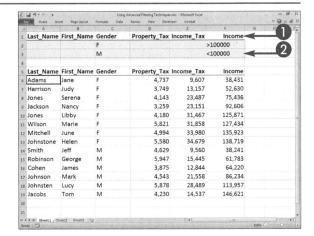

③ Click the Data tab.

④ Click Advanced.

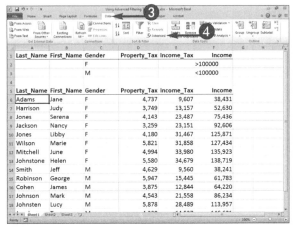

The Advanced Filter dialog box appears.

5 Click a radio button option to indicate where to place the filtered list (◉ changes to ◉).

You can click Copy to another location to copy the list to another location and retain the original list.

6 Enter the range for the list. Include labels.

7 Enter the range for the criteria defined in Step 2. Include labels.

● If you chose to copy the filtered list in Step 5, enter the first cell in the range where you want to place the copy.

8 Click OK.

● The filtered list appears.

Click Clear on the Data tab in the Sort & Filter group to clear your filter.

Advanced Filter dialog box:
- Action: Filter the list, in-place / Copy to another location
- List range: $A$5:$F$19
- Criteria range: $A$1:$F$3
- Copy to:
- Unique records only
- OK / Cancel

	Last_Name	First_Name	Gender	Property_Tax	Income_Tax	Income
1	Last_Name	First_Name	Gender	Property_Tax	Income_Tax	Income
2			F			>100000
3			M			<100000
4						
5	Last_Name	First_Name	Gender	Property_Tax	Income_Tax	Income
10	Jones	Libby	F	4,180	31,467	125,871
11	Wilson	Marie	F	5,821	31,858	127,434
12	Mitchell	June	F	4,994	33,980	135,923
13	Johnstone	Helen	F	5,580	34,679	138,719
14	Smith	Jeff	M	4,629	9,560	38,241
15	Robinson	George	M	5,947	15,445	61,783
16	Cohen	James	M	3,875	12,844	64,220
17	Johnson	Mark	M	4,543	21,558	86,234

Using Advanced Filtering Techniques.xlsx - Microsoft Excel

Ready   8 of 14 records found

Apply It

By default, the criteria you enter are not case-sensitive. Excel considers "JONES" the same as "jones". You can, however, use the EXACT function to create criteria that are case-sensitive. To start, create a column label in your criteria range and name it **Exact Match**. In the field below the Exact Match column label, type the EXACT function. For example, type =EXACT(A10, "Jones"). A10 refers to the column you want to filter, A, and the first row under the label of the list range, 10.

Now, click the Data tab. Click Advanced in the Sort & Filter group. The Advanced Filter dialog box appears. Click the Filter the list, in-place or Copy to another location radio button (◉ changes to◉). Type the list range into the List range field. Type the criteria range into the Criteria range field. Enter a Copy to location if necessary and then click OK. Excel filters your list, finding only exact matches.

If you name your list range **Database**, your criteria range **Criteria**, and your Copy to range **Extract**, Excel automatically places these values into the Advanced Filter dialog box.

Filter Duplicate Records

E xcel provides many tools for managing long lists. With such lists, you may need to identify and display unique records. You might, for example, want to have a unique list of your female customers.

Excel provides tools for displaying unique records that meet your criteria. You start with a worksheet formatted as a list, in which some of the records are duplicates, meaning the values in two or more rows are the same. Then use Excel's advanced filtering tool to identify and filter the duplicates. You must specify the criteria by which you want to filter your data. Your criteria consist of a least two rows, one with one or more labels and the other with criteria. See the section, "Enter Criteria to Find Records" for detailed information on how to set up your criteria. Because Excel hides the duplicate rows, the best

placement for your criteria is above your list or on another worksheet. Place at least one blank row between your criteria range and your list.

You have two options when you create a filtered list using Excel's advanced filtering tool. You can have your filtered list appear in place — under the column heads of your unfiltered list — thereby temporarily replacing your unfiltered list, or you can place your filtered list in another location. Use the Copy to field in the Advanced Filter dialog box to specify the location. If you copy your list to another location, you can specify which fields you want to copy by typing the column labels into the area you specify in the Copy to field.

Filter Duplicate Records

① Type the labels for the columns you want to filter.

② Type the criteria by which you want to filter.

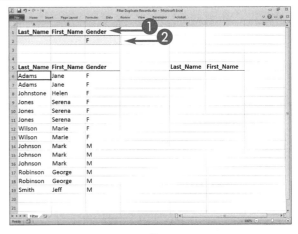

③ Click the Data tab.

④ Click Advanced.

The Advanced Filter dialog box appears.

⑤ Click a radio button to indicate where to place the filtered list (◎ changes to ◉).

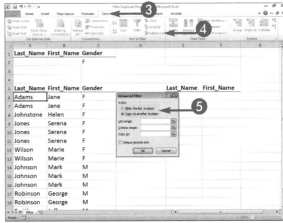

6 Enter the range for the list. Include labels.

7 Enter the range for the criteria defined in Step 2. Include labels.

8 If you chose to copy the filtered list in Step 5, enter the range where you want to copy the information.

9 Click Unique records only (☐ changes to ✔).

10 Click OK.

● The filtered list appears.

Click Clear on the Data tab in the Sort & Filter group to clear your filter.

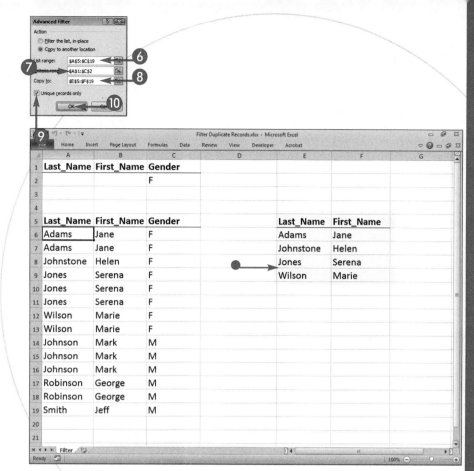

You can use Excel's advanced filtering feature to display a unique list — a list with just one copy of rows in which every field in every column is the same. Click the Data tab. Click Advanced in the Sort & Filter group. The Advanced Filter dialog box appears. Select whether you want to filter your list in place or to another location (◉ changes to ◉). Complete the List range field. Do not enter a Criteria range. Enter a Copy to location if Excel is not filtering in place. Click Unique records only (☐ changes to ✔), and then click OK. Excel displays unique records.

Filtering duplicate records temporarily removes them from view. If you want to delete duplicate records permanently, select your list, and click the Data tab. Then in the Data tools group, click Remove Duplicates. The Remove Duplicates dialog box appears. If your list has headers, click My data has headers (☐ changes to ✔). Select the columns you want to check for duplicates and then click OK. Excel deletes the duplicate records.

Count Filtered Records

Like standard worksheet functions, database functions enable you to perform calculations and summarize data patterns. Database functions are meant for lists and are especially good at summarizing the subsets you create by filtering your list. Most database functions combine two tasks: they filter a group of records based on values in a single column, and then they count the records or perform another simple operation on the filtered data.

DCOUNT is a database function that counts the number of cells containing numbers. DCOUNT takes three arguments. The first argument, Database, identifies the cell range for the entire list. The second argument, Field, identifies the column you want to count. You can enter the column label enclosed in quotes; for example, "Income", or you

can enter the column number. The first column in the list is 1, the second is 2, and so on. In the third argument, Criteria, you provide Excel with the range location of your criteria for extracting information. For example, your criteria could be Income >100000, where Income is the column label. You build the criteria manually, copying column labels and defining the conditions in the cells below them. You then place the range in your formula. You can use any range as long as the range includes at least one column label and one cell below it. If you want to count every record in the list, leave the cells in your criteria range below your label blank. If your criteria is text, enter it in the format = "= Text Value". If you do not, Excel may calculate improperly.

Count Filtered Records

1 Type the labels for the criteria.

2 Type the criteria for counting records.

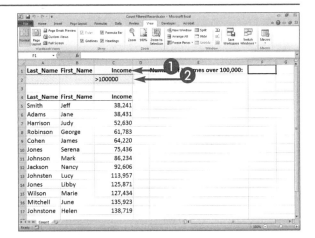

3 Type =DCOUNT(.

Alternatively, click the function on the AutoComplete list.

4 Click the Insert Function button.

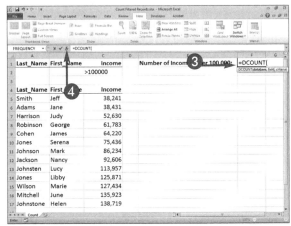

The Function Arguments dialog box appears.

5 Enter the range for the list. Include labels.

6 Type the column name within quotation marks.

Or type the column's number or the column's range.

7 Enter the range for the criteria defined in Step 2. Include labels.

8 Click OK.

● Excel calculates the result.

Click Clear on the Data tab in the Sort & Filter group to clear your filter.

Note: *The* DCOUNT *function counts only cells containing numbers. For non-numeric data, use the* DCOUNTA *function.*

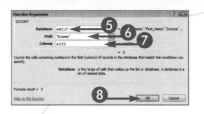

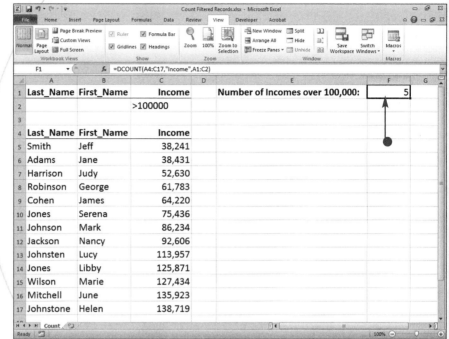

Extra

The names of database functions begin with a D to distinguish them from worksheet functions. As with worksheet functions, you can use the Function Wizard to build database functions. Type the function into a cell — for example, =DCOUNT() — and then click the Insert Function button.

Excel offers several database functions. They all take the same arguments: Database, Field, and Criteria. The table that follows lists a few:

FUNCTION	DESCRIPTION
DCOUNTA	Counts nonblank cells that match the criteria you specify
DGET	Extracts the one record that meets the criteria you specify
DMAX	Returns the largest number that meets the criteria you specify
DMIN	Returns the smallest number that meets the criteria you specify
DAVERAGE	Returns the average of the numbers that meet the criteria you specify
DSUM	Returns the sum of the numbers that meet the criteria you specify

Subtotal Records

After you sort, you can group your data into categories, such as quarter and region, and you can perform calculations so that you can compare one category with another. If you have a sort defined for at least one column, you can find the average, sum, min, max, number of items, and more for that column or another column. Excel calls this feature *subtotaling*.

When you apply the subtotaling feature to a list, Excel outlines the data. You can expand and collapse the outline to see different views of the data. For example, if you subtotal by region, you can collapse the data so that you only see regional and grand totals. Your subtotals and grand totals can appear either above or below each category. If you want them to appear below the category, select Summary below data. You can choose to enter a

page break after each subtotal. This feature places each category on a separate page when you print.

You can create several levels of subtotals for a single sorted list. You start by using the Subtotal dialog box to create the highest-level subtotal. Then you open the Subtotal dialog box again to create the next-level subtotal. You can create up to eight levels. Make sure you have not checked the Replace current subtotals check box in the Subtotal dialog box as you create each level.

You can create subtotals on columns other than the one defining the sort. For example, if you sort by quarter, you can subtotal sales. You can also do a count on a column with text entries. To remove subtotals, click the Remove All button in the Subtotal dialog box.

Subtotal Records

1. Click a cell in your sorted list.

2. Click the Data tab.

3. Click Subtotal.

   The Subtotal dialog box appears.

4. Click the ☑ and then select the category by which you want to subtotal.

5. Click the ☑ and then select a calculation type.

6. Click one or more columns to subtotal (☐ changes to ✔).

7. Click the options you want (☐ changes to ✔).

8. Click OK.

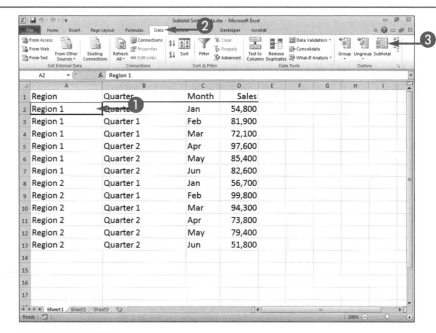

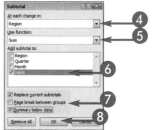

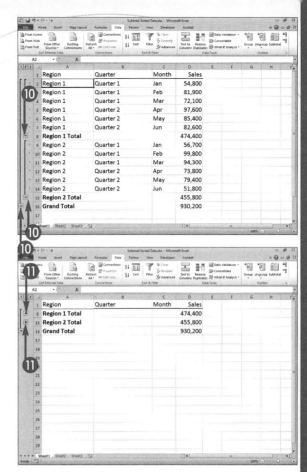

9 Repeat Steps 4 through 7 to create additional groups.

Make sure the Replace current subtotals box is not selected.

The list appears with the outlining controls that enable you to compare the results.

10 To compare results in different rows, click the minus signs (−).

Only the result rows appear.

11 To redisplay all results, click the plus signs (+).

Excel displays all results.

Apply It

You can manually group the rows and columns in your worksheet. For example, you can hide the details related to daily sales so that you can compare monthly sales. Select the columns or rows you want to group. Click the Data tab. Click Group in the Outline group. A menu appears. Click Group. The Group dialog box appears. Click a radio button option to select either the Columns or Rows option. Click Rows if you want to group rows (○ changes to ◉). Click Columns if you want to group columns (○ changes to ◉). Click OK. Excel places Collapse buttons (−) above the worksheet column labels if you chose columns or to the left of the worksheet row labels if you chose rows. When you click a Collapse button, Excel hides the columns or rows and the Collapse button turns into an Expand button (+). When you click an Expand button, Excel reveals the columns or rows and the Expand button turns into a Collapse button.

To remove a group, click the Data tab. Click Ungroup in the Outline group. A menu appears. Click Ungroup. The Ungroup dialog box appears. Click a radio button option to select either Columns or Rows. Click Columns if you want to ungroup columns. Click Rows if you want to Ungroup rows. Click OK.

Using Auto Outline

When you outline a worksheet, Excel places buttons above the worksheet column labels and to the left of the worksheet row labels. You can use these buttons to collapse and expand areas of your worksheet. The collapse buttons appear as minus signs (–). The expand buttons appear as plus signs (+). When you click a minus sign, Excel hides columns or rows. When you click a plus sign, Excel reveals columns or rows.

Excel can automatically outline your worksheet for you. For example, if you have a worksheet with sales data in columns for January, February, and March and a formula that calculates quarterly totals by summing January, February, and March and then does the same for April, May, and June, you can outline your columns by quarter. If on that same worksheet, you have data on rows for two divisions, Division A and Division B, and you have

formulas that calculate totals by division, you can outline your rows by division.

The Auto Outline feature uses formulas to determine where to place expand and collapse buttons. Expand and collapse buttons appear on columns with formulas. So, to create an outline, enter formulas where you want the collapsible buttons to appear. If, for example, you want to collapse your worksheet so that you only see quarterly summaries and division totals, enter formulas to calculate the quarterly summaries and the division totals.

The Auto Outline feature gives you a great deal of flexibility. You can expand or collapse each area individually. For example, you can collapse Quarter 1 so that you only see the summary, while leaving the details of Quarter 2 available for viewing.

Using Auto Outline

① Enter formulas to summarize your data.

② Click the Data tab.

③ Click the ⬒ under Group.

④ Click Auto Outline.

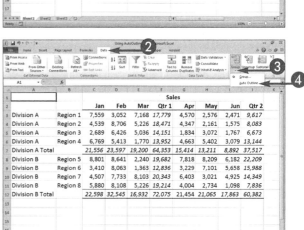

Excel outlines the worksheet.

⑤ Click the minus signs (⊟) to collapse the outline.

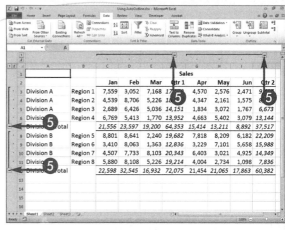

Excel collapses the outline.

⑥ Click the plus signs (⊞) to expand the outline.

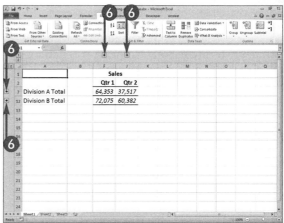

Apply It

To remove an Auto Outline, click the Data tab. Click the down arrow under Ungroup in the Outline group. A menu appears. Click Clear Outline.

If you want to outline a range of cells instead of an entire worksheet, select the range you want to outline. Click the Data tab. Click the down arrow under Group. A menu appears. Click Auto Outline. Excel outlines the range. You can now use the Expand (⊞) and Collapse buttons (⊟).

You can have Excel automatically apply a style each time you create an outline. Click the Data tab. Click the launcher in the Outline group. The Settings dialog box appears. Click Automatic Styles. Click OK. Now when you create an outline, Excel automatically applies a style. If you want to apply a style to an Auto Outline manually, select the range. Click the Data tab. Click the launcher in the Outline group. The Settings dialog box appears. Click Apply Styles. Excel applies the style.

You can use the Expand and Collapse buttons on the Ribbon to expand and collapse your outline. Select the area you want to expand or collapse and then click the Expand button (⊞) to expand the area or the Collapse button (⊟) to collapse it.

Define Data as a Table

I n Excel, a table is a special type of list. Like all lists, a table is a set of columns and rows where each column represents a single type of data. To create a table, you simply define a list as a table. When you define a list as a table, Excel adds AutoFilter buttons to each column label, enabling you to readily sort and filter your data. To learn how to use these AutoFilter buttons, see section, "Perform Simple Sorts and Filters."

Tables have a unique quality. When you enter a formula into a table column that does not have any data in it, it becomes a calculated column. Calculated columns automatically calculate when you create a new row. However, if you type a formula in a table column that already contains data, Excel does not automatically create a calculated column. You, however, can turn the column into a calculated column by clicking the Create Calculated Column button that appears after you type the formula.

By selecting Total Row on the Design tab, you can easily add totals to your Excel table. Totals enable you to find the sum, count, max, min, or other value based on a column. You can calculate a different value for each column in your table.

You can create a new table row by pressing the Tab key while in the last field in the last row of your table. To create a new table column, type the label name next to the last label in the last column of the table.

Define Data as a Table

1 Click a cell in your list.

2 Click the Home tab.

3 Click Format as Table.

The Format gallery appears.

4 Click a format.

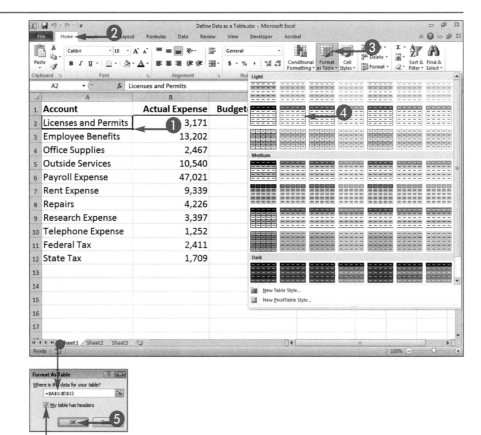

The Format as Table dialog box appears.

● Your list's range.

● Deselect this check box if your list does not have column labels.

5 Click OK.

Excel formats your list as a table.

● AutoFilter buttons appear next to each column label.

● The Table Tools appear.

Note: *Refer to section, "Perform Simple Sorts and Filters" to learn how to use AutoFilter buttons.*

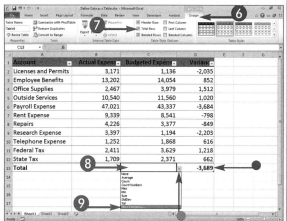

⑥ Click the Design tab.

⑦ Click Total Row (☐ changes to ☑).

● Excel places a total row at the end of your table.

⑧ Click a field in the total row.

● A ▾ appears next to the field.

⑨ Click the ▾ and then select how you want to total the column.

Excel creates a total.

Extra

If you want to add a formula to your table but you do not want it to be a calculated column, click Undo Calculated Column on the AutoCorrect Options menu that automatically appears when you complete the entry of your formula.

If you do not want Excel to create calculated fields automatically, click the File tab. A menu appears. Click Options. Click Proofing. Click the AutoCorrect Options button. The AutoCorrect dialog box appears. Click the AutoFormat As You Type tab. Deselect Fill formulas in tables to create calculated columns (☑ changes to ☐).

You can use the Insert and Delete options on the Home tab in the Cells group to insert and delete rows and columns in your table. To insert rows or columns, click anywhere in your table. Click the Home tab. Click the down arrow next to Insert in the Cells group and then click Insert Table Rows Above or Insert Table Columns to Left.

To delete rows or columns, click anywhere in your table. Click the Home tab. Click the down arrow next to Delete in the Cells group and then click Delete Table Rows or Delete Table Columns.

Modify a Table Style

Table styles format the rows and columns of your table to make your table easier to read. When you create a table, you apply a style. You can use the style gallery to change or remove a style. The style gallery provides a large number of styles from which to choose. As you move your mouse pointer over each style in the gallery, Excel gives you a live preview of how that style will appear when you apply it. You can use the Clear button at the bottom of the Style gallery to remove a style.

Excel also provides a number of table-style options you can use to modify a table style. By choosing banded rows or banded columns, you can have every other row or every other column appear in a different color. You can

also apply special formatting to the last column or the first column in your table if you want the titles, totals, or whatever information you have in those columns to stand out.

Table styles make your table more attractive and user friendly. If you have a favorite style, you can set that style to be the default. Then, whenever you define a list to be a table, Excel will apply that style.

If you do not want your data formatted as a table, you can change a table back to a regular range of cells. If you need to add columns or rows to your table, you can make your table larger. And, if you do not see a table style you like in the gallery, you can modify an existing style and create a new style.

Modify a Table Style

1. Click any cell in your table.

2. Click the Design tab.

3. Click the More button (☴) in the Table Styles group.

A gallery of styles appears.

4. Click a style to apply it to your table.

● Click Clear to remove a style from your table.

5 Right-click a style.

A menu appears.

6 Click Set As Default.

Excel makes the style the default style.

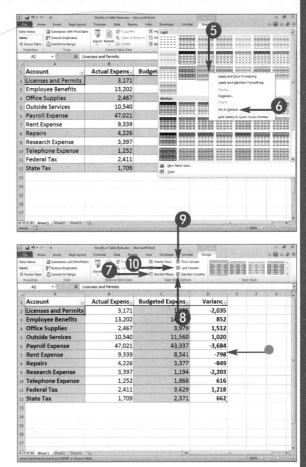

7 Click this check box to remove banded rows (☑ changes to ☐).

8 Click this check box to add banded columns (☐ changes to ☑).

9 Click this check box to apply special formatting to the first column (☐ changes to ☑).

10 Click this check box to apply special formatting to the last column (☐ changes to ☑).

● Excel reformats the table.

Apply It

You can convert a table back to a regular range of cells. Click anywhere in your table, click the Design tab, and then click Convert to Range in the Tools group. At the prompt, click Yes. Excel converts the table to a normal range and removes the AutoFilter buttons.

You can easily add columns your table. Click any cell in your table. The Table tools appear. Click the Design tab and then click Resize Table in the Properties group. The Resize Table dialog box appears. Enter a new range in the Select the New Data Range for Your Table field and then click OK.

You can create your own table style by modifying an existing style. Click in your table. Click the Design tab. Click the More button (▾) in the Table Styles group. Click the style you want to modify and then right-click. A menu appears. Click Duplicate. The Modify Table Quick Style dialog box appears. Type a name in the Name field. In the Table Elements box, click the element you want to modify and then click Format. The Format Cells dialog box appears. Use it to change the existing format.

Using Database Functions with a Table

Database functions were designed to be used with lists. A table is a type of list. Using database functions with a table provides advantages because every table has a name and Excel will use the table's name in the database function. Because the function is referencing a table name, the table can grow to an unlimited number of rows and the reference will still be valid. In fact, no matter how many records you add or delete, your table reference remains valid.

DSUM is a database function that totals the numbers of cells in a column that match the criteria you enter. DSUM takes three arguments. The first argument, `Database`, is the table range. The second argument, `Field`, identifies the the column you want to sum. You can enter the

column label enclosed in quotes; for example, `"Income"` or you can enter the column number. The first column in the table is 1, the second is 2, and so on. In the third argument, `Criteria`, you provide Excel with the range location of your criteria. For example, your criteria could be `Gender = "=F"`, where Gender is the column label. You build the criteria manually, copying column labels and defining the conditions in the cells below them. You then place the range in your formula. You can use any range as long as the range includes at least one column label and one cell below it. If you want to add every record in the list, leave the cells in your criteria range below your labels blank. If your criteria is text, enter it in the format `= "= Text Value"`.

Using Database Functions with a Table

1. Define your list as a table.

2. Create the criteria range.

3. Click anywhere in your list.

- The Table tools appear.

4. Click the Design tab.

5. Type a table name.

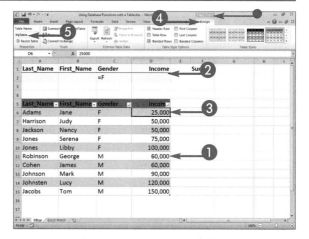

6. Type **=DSUM(**.

   Alternatively, click the function on the AutoComplete list.

7. Click the Insert Function button.

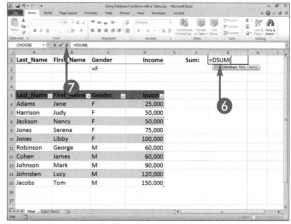

The Function Arguments dialog box appears.

⑧ Enter the range for the table. Include column labels.

Excel enters the table name.

⑨ Type the column name within quotation marks.

Or type the column's number or the column's range.

⑩ Enter the range for the criteria defined in Step 2. Include labels.

⑪ Click OK.

● Excel calculates the result.

Click Clear on the Data tab in the Sort & Filter group to clear your filter.

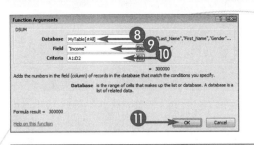

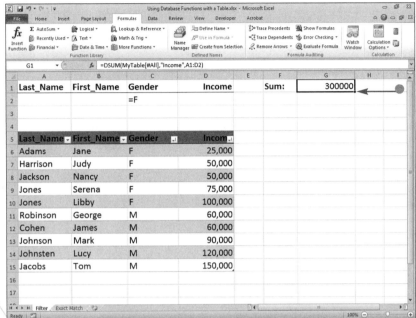

	Last_Name	First_Name	Gender		Income		Sum:	300000
1	Last_Name	First_Name	Gender		Income		Sum:	300000
2			=F					
5	Last_Name	First_Name	Gender		Income			
6	Adams	Jane	F		25,000			
7	Harrison	Judy	F		50,000			
8	Jackson	Nancy	F		50,000			
9	Jones	Serena	F		75,000			
10	Jones	Libby	F		100,000			
11	Robinson	George	M		60,000			
12	Cohen	James	M		60,000			
13	Johnson	Mark	M		90,000			
14	Johnsten	Lucy	M		120,000			
15	Jacobs	Tom	M		150,000			

=DSUM(MyTable[#All],"Income",A1:D2)

Extra

Avoid entering data in the column immediately after the last column in the table because if you enter data into that column, it may become part of the table.

You do not have to name your table. Excel automatically names every table Table#, where # is a number that designates the order in which the table was created. The first table you create is Table1, the next table is Table2, and so on.

As you add, delete, or change the data in your table, the database function automatically updates. The same is true for the criteria. As you change your criteria, the results of the formula update. You can find, for example, the sum of female incomes and then find the sum of male incomes without making any changes to your formula.

Create a PivotTable

xcel offers you much more than just a way of keeping track of your data and doing calculations. It also provides tools to analyze your data so that you can understand it and use it to make more effective decisions.

One of the most useful tools, the PivotTable, is also one of the least understood. PivotTables help you answer questions about your data. Similar to a cross-tabulation in statistics, a PivotTable shows how data is distributed across categories. For example, you can use a PivotTable to see how different products sell by region and by quarter.

You base PivotTables on lists. Lists are made up of rows and columns. You can use a worksheet list or you can connect to a list from another data source, such as Access.

For more information on lists, see Chapter 8. For more information on external data sources, see Chapter 11.

The row and column labels of a PivotTable usually contain discrete information, meaning the values fall into categories. For example, gender is a discrete category because all values are either male or female. Quarter is another discrete category because all values fall into one of four quarters: Quarter 1, Quarter 2, Quarter 3, or Quarter 4. Salary and weight are not discrete (they are continuous) because a wide range of values is possible for each.

The body of a PivotTable — the data area — usually has continuous data and shows how the data are distributed across rows and columns. For example, you could show how the number of units sold is distributed among sales regions in different quarters.

Create a PivotTable

① Select the data you want to include in your PivotTable.

Note: *Make sure to include the row and column labels.*

If you are going to use an external data source, skip this step.

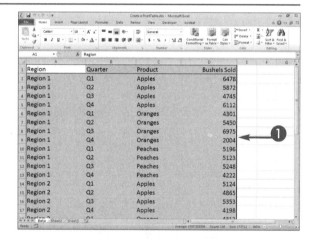

② Click the Insert tab.

③ Click PivotTable.

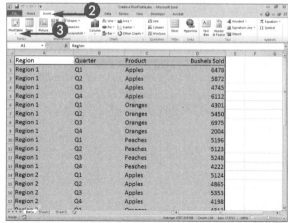

The Create PivotTable dialog box appears.

④ Click a data source
(○ changes to ◉).

● If you selected a range in the current workbook, the range appears here.

● If you are going to use an external data source, click here.

⑤ Click a worksheet option (○ changes to ◉) to select where to place the report.

● If you want to place the PivotTable on the existing worksheet, click the cell in which you want to place the PivotTable, or type a location.

⑥ Click OK.

● Excel opens the PivotTable Field List.

● The PivotTable tools appear.

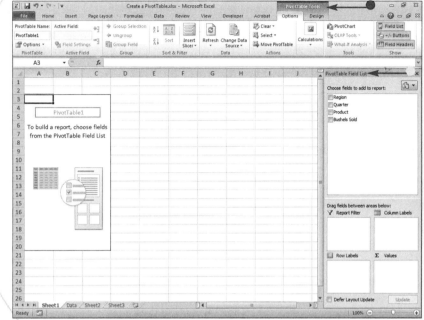

Extra

If you want the clear a PivotTable, click anywhere in your PivotTable. The PivotTable tools appear. Click the Options tab. Click Clear in the Actions group. A menu appears. Click Clear All. Excel removes all formatting, filters, labels, and values from your report. You can rebuild your report by using the PivotTable Field List.

If you want to remove a PivotTable from your worksheet, click anywhere in the PivotTable. The PivotTable tools appear. Click the Options tab. Click Select in the Actions group. A menu appears. Click Entire Table. Excel selects the entire table. Press the Delete key. Excel deletes your PivotTable.

When you create a PivotTable, you must base it on data structured as a list. Your list should include column headings in the first row. Tables are structured as lists. So, you can base your PivotTable on a table. To learn more about lists and tables, see Chapter 8. When creating a PivotTable, do not use a worksheet list with blank columns or rows. If you do, Excel may not create the PivotTable correctly.

continued ➡

A PivotTable consists of several elements: report filters, data, column labels, and row labels. To organize the elements, use the PivotTable Field List. When working with a PivotTable, you can bring the Field List into view by clicking anywhere in the PivotTable, clicking the Options tab, and then clicking Field List in the Show/Hide group.

To construct a PivotTable, choose the fields you want to include in your report and then drag fields from the PivotTable Field List into the Report Filter, Column Labels, Row Labels, and Σ Values boxes. You can click and drag more than one field into an area. By using Report Filter fields, you can filter the data that appears in your report. Row Label fields appear as row labels down the left side of your PivotTable, and Column Label fields appear as column labels across the top of your PivotTable.

Place your continuous data fields in the Σ Values box. Fields placed in the Σ Values box make up the data area. You can sort and filter your PivotTable column and row data, and you can arrange and rearrange field layouts.

Column and row labels display in the order you place them in the Column and Row Labels boxes. You can change the display order by clicking and dragging the fields within the box.

When you create a PivotTable, you can place it on a new worksheet or on the existing worksheet. If you choose New Worksheet in the Create PivotTable dialog box, Excel creates and moves you to a new worksheet in your workbook and opens the PivotTable Field List. If you choose Existing Worksheet, Excel opens the PivotTable Field List so you create your PivotTable on the current worksheet.

Create a PivotTable (continued)

⑦ Click to select the fields you want to include in your PivotTable (☐ changes to ✔).

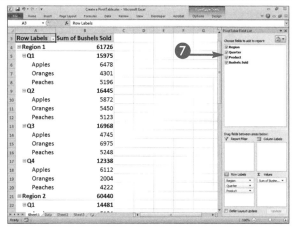

⑧ Click and drag fields among the boxes.

● Click and drag the fields you want to filter by to the Report Filter box.

● Click and drag fields you want to display as columns to the Column Labels box.

● Click and drag fields you want to display as rows to the Row Labels box.

● Click and drag fields you want to display as data to the Σ Values box.

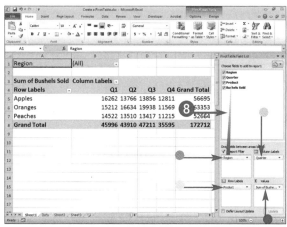

- As you build the PivotTable, your changes instantly appear.

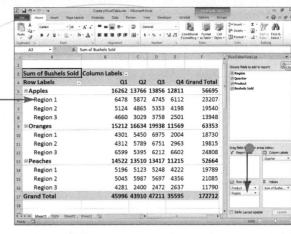

9 Click the ▾ next to Row Label or Column Label then choose your sort and filter options.

Note: For more information on sorting and filtering, see Chapter 8.

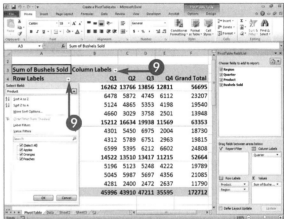

Extra

By default, Excel has divided the PivotTable Field List into two sections: Field and Areas. The Field section lists all the fields available for you to use when creating your PivotTable. The Areas section gives you the ability to design your report.

To change the way the PivotTable Field List displays, click the Field List button (▦▾) located in the upper-right corner of the PivotTable Field List box. A menu appears. Choose from the following options: Fields Section and Areas Section Stacked, Fields Section and Areas Section Side by Side, Fields Section Only, Areas Section Only (2 by 2), and Areas Section Only (1 by 4).

The Fields Section and Areas Section Stacked option places the Field section at the top of the PivotTable Field List box and the Area section directly below it. The Fields Section and Areas Section Side by Side option places the Field section on the left side of the PivotTable Field List box and the Area section to the right of it. The Fields Section Only option only displays the Fields section and the Areas Section Only option only displays the Area section; both display in either a two-by-two or one-by-four format.

Modify a PivotTable Layout

W hen you create a PivotTable, Excel groups the data for you. All items with the same row label are grouped together and all items with the same column label are grouped together. You can add subtotals to your PivotTable. For example, if you sell apples, oranges, and peaches, in Regions 1, 2 and 3, you can subtotal by product to find the total number of apples, the total number of oranges, and the total number of peaches sold.

You should structure your data so that Excel groups by product, shows the total number of products sold in Region 1, the total number of products sold in Region 2, and the total number of products sold in Region 3. You can then then have Excel show a subtotal for each

product. By default, subtotals appear at the top of each group. You can place them at the bottom of each group or you can eliminate them.

By including grand totals you can easily see totals across all groupings. You can calculate grand totals for both rows and columns, for just rows, for just columns, or for neither rows nor columns. For example, if you sell three products and they are shown in the rows, you can use a row grand total to show the total amount sold. If there are subtotals in your PivotTable, the grand total is equal to the sum of the subtotals. If the columns in your PivotTable show the number of products sold by quarter, you can use a column grand total to show the total amount sold for the year.

Modify a PivotTable Layout

Modify a Subtotal

1. Click in any PivotTable cell.

   The PivotTable tools appear.

2. Click the Design tab.

3. Click Subtotals.

   A menu appears.

4. Click the Subtotals option you want.

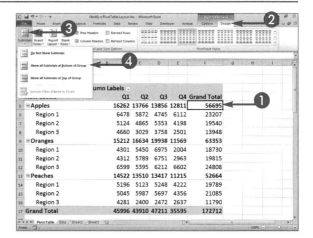

● Excel adds, removes, or moves the subtotal.

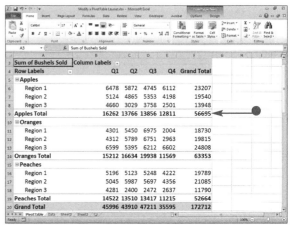

Modify a Grand Total

① Click in any PivotTable cell.

  The PivotTable tools appear.

② Click the Design tab.

③ Click Grand Totals.

  A menu appears.

④ Click the Grand Totals option you want.

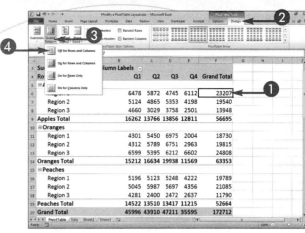

  Excel adds or removes Grand Totals.

● In this example, Excel removes the Grand Totals.

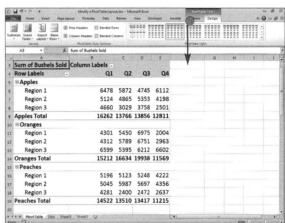

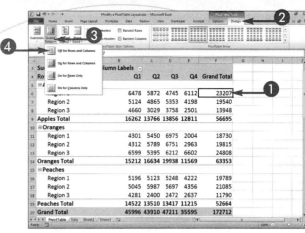

Apply It

The data in a PivotTable can get crowded and difficult to read. To remedy this situation, you can choose to have Excel show a blank row after each group in your Pivot table. Click anywhere in your PivotTable. The PivotTable tools appear. Click the Design tab. Click Blank Rows in the Layout group. A menu appears. Click Insert a Blank Line after Each Item.

By default, Excel creates or modifies your PivotTable as you click and drag fields among the Report Filter, Column Labels, Row Labels, and Sum Values fields. If you do not want your PivotTable created or modified dynamically, click the Defer Layout Update check box (☐ changes to ✔) at the bottom of the PivotTable Field List and then click the Update button when you are ready to create or modify your PivotTable.

You can display a PivotTable in compact, tabular, or outline form. Click anywhere in your PivotTable. The PivotTable tools appear. Click the Design tab and then choose Report Layout in the Layout group. A menu appears. Click the PivotTable layout you want.

Summarize PivotTable Values

You can use PivotTables to compare categories of data. Column and row intersections divide data into categories. By default, for numeric fields the intersection of row and column labels is the sum of the values of the field in the Σ Values box. For example, if you have a column labeled Quarter 1 and a row labeled Region 1, by default the intersection of Quarter 1 and Region 1 is the sum of the Quarter 1, Region 1 values for the field in the Σ Values box of the Pivot Table field list. If the field in the Σ Values box is a text field, Excel performs a count.

In addition to sum, there are a variety of other calculations you can perform on Σ Values. To tell Excel which calculation to perform, click the Calculations option on the Options tab and then select Summarize Values By.

A menu will appear. You can choose from Sum, Count, Average, Max, Min, Product or More Options. Choosing More Options opens the Value Field Settings dialog box, which provides you with additional options, such as standard deviation and variance.

Calculations used to generate values can result in poorly formatted data. To remedy this, use the Number Format button in the Value Field Settings dialog box to access the number-formatting capabilities of the Format Cells dialog box. You might, for example, want to reduce the number of decimal places so you see 1235 instead of 1234.56789.

If you are using an Online Analytical Processing (OLAP) data source, you cannot change the calculation.

Summarize PivotTable Values

1 Click in any field in your PivotTable.

The PivotTable tools appear.

2 Click the Options tab.

3 Click Calculations.

4 Click Summarize Values By.

A menu appears.

5 Click More Options.

Alternatively, click the option you want and Excel performs the calculation.

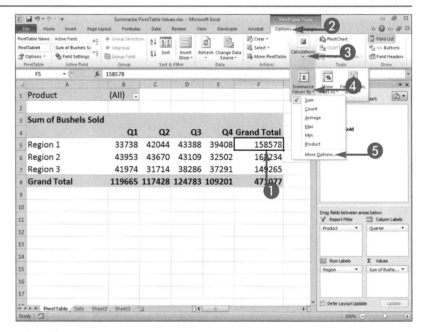

The Value Field Settings dialog box appears.

6 Click the option you want.

7 Click Number Format.

The Format Cells dialog box appears.

8 Format the number.

Note: See Chapter 2 to learn how to format numbers.

9 Click OK to close the Format Cells dialog box.

10 Click OK to close the Value Field Settings dialog box.

Excel recalculates the PivotTable using the function you chose.

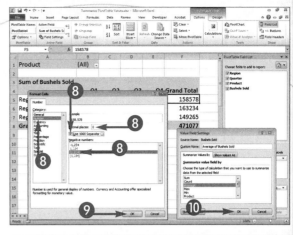

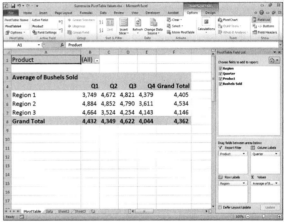

Extra

To access additional calculation options, click anywhere in your PivotTable, click the Options tab, click Calculations, click Show Values As and then click an option. The following table describes some of the options available.

OPTION	DESCRIPTION
% of Grand Total	Finds the percentage of the cell value to the grand total value
% of Column Total	Finds the percentage of the cell value to the column total
% of Row Total	Finds the percentage of the cell value to the row total
% Of	Determines the percentage of the current PivotTable cell to the selected base value
Difference From	Calculates the difference between two PivotTable cells
% Difference From	Determines the percentage difference between two cell values
Running Total In	Shows the running total in each cell
Index	Calculates by using the following formula ((value in cell) x (Grand Total of Grand Totals))/((Grand Row Total) x (Grand Column Total))

Create a PivotTable Calculated Field

Within a PivotTable, you can create new fields, called *calculated fields*, which you can base on the values in existing fields. You create a calculated field by creating a formula. Your formula can include functions; operators such as +, −, *, and /; and existing fields, including other calculated fields; but your formula cannot use cell references. For example, you could enter the following formula:

```
= 'Bushels Sold' + 2000
```

You usually use calculated fields with continuous data such as incomes, prices, miles, and sales. For example, you can add a value to each value in a field called Bushels to create a calculated field called Projection.

Use the Insert Calculated Field dialog box to name your calculated field and to enter the formula you want to use. You can also use this dialog box to modify existing calculated fields or delete fields you no longer want to use. Once created, your calculated fields are available in the PivotTable Field List for use in your PivotTable. You cannot place calculated fields in report filters, column labels, or row labels. You can only place calculated fields in the data area, therefore place your calculated field in the Σ Values box.

If you want to see a list of all the formulas used by your PivotTable, choose the List Formulas option under Calculations; Field, Items, and Sets on the Options tab.

Create a PivotTable Calculated Field

① Click any field in your PivotTable.

The PivotTable tools appear.

② Click the Options tab.

● If the PivotTable Field List does not open, click Field List.

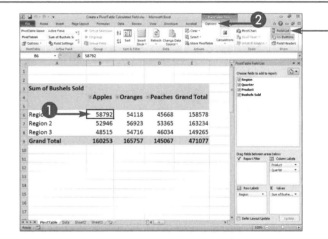

③ Click Calculations.

④ Click Fields, Items, & Sets.

A menu appears.

⑤ Click Calculated Field.

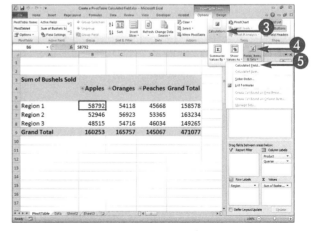

The Insert Calculated Field dialog box appears.

6 Type a name for the new field.

7 Double-click an existing field to use in defining the field.

8 Type an operator and the value, such as **+2000**.

9 Click OK.

● The calculated field appears at the end of the Field List.

● You can place the calculated field in the Σ Values box.

● Values for the calculated field fill the data area.

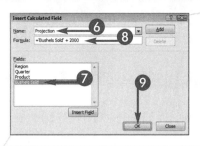

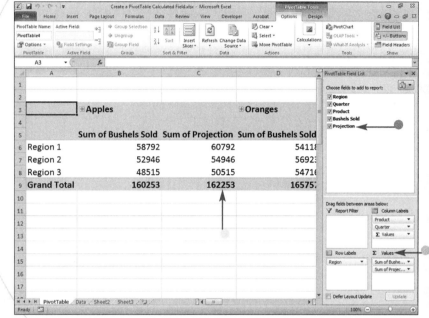

If you no longer want to include a calculated field in your PivotTable report, you can delete it. If you want to change the formula, you can modify it. Click anywhere in your PivotTable. Click the Options tab. Click Calculations. Click Fields, Items, & Sets and then click Calculated Field. The Insert Calculated Field dialog box appears. Click the ▼ next to the Name field. Click the field you want to modify or delete. Click Modify if you want to modify the field. Excel makes the formula available for modification. Click Delete if you want to delete the field. Excel deletes the field.

You can base one calculated field on another calculated field. If you do, you may want to use the Calculated Item Solve Order dialog box to tell Excel the order in which you want it to perform your calculations. Click a cell in your PivotTable. The PivotTable tools appear. Click the Options tab. Click Calculations. Click Fields, Items, & Sets and then click Solve Order. The Calculated Item Solve Order dialog box appears. Use the Move Up button to move a calculation up in the solve order. Use the Move Down button to move a calculation down in the solve order.

Group the Rows or Columns in a PivotTable

Grouping enables you to compare groups of data. For example, if your PivotTable shows each month as a column, you can group the months so that you can compare quarters. When you group columns or rows, Excel totals the data, creates a field header, and creates a field with an expand/collapse button. If the expand/collapse button displays a plus (+), you can click it to expand the group. If the expand/collapse button displays a minus (–), you can click it to collapse the group. If you do not want to display the button, you can click Buttons in the Show/Hide group on the Options tab to toggle the button display off. If after grouping your data, you want to ungroup it, you can.

Apply It

To group dates, click a cell that contains a date. Click the Options tab. Click Group Field. The Grouping dialog box appears. Type the date to start the grouping in the Starting At field and the date to end the grouping in the Ending At field. In the By box, select one or more time periods. If you are grouping by days, enter a number in the Number of Days field.

Group the Rows or Columns in a PivotTable

① Click and drag the row or column labels to select the rows or columns you want to group.

② Click the Options tab.

③ Click Group Selection.

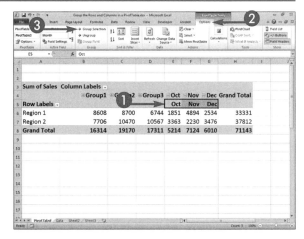

● A new group appears, with an expand/collapse button.

Note: Click minus (–) to collapse the group. Click the plus (+) to expand the group.

Note: To remove a group, click in the cell that contains the group header and then click Ungroup.

Excel removes the group.

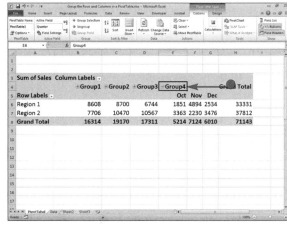

Apply a Style to a PivotTable

PivotTable styles format the cells in the rows and columns of your PivotTable to make your PivotTable attractive and easier to read. You can use PivotTable styles to change the look of your PivotTable. Excel has a number of predesigned styles from which to choose.

When you create a PivotTable, Excel applies the default style. You can change the style by using the Style gallery. There are three buttons along the side of the Style gallery. To move up and down through the gallery, use the Up and Down buttons. To open the gallery, use the More button. As you position your mouse pointer over each style in the gallery, Excel provides you with a live preview of how the style will appear when you apply it.

Apply It

The PivotTable Tools Design tab provides a number of PivotTable Style Options that you can use to modify your table. By choosing Banded Rows or Banded Columns you can have every other row or every other column appear in a different color. You can also apply special formatting to the Column Headers or Row Headers in your table if you want titles or totals to stand out.

Apply a Style to a PivotTable

1 Click in any cell in your PivotTable.

The PivotTable tools appear.

2 Click the Design tab.

3 Click the More button (▼).

The PivotTables style gallery appears.

4 Click the style you want.

Excel applies the style to your PivotTable.

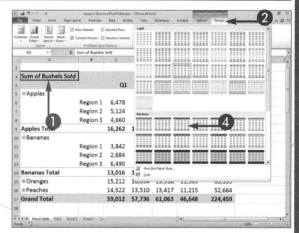

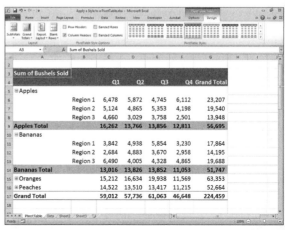

Filter a PivotTable

W hen you create a PivotTable, you can place fields in the Report Filter box and use those fields to filter your data. Filtering enables you to view only the data that is relevant to you. For example, if your data consists of Quarters 1 through 4 and you want to focus on Quarter 1; you can filter your PivotTable so only Quarter 1 data appears.

Down arrows appear next to Row Label, Column Label, and Report Filter fields in a PivotTable. You can click these down arrows and use the options in the box that appears to filter. You can search for the item you want to filter by or click check boxes to select the fields.

Filter a PivotTable

1 Click the ▾ to filter.

2 Click the Select Multiple Items option to select multiple items (▢ changes to ✔).

3 Click check boxes to deselect items (✔ changes to ▢).

● Alternatively, search for the item you want.

4 Click OK.

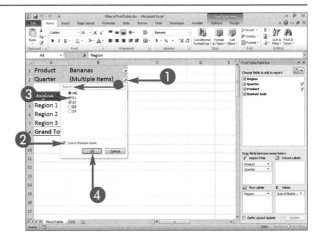

Excel filters the PivotTable.

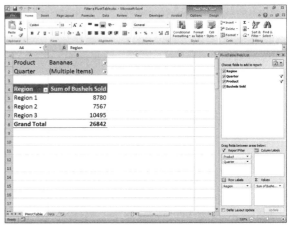

Sort a PivotTable

Putting a list in alphabetical order can make finding data easier. Ordering numerical data can help you spot trends. You can sort PivotTables by field labels or by data values. When you sort by field labels, the corresponding data values are sorted as well. The opposite is also true: sorting the data values rearranges the field labels.

You can sort your PivotTable in either ascending or descending order. You can also specify the sort direction: top to bottom or left to right.

You can manually rearrange column and row labels by clicking and dragging them to a new location. As you move your mouse pointer over the border of a cell, a four-sided arrow indicates that you can click and drag the cell.

Apply It

You can click the down arrow next to the field header to sort your PivotTable data. For example, to sort by row label or column label, click the down arrow next to Row Labels or Column Labels and then select a sort option from the menu. Click More Sort Options to open the Sort dialog box. You can use the Sort dialog box to sort by a value.

Sort a PivotTable

Sort Field Labels

1. Click and drag to select the field labels you want to sort.

2. Click the Options tab.

3. Click the A to Z (ascending) or Z to A (descending) button.

- Excel sorts your field labels.

Sort Data Fields

1. Click and drag to select the data you want to sort.

2. Click the Options tab.

3. Click Sort.

    The Sort By Value dialog box appears.

4. Click a Sort option (◉ changes to ◉).

5. Click a Sort direction (◉ changes to ◉).

6. Click OK.

    Excel sorts your data fields.

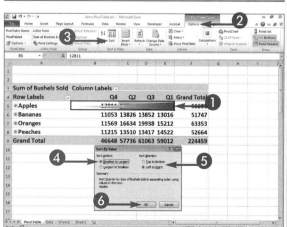

181

Retrieve Values from a PivotTable

When you create a PivotTable, down arrows appear next to Row Label, Column Label, and Report Filter fields. You can use these down arrows for filtering. Filtering enables you to view only the data that is relevant to you. For example, if your data consists of Regions 1 to 4 and you want to focus on Region 4, you can filter your PivotTable so only Region 4 data appears. As you filter your data, Excel changes the cell in which the data is located. If you use cell references to retrieve data from your PivotTable, filtering can cause you to retrieve the wrong data. To avoid this problem, use the GETPIVOTDATA function to retrieve data from your PivotTable.

The GETPIVOTDATA function is complex. You must supply two required arguments: a data field that contains the results you want to retrieve and the cell address of a cell in your PivotTable. You may also need to supply up to 126 pairs of fields that describe the data you want to

retrieve. The easiest way to create a GETPIVOTDATA function is to type an equal sign (=) and then click the PivotTable cell whose value you want. Excel automatically generates the GETPIVOTDATA function.

PivotTables summarize data. You should use the GETPIVOTDATA function whenever you want to create a report based on the summary data found in a PivotTable. If the data you want to retrieve is not visible in the PivotTable, Excel will display a #REF! error.

If you want to create a formula that uses PivotTable data, use the GETPIVOTDATA function. By default, Excel automatically generates the GETPIVOTDATA function whenever you create a formula by clicking in a cell in a Pivot table. If the GETPIVOTDATA function does not automatically generate, click Options in the PivotTable group on the Options tab and make sure that Generate GetPivotData is selected.

Retrieve Values from a PivotTable

① Click in the cell in which you want to place the retrieved data.

② Type =.

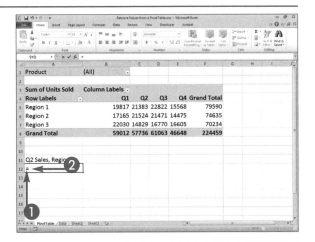

③ Click the cell value you want to retrieve.

● Excel creates the GETPIVOTDATA function.

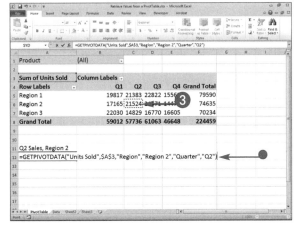

- The data field that contains the results you want to retrieve.

- The cell address of a cell in your PivotTable.

- The field that describes the data you want to retrieve.

- The item that describes the data you want to retrieve.

④ Press Enter.

Excel retrieves the value you entered into your function.

If the cell location changes because of filtering, Excel is still able to retrieve the value.

Note: Excel cannot retrieve a value that does not appear on-screen.

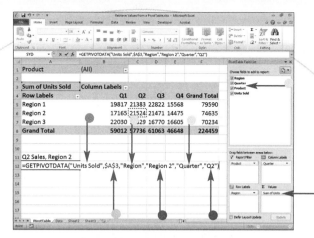

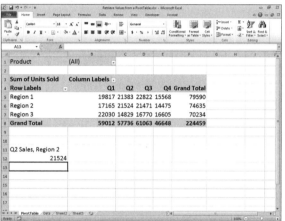

Using Slicer

Filtering enables you to view only the data that is relevant to you. You can use the down arrows that appear next to Row Label, Column Label, and Report Filter fields to filter a PivotTable. You can also use Slicer. With Slicer, you can dynamically filter your data and quickly zero in on just the data you want.

Slicer creates a panel for each field you select. The panel displays every item in the field. You can use the panel to select the items you want to see. For example, if you have Customer, Quarter, and Product panels, you can select the customers, quarters, and products you want to see in your PivotTable.

A Slicer panel can also provide you with useful information. The state of each item can be represented by a different format. For example, selected items can have a

dark blue fill, unselected item can have a gray fill, items with data can appear with regular type, items with no data can appear with italic type, and when you hover you mouse pointer over an item, it can appear with a gradient fill. How items in a panel appear depend on the style you apply.

You can resize a Slicer panel. When you click a Slicer panel a border appears around it. There are sets of dots on the sides and corners of the border. If you hover your mouse pointer over the dots, the mouse pointer turns into a double-sided arrow. You can then click and drag to resize the panel. You can also move a slider panel. If you hover your mouse pointer over a solid section of the border, the mouse pointer turns into a four-sided arrow. You can then click and drag to move the panel.

Using Slicer

① Click in any cell in a PivotTable.

The PivotTable tools appear.

② Click the Options tab.

③ Click Insert Slicer.

A menu appears.

④ Click Insert Slicer on the menu.

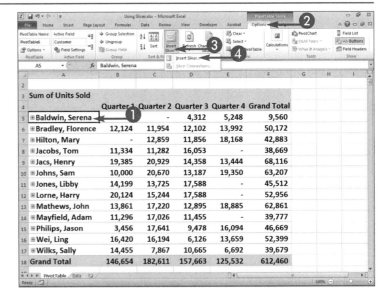

The Insert Slicers dialog box appears.

⑤ Click the fields for which you want to create a Slicer panel (☐ turns into ✔).

⑥ Click OK.

Excel creates a Slicer panel for each of the fields you selected.

⑦ Hover over the portion of the border without dots.

The mouse pointer turns into a four-sided arrow.

⑧ Drag the Slicer pane to a new location.

⑨ Hover over the series of dots that appear on the border.

The mouse pointer turns into a double-sided arrow.

⑩ Click and drag to resize the panel.

⑪ Click to select the items you want to see in your PivotTable.

● Customers that are greyed out do not appear in PivotTable because there is no available data.

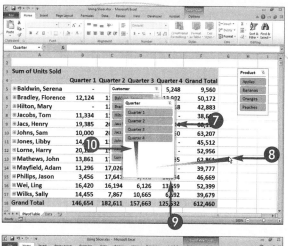

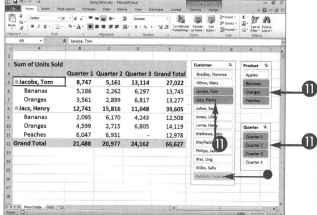

Extra

To select multiple non-adjacent items in a Slicer panel, hold down the Ctrl key and then click each option. To select multiple adjacent items in a Slicer panel, click the first option and then hold down the Shift key and click the last option.

To apply a style to a Slicer panel, click the Slicer panel. The Slicer tools appear. Click to select a slicer style from the Slicer Styles gallery. Excel applies the style to the panel. To create a new style, click New Slicer Style at the bottom of the Slicer Style gallery. The New Slicer Quick Style dialog box appears. Click the Slicer element you want to format and then click the Format button. The Format Cells dialog box appears. Use it to format the element.

You can use the Slicer Setting dialog box to set a number of slicer options, such as the number of columns in a panel, the width and height of the buttons, and the position and sort order of the panel. To open the Slicer Settings dialog box, click a Slicer panel. The Slicer tools appear. Click Slicer Settings.

Create
a Chart

With Excel, you can quickly create a chart. A chart is a visual representation of the numbers in your worksheet. Charts can clarify patterns that can get lost in columns of numbers and text, and they make your data more accessible to people who are not familiar with, or do not want to delve into the details. Charts can be easier to understand than rows and columns of numbers because the mind perceives, processes, and recalls visual information more quickly than textual or numerical information.

In Excel, you can create charts with dramatic visual appeal quickly and easily. Your data should be organized into rows and columns with each row and column labeled. When you select the data, include the row and column labels. You must choose a chart type. Excel

provides several chart types from which to choose, including column, line, pie, bar, area, and scatter charts. In addition, each chart type has a number of subtype options.

After you create a chart, Excel makes Chart tools available to you through the Design, Layout, and Format contextual tabs. Using the Chart tools, you can choose a chart style and layout. You can change the color scheme of your chart by applying a chart style. You can use layouts to add a chart title, axis labels, a legend, or a data table to your chart. A chart title summarizes chart content, axis labels explain each axis, a legend explains the colors used to represent data, and a data table displays the data presented in the chart. You can edit the chart title and axis labels.

Create a Chart

1 Click and drag to select the worksheet data you want to chart.

   Include row and column labels.

2 Click the Insert tab.

3 Click a chart type.

4 Click a chart subtype.

   Excel creates a chart based on the data you selected.

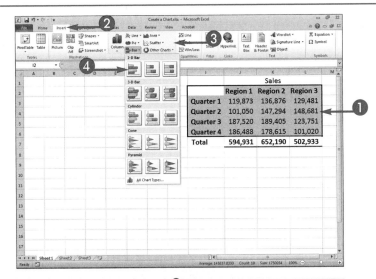

● The Chart tools appear.

5 Click the Design tab.

6 Click the Chart Style button (⬇) and then select a chart style.

   Excel applies the style to your chart.

7 Click the Chart Layout button (⬇) and then select a chart layout.

   Excel applies the layout to your chart.

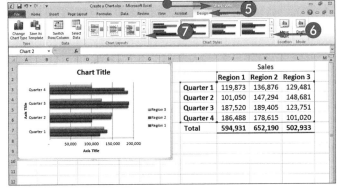

8 Right-click the chart title or an axis title.

A context menu appears.

9 Click Edit Text.

10 Select the current text and then type to change the title or axis label.

11 Repeat Steps 8 and 9 to change the remaining title and axis labels.

● Excel changes the labels on the chart.

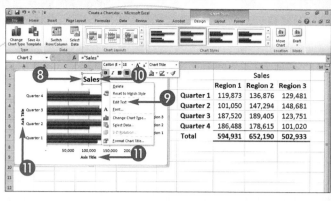

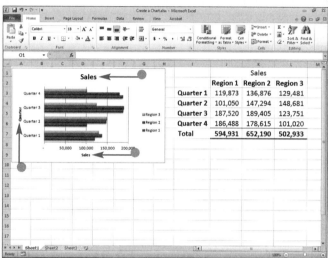

Extra

Excel ships with the Column chart as the default chart type. You can change the default chart type by clicking the launcher in the Insert tab's Chart group to open the Insert Chart dialog box. Click a chart type and a subtype, and then click the Set as Default Chart button located at the bottom of the Insert Chart dialog box.

To create a chart quickly and easily using all of Excel's charting defaults, select the data you want to chart and then press F11. Excel creates a chart on a new chart sheet. You can modify the chart by using any of the Chart tools. If you want your chart embedded in your current worksheet instead of on a chart sheet, press Alt+F1.

You can manually change the placement of the various elements that make up your chart. For example, you can move the legend from the left side of your chart to the right side. Position your mouse pointer over the element you want to move. When your mouse pointer turns into a four-sided arrow, click and drag the element to a new location.

Add Chart Details

A fter you create a chart in Excel, modifying it or adding details is easy. In fact, you can modify virtually all the elements of a chart. For example, when you create a chart, Excel places it on the same worksheet as the data from which you created it. You can move the chart to another worksheet or to a special chart sheet. If you choose to move your chart to a chart sheet, you must name the sheet. Excel creates the chart sheet and places the name you gave it on the sheet's tab.

Many chart types have a 3-D option. To make a 3-D chart easier to read, you can use the X and Y fields in the 3-D Rotation pane to change the chart rotation. The X field

rotates the horizontal axis of your chart and the Y field rotates the vertical axis of your chart.

As you rotate your chart, Excel provides a live preview of your changes. If at any time you want to return to the default rotation, click the Default Rotation button near the bottom of the Format Chart Area dialog box. In addition to changing your chart's rotation, you may also want to change your chart's perspective. Changing the rotation and/or perspective is useful if the bars in the front of your bar chart hide bars in the back of your bar chart. Use the Perspective field in the 3-D Rotation dialog box to change the perspective.

Add Chart Details

Change Chart Location

1 Click your chart.

● The Chart tools appear.

2 Click the Design tab.

3 Click Move Chart.

The Move Chart dialog box appears.

4 Click the New sheet option (◎ changes to ◉).

● Alternatively, click Object in (◎ changes to ◉) to place the chart on another worksheet.

◉ If you click Object in, click the down arrow (▾) and select the sheet on which you want to place the chart.

5 Type a name for the sheet.

6 Click OK.

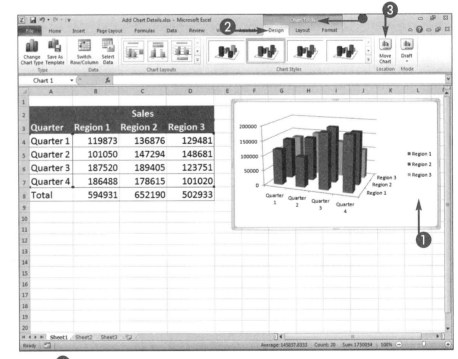

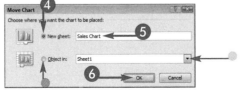

- Excel places the chart on a chart sheet.

Change Rotation and Perspective

1. Click the Layout tab.

2. Click 3-D Rotation.

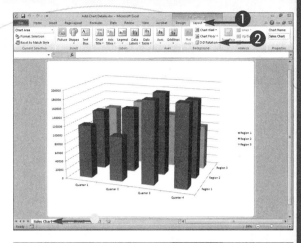

The Format Chart Area dialog box appears.

3. Type a value to increase or decrease the X rotation.

4. Type a value to increase or decrease the Y rotation.

- Click Default Rotation to return to the default rotation.

5. Type a value to increase or decrease the perspective.

6. Click Close.

Excel rotates and changes the perspective of your chart.

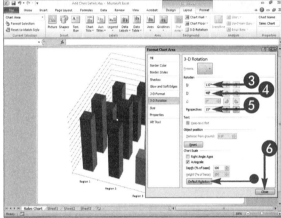

Apply It

You can add, remove, or change the plot area's fill when working with two-dimensional charts. Just click the chart, click the Layout tab, and then click Plot Area in the Background group. A menu of options appears. From the menu, click More Plot Area Options. The Format Plot Area dialog box appears. Click Fill. Click Solid Fill to place solid color in the fill area. Use the color box to select the color you want.

Click Gradient Fill to place a gradient fill in the plot area. Use the Gradient Fill pane to set the colors, type, and direction of your gradient fill.

Click Picture or Texture Fill to fill your plot area with a picture or texture. You can select a texture from the menu or you can click the File button to locate a picture or texture you want to insert. Click the Clipboard button to fill the plot area with the item currently on the Clipboard. Click the Clip Art button and then double-click the clip-art item with which you want to fill the plot area. Regardless of what you fill the plot area with, you can adjust the transparency.

continued →

Add Chart Details
(continued)

To make your chart more readable, you may want to change some of the attributes of your chart. You can easily change the walls and floor of your three-dimensional charts. The walls are the side and back of your chart, and the floor is the bottom of your chart. You can choose to show the chart walls and/or floor, not show the walls and/or floor, or fill the chart walls and/or floor with a color, gradient, or picture. Choose Solid Fill in the appropriate format dialog box to fill with a color, choose Gradient Fill to fill with a gradient, or choose Picture or Texture Fill to fill with a picture or texture.

Excel bases axis values on the range of values in your data. Axis values encompass the range. For example, if the lowest value represented in your chart is 101,020 and the highest value represented in your chart is 189,405, your axis values

might range from 0 to 200,000. Axis labels describe the data displayed on each axis. Excel provides several options for choosing whether to display axis values and how to display the axis values and labels on each axis, including the horizontal, vertical, and depth axis of a 3-D chart.

When you create a chart in Excel, Excel creates horizontal and vertical gridlines to mark major and minor intervals in your data series. If your axis values run from 0 to 200,000, major gridlines might be at 20,000, 40,000, 60,000, and so on. Minor gridlines might be at 2,000, 4,000, 6,000, and so on. You can remove gridlines with the None option, display major units only with the Major Gridlines option, display minor units only with the Minor Gridlines option, or display major and minor units with the Major and Minor option.

Add Chart Details *(continued)*

Change the Wall and Floor

1 Click your chart.

● The Chart tools appear.

2 Click the Layout tab.

3 Click Chart Wall.

   A menu appears.

4 Click More Wall Options.

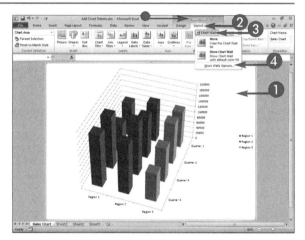

The Format Walls dialog box appears.

5 Click a Fill option (⚪ changes to ⦿).

6 Click Close.

● Excel changes the fill of the chart wall.

   Click Chart Floor in the Background group and repeat Steps 4 to 6 to change the chart floor.

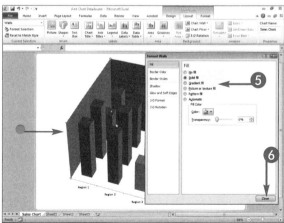

Adjust the Axis

① Click the Layout tab.

② Click Axes.

③ Click Primary Horizontal Axis.

Note: *To change the vertical axis, click Primary Vertical Axis. To change the depth axis, click Depth Axis.*

④ Click a Primary Horizontal Axis option.

◉ Excel changes the display of your horizontal axis.

Change the Gridlines

① Click the Layout tab.

② Click Gridlines.

③ Click Primary Horizontal Gridlines.

Note: *To change the vertical gridlines, click Primary Vertical Gridlines and choose a menu option. To change the depth gridlines, click Depth Gridlines and choose a menu option.*

④ Click a menu option.

◉ Excel changes the display of your horizontal axis.

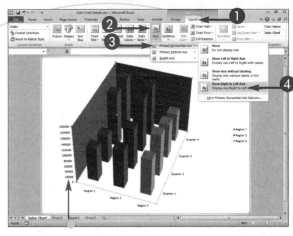

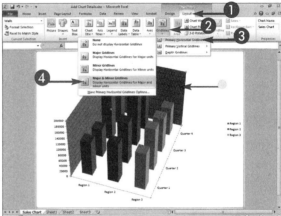

Apply It

To resize your chart, click your chart. A border surrounds it, with dots on the sides and corners. Place the mouse pointer over the dots. When a double arrow appears, click and drag to resize your chart.

You can also use the Ribbon to resize your chart. Click your chart. The Chart tools appear. Click the Format tab. Use the Shape Height field to adjust the height of your chart. Use the Shape Width field to adjust the width of your chart. Be careful when resizing because it may skew the chart and distort the presentation of the content.

You can use the menu options that appear when you click one of the buttons in the Labels group on the Layout tab to tell Excel things such as whether, where, and how to display a chart title, axis titles, legend, data labels, or data tables. Click the More option at the bottom of the menu to open a dialog box in which you can format a chart title, a legend, axis titles, data labels, or data tables.

Create a
Combination Chart

If you show two or more data series in a single chart, you can change the chart type for one or more series and create a combination chart. Using different chart types can make it easier to distinguish different categories of data shown in the same chart. For example, you can create a combination chart that shows the number of homes sold as a line chart and the average sales price as a column chart.

When you plot two different types of data in the same chart, the range of values can vary wildly. For example, the range of values for homes sold might be between 9 and 15, while the range of values for the average sales price might be between 750,000 and 950,000. You can

plot each of these data series on a different vertical axis to make it easier for the user to see values for the associated series. In the example, you could plot average sales prices on one vertical axis and number of homes sold on the other vertical axis.

To create a combination chart, you first create a chart with both data series shown as the same chart type. Then if the data series' values vary wildly, you can change the legend and chart type for one of the data series.

The chart legend changes to reflect the changes you have made to your chart. For example, if a chart changes from a line chart to a bar chart, an appropriate colored bar displays in the legend.

Create a Combination Chart

Chart Your Data

1. Select the data you want to chart.

2. Click the Insert tab.

3. Click a chart type.

4. Click a chart subtype.

   Excel charts your data.

● The Homes Sold data series.

● The Average Sales Price data series.

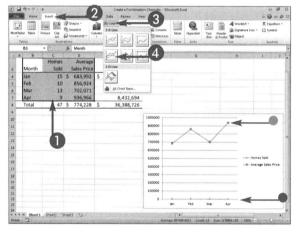

Create a Secondary Axis

1. Click a data point in the series you want to place on a secondary axis.

   The Chart tools appear.

2. Click the Format tab.

3. Click Format Selection.

   The Format Data Series dialog box appears.

4. Click the Secondary Axis option (◎ changes to ◉).

5. Click Close.

● Excel plots the data you chose on a secondary axis.

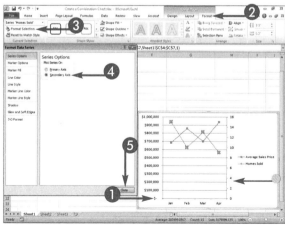

Change Chart Type

1 Click a data point in the series you want to change.

The Chart tools appear.

2 Click the Design tab.

3 Click Change Chart Type.

The Change Chart Type dialog box appears.

4 Click a new chart type.

5 Click a new chart subtype.

6 Click OK.

○ Excel changes the chart type for the series.

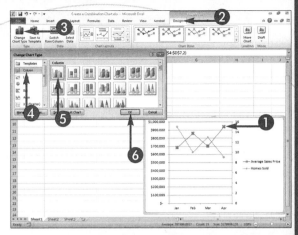

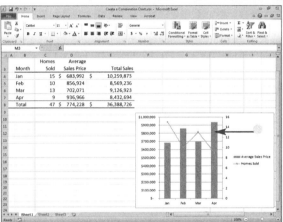

You can modify the location, style, or layout of a combination chart just as you can any other chart. See section, "Add Chart Details" in this chapter to learn more about changing a chart location, style, or layout. When you change the chart style, the styles associated with both data series change.

You can add a title to your secondary axis. Click anywhere in your chart. The Chart tools appear. Click the Layout tab, click Axis Titles in the Labels group, click Secondary Vertical Axis Title, and then choose an option from the menu. Choose None if you do not want to display an axis title. Choose Rotated if you want to display a rotated text and you want Excel to resize the chart. Choose Vertical if you want to display vertical text and you want Excel to resize the chart. Choose Horizontal if you want to display horizontal text and you want Excel to resize the chart. If you chose to include a title, Excel places a text box in your chart. Delete the text in the text box and then type the title you want to give the axis.

Change the Chart Type

xcel provides a variety of chart types and subtypes from which to choose. If you are not satisfied with the chart type you have chosen, you can easily make another choice.

Use a column or bar chart to plot data arranged in rows and columns. Both types are useful when your data changes over time or when you want to compare data values. Use a stacked bar or a stacked column chart to show the relationship of individual items to the whole. Use a 3-D chart to show data on two axes. The cylinder, cone, and pyramid bar and column subtypes all provide you with interesting ways to present your charts.

Area and line charts are also good for plotting data organized into columns and rows. Use an area chart to show how values change over time and how each part of

the whole contributes to the change. Line charts are ideal for showing trends in your data; consider using a line chart to show changes measured at regular intervals.

Pie charts are useful when you want to display data arranged in one column or one row. Each data point in a pie chart represents a percentage of the whole pie. Like pie charts, each data point in a doughnut chart represents a percentage of the whole pie; however, a doughnut chart can display more than one column or row of data.

Excel stock charts display the high, low, and close; open, high, low, and, close; volume, high, low, and close; and volume, open, high, low, and close values of a stock. When creating a stock chart, you must arrange your columns of data with the date in the first column followed by the order given in the chart name; for example, date, high, low, close.

Change the Chart Type

1 Click your chart.

● The Chart tools appear.

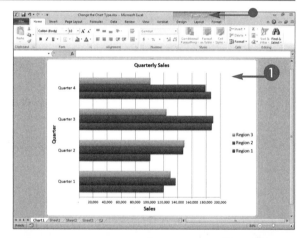

2 Click the Design tab.

3 Click Change Chart Type.

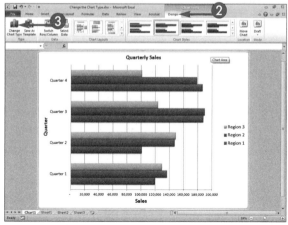

The Change Chart Type
dialog box appears.

④ Click a chart type.

⑤ Click a subtype.

⑥ Click OK.

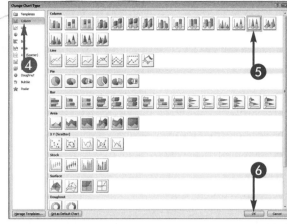

● The chart appears,
formatted in the new
chart type and subtype.

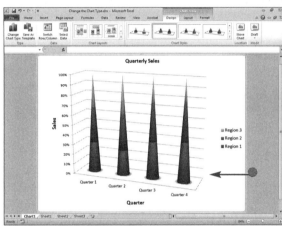

Apply It

Once you have your chart designed
exactly the way you want it, you can
save your design as a template. By
using templates, you can save your
settings and apply them to other
charts. To create a template, click
your chart. The Chart tools appear.
Click the Design tab. Click Save as
Template in the Type group. The
Save Chart Template dialog box
appears. Make sure you are in the
Charts folder; then type the name
you want to give your template and
click Save.

To use your template, select the
data you want to chart, click the
Insert tab, and then click the
launcher in the Charts group. The
Insert Charts dialog box appears.
Click Templates, click your
template, and then click OK. Excel
creates a chart based on the
settings in your template.

To apply your template to an
existing chart, click your chart. The
Chart tools appear. Click the
Design tab. Click Change Chart
Type in the Type group. The
Change Chart Type dialog box
appears. Click Templates, click your
template, and then click OK. Excel
applies your template to your chart.

Add or Remove Chart Data

If you want to include new data in your chart or exclude data from your chart, you can use the Select Data Source dialog box to add and remove entire columns or rows of information or to change your data series entirely without changing your chart's type or other properties. Excel defines a *data series* as the related data points you plot in a chart. Excel gives each data series in your chart a unique color or pattern and provides a key to each data series in the chart legend. It also creates a series formula for each data series. If you select a series in a chart by clicking a data point, you can see the series formula in the formula bar. For example, if you click a bar in a bar chart, you can see the series

formula in the formula bar. You can edit the series formula, but it is easier to change the data in a chart by using the Select Data Source dialog box.

The Select Data Source dialog box Legend Entries (Series) box lists the names of your data series. You can use this box to add, edit, or remove a data series. When you click the Add button, the Edit Series dialog box appears. You can use it to select new ranges or to define your series name and your series values; or you can type a name in the Series Name field and/or enter an array in the Series Values field. An array is a series of values, separated by commas. You must enclose arrays in curly braces; for example, {100000, 110000, 90000}.

Add or Remove Chart Data

Change the Data Area

● Charted data.

① Click your chart.

The Chart tools appear.

② Click the Design tab.

③ Click Select Data.

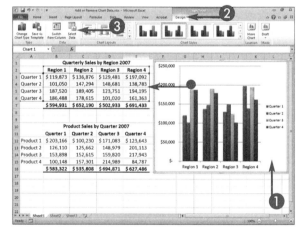

The Select Data Source dialog box appears.

④ Enter the range you want to include in your chart.

⑤ Click OK.

● Excel redefines the data series area.

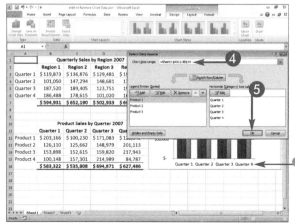

Add a Legend Item

1. Perform Steps 1 to 3 under the Change the Data Area section.

   The Select Data Source dialog box appears.

2. Click Add.

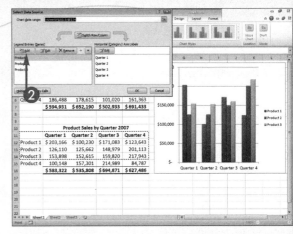

The Edit Series dialog box appears.

3. Click the cell with the name you want for your new data series, or type the cell address.

4. Enter the data series range or type an array.

5. Click OK.

- Excel adds the data series and legend name to your chart.

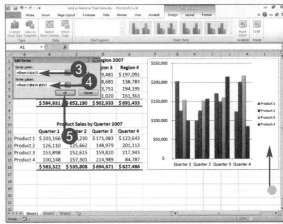

Add Sparklines

parklines enable you to see trends in your data at a glance. *Sparklines* are charts that appear in a single cell. There are three types of sparklines: Line, Column, and Win/Loss. If you choose Line as your sparkline type, Excel creates a line chart. If you choose Column as your sparkline type, Excel creates a bar chart. If you choose Win/Loss as your sparkline type, Excel creates a Win/Loss chart.

A line chart shows each point in a data series on a line. With a line chart, you can easily see how your data fluctuates. A column chart is a bar chart. Negative values appear below the zero line; positive values appear above the zero line. The size of each bar corresponds to the relative size of the value it represents. A Win/Loss chart

is also a bar chart. And, as with a column chart, negative values appear below the zero line and positive values appear above the zero line. However, with a Win/Loss chart, the size of each bar is the same.

You can mark points on a sparkline. There are six point types: High Point, Low Point, Negative Points, First Point, Last Point, and Markers. The High Point is the highest value, the Low Point is the lowest value, Negative Points are points that are below zero, the First Point is the first value, and Last Point is the last value. Markers can only be used with line charts. They mark every point in the series. You can specify the color of each point type. For example, you can have the high point appear in green and the low point appear in red.

Add Sparklines

1. Select the data range you want to chart.

2. Click Insert.

3. Click a Sparkline type.

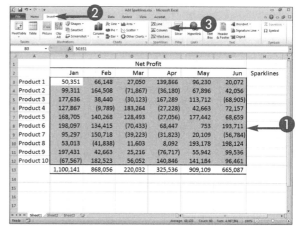

The Create Sparklines dialog box appears.

● The data range you selected appears in the data range field.

4. Enter the location where you want to place the sparklines.

5. Click OK.

- The Sparklines appear.

  The Sparkline tools appear.

6️⃣ Click Marker Color.

7️⃣ Click the type of marker you want to add.

8️⃣ Select a color from the color palette.

  Repeat Steps 7 and 8 if you want to add additional markers.

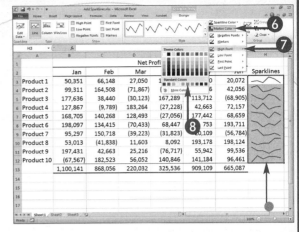

- Excel adds the markers.

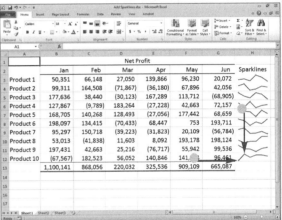

Apply It

When you click in a field that contains a sparkline, the Sparkline Tools appear. If you activate the Design tab, you can use the Style gallery to apply a style to your sparklines. In addition, you can use the Sparkline Color field to change the color or weight of your sparklines. Click Sparkline Color and then choose the color, if you want to change the color or click Sparkline Color and then choose the weight, if you want to change the weight.

You can also change the sparkline type. Click in a cell that contains a sparkline. The Sparkline tools appear. Activate the Design tab. In the Type group, click the sparkline type you want.

If you create your sparklines by selecting a cell range, Excel groups the sparklines. You can clear sparklines from a cell, cell range, or cell group. Click in a cell or cell range that contains sparklines. The Sparkline tools appear. Activate the Design tab. Click the down arrow (⬇) next to Clear. Click Clear Selected Sparklines to clear the sparklines in the cell or cell range you selected or click Clear Selected Sparkline Groups to clear all the sparklines in the group.

Create a Trendline

Trendlines help you see both the size and direction of changes in your data, and you can use them to forecast future or past values based on available data. A *trendline* is the line through your data series that is as close as possible to every point in your data series. You can add a trendline to any chart type except 3-D, stacked, radar, pie, surface, and doughnut charts. Excel superimposes the trendline over your chart.

Excel provides the following trendline types: linear, logarithmic, polynomial, power, exponential, and moving average. You choose a trendline type based on the type of data you have. Excel generates a statistic called *R-squared*. R-squared represents the fraction of the observed data that is explained by the fitted trendline/curve. The closer R-squared is to 1, the better the line fits your data. You can choose to have the R-squared value appear on your chart.

Use a linear trendline if your data increases or decreases at a steady rate. Use a logarithmic trendline when your data increases or decreases quickly and then levels out. Use a polynomial trendline when your data fluctuates up and down. Generally, you can estimate the order of a polynomial by the number of hills or valleys that occur. If your data has one hill or valley, it is usually somewhere around an order-2 polynomial. If it has two hills or valleys, it is usually somewhere around an order-3 polynomial, and so on. Use a power trendline to compare data that increases at a specific rate. Use a moving average trendline to smooth out your data so you can see fluctuations in your data. A moving average trendline averages groups of sequential points in your data and then creates a trendline. Use the Period field in the Format Trendline dialog box to tell Excel how many fields to average.

Create a Trendline

① Click your chart.

The Chart tools appear.

② Click the Layout tab.

③ Click Trendline.

A menu appears.

④ Click More Trendline Options.

Alternatively, click a menu option.

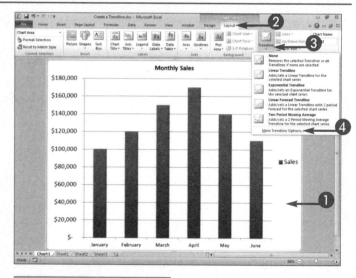

The Format Trendline dialog box appears.

⑤ Click Trendline Options.

6. Click a regression type
   (⊙ changes to ◉).

7. Set the number of periods to
   forecast.

8. Click Display R-squared value
   on chart (☐ changes to ✔).

9. Click Close.

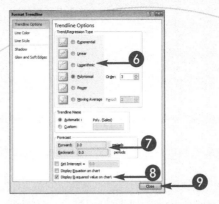

- The trendline appears on
  the chart.

- If you selected R-squared in
  Step 8, the R-squared value
  appears on the chart.

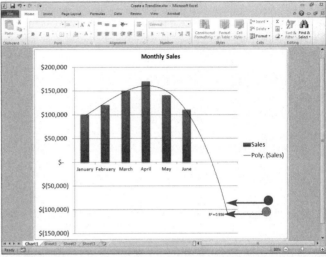

Extra

You can use a linear series to project future values. To create a linear series, you add the difference between the first value and the second value to the second value to create the next value. You then add the difference between the first and second values to each subsequent value. For example:

INITIAL VALUES	LINEAR SERIES
1,2	3,4,5
1,3	5,7,9
25,0	−25,−50,−75

If you want to project future values for a simple linear trend, you can use the fill handle. Select at least the last two rows of your data and then drag the fill handle. To learn more about the AutoFill feature and the fill handle, see Chapter 12.

You can use a growth series to project future values. To create a growth series, you divide the second value by the starting value. You then multiply the result by each subsequent value. For example:

INITIAL VALUES	GROWTH SERIES
3,6	12,24,48
2,5	12.5,31.25,78.125
2,3	4.5,6.75,10.125

You can also use the fill handle to predict a growth trend. Select at least the last two rows of your data, hold down the right mouse button, and then drag. Release the right mouse button and click Growth Trend on the shortcut menu that appears.

Add
Error Bars

With Excel, you can generate error bars to provide an estimate of the potential error in experimental or sampled data. In science, marketing, polling, and other fields, people make conclusions about the real world by sampling or devising controlled experiments. When you sample data or generate data under laboratory conditions, the resulting numbers are approximates. If the entire population were surveyed, the actual results could be higher or lower. An error bar shows the range of possible values that could have occurred.

With Excel, you can show the range of possible values in several ways, including as a fixed number, as a percentage of the data point, or in terms of standard deviation units. Use the Format Error Bars dialog box to make your choice. If you choose Fixed value, you specify the constant value Excel displays as the error amount for

each data point. If you choose Percentage, Excel uses the percentage you specify in the Percentage box to calculate the possible error amount as a percentage of the value of the data point. If you choose Standard deviation(s), Excel calculates the standard deviation, multiplies it by the number you enter into the Standard deviation(s) box, and then uses the result. If you choose Standard error, Excel calculates and uses the standard error. If you choose Custom, you can specify the error values Excel uses.

You can choose how Excel displays error bars. Choose Both if you want to display the actual data point plus and minus the error amount. Choose Minus if you want to display the actual data point minus the error amount. Choose Plus if you want to display the actual data point plus the error amount. You can display your error bar with or without caps on the ends.

Add Error Bars

① Click your chart.

● The Chart tools appear.

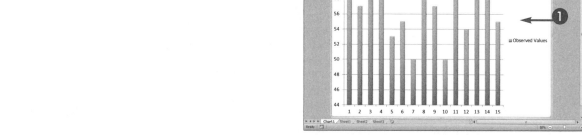

② Click the Layout tab.

③ Click Error Bars.

A menu appears.

④ Click More Error Bars Options.

Alternatively, click the appropriate menu option.

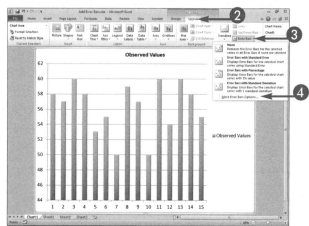

The Format Error Bars dialog box appears.

5 Click a Direction option (◉ changes to ◉).

6 Click an End style option (◉ changes to ◉).

7 Click an Error Amount option (◉ changes to ◉).

8 Type a value if you chose Fixed value, Percentage, or Standard deviation(s) in Step 7.

9 Click Close.

● Your chart appears with error bars.

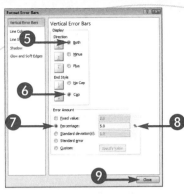

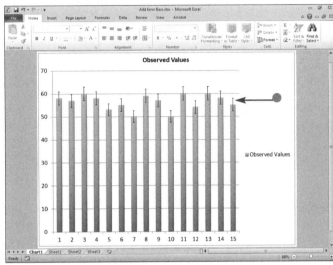

Extra

Standard deviation units indicate whether an experimental number is reasonably close to the population characteristic you are studying. For example, you can have a confidence level of 95 percent that the populations mean falls within two standard deviation units of the sampled mean, which you know. Your confidence level in estimating population characteristics assumes that the sampled values are normally — or evenly — distributed around the mean, as in a bell curve.

Only certain chart types support error bars, including 2-D area, bar, column, line, and XY scatter charts. These types let you create error bars for the values measured by the y-axis. For the scatter chart, you can create both X and Y error bars.

You can add error bars and trendlines to a PivotChart. However, if you make changes to your PivotChart, Excel may remove the error bars or trendlines. Changes that may result in the loss of error bars or trendlines include changing the layout, removing fields, and hiding or displaying items.

You can use the Line Color, Line Style, and Shadow options in the Format Error Bars dialog box to change the line color or line style of your error bars or to add shadows to your error bars.

Create a Histogram

With Excel, you can use histograms to group a list of values into categories and compare the categories. Excel calls these categories bins. To display the test scores for a group of students, for example, your first bin might be <=60, representing scores lower than or equal to 60 percent, your second bin might be 70, and so on, up to a bin for test scores higher than 100 percent. Excel counts the number of occurrences in each bin.

When creating a histogram, you must provide three pieces of information: the data you want to categorize, the bins, and the cell ID of the cell in the upper-left corner of the range in which you want the results to appear. Your bins must be in lowest to highest order. The results can appear in the current worksheet, in a new worksheet, or in a new workbook.

To create a histogram and a chart at the same time, click the Chart Output option in the Histogram dialog box. You can modify the chart just as you would any other chart. Click the Cumulative Percentage option in the Histogram dialog box to create a histogram output table that includes cumulative percentages. Click the Pareto (sorted histogram) option to create a histogram output table that includes frequency data sorted from highest to lowest.

As you make changes to your data, Excel does not automatically make changes to your histogram. You must regenerate your histogram when you make changes to your data.

The histogram tool is part of the Data Analysis Toolpak, which you may need to install as explained in the Extra portion of this section.

Create a Histogram

1. Place your data in a worksheet.

2. Type the values that define the bins.

Note: *The bins must be ordered from lowest to highest but need not be the same size.*

3. Click the Data tab.

4. Click Data Analysis.

The Data Analysis dialog box appears.

5. Click Histogram.

6. Click OK.

The Histogram dialog box appears.

7 Enter the cell range for the numbers you want to categorize.

8 Enter the cell range for the bins.

9 Click an Output option where you want to place your output (⊙ changes to ◉).

10 Enter the cell where you want the results to start.

11 Select a histogram options (☐ changes to ✔).

12 Click OK.

The results appear.

● Number of values per bin.

● Uncategorized values above the highest bin.

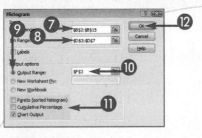

Extra

Before you create a histogram, you must install the Data Analysis Toolpak add-in. Click File. A menu appears. Click Options. The Excel Options dialog box appears. Click Add-Ins. In the View and Manage Microsoft Office Add-ins pane, click Analysis Toolpak and then click Go. The Add-Ins dialog box appears. Select Analysis Toolpak and then click OK. The Data Analysis Toolpak appears on the Data tab.

You can use the FREQUENCY function to create a histogram. You must supply the function with two pieces of information: Data_array and Bins_array. The Data_array is the list of data you want to place in bins. The Bins_array is the list of bins you want to use. To use the FREQUENCY function, you must select the cells into which you want to place your results. If you have five bins, select six cells — one more cell than the number of bins you have. Type the function or enter it into the Function Arguments dialog box. Frequency is an array function, so press Ctrl+Shift+Enter after you have entered your arguments instead of clicking OK. Refer to Sheet2 of Histogram.xlsx, which is on the Web site for this book, to see an example.

Chart
Filtered Data

With Excel, you can quickly create a chart of the information in a worksheet. Charts show trends and anomalies that may be otherwise difficult to detect in columns of numbers. By choosing the appropriate type of chart and formatting the chart features, you can share your results with others and convey patterns in your data.

To create a chart, use the options in the Charts group on the Insert tab. See the section, "Create a Chart" in this chapter to learn more. You can position your chart next to the data on which you base it, so when you change the data, you can instantly observe the changes in the chart.

By using Excel's filtering features, you can filter your data. Filtering your data enables you to limit the data you

see. For example, if your worksheet has data for Quarter 1, Quarter 2, Quarter 3, and Quarter 4, you can filter your data so you see only Quarter 1 and Quarter 2. You can use the Filter option on the Data tab to filter your data, you can define your data as a table and use the table filtering options, or you can use functions to filter your data. To learn more about filtering, see Chapter 8.

By default, as you filter your data, Excel removes the filtered data from your chart. If you do not want Excel to remove filtered data, use the Show Data in Hidden Rows and Columns option in the Hidden and Empty Cell Settings dialog box to instruct Excel to display all the data in your chart.

Chart Filtered Data

① Create a chart.

② Filter the data.

A filter (⊤) on the button indicates that you have filtered data.

By default, only the unfiltered data displays in the chart.

In this example, only Quarter 1 and Quarter 2 display.

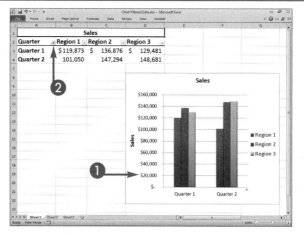

③ Click your chart.

The Chart tools appear.

④ Click the Design tab.

⑤ Click Select Data.

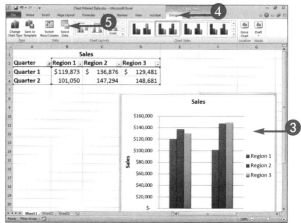

The Select Data Source dialog box appears.

6 Click the Hidden and Empty Cells button.

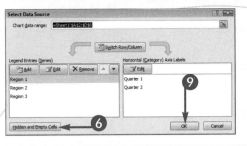

The Hidden and Empty Cell Settings dialog box appears.

7 Click the Show data in hidden rows and columns option (☐ changes to ✔).

8 Click OK.

9 Click OK in the Select Data Source dialog box.

● Excel displays the hidden data in your chart.

In this example, Quarter 1, Quarter 2, Quarter 3, and Quarter 4 display.

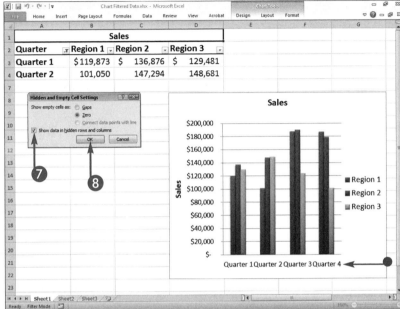

Extra

Sometimes you find yourself without a value for a period, transaction, or whatever you happen to be tracking. Perhaps the data was not recorded, was not validly recorded, or is just missing. The term missing data means a data series has no value for one or more cells. Excel makes it easy for you to show that data is missing.

The Hidden and Empty Cell Settings dialog box has three options for representing missing data: Gaps, Zero, and Connect data points with line. You can only use Connect data points with line when you are working with a line chart.

The default is Gaps. If you choose Gaps, Excel does not plot the missing data. This option makes it clear that data is missing, which is important when precision is important or not much data is missing. If you choose Zero, Excel treats the missing data as a zero, which can be misleading but may be desirable if you rely on functions that cannot handle a missing value. If you choose Connect data points with line, Excel interpolates the data, constructing a data series based on the values of neighboring points.

Create a PivotChart

A PivotChart is a graphical representation of a PivotTable. PivotCharts combine the cross-tabulation capabilities of a PivotTable with the visual appeal of a chart. PivotTables reveal patterns in your data. PivotCharts can make patterns even more apparent. Like all Excel charts, PivotCharts have a chart type, axis, legend, and data, all of which you can modify.

You can create a PivotChart by creating a PivotTable and then selecting a chart type from the Insert Chart dialog box. The option for creating a PivotChart is located on the Options tab, which is a contextual tab that appears when you click in a PivotTable. Most of the standard chart types are available to you, including column, line, pie, bar, and area charts. In addition, each chart type has a number of subtype options from which you can choose.

Most of the standard chart subtypes are available to you as well.

After you create a PivotChart, Excel makes PivotChart tools available to you through the Design, Layout, Format, and Analyze contextual tabs. The Design, Layout, and Format tools provide you with all the same options you have when creating a standard chart. These options are explained in this chapter. You can use them to layout and format your chart. The Analyze contextual tab is unique to PivotCharts. It has options that you can use to work with your PivotChart and PivotTable data.

By default, Excel embeds your PivotChart in the same worksheet where your PivotTable is located. You may want to move your PivotChart to make it easier to work with.

Create a PivotChart

① Click any cell in your PivotTable.

● The PivotTable tools appear.

② Click the Options tab.

③ Click PivotChart.

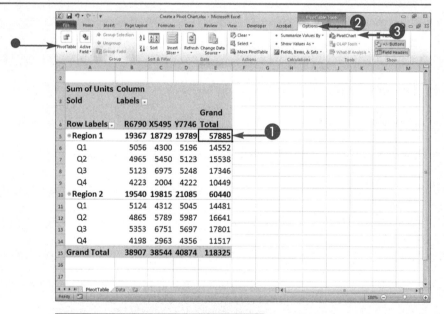

The Insert Chart dialog box appears.

④ Click a chart type.

⑤ Click a chart subtype.

⑥ Click OK.

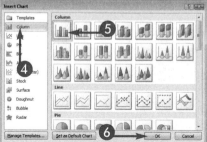

- The PivotChart appears.

7 Click the Design tab.

8 Click Move Chart.

The Move Chart dialog box appears.

9 Click where you want to move the chart (○ changes to ◉).

10 Type a Name.

11 Click OK.

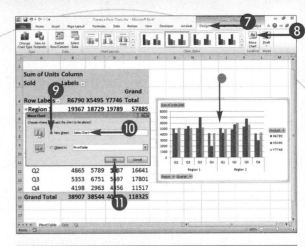

Excel moves the chart.

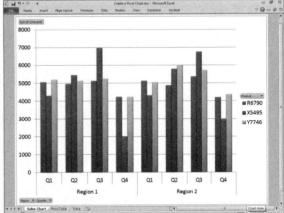

Extra

To save time, you can create a PivotChart when you create a PivotTable. Select the data on which you want to base your PivotTable. Click the Insert tab. Click the down arrow (▾) under PivotTable. Click PivotChart. The Create PivotTable with PivotChart dialog box appears. Choose where you want to place the PivotTable and PivotChart. Click OK. Excel creates the structure for PivotTable and PivotChart. Use the PivotTable Field List to create your PivotTable. As you do, Excel creates your PivotChart.

With a Standard Chart, you can click the Design tab. Click Select Data in the Data group and then click Switch/Row column to switch the row/column orientation. You cannot use the Select Data Source dialog box to switch the row/column orientation in a PivotChart. However, you can click the Switch Row/Column button in the Data group to make the switch.

In a standard chart, you can use the Select Data Source dialog box to change the chart data range. You cannot change the data range for a PivotChart by using the Select Data Source dialog box.

Filter a PivotChart

PivotCharts have filter buttons that you can use to sort and filter the data in your PivotChart. Changes you make to your PivotChart are automatically reflected in your PivotTable. For example, if your chart displays Region 1 and Region 2, you can filter it so that it only displays Region 1. When you filter your PivotChart, you also filter your PivotTable. Therefore, your PivotTable will also only display Region 1.

PivotCharts have Axis fields and Legend fields. You can use these fields to filter your PivotChart. Axis fields correspond to the Row Label fields in the PivotTable Field List. Axis Field categories appear on an axis of a PivotChart. For example, if the Row Labels in your

PivotTable are Region and Quarter, Region and Quarter will appear on the Axis of your chart. You can use the Axis filter button to filter the data on the axis.

Legend fields correspond to the Column Label fields in the PivotTable Field List. Legend fields appear in the Legend of your PivotChart. They are the data series in your chart. You can use Legend filter buttons to filter the legend data. For example, if the Column Label in your PivotTable is Product, you can use the Legend filter button to filter products.

If your PivotTable has a report filter, you can also use it to filter your PivotChart. Report filters appear in the Report Filter box of the PivotTable Field List.

Filter a PivotChart

① Click a filter button.

● Axis Filter buttons

● Legend Filter buttons

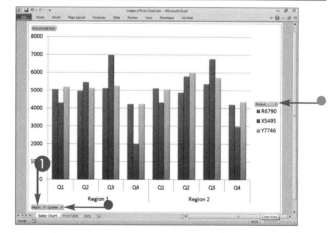

● The Sort and Filter dialog box appears.

② Click an option to deselect the fields you want to filter (☑ change to ☐).

③ Click OK.

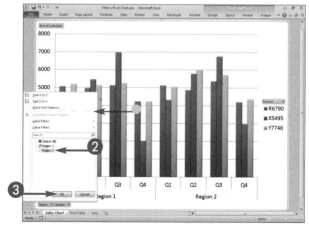

- Excel Filters your PivotChart.

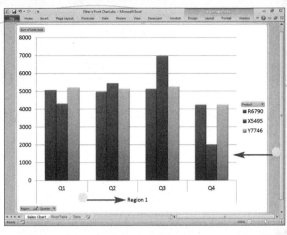

- Excel filters your PivotTable.

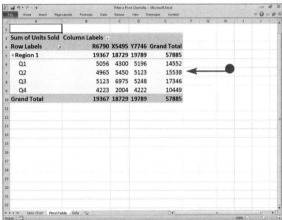

Paste Link into Word

You can place Excel data in other programs. In Word, for example, you can use Excel worksheet data to present quarterly reports or other financial documents. In PowerPoint, you can use Excel worksheet data to illustrate your presentations.

You can add Excel worksheet data to Word or PowerPoint by using the Copy and Paste commands. The Copy command copies the Excel data. The Paste command places the copy in another document. When you copy and paste, if you make changes to the original Excel document, you must go into the Word or PowerPoint document and update it as well.

You can also place Excel data in Word or PowerPoint by using a paste link. When you use a paste link, if you alter Excel data from Word or PowerPoint, Office automatically

updates the Excel source document. The opposite is also true. When you alter paste-linked data in Excel, Office automatically updates the linked Word or PowerPoint document. Paste linking enables you to keep your documents in sync because you do not have to worry about coordinating the changes in one document with changes in the other document. To paste link your documents, use the Paste Special command. You have two options when paste linking data: paste link as a picture or as an icon. Choosing picture displays a picture of your worksheet. Choosing icon displays an icon.

To edit a paste-linked Excel worksheet in Word or PowerPoint, double-click the worksheet picture or icon. When you do, Microsoft Word or PowerPoint automatically opens the document in Excel and makes all the Excel commands available so you can edit the document.

Paste Link into Word

① Select the range you want to paste link.

② Click the Home tab.

③ Click the Copy button (📋).

● Switch to the Word or PowerPoint document.

④ Click the Home tab.

⑤ Click the down arrow (▼) under Paste.

⑥ Click Paste Special.

The Paste Special dialog box appears.

⑦ Click the Paste link option (◉ changes to ◉).

● Click the Display as icon option if you want to display your document as an icon (☐ changes to ✔).

⑧ Click Microsoft Office Excel Worksheet Object.

⑨ Click OK.

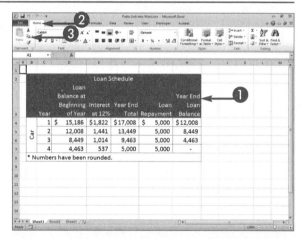

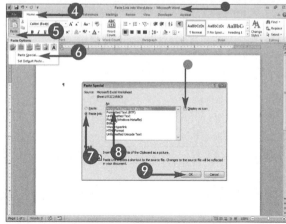

A picture of the worksheet appears in Word.

If you chose Display as Icon, the icon appears.

⑩ Double-click the worksheet to edit it.

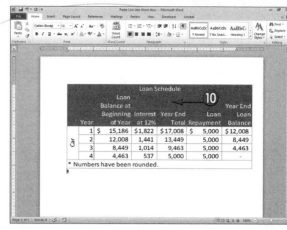

● Your worksheet opens in Excel and you can make any necessary edits.

When you have completed your edits, save and close your Excel document and return to your Word document.

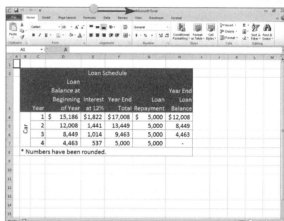

Extra

If you paste linked your worksheet as a picture and you want to display it as an icon instead, or vice versa, right-click the icon or picture. A menu appears. Click Linked Worksheet Object and then click Convert. The Convert dialog box appears. Select Display as icon (☐ changes to ✔) to display your worksheet as an icon. Deselect Display as Icon (✔ changes to ☐) to display your worksheet as a picture.

You can paste link a Word document into Excel. You select the data in Word you want to paste link, click the Home tab, and then click the Copy button. You then move to Excel and click the Home tab, click the down arrow under Paste, and then click Paste Special. The Paste Special dialog box appears. Click Paste Link, click Microsoft Office Word Document Object, and then click OK. Your Word document appears in Excel, and you can double-click your Word document to edit it.

Embed a Worksheet

As you present a PowerPoint presentation or change a Word document, you can edit Excel worksheets without leaving PowerPoint or Word. This means you can demonstrate different business scenarios as you give your PowerPoint presentation or do sophisticated mathematical calculations while in Word. To use this feature, you must embed your Excel worksheet into your PowerPoint or Word file.

When you embed an Excel worksheet, the embedded Excel worksheet becomes part of the PowerPoint or Word document and is accessible only through PowerPoint or Word. There is no link between the embedded document and the original document and, in that way, embedding differs from paste linking. When you make changes to an embedded Excel document, the changes only affect the

PowerPoint or Word document. When you make changes to a paste linked Excel document, the changes affect both the original Excel document and the Word or PowerPoint document. See the previous section, "Paste Link into Word," for more information on paste linking.

You can embed an existing Excel file or generate a new file entirely within PowerPoint or Word. To embed an Excel file, use the Insert Object dialog box. You can choose to have embedded worksheets display as a picture or as an icon. As with paste-linked worksheets, if you choose Display as Icon, Excel gives you several icons from which to choose. You just click the Change Icon button and then select an icon.

If you choose to embed an existing file, you can use the Insert Object dialog box to browse for the file.

Embed a Worksheet

① Open PowerPoint.

Note: *This example uses PowerPoint. You can follow similar steps to embed your document in Word.*

② Click the Insert tab.

③ Click Object.

The Insert Object dialog box appears.

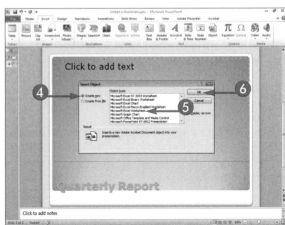

④ Click the Create new option (⬜ changes to ◉) to generate a new worksheet.

Alternatively, click Create from file to open an existing workbook.

⑤ Click Microsoft Office Excel Worksheet.

⑥ Click OK.

A blank worksheet appears.

- All the Microsoft Excel commands are available to you.

⑦ Create your worksheet.

⑧ Click outside the worksheet when you have finished.

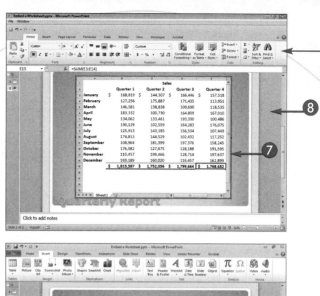

- Your completed worksheet appears in your PowerPoint presentation.

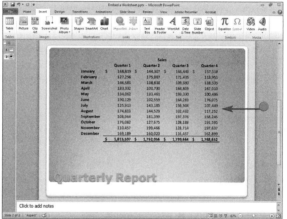

Hyperlink a Worksheet

You are probably familiar with the many benefits of hyperlinks on Web pages. When you click a link, you jump to a new Web page with more links, creating an enormous and seamless web of information. Like most Office applications, Excel also lets you create links. These links can take users to a place in the same workbook, to a document created by another Office application, or even to a Web page. For example, creating a hyperlink to a Word document provides an alternative to annotating worksheets by using comments and text boxes. Unlike comments, a linked Word document can be of any length and complexity. Unlike text boxes, hyperlinks do not obstruct worksheets or distract readers.

Hyperlinking a document is different from paste linking. Instead of pulling data created by another application into

Excel, a hyperlink jumps you from a worksheet to a related document.

To create a hyperlink, use the Insert Hyperlink dialog box. In the Text to display field, type the text you want to appear in the hyperlinked cell. The ScreenTip button opens the Set Hyperlink ScreenTip dialog box. Use this dialog box to enter the text that appears as users move the mouse pointer over the hyperlink. By default, the address of the linked-to file appears. In the Address field, type the filename of the file to which you want to link or the Web address of the Web page to which you want to link. The Edit Hyperlink dialog box has buttons to help you find the file or Web page you want. Click Current Folder to search the current folder, click Browsed Pages to review files you have browsed, and click Recent Files to review files you have recently opened.

Hyperlink a Worksheet

1 Click in a cell.

2 Click the Insert tab.

3 Click Hyperlink.

   The Insert Hyperlink dialog box appears.

4 Click a Link to location.

5 Type the text you want to display.

6 Click the ▼ and then select a folder.

7 Click a Look in option to choose where to search.

8 Click a file.

   You can click the ScreenTip button to enter the text that appears when you hover your mouse pointer over the hyperlink.

9 Click OK.

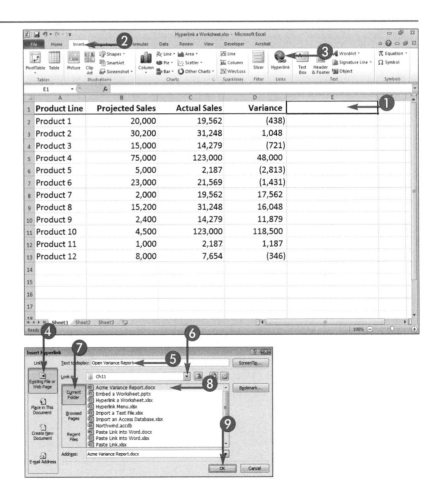

Your Text to display entry appears as a hyperlink.

⑩ Click the link.

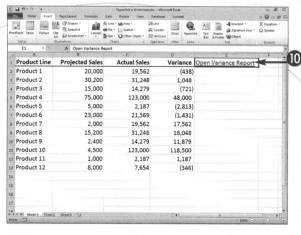

The linked-to document appears.

⑪ Click the Close button (⊠) to close the document.

Office returns you to Excel.

To remove the hyperlink, right-click the linked worksheet cell and then click Remove Hyperlink.

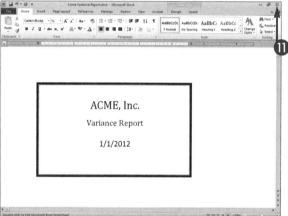

Apply It

Adding a hyperlink to another area of your workbook can help you move around your workbook quickly. For example, if you have sales figures for different regions in a single workbook on separate worksheet, you can create a menu of links that will quickly take you to the information you want.

To create an internal workbook hyperlink, move to the cell in which you want to place the link. Click the Insert tab. Click Hyperlink. The Insert Hyperlink dialog box appears. Click Place in This Document in the Link To area. Type the text you want to appear in the cell in the Text to display field. Type the cell you want to move to in the Type the Cell Reference field. Alternatively, click the sheet name in the Or Select a Place in this Document box to move to cell A1 of a particular sheet. If you have named ranges, you can also click a range name in the Or Select a Place in this Document box. When you have completed your entries, click OK. Excel creates your hyperlink.

Query a Web Site

nce you place data in Excel, you have complete access to Excel's data analysis and presentation tools, including functions, PivotTables, and charts. Excel gives you two options for placing Web-based tabular data in Excel. You can copy and paste the data from the Web into Excel or you can use a Web query.

Both techniques enable you to view and edit numbers, but querying a Web site has advantages. When you import data as a Web query, you can filter the data and view only records of interest. A Web query also enables you to refresh data if it is subject to updates.

The New Web Query dialog box works much like any Web browser. You type the address of a Web site and view the associated Web pages. The dialog box analyzes

each Web page and breaks the page into individual tables of data. Yellow arrow buttons display next to each section of the Web page. You click the buttons to identify the portion of the Web page you want to import. Excel only imports the text portion of the Web page. If you want to capture any of the graphics, you must do so by using the Copy and Paste commands.

You must tell Excel where to place Web data. By default, Excel selects the active cell. If the existing worksheet contains data, Excel adds enough columns to hold the imported data. Any existing worksheet data moves to the right, into new columns. Alternatively, you can select the New worksheet option to create a new worksheet for the data. If you create a new worksheet, Excel inserts the worksheet in the current workbook.

Query a Web Site

① Click the Data tab.

② Click From Web.

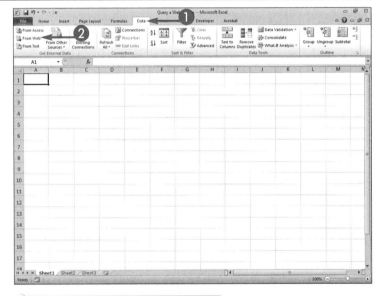

The New Web Query dialog box appears.

③ Type the Web address.

This example uses www.fec.gov/finance/precm8.htm.

④ Click Go.

The Web page appears in the dialog box.

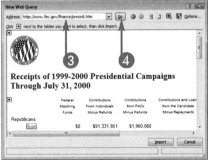

⑤ Click the elements that you want to appear in your worksheet.

A check mark indicates you want an element.

● An arrow indicates you do not want an element.

⑥ Click Import.

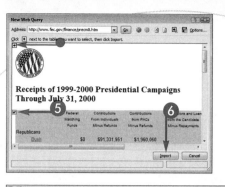

The Import Data dialog box appears.

⑦ Click a worksheet option to select a location for the imported page (◎ changes to ◉).

● If you select Existing worksheet, enter the cell that represents the upper-left cell of the data area.

⑧ Click OK.

● The selected Web elements appear within Excel, ready for analysis, charting, and so on.

● Click Refresh All on the Data tab to refresh your data.

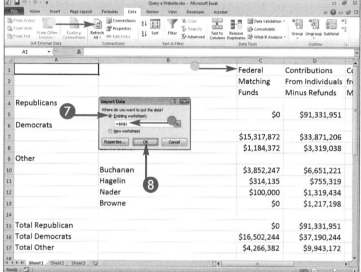

Extra

You can import the text formatting along with the Web page data. Click the Options button in the upper-right corner of the New Web Query dialog box. In the Web Query Options dialog box that appears, select one of the following formatting options.

FORMATTING	DESCRIPTION
None	Imports the text only and applies the Normal format style
Rich Text	Imports the text with the formatting on the Web page
Full HTML	Imports the text with all HTML styles, including links

A *query* is a file containing a definition of the data you import into Excel from an external source. The query definition indicates the data source, the rows to include, how rows added to the source are accommodated by the query, and the frequency with which the data is updated. You can view and modify query properties by clicking the Data tab and then clicking Properties.

Import a Text File

Many software applications have an option you can use to export the application's data to a text file. You can import text files from other applications into Excel by using the Text Import Wizard. You can then use Excel's sophisticated data analysis capabilities to analyze the data. In fact, once you have imported the data, you can use it in a PivotTable, create charts with it, or manipulate it just as you would any other Excel data.

The Text Import Wizard can handle any delimited or fixed-width file. A *delimited* file uses a comma, semicolon, tab, space, or other character to mark the end of each column. A *fixed-width* file aligns each column and gives each column a defined width. A space usually separates the columns.

You start the import of a text file by using the Import Text File dialog box to locate the file you want to import. Text files created by other software applications may be in one of many popular file formats. You can identify the file format by the file extension. Programs usually use commas to delimit files with a .csv extension. Another popular extension is .txt. The exporting program usually delimits .txt files with tabs.

After you locate your file, Excel opens the Text Import Wizard. You must tell Excel whether you are importing a fixed-width file or a delimited file. If you are importing a fixed-width file, you tell Excel exactly where each column begins by clicking the location in the Data Preview window. Excel inserts a break line. You can adjust the location of the line or delete the line.

Import a Text File

① Click the Data tab.

② Click From Text.

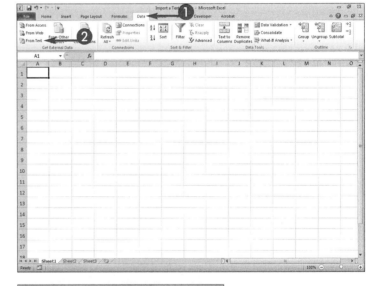

The Import Text File dialog box appears.

③ Click here and then locate the folder in which you stored your file.

④ Click the file.

⑤ Click Import.

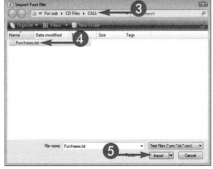

The Text Import Wizard appears.

⑥ Click a file type to select the one that best describes your data (◉ changes to ◉).

⑦ Type the row at which to begin importing.

⑧ Click Next.

⑨ Click a delimiter to select the type your data uses (☐ changes to ✔).

⑩ Click the ▾ and then select the text qualifier your data uses.

⑪ Click Next.

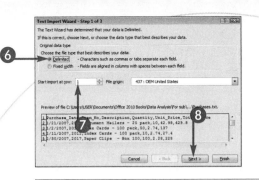

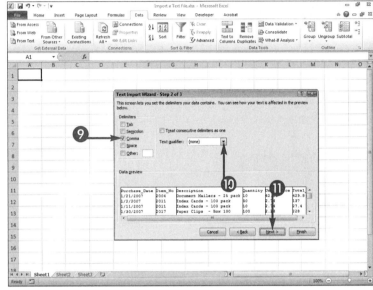

Apply It

You may find you want to import Excel data into another application that accepts text files. You can use the following steps to export an Excel file as a text file. Click the File tab. A menu appears. Click Save As. The Save As dialog box appears. In the Save In field, select the folder in which you want to save your file. In the Save as Type field, select a text format such as Formatted Text (Space delimited) (*.prn), CSV (Comma delimited) (*.csv), or any one of the many other text formats, including the *.txt formats. Type the filename you want to give the file in the Filename field and then click Save. A dialog box appears telling you Excel will only save the active sheet. Click OK. Another dialog box appears warning you that any feature incompatible with a text file will be lost. Click Yes. Excel saves your file as a text file.

continued ➡

ou can use the Start Import at Row field to specify the row that you want to begin the import with. If your data has titles or other information you do not want to import at the top of the file, you can skip those rows. Excel uses the Preview window to provide you with a preview of the import file. The Preview window numbers each row.

If you are importing a delimited file, you tell Excel the type of delimiters the file uses on the second page of the Text Import Wizard. You can specify more than one delimiter. Some delimited file formats surround text data with a text qualifier, such as single or double quotes. You can use the Text Qualifier field to tell Excel whether your data has a text qualifier and, if so, what the qualifier is.

After you have defined the layout of your data, you must define the data type contained in each column. You have three options: general, text, and date. General converts numeric data to numbers, dates to dates, and everything else to text. If you have numeric data that is text, use the text option to have Excel convert the data to text. If you have dates, click the date option and specify the format you want to use. If there is a column you do not want to import, click the Do not import column option.

In the Import Data dialog box, you must tell Excel where you want to place your imported text file. You can choose an existing worksheet or a new worksheet. If you choose Existing worksheet, you must specify the starting cell. If you choose New worksheet, Excel begins the data placement in cell A1 of a new worksheet.

Import a Text File (continued)

⑫ Click the column head.

⑬ Click a column data format option to select a data type or to skip a column (◉ changes to ◉).

Repeat Steps 12 and 13 for each column.

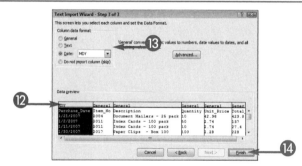

⑭ Click Finish.

The Import Data dialog box appears.

⑮ Click a worksheet option to select where you want to put your data (◉ changes to ◉).

● If you selected Existing worksheet, click a cell or type a cell address.

⑯ Click OK.

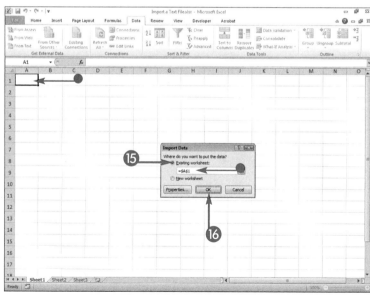

Excel imports the data.

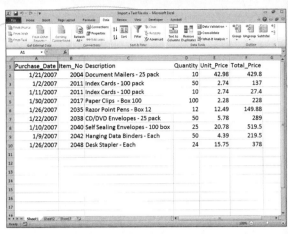

You can format and analyze your data.

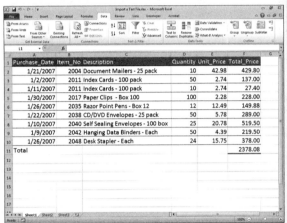

Apply It

Excel has an option you can use to break cells into columns. The feature works a lot like the Text Import Wizard. You select the cells you want to divide and then click the Data tab. In the Data Tools group, click Text to Columns. The Convert Text to Columns Wizard appears. Select whether your cells are delimited or of fixed width. Click Next.

If your cells are delimited, on page 2 of the wizard, select the delimiter and enter the text qualifier. Click the Treat consecutive delimiters as one check box (□ changes to ✔) if that is what you want to do. Click Next. Assign formats to each column, select a destination for the output, and then click Finish. Excel breaks your cells into columns.

If your cells are fixed width, on page 2 of the wizard, click in the Data Preview box to place a line between columns. Click Next. Assign formats to each column, select a destination for the output, and then click Finish. Excel breaks your cells into columns.

Import an Access Database

Many organizations use more than one application to manage tabular data. Excel is best for managing, analyzing, and presenting numbers. Databases such as Access help you store, filter, and retrieve large quantities of data of every type. With Excel, you can apply easy-to-use data analysis techniques to complex Access databases.

Instead of using worksheets, in Access, you must carefully organize your information into data tables, each of which stores information about one part of the entity of interest to you: customers, products, employees, transactions, and so on. To help keep track of these tables in Access, you create unique identifiers, called *keys*. Access can automatically assign keys to each customer, product, employee, transaction, and so on. The keys link tables to each other.

You can import an Access data table and analyze your Access data in Excel. You start the import process by selecting the Access database from which you want to import data. Excel presents you with a list of the tables found in that database. You select the table you want to import. You then choose how you want to view the data. You can choose from Table, PivotTable Report, and PivotChart and PivotTable Report. The Table option brings the data into your worksheet as a table. See Chapter 8 to learn more about tables. The PivotTable Report option connects to your table and makes your data ready for you to use in a PivotTable report. It does not import the table as a list. See Chapter 9 to learn more about PivotTables. The PivotChart and PivotTable Report option connects to your table and imports your data, ready to be used in a PivotChart and PivotTable. It does not import the table as a list. See Chapter 10 to learn more about PivotCharts.

Import an Access Database

① Click the Data tab.

② Click From Access.

   The Select Data Source dialog box appears.

③ Click here and locate the folder in which your Access database is located.

④ Click to select your database.

⑤ Click Open.

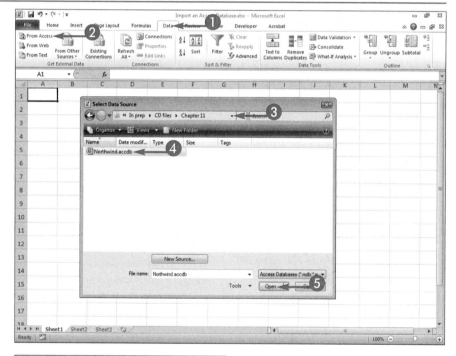

   The Select Table dialog box appears.

⑥ Click the table you want to open.

⑦ Click OK.

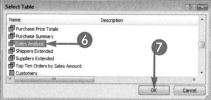

The Import Data dialog box appears.

8 Click an import option to select how you want to view your data (◎ changes to ◉).

9 Click a worksheet option to select where you want to put your data (◎ changes to ◉).

● If you selected Existing worksheet, click a cell or type a cell address.

10 Click OK.

Your data appears in Excel.

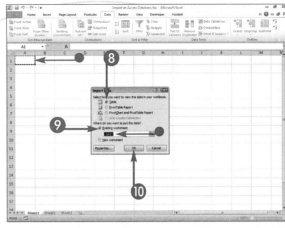

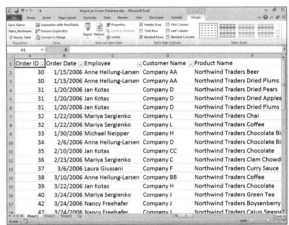

Extra

You can copy and paste Access data into Excel. In Access, click the Home tab, click View, and then click Datasheet View. Drag your mouse pointer over the column labels to select the columns you want to copy. On the Home tab, click the Copy button. Move to Excel. Click where you want to place your Access table. On the Home tab, click Paste. Excel pastes your data.

Importing your data into Excel has an advantage over copying and pasting your data into Excel. When you import your data, you make a connection between your data and the Access database. You can refresh your data so that any changes made to the Access database appear in Excel. To refresh your data manually, click Refresh All on the Data tab and then click Refresh.

You can tell Excel how you want to refresh your data. Click the Properties button in the Import Data dialog box. The Connection Properties dialog box appears. If you want to be able to use Excel while your data is refreshing, click Enable Background Refresh. If you want to refresh at certain intervals, click Refresh and enter the interval in minutes. If you want to refresh when the file opens, click Refresh Data When Opening File.

Query an
Access Database

The Query Wizard is part of Microsoft Query, a separate application that comes with Microsoft Office. Microsoft Query makes it easy for you to generate queries in Structured Query Language (SQL), a standard in the corporate world.

The Query Wizard provides a point-and-click interface for importing tables or selected columns into Excel. You start the process in the Choose Data Source dialog box by selecting MS Access Database as your data source and telling Excel you want to use the Query Wizard to create or edit queries. You then locate the database you want to use. The Query Wizard displays a list of tables and columns found in the database. You can select one or more tables and/or columns to query. You can also preview the data in the individual fields of your tables. Your columns will appear in Excel in the order listed in

the Columns in Your Query field in the Choose Columns dialog box. You can adjust the order of the fields.

Once you have selected the columns or tables you want, you can filter and sort. The Query Wizard provides 16 comparison operators. In addition, you can create multiple filters by using And and Or.

Use Or when you want the wizard to select data that meets either of the specified conditions. For example, ask the wizard to select all dresses that are blue or all dresses that have red buttons. The wizard returns every blue dress and every dress with red buttons. Alternatively, ask the wizard to select all dresses that are blue and have red buttons. The And selection criteria are more restrictive. The wizard returns only items that meet both selection criteria: blue dresses with red buttons.

Query an Access Database

Note: You must install the New Database Query button (🗔) on the Quick Access Toolbar or on a Custom tab. See Chapter 17 to learn how.

1. Click the New Database Query button (🗔).

   The Choose Data Source dialog box appears.

2. Click the Databases tab.

3. Click MS Access Database.

4. Click OK.

   The Select Database dialog box appears.

5. Click the folder in which you stored your database.

6. Click your database.

7. Click OK.

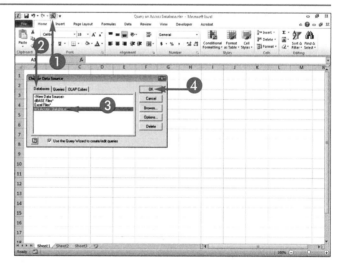

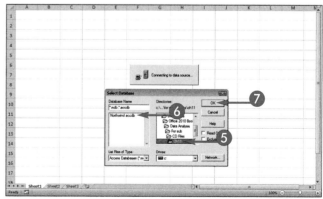

The Query Wizard - Choose Columns dialog box appears.

⑧ Click the table and/or fields you want to import.

⑨ Click the Add button.

If you want to open more than one table, repeat Steps 8 and 9.

⑩ Click Next.

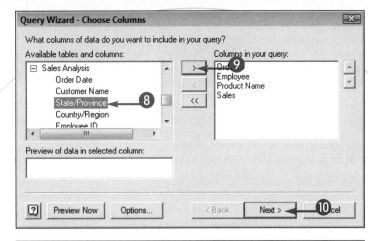

The Query Wizard - Filter Data dialog box appears.

⑪ Click the column by which you want to filter.

⑫ Click the ▾ and select a comparison operator.

⑬ Click the ▾ and then select the criteria by which you want to filter.

● You can apply additional filters.

● You can use And and/or Or (◉ changes to ◉).

⑭ Click Next.

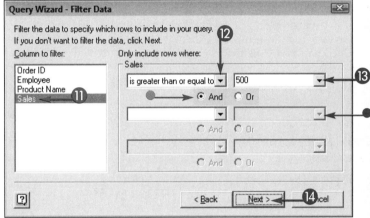

Extra

You use the Choose Data Source dialog box to import an Access database. To open the Choose Data Source dialog box, you click the New Database Query button on the Quick Access Toolbar or you click the Data tab, click From Other Sources in the Get External Data group, and then click From Microsoft Query.

If you import fields from more than one table, you may need to tell Microsoft Query how to join the tables. Microsoft Query provides a sophisticated interface to help you. On the final page of the wizard, if you click View Data or Edit Query In (◉ changes to ◉) and then click Finish, the Microsoft Query interface appears. You can use it to edit your query. Click Help on the Microsoft Query menu to learn how to use this function.

Filtering data improves performance when you are working with large databases. Using Microsoft Query can speed up performance. If you work with large databases and want to apply numerous filters and sort orders, MS Query is worth learning.

continued ➡

With the Query Wizard, you can sort your data and create sorts within sorts. For example, you can alphabetize a list of employees and products as follows: first in alphabetical order by employee, then in alphabetical order by product.

After you import the data into Excel, you can use Excel's tools to further sort and filter. You can go beyond the wizard and directly manipulate the Access tables.

On the final page of the Query Wizard, click View Data or Edit Query in Microsoft Query and then click Finish for a graphical view of the underlying data tables. You can work directly with criteria fields, add tables, and connect tables by shared fields. You can also run and view queries. When you have finished, you can save the query.

Saved queries become available in Excel for viewing, analyzing, charting, and so on.

You can choose how you want to view your data in Excel. You can view it as a table, a PivotTable report, or a PivotChart and PivotTable report. The Table option brings the data into your worksheet as a table. See Chapter 8 to learn more about tables. The PivotTable Report option connects to your table and makes your data ready for you to use in a PivotTable report. It does not import the table as a list. See Chapter 9 to learn more about PivotTables. The PivotChart and PivotTable Report option connects to your table and imports your data, ready to be used in a PivotChart and PivotTable report. It does not import the table as a list. See Chapter 10 to learn more about PivotCharts.

Query an Access Database (continued)

⑮ Click the ▾ and select the column by which you want to sort your data.

⑯ Click Ascending or Descending order (◉ changes to ◉).

● Optionally, you can add additional sort criteria.

⑰ Click Next.

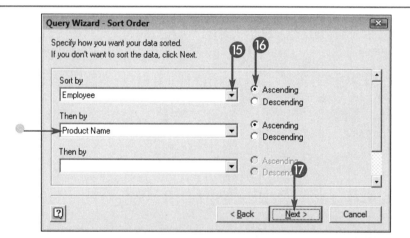

The Query Wizard – Finish dialog box appears.

⑱ Click Return Data to Microsoft Office Excel (◉ changes to ◉).

○ Click View data or edit query in Microsoft Query and then click Finish for a graphical view of the underlying data tables.

● Click here to save your query.

⑲ Click Finish.

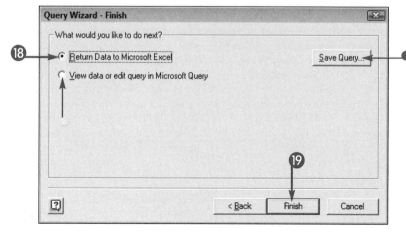

The Import Data dialog box appears.

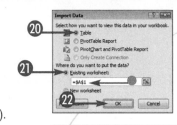

20 Click an import option to select how you want to view your data (◉ changes to ◉).

21 Click to select where you want to place your data (◉ changes to ◉).

● If you chose Existing worksheet, click and drag to select a range, or type a range.

22 Click OK.

Your Access data appears in Excel.

	A	B	C	D	E	F
1	Order ID	Employee	Product Name	Sales		
2	79	Andrew Cencini	Northwind Traders Dried Apples	1590		
3	79	Andrew Cencini	Northwind Traders Dried Pears	900		
4	30	Anne Hellung-Larsen	Northwind Traders Beer	1400		
5	77	Anne Hellung-Larsen	Northwind Traders Boysenberry Spread	2250		
6	76	Anne Hellung-Larsen	Northwind Traders Cajun Seasoning	660		
7	38	Anne Hellung-Larsen	Northwind Traders Coffee	13800		
8	51	Anne Hellung-Larsen	Northwind Traders Crab Meat	552		
9	51	Anne Hellung-Larsen	Northwind Traders Olive Oil	533.75		
10	39	Jan Kotas	Northwind Traders Chocolate	1275		
11	31	Jan Kotas	Northwind Traders Dried Apples	530		
12	58	Jan Kotas	Northwind Traders Marmalade	3240		
13	37	Laura Giussani	Northwind Traders Curry Sauce	680		
14	75	Mariya Sergienko	Northwind Traders Chocolate	510		
15	36	Mariya Sergienko	Northwind Traders Clam Chowder	1930		
16	32	Mariya Sergienko	Northwind Traders Coffee	920		
17	48	Mariya Sergienko	Northwind Traders Curry Sauce	1000		
18	40	Mariya Sergienko	Northwind Traders Green Tea	598		

Extra

By saving your query, you can quickly retrieve data. To save, click Save Query on the final page of the Query Wizard. The Save As dialog box appears. In the Save In field, locate the folder in which you want to save your query. Name your query in the Filename field. Click Save. Excel saves your query.

To retrieve a saved query, click the Data tab and then click Existing Connections in the Get External Data group. The Existing Connections dialog box appears. Click the name of your saved query. Click Open. The Import Data dialog box appears. Click a radio button (◉ changes to ◉) to select how you want to view your data. Click a radio button (◉ changes to ◉) to select where you want to place your data. Click OK. Excel imports your data.

Refreshing updates the data so you can see any changes made to your data in Access since the last refresh. To refresh your data, click the Data tab and then click Refresh All. Excel refreshes your data.

To delete a saved query, click the New Database Query button on the Quick Access Toolbar to open the Choose Data Source dialog box. Click the Queries tab. Click your query and then click Delete.

Perform
What-If Analysis

By using the Internal Rate of Return (IRR) function, you can find out how a change in the amount loaned, payment amount, or payment date — or some combination of these factors — affects the interest received. You can type in different amounts at different payment dates to see how different scenarios affect the interest rate.

What-if analysis is a systematic way of finding out how a change in one or more scenarios affects the result. The Scenario Manager lets you vary one or more inputs into any formula or function to see how the result changes.

There are two ways to use the scenario manager. You can click a scenario in the Scenario Manager dialog box and then click Show. Excel displays the scenario and the result in your worksheet. When you use this method, Excel

changes the values in your worksheet to the values in your scenario. If your original worksheet data is not one of your scenario options, it will be lost. Alternatively, you can create a summary report. A summary report displays each of your scenarios in a different column, in a new worksheet. With a summary report, you can compare scenarios side by side.

The beauty of the Scenario Manager is that it stores a series of values so you can see how each value or combination of values influences the result. You can also present your information as a PivotTable and thereby give yourself all the flexibility a PivotTable offers. To learn more about PivotTables, see Chapter 9.

To create scenarios, you must first enter the values required into a worksheet and type a formula that calculates the answer. The example uses the IRR function.

Perform What-If Analysis

① Click and drag to select the cells that contain the values you want to vary.

② Click the Data tab.

③ Click What-If Analysis.

④ Click Scenario Manager.

The Scenario Manager dialog box appears.

⑤ Click Add.

● The Add Scenario dialog box appears, showing the cells selected in Step 1.

⑥ Type a name for your scenario.

⑦ Click OK.

The Scenario Values dialog box appears.

⑧ Type the scenario values.

⑨ Click Add to create more scenarios.

The Add Scenario dialog box reappears.

⑩ Click OK instead of Add when you finish entering scenarios.

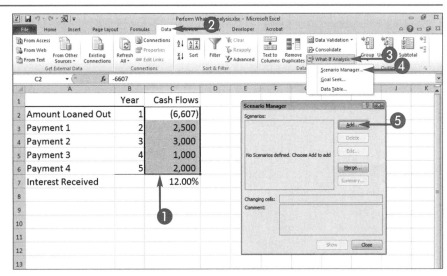

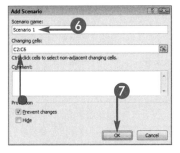

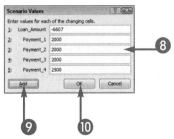

The Scenario Manager dialog box appears.

⑪ Click Summary.

The Scenario Summary dialog box appears.

● Alternatively, click a scenario and then click Show to display the scenario in your worksheet.

⑫ Click a Report type option (☐ changes to ✔).

⑬ Enter the field that calculates the results.

⑭ Click OK.

The type of report you requested appears in a new worksheet, displaying how each value affects the result.

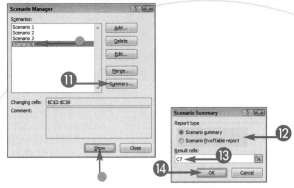

1 2		Scenario Summary						
			Current Values:	Scenario 1	Scenario 2	Scenario 3	Scenario 4	
		Changing Cells:						
		Loan_Amount	(6,607)	(6,607)	(6,607)	(6,607)	(6,607)	
		Payment_1	2,500	2,000	2,500	5,000	1,000	
		Payment_2	3,000	2,000	2,000	1,000	1,000	
		Payment_3	1,000	2,000	2,000	1,000	1,000	
		Payment_4	2,000	2,500	2,000	1,500	5,000	
		Result Cells:						
		Interest_Received	12.00%	10.50%	11.36%	15.12%	6.13%	

Notes: Current Values column represents values of changing cells at time Scenario Summary Report was created. Changing cells for each scenario are highlighted in gray.

Apply It

If you name the cells in your original worksheet, your Scenario Summary becomes easier to read because Excel displays the cell name instead of the cell address. For example, in this section, cell C2 is named Loan_Amount, cells C3 through C6 are named Payment_1 through Payment_4, and cell B7 is named Interest_Received. To learn how to name cells, see Chapter 4.

If you share copies of a workbook and people add their own scenarios, you can merge these scenarios into a single list. To do so, open the workbooks and click Data and then Scenario Manager. In the Scenario Manager, click Merge. In the Merge Scenarios window, select the workbooks and individual worksheets to consolidate, and then Click OK.

You can use the Scenario Manager dialog box to edit and delete scenarios. Click the Data tab, click What-If Analysis in the Data Tools group, and then click Scenario Manager. The Scenario Manager dialog box appears. Click a scenario and then click Delete to delete a scenario. Click a scenario and then click Edit to edit a scenario.

Optimize a Result with Goal Seek

Goal Seek is a powerful tool you can use to find a way to reach your goals. With Goal Seek, you tell Excel which value in your formula you want to change; Excel then adjusts that value to give you the result you want. For example, if you need a loan for a new home and your goal is to make a monthly payment of a specific amount, you can use Goal Seek to show you how you can reach your goal by adjusting one of the loan terms. You can have Goal Seek find the interest rate required to reach your payment goal, given a loan amount and number of payments, find the loan amount required to reach your goal, given an interest rate and number of payments, or find the number of payments required to reach your goal, given an interest rate and loan amount.

In the Goal Seek dialog box, the Set Cell field tells Excel which cell contains the formula with a value you want to manipulate to achieve your goal. The To Value field tells Excel what your goal is. The By Changing Cell field tells Excel the cell that contains the value you want to change. The cell address you enter in the By Changing Cell field must be included in the formula you reference in the Set Cell field. If you are not getting a result, you can try clicking the Office button, clicking Excel Options, and then clicking Formulas. Then in the Calculations Options area, increase the maximum iterations. This example uses the Payment (PMT) function.

Optimize a Result with Goal Seek

1. Click the cell that contains the value you want to reach.

2. Click the Data tab.

3. Click What-If Analysis.

   A menu appears.

4. Click Goal Seek.

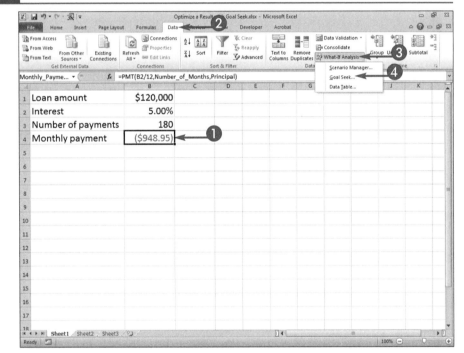

The Goal Seek dialog box appears.

5. Enter the value you want to reach.

6. Enter the value you want to change to reach your goal.

7. Click OK.

The results appear in the worksheet.

8 Click OK to accept the change.

● Alternatively, you can click Cancel to restore the original values.

Excel changes you worksheet.

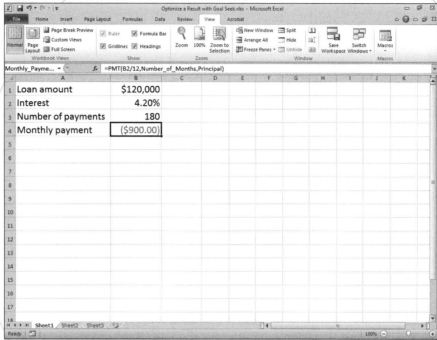

	A	B
1	Loan amount	$120,000
2	Interest	4.20%
3	Number of payments	180
4	Monthly payment	($900.00)

Extra

Not all goals can be reached. If Goal Seek returns the message saying it cannot find a solution, you may have entered a goal that cannot be reached or Excel may need more iterations to solve the problem. To change the maximum iterations, click the Microsoft Office button. A menu appears. Click Options. The Excel Options dialog box appears. Click Formulas. The Change Options Related to Formula Calculations, Performance, and Error Handling pane appears. Increase the Maximum Iterations. Click OK and then try Goal Seek again.

To vary multiple inputs to achieve a specific goal, you must use Solver. To add the Solver add-in to Microsoft Excel, click the Office button. A menu appears. Click Options. The Excel Options dialog box appears. Click Add-Ins. The View and Manage Microsoft Office Add-Ins dialog box appears. Click the add-in you want. In this case, click Solver Add-in. Click Go. The Add-ins dialog box appears. Click Solver-Add-in. Click OK. The Solver add-in appears on the Add-Ins tab ready for you to use.

Using Solver

To vary multiple inputs to achieve a specific goal, use Solver. For example, if you want to find out how to adjust both the loan amount and interest rate so that you can reduce a monthly loan payment to from $900.00 to $850.00, you can use Solver.

When using Solver, you must establish a *target* cell. The target cell is the cell that contains the formula that calculates the goal you want to reach. In this example, it is the cell that contains the payment amount. You must also establish one or more *adjustable* cells. These are the cells that Solver can change to reach your goal. In this example, the adjustable cells would be the loan amount and the interest rate. The formula in the target cell must directly or indirectly reference the adjustable cells.

You enter Solver parameters in the Solver Parameters dialog box. In the To field, select Max if you want the target field to be the highest possible value; select Min if you want the target field to be the lowest possible value; and select Value if you want the target field to be a specific value, and then type the value in the field.

When Solver finds a solution, you can choose either Keep Solver Solution or Restore Original Values. If you choose Keep Solver Solution, Excel permanently changes the worksheet. You cannot undo the changes.

Solver is an add-in. By default, it is not loaded. See Chapter 7 to learn how to load add-ins. Once loaded, Solver appears on the Data tab.

Using Solver

① Click the target cell.

② Click the Data tab.

③ Click Solver.

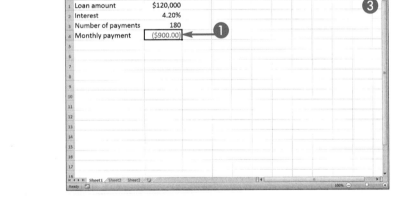

The Solver Parameters dialog box appears.

④ Enter the target cell.

⑤ Click the Value Of option (◎ changes to ◉) and enter the target amount.

⑥ Enter the adjustable cells.

⑦ Click Solve.

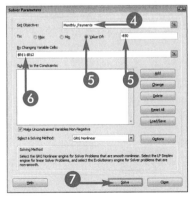

The Solver Results dialog box appears.

⑧ Click the Keep Solver Solution option to apply changes (◉ changes to ◉).

● Alternatively, click Restore Original Values to restore original values.

⑨ Click OK.

● Excels places the results in the worksheet.

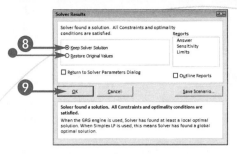

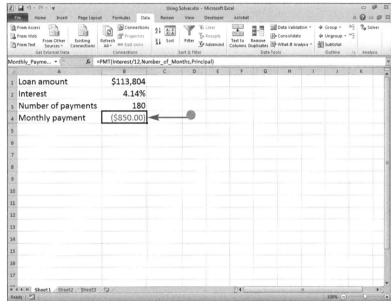

Extra

When using Solver, you can also enter *constraints*. Constraints limit the values Solver can use. For example, in the loan payment problem, a constraint might be that the loan amount must less than or equal to $100,000.

To define constraints, click the Add button in the Solver Parameters dialog box. The Add Constraints dialog box appears. In the Cell Reference field, specify the reference field. In the next field, select an operator. In the Constraint field, specify a comparison value. For example, you can enter the following:

CELL REFERENCE	OPERATOR	CONSTRAINT
B1	<=	100000

If B1 is the loan amount, this entry constrains the loan amount to <= 100000.

Solve a Formula with a Data Table

When you need to find out how changing certain values in your formula affects the outcome, you can use a data table. For example, if you want to create a worksheet that shows how different interest rates affect the amount you must pay monthly on a loan, use a data table. With a data table, you can create your worksheet without having to enter the same formula multiple times.

A data table contains at least two columns or two rows. If you use columns, the first column consists of the values you want to substitute into a formula. The first cell of the second column contains the formula you want to use. The formula must reference the first value in the first column. If you are varying interest rates so you can compare loan payments, and the first column (column A) contains the

interest rate you want to substitute in the PMT function, the Rate argument must reference column A, as shown in the following formula:

```
=PMT(A5/PeriodsPerYear, LoanTerm, -LoanAmount)
```

If you use rows to create your data table, place your substitution values in the first row. Place your formula in the first cell of the second row and reference the first cell of the first row in your formula.

If your data is set up in columns, use the Column input cell field in the Data Table dialog box to tell Excel the location of the cell referenced in your formula. If your data is set up in rows, use the Row input cell field in the Data Table dialog box to tell Excel the location of the cell referenced in your formula.

Solve a Formula with a Data Table

① Type the substitution values in a column.

You can also place values in a row.

② Type the formula in the first cell of the next column.

If your values are in a row, type the formula in the first cell in the row under the values.

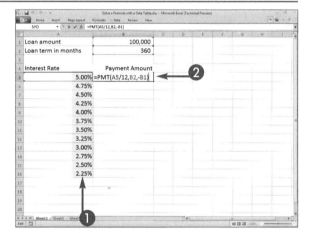

③ Select the cells containing substitution values, the formula, and the cells you want to fill.

④ Click the Data tab.

⑤ Click What-If Analysis.

A menu appears.

⑥ Click Data Table.

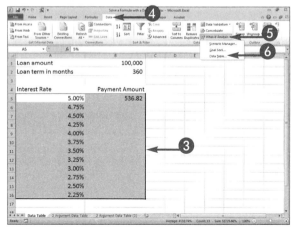

The Data Table dialog
box appears.

7 Click the cell, or type
the cell reference for
the first substitution
cell if you are using
columns.

● Type the cell reference
in this field if you are
using rows.

8 Click OK.

● Excel displays the
comparison results in
the second column of
the data table.

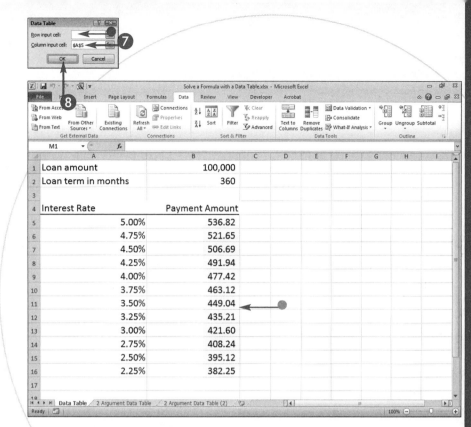

Apply It

If you want to substitute values for two arguments, you can create a two-input data table. In a two-input data
table, you specify the first set of substitution values in the column under the formula cell and the second set of
substitution values in the row to the right of the formula. For example, if you want to see how both interest rates
and length of the loan affect your payments, you specify the interest rates in the column under the formula and
the length of the loan values in the row next to the formula.

When you create a two-input data table, your formula must initially reference cells located outside the data table.
This means if your data table contains interest rates in a column, the formula must initially reference a cell outside
the column containing an interest rate value. In the Data Table dialog box, you specify both the row and column
initial input cells. To see an example of a two-input data table, refer to Solve a Formula with a Data Tables.xlsx,
which is on the Web site for this book.

Extend a Series with Auto Fill

Auto Fill gives you a way to enter data quickly when the data series follows a well-known pattern. For example, you can use Auto Fill to enter the days of the week, the months of the year, or numeric increments of two. All you have to do is enter the initial values and then drag the fill handle. Excel automatically fills the cell with the series. For example, if you want to enter the months of the year, type **January**, drag the fill handle and as you drag; Excel enters February, March, April, May, and so on. The Fill handle is the small black square in the lower-right corner of the selection area. When you move your mouse pointer over the fill handle, your mouse pointer turns into a cross.

Your fill can consist of numbers, dates, times, months of the year, days of the week, text, or formulas. By default,

when filling, Excel also copies the format. For example, if you type **Jan** in red and then click and drag the fill handle two cells, Excel fills Jan, Feb, Mar using red text. If you type **January** in a cell with a green background and white text, Excel fills January, February, March using a green background and white text.

After you fill the cells, the AutoFill button appears. Click the button to open a menu that enables you to change the fill. You can copy the initial value to each cell in the fill, fill with formatting only, fill without formatting, or fill with weekdays, months, or years, depending on the type of fill you created.

Extend a Series with Auto Fill

Fill with a Series

① Type the initial value for the series you want to create.

② Select a cell or cells.

③ Click the fill handle.

④ Drag the desired number of cells and then release the mouse button.

Excel fills the cells with a series.

The AutoFill Options button appears.

⑤ Click the AutoFill Options button (⊞▾).

A menu appears.

Use the menu to change the manner in which Excel fills the cells.

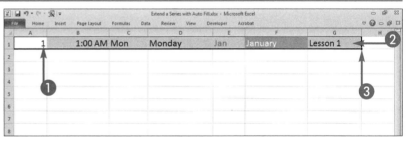

Fill with a Pattern

① Type a pattern.

② Repeat Steps 2 to 4 under Fill with a Series.

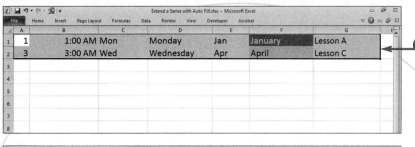

Excel fills the cells with the pattern.

Extra

When you release the mouse button after creating a series, the Auto Fill Options button appears. Click the button to view a menu of options. If you want to fill with the days of the week, you can click Fill Days to fill with Sunday through Saturday or Fill Weekdays to fill with Monday through Friday. You can also click the Fill Formatting Only option to change the formatting of the cell without changing the contents. Click the Fill Without Formatting option to change the contents of the filled cells without changing the formatting.

You can fill cells with a growth trend, such as 1, 3, 9, 27 or 2, 4, 8, 16. Type the first two values of the growth trend. Select the values you typed and all the cells you want to fill. Click the Home tab and then click the Fill button ( ). A menu appears. Click Series. The Series dialog box appears. Click Growth, click Trend, and then click OK. Excel fills the cells with your growth trend. To learn more about growth trends, see the section "Create a Trendline" in Chapter 10.

Join Text

I n Excel, you can join text, numbers, and cell references to form a single string of text. For example, if you list first names in one column, and last name in another column, but you need names formatted, last name, comma, first name as in "Smith, John" you can use the you can use the CANCATENATE function to join text so that it is formatted the way you want.

With the CANCATENATE function you can join up to 255 items to form a single string of text. If you need to include a literal value, enclose it in quotes. If you need to include blank spaces, place them between quotes. Separate each value you want to join with a comma.

Join Text

1. Type **=CONCATENATE(**.

2. Click the Insert Function button.

   The Function Arguments dialog box appears.

3. Enter a cell where an argument is located.

4. Enter a literal value.

5. Enter a space.

6. Repeats Steps 3 to 5 if needed.

7. Click OK.

- Excel displays the result.
- You can copy and paste.

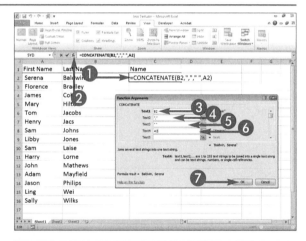

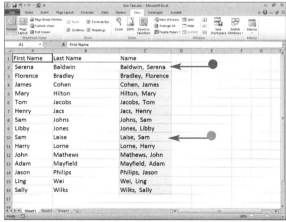

240

Add a Calculator

I f you want to do quick calculations without using a formula or function, use a calculator. In Excel, you can place a calculator on the Quick Access Toolbar or on the Ribbon. See Chapter 17 to learn how.

You can use the calculator as you would any electronic calculator. Click a number, choose an operator — such as the plus key (+) to do addition — and then click another number. Press the equal sign key (=) to get a result. Use MS to remember a value, MR to recall it, and MC to clear memory.

Statistical and mathematical functions are available in the calculator's scientific view when you click View and then Scientific. In this view, you can cube a number, find its square root, compute its log, and more.

Extra

In both standard and scientific views, you can transfer a value from the calculator to Excel by displaying it, copying it, and pasting it into a cell. For complete instructions on using the Excel calculator, open the calculator. On the calculator's menu, click Help and then click Help Topics. The Calculator dialog box appears. Click the Contents tab and then Calculator. A list of topics appears.

Add a Calculator

Note: *Before you can use the calculator, you must add it to the Ribbon or to the Quick Access Toolbar. You can find the Calculator button under the Commands not in the Ribbon option in the Choose Commands From field.*

① Click Calculator.

The calculator appears in Standard mode.

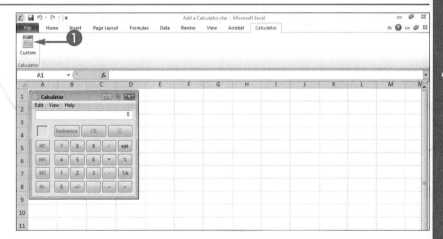

② Click View.

③ Click Scientific.

The calculator appears in Scientific mode.

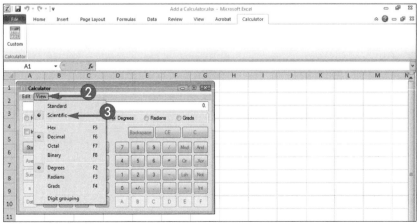

Consolidate Worksheets

If you keep related data in separate worksheets — or for that matter, separate workbooks — you may eventually want to consolidate the worksheets. For example, if you keep sales information for several regions on separate worksheets, you may want to consolidate the worksheets to find the total sales for all regions. With Excel's Consolidate feature, you can do just that. Excel provides a variety of functions you can use to consolidate, including SUM, COUNT, AVERAGE, MAX, MIN, and PRODUCT.

You start the consolidation process by selecting a location for your consolidated data. You can format the cells so the incoming data displays properly. Then select the function you want to use to consolidate your data. The SUM function takes the data from each location you specify and adds it together. You tell Excel the locations

of the data you want to consolidate. You can type the range in the Reference field of the Consolidate dialog box or click and drag to select the area. If you type the range, remember to include the worksheet name in single quotes followed by an exclamation point and the range. For example, to refer to the range $B$3:$D$7 on a sheet named Region 1, type **'Region 1'!$B$3:$D$7**. Excel takes the data and consolidates it.

If you want to include data from another workbook in your worksheet, open the other workbook. Then in the Consolidate dialog box, place your cursor in the Reference field. Use the View tab to switch windows and choose the other workbook. Once in the workbook, you can click and drag to select the data you want to consolidate.

Consolidate Worksheets

① Click in the top-left cell of the range into which you want to consolidate your data.

② Click the Data tab.

③ Click Consolidate.

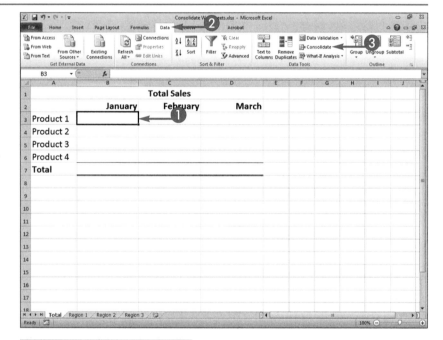

The Consolidate dialog box appears.

④ Click the ▾ and then select the function you want to use to consolidate your data.

⑤ Click and drag to select the location of your data or type the cell range.

⑥ Click Add.

⑦ Repeat Steps 5 and 6 for each location you want to consolidate.

⑧ Click OK.

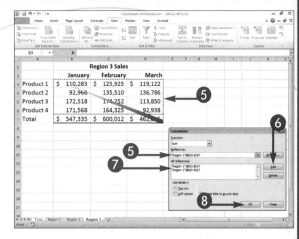

Excel consolidates your data.

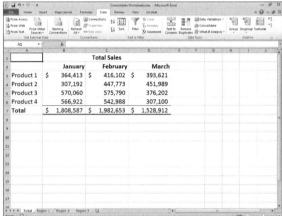

Extra

If you click Create links to source data (☐ changes to ✔) in the Consolidate dialog box, Excel updates your consolidated data each time you make a change to the data on which you base your consolidation. If you select this option, you cannot change the cells and ranges included in the consolidation. If you later want to update your consolidation, do not select Create links to source data.

If you click Top row and/or Left column (☐ changes to ✔) in the Use labels in section of the Consolidate dialog box, Excels copies the row or column labels in the source ranges to the consolidation. If a label does not match a label already in the consolidation, Excel creates a new column or row. If you have a column or row you do not want to consolidate, give it a unique name. Use this option if you have arranged the data you want to consolidate differently on each worksheet but you have given your data the same column or row labels.

Highlight Cells that Meet Your Criteria

I f you want to monitor your data by highlighting a condition, Excel's conditional formatting feature can aid you. For example, if your company offers a bonus when sales exceed $100,000, you can have Excel highlight sales figures whenever cell values in a range of cells are more than $100,000. You can also have Excel highlight a cell when the value is less than, equal to, or between specified values. You can use Excel's conditional formatting feature to monitor numbers, text, and dates. In addition, the conditional formatting feature can check for duplicate values, text that contains a specified series of characters, or a date occurring in a specified time period, such as yesterday, today, tomorrow, or last month.

To highlight a condition, you tell Excel the criteria and the format you want to apply if the criteria are met. For

example, for sales greater than $100,000, you can choose greater than and enter $100,000 as the value and then choose to display sales that meet that criterion with a light red fill with dark red text, with a yellow fill with dark yellow text, with a green fill with dark green text, with a light red fill, with red text, or with a red border. If none of those formats suit you, you can create a custom format. Your custom format can consist of number formatting, font formatting, border formatting, and/or fill formatting. Excel applies the format you choose to cells that meet the criteria and leaves cells that do not meet the criteria unchanged. You can apply conditional formatting to a cell range, an Excel table, or a PivotTable.

Highlight Cells that Meet Your Criteria

Create a Conditional Format

1. Click and drag to select the data you want to monitor.

2. Click the Home tab.

3. Click Conditional Formatting.

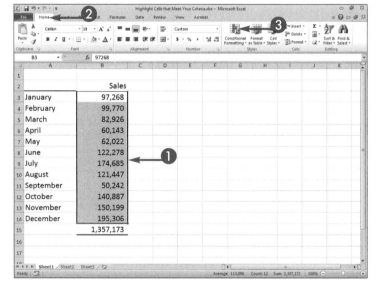

A menu appears.

4. Click Highlight Cells Rules.

A menu appears

5. Click a menu option.

A dialog box appears.

⑥ Enter your criteria.

⑦ Click the ▾ and then select a format.

● Choose Custom Format to create a custom format.

⑧ Click OK.

Excel highlights all the data that meets your criteria.

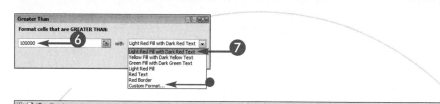

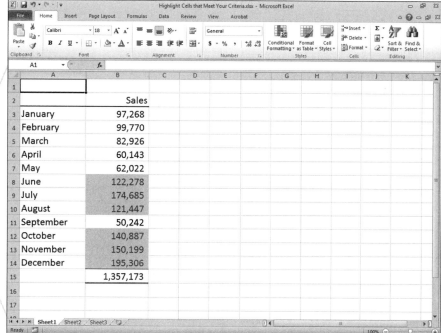

	A	B
1		
2		Sales
3	January	97,268
4	February	99,770
5	March	82,926
6	April	60,143
7	May	62,022
8	June	122,278
9	July	174,685
10	August	121,447
11	September	50,242
12	October	140,887
13	November	150,199
14	December	195,306
15		1,357,173
16		
17		

Apply It

You can highlight duplicate values. To make sure you do not delete values you want to keep, use this feature before you delete duplicates. Select the cells you want to check for duplicates. Click the Home tab. Click Conditional Formatting in the Styles group. A menu appears. Click Highlight Cells Rules. A menu appears. Click Duplicate Values. The Duplicate Values dialog box appears. Choose the format you want to apply to duplicate values. Click OK. Excel highlights all the duplicate values. Note that Excel evaluates each column individually. Also, you may want to click Undo to remove the formatting before you delete.

To delete the duplicates, select the cells from which you want to remove duplicates. Click the Data tab. Click Remove Duplicates in the Data Tools group. The Remove Duplicates dialog box appears. Click the check box to deselect the columns you do not want to check for duplicates (☑ changes to ☐). Click OK. Excel deletes the duplicates. You can also use the Duplicate Values dialog box to check for unique values by selecting Unique in the Criteria field.

Find the Highest or Lowest Ranked Values

You can use conditional formatting to find the highest or lowest ranked values. For example, you can use conditional formatting to find the top three sales people or the bottom three sales people. When trying to find the rank, you have several options to choose from. If you choose Top 10, you can highlight the highest numbers in the selected range. You set the criteria: top 3, top 10, or whatever number you want. If you choose Bottom 10 items, you can choose the lowest number in the selected range, again you choose the criteria. If you want to find the top values or bottom values based in a percentage, choose Top 10 % or Bottom 10 % or enter the exact percentage you want.

Apply It

You can also use conditional formatting to highlight values that are above or below average. Click the Home tab. Click Conditional Formatting. Click Top/Bottom Rules, and click Above Average or Below Average depending on what you want. The Above Average or Below Average dialog box appears. Select the format you want to apply. Excel calculates the average and applies the format.

Find the Highest or Lowest Ranked Values

1. Click and drag to select the cells where you want to find values.

2. Click the Home tab.

3. Click Conditional Formatting.

4. Click Top/Bottom Rules.

5. Click the rule you want.

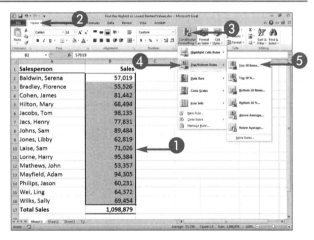

6. Enter your criteria.

7. Click the ▼ and then select a format.

8. Click OK.

   Excel highlights the cells that meet your criteria.

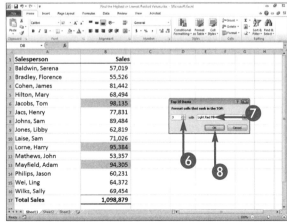

Add Data Bars to Your Worksheet

Data bars are a type of conditional formatting. You use data bars to indicate the relative size of a number — the longer the bar, the higher the number. Because each bar represents the relative size of the data, you can compare things such as sales performance with a glance.

Like all conditional formats, data bars can be applied to columns of data, rows of data, or a grid of data. When you add data bars to rows of data, make sure that the columns are the same size. Differences in the width of cells can distort the size of the bars. You can choose from several colors when you add data bars to your worksheet, and you can choose from solid color or gradient color.

Extra

You can also use color scales to conditionally format data. Color scales use gradations of color. For example, if you use Excel's yellow and green color scale, yellow represents higher values and green, lower values. To apply a color scale, select the cells to which you want to apply the scale, click the Home tab, click Conditional Formatting, click Color Scales, and then click the color scale you want to apply.

Add Data Bars to Your Worksheet

1 Click and drag to select the cells where you want to add data bars.

2 Click the Home tab.

3 Click Conditional Formatting.

4 Click Data Bars.

5 Click your color choice.

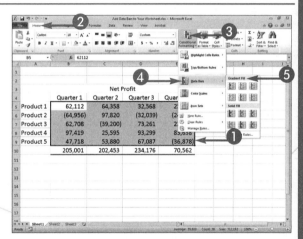

Excel applies the data bars.

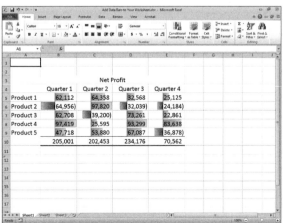

Add Icon Sets to Your Worksheet

You can conditionally format your data by using icon sets. Icon sets make it easy to see trends in your data at a glance and they make it easy to see how data values relate to one another. Icon sets comes in sets of three, four, and five icons. You can use them to divide your data into three, four, or five categories. You choose the icon set you want to use. Excel automatically categorizes cells and places the correct icons in the cell. By default, Excel uses percentages to divide cells into categories.

Icons sets are a great way to group data. Each icon tells you a cell's value relative to all other values in the selected range.

Apply It

You can display icon sets without displaying the underlying data. Click the Home tab. Click Conditional Formatting in the Styles group. A menu appears. Click Icon Sets. Click More Rules. The New Formatting Rule dialog box appears. Click the down arrow (▾) in the Icon Style field and then select the icon set you are using. Click the Show Icon Only check box (☐ changes to ✔). Click OK. Excel displays the icon without the data.

Add Icon Sets to Your Worksheet

① Click and drag to select the cells where you want to add icon sets.

② Click the Home tab.

③ Click Conditional Formatting.

④ Click Icon Sets.

⑤ Click the set you want.

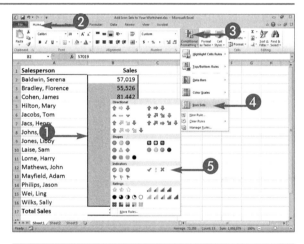

Excel applies the icon set.

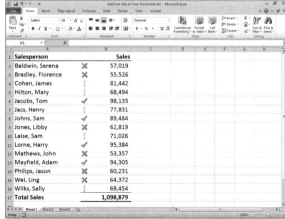

Remove Conditional Formatting

You can apply several types of conditional formats. *Formats* that highlight values that meet a criteria, data bars, color scales, and icon sets. When formats are no longer needed, you can remove them. When removing conditional formats you have four options: Remove Rules from Selected Cells, Clear Rules from Entire Sheet, Clear Rules from This Table, and Clear Rules from This PivotTable. Remove Rules from Selected Cells removes conditional formatting from the cells you have selected. Clear Rules from Entire Sheet removes all the conditional formatting on the worksheet. Clear Rules from This Table removes conditional formatting from the table you have selected. Clear Rules from This PivotTable removes conditional formatting from the PivotTable you have selected.

Extra

Changes affect conditionally formatted data. When you are highlighting data that meets a condition, if you make a change so a cell no longer meets the condition, Excel removes the format. With data bars, changes to a cell value can change the length of the data bar. With color scales, changes to a cell value can change the color of the cell. With icon sets, changes to a cell value can change the icons.

Remove Conditional Formatting

① Click and drag to select the cells where you want to remove conditional formatting.

② Click the Home tab.

③ Click Conditional Formatting.

④ Click Clear Rules.

⑤ Click the option you want.

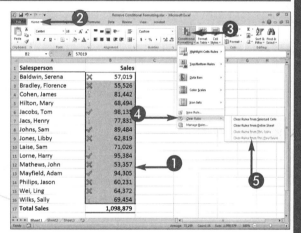

● Excel removes the conditional formatting.

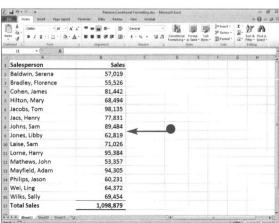

Change Conditional Formatting Rules

The Highlight Cells Rules and Top/Bottom Rules options under Conditional Formatting highlight cells that meet your criteria. You can, for example, use Highlight Cells Rules to find the top three sales people. A *data bar* is a colored bar you place in a cell. With data bars you can discern at a glance how large a value in one cell is relative to the values in other cells. The length of the bar represents the value of the cell relative to other cells — the longer the bar, the higher the value. Excel provides you with several bars from which to choose. *Color scales* and *icon sets* are similar to data bars, except color scales use gradations of color to represent the relative size of the value, and icon sets use icons to represent the relative size of the value.

Highlight cells rules, top/bottom rules, data bars, color scales, and icon sets all use rules to determine when to display what. You can use the rules defined by Excel or you can create your own. At the bottom of the Highlight Cells Rules, Top/Bottom Rules, Data Bars, Color Scales, or Icon Sets submenu, click More Rules to adjust and create rules. You can create rules that format cells based on their values, what they contain, how they rank, whether they are above or below average, and whether they are unique or duplicate values; or you can also use a formula to tell Excel which cells to format.

Change Conditional Formatting Rules

1. Click and drag to select the data you want to monitor.

2. Click the Home tab.

3. Click Conditional Formatting.

    A menu appears.

4. Click an option.

    A submenu appears.

5. Click More Rules.

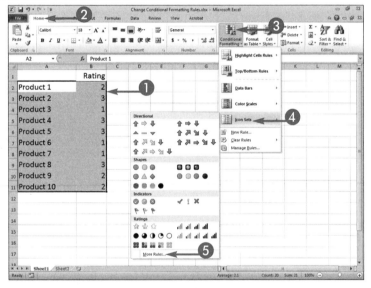

The New Formatting Rule dialog box appears.

6. Click a rule.

7. Click the ▼ and select a format style.

8. Click the ▼ and select an icon style.

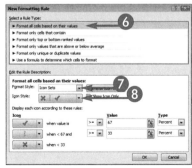

⑨ Click the ▾ and select an operator.

⑩ Click the ▾ and select a type.

Note: *You can choose Number, Percent, Formula, or Percentile.*

⑪ Enter a value.

Repeat Steps 9 through 11 for each icon, as needed.

⑫ Click OK.

Excel displays the results of your rule.

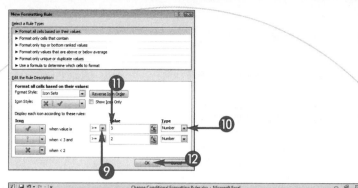

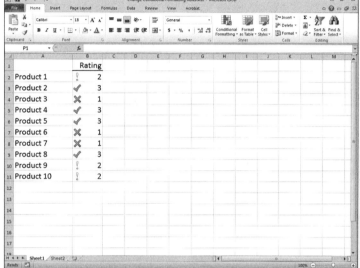

Extra

You can apply multiple conditional formatting rules to a range of cells. When you apply conditional formatting rules to cells, Excel executes them in order of precedence. By default, rules stack in the order you create them. Excel gives the most recently created rule the highest precedence. If two rules conflict, Excel applies the rule with the highest precedence. For example, if one rule formats text green and another rule formats text blue, Excel applies the rule with the highest precedence. You can click the Home tab, click Conditional Formatting, and then click Manage Rules to open the Conditional Formatting Rules Manager. The manager lists rules in order, putting the rule with the highest precedence on top. Use the Up and Down arrow keys (⬆ and ⬇) to change the order. You can also use the Conditional Formatting Rules Manger to delete a rule, edit a rule, or create a new rule.

If you manually apply a format to a cell and the format conflicts with a conditional format rule, the conditional format rule overrides the manual format. If you remove the conditional format, Excel reapplies the manual format.

Paste with Paste Special

By clicking the Copy button on the Home tab, pressing Ctrl+C, or clicking Copy on a context menu, you can easily copy the contents of a range of cells so you can paste the contents somewhere else in your worksheet. Cells can contain a lot of information. When you paste with Paste Special, you decide exactly what information you want to paste.

You can choose to paste everything or you can choose to paste just one element of the cell's contents, such as the formula, value, format, comment, validation, or column width. You can use the Paste Special dialog box to choose what you want to paste; however, you do not have to open the Paste Special dialog box to perform some paste special options, such as paste formulas, paste without borders, transpose, or paste-link. You can select these options and others directly from the Paste menu.

When you paste without borders, Excel pastes all your formatting but does not include any borders. When you transpose, Excel changes a row to a column or vice versa. You can use the paste link option in the Paste Special dialog box to keep your source and destination data synchronized. If you click the Paste Link button when pasting, Excel automatically updates the destination data when you make changes to the source data.

You can paste more than once. For example, when you paste by clicking Paste on the Home tab, Excel pastes the values, formulas, and formats but does not adjust the column widths. You can remedy this problem by pasting in two steps. In the first step, paste column widths. Excel adjusts the column widths. In the second step, paste your values, formulas, and formats.

Paste with Paste Special

Open the Paste Special Dialog Box

1. Click and drag to select the cells you want to copy.

2. Click the Home tab.

3. Click the Copy button (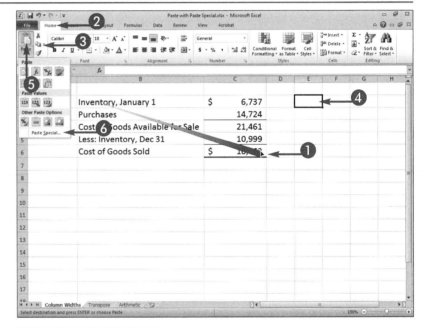).

4. Place the cursor in the upper-left corner of the cell(s) where you want to paste.

5. Click the Paste button (📋).

   A menu appears.

6. Click Paste Special.

The Paste Special dialog box appears.

Paste Column Widths

1. Follow Steps 1 to 6 under the "Open the Paste Special Dialog Box" section.

2. In the Paste SpeClick Column widths (⊙ changes to ◉) in the Paste Special dialog box.

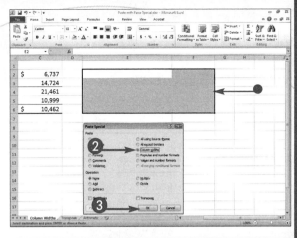

3. Click OK.

● Excel copies the column widths from the source to the destination.

4. Click Paste.

● Excel pastes the contents of the cells.

You can press Esc to end the copy session.

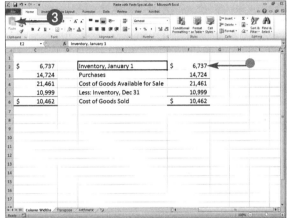

Extra

The following table lists Paste Special options:

OPTION	FUNCTION
All	Pastes the contents and the formatting in the copied cells.
Formulas	Pastes the formulas included in copied cells.
Values	Pastes the results of formulas or the data displayed in a cell.
Comments	Pastes the comments attached to a cell.
Validation	Pastes the validation rules from copied cells.
All using Source theme	Pastes the cell contents using the document theme applied to the copied data.
All except borders	Pastes all of the cell contents except borders.
Column widths	Pastes the column widths of the copied cells.
Formulas and number formats	Pastes only the formulas and number formats.
Values and number formats	Pastes only the values and number formats.

continued ➡

Y ou can use the Format Painter to copy formats from one cell to another. You can also use Paste Special. Simply copy a cell with the format you want, and then use Paste Special to paste the format into other cells. This feature is useful when you want to use the same format but different data in a range of cells. See Chapter 2 to learn more about the Format Painter.

You can use Paste Special to copy formulas or values from one location in your worksheet to another. When you want to use a cell's formula in adjacent cells in your worksheet, you can drag the fill handle to fill adjacent cells with the formula. However, when you want to use a formula in a nonadjacent cell, you must paste the formula with Paste Special. To learn more about using the fill

handle, see the section "Extend a Series with AutoFill" in this chapter. When you want the results of a formula but not the formula, paste the value.

You can also use Paste Special to perform simple arithmetic operations on each cell in a range. For example, in a list of salaries, you may want to increase every salary by 1 percent. You can use Paste Special to make the change quickly. Just type **1.01** in a cell and then select Multiply in the Paste Special dialog box.

You can choose the Skip Blanks option in the Paste Special dialog box if your source data includes any blanks. If you choose this option, Excel will not overwrite a destination cell with a blank if the destination cell has data in it.

Paste with Paste Special (continued)

Transpose Data

1. Follow Steps 1 to 6 under the "Open the Paste Special Dialog Box" section.

2. In the Paste Special dialog box, click the Transpose option (▢ changes to ✔).

3. Click OK

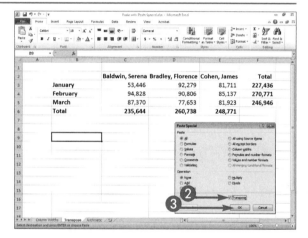

Excel transposes the data.

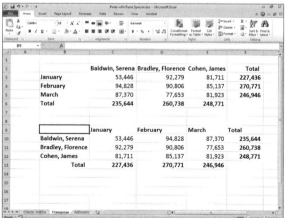

Perform Simple Arithmetic

1. Click in the cell that contains the number you want to use to add, subtract, multiply, or divide.

2. Click the Home tab.

3. Click the Copy button (📋).

4. Click and drag to select the cells where you want to paste.

5. Click Paste.

6. Click Paste Special.

   The Paste Special dialog box appears.

7. Click the option you want to perform.

8. Click OK.

   ● Excel performs the calculation.

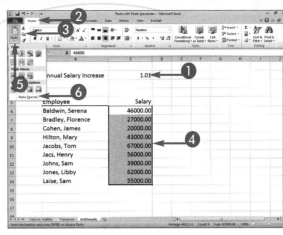

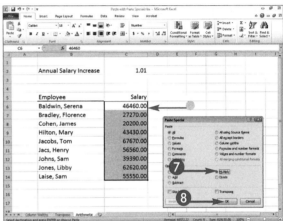

Extra

The following table lists Paste Special options:

OPTION	FUNCTION
None	No mathematical operation is performed.
Add	Adds the copied data to the destination cell.
Subtract	Subtracts the copied data from the destination cell.
Multiply	Multiplies the copied data by the data in the destination cell.
Divide	Divides the copied data by the data in the destination cell.
Skip blanks	Does not overwrite a destination cell with a blank if the destination cell has data in it and the copied cell does not.
Transpose	Changes columns to rows and vice versa.
Paste Link	Links the destination cells to the copied data. When you change the copied cell, the destination cell changes.

Validate with a Validation List

I n Excel, you can restrict the values a user can enter into a cell. By restricting values, you help ensure that all worksheet entries are valid and that calculations based on them are valid as well. During data entry, a validation list forces anyone using your worksheet to select a value from a drop-down list rather than typing and potentially entering the wrong information. Validation lists save time and reduce errors.

There are two methods that you can use to create a data validation list. First, if your list is short and does not change, you can type your list into the Source field of the Data Validation dialog box. For example, if your field collects gender, you can type "Male, Female" into the Source field. You must separate values with a comma. Second, if your list is long or if it changes, you can type

the values into adjacent cells in a column or row. You may want to place the list in an out-of-the-way place on your worksheet or on a separate worksheet. With this method, if your list changes, just type the new values into the cells you have designated as the validation list. You can name the range. See Chapter 4 to learn how to name ranges. After you create your list of values, use the Source field in the Data Validation dialog box to assign the values to your validation list. You can click and drag to select the valid entries, or you can type = followed by the range, or type = followed by the range name.

After you have created a validation list, you can copy and paste it into other cells by using Paste Special's Validation option.

Create a Validation List

1. Click in a cell.

2. Click the Data tab.

3. Click Data Validation.

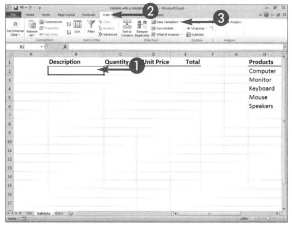

The Data Validation dialog box appears.

4. Click the ▾ and then select List.

5. Enter the range where the valid entries are located.

   Alternatively, type the list of valid entries, with each entry followed by a comma.

6. Click OK.

● Excel creates a validation list in the cell you selected.

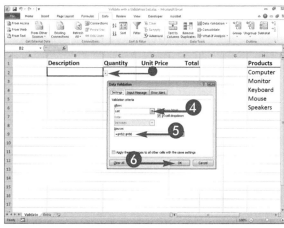

Paste a Validation List

1. Copy the cell with the validation list.

2. Select the cells where you want to place the validation list.

3. Click the ☑ under Paste.

   A menu appears.

4. Click Paste Special.

   The Paste Special dialog box appears.

5. Click the Validation option (◎ changes to ◉).

6. Click OK.

   Excel places the validation list in the cells you selected.

- When you make an entry, you must pick from the list.

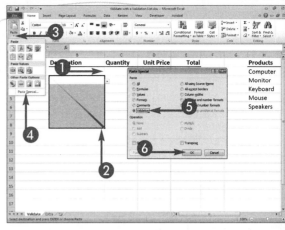

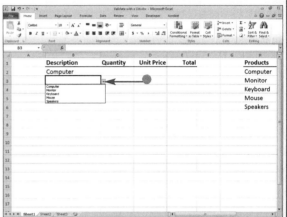

Extra

To remove a validation list, click in any cell that contains the validation list you want to remove, click the Home tab, and then click Find and Select in the Editing group. A menu appears. Click Go To Special. The Go To Special dialog box appears. Click Data Validation, click Same, and then click OK. The Go To Special dialog box closes. Click the Data tab and then click Data Validation in the Data Tools group. The Data Validation dialog box appears. Click the Settings tab. Click Clear All and then click OK.

If you base your validation list on a range of cells and any cell in that range is blank, and if you select the Ignore Blank check box (☐ changes to ☑) on the Settings tab of the Data Validation dialog box, you can enter any value into the cells you validate with your list. Otherwise, entry into the cells is restricted to items in your list, and if you try to enter another value, you cannot do so.

Validate with Data Entry Rules

You can use data entry rules to ensure data is entered in the correct format, and you can restrict the data entered to whole numbers, decimals, dates, times, or a specific text length. You can also specify whether the values need to be between, not between, equal to, not equal to, greater than, less than, greater than or equal to, or less than or equal to the values you specify.

In addition, you can create an input message that appears when the user enters the cell and an error alert that displays if the user makes an incorrect entry. Error alerts can stop users, provide a warning, or just provide information. For example, when a user makes an incorrect entry, the Stop Error Alert style displays the error message you entered and the user cannot make

an entry that does not meet your criteria. The Warning Alert style and the Information Alert style display a message but the user can still make an entry that does not meet your criteria. Input messages and error alerts consist of a title and a message.

After you create your data entry rule, you can copy and paste it into the appropriate cells by using the Paste Special Validation option. Refer to "Paste a Validation List" in the section "Validate with a Validation List" to learn how to copy and paste your data entry rule. If you click and drag to select the cells to which you want to apply your data validation rules and then open the Data Validation dialog box and create your data validation, Excel applies your validation to all the cells you selected.

Validate with Data Entry Rules

① Select the cells where you want to place validation rules.

② Click the Data tab.

③ Click Data Validation.

The Data Validation dialog box appears.

④ Click the ▾ and then select the Allow and Data validation criteria.

⑤ Type the criteria or click and drag to select the cells with the criteria you want to use.

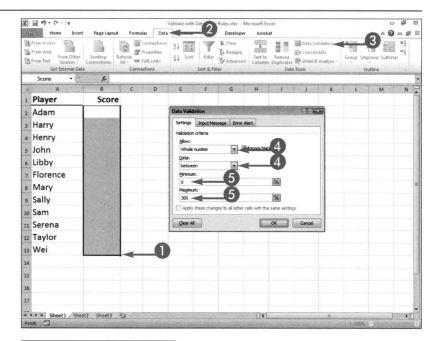

⑥ Click the Input Message tab.

⑦ Type a message title.

⑧ Type a message.

⑨ Click the Error Alert tab.

⑩ Click the 🔽 and then select a style.

Choose Stop if you want to stop the entry of invalid data.

Choose Warning if you want to display a warning to the user, but not prevent the data entry.

Choose Information to provide information to the user.

⑪ Type a title.

⑫ Type an error message.

⑬ Click OK.

Excel creates the data entry rule.

● When a user clicks in the cell, Excel displays the input message.

● When a user enters invalid data, Excel displays the error alert.

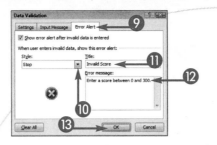

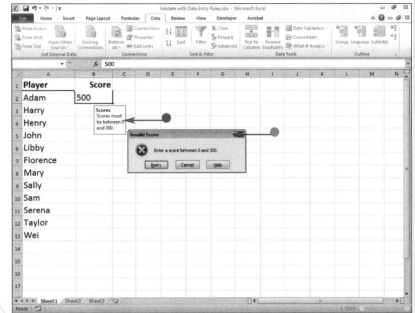

Extra

If you select Custom in the Allow field on the Settings tab of the Data Validation dialog box, you can create a formula that validates an entry. Place your formula in the formula field. Your formula must resolve to a logical value.

PURPOSE	FORMULA
Restrict the cell entry to text. B2 is the current cell.	`=ISTEXT(B2)`
You can only make an entry if cell A2 is less than 1,000.	`=AND(A2<1000)`
You can only make an entry if cell A2 is less than 1,000 and cell A3 is 0.	`=AND(A2<1000, A3=0)`
You can only make an entry if your entry is less than cell A2 plus 100.	`=IF(C5<A2+100,TRUE,FALSE)`

Cell C5 is the current cell. See the file Validate with a List.xlsx, the Extra sheet for a demonstration of these formulas, on the Web site for this book.

Add Comments to Your Worksheet

A *comment* is a bit of descriptive text that enables you to document your work. If someone else maintains your worksheet, or others use it in a workgroup, your comments can provide useful information. You can enter comments in any cell you want to document or otherwise annotate.

Comments in Excel do not appear until you choose to view them. Excel associates comments with individual cells and indicates their presence with a tiny red triangle in the cell's upper-right corner. View an individual comment by clicking in the cell or positioning your cursor over it. View all comments in a worksheet by clicking the Review tab and then clicking Show All Comments.

When you track your changes, Excel automatically generates a comment every time you copy or change a cell. The comment records what changed in the cell,

who made the change, and the time and date of the change. To learn more about tracking changes, see the next section, "Track Changes."

When a comment gets in the way of another comment or blocks data, you can move it. Just position your cursor over the comment box border until the arrow turns into a four-sided arrow, click and drag the comment to a better location, and then release the mouse button. Your comment will remain in this position until you display all comments again.

When you sort, cut and paste, or copy and paste, comments move with the cell. Once you have created a comment, you can edit or delete it. You can also cycle through the comments in your worksheet by clicking Previous and Next on the Review tab.

Add Comments to Your Worksheet

Add a Comment

① Click a cell.

② Click the Review tab.

③ Click New Comment.

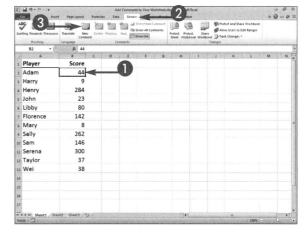

● A comment box appears.

● A red triangle appears.

④ Type your comment.

   Note: To apply bold or other formatting, select the text, right-click, click Format Comment, and then make changes as appropriate.

⑤ Click outside the comment box when you finish.

   The comment box disappears.

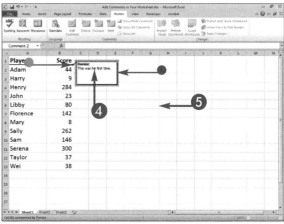

Position the cursor over the cell to display your comment again.

⑥ Click Edit Comment to edit a comment.

⑦ Click Delete to delete a comment.

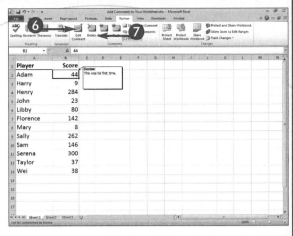

Display All Comments

⑧ Click Show All Comments.

● You can now see all the comments in the worksheet.

To close the comment boxes, click Show All Comments again.

⑨ Click Previous or Next.

Excel cycles through the comments.

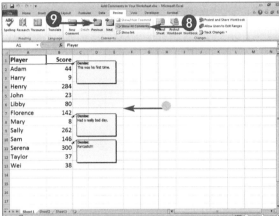

Extra

A name displays each time you enter a comment. To set the name, click the File tab, and then click Options. The Excel Options dialog box appears. Click General and then type the name you want to appear in the comment box in the User Name field.

To delete a name or any other part of a comment, select it and press the Delete key.

If your worksheet has comments, you can print the comments as they appear in your worksheet or you can print the worksheet with the comments listed at the end of the sheet. To print the comments, click the Review tab. Click Show All Comments in the Comments group to show your comments. Click the Page Layout tab. Click the launcher in the Page Setup group. The Page Setup dialog box appears. Click the Sheet tab. In the Comments field, click As displayed on sheet to print your comments as they appear in your worksheet or click At end of sheet to print your comments at the end of the sheet. To see how your comments will appear, you can click Print Preview before you print.

Track Changes

By using change tracking, you can monitor the changes made to a *shared workbook*. A shared workbook is a workbook that can be edited by multiple people at the same time. When you turn on change tracking, your workbook automatically becomes a shared workbook. Change tracking keeps a log of changes. You can except or reject each change. This feature is especially useful when you have a workbook that needs to be reviewed by others. You can review each person's comments and changes and then finalize the workbook.

You can use the Highlight Changes dialog box to turn on change tracking. The Highlight changes dialog box has When, Who, and Where options. Use When to define the time after which edits are tracked — for example, after a specific date or since you last saved. Use Who to identify the group whose edits you want to track — for example,

everyone in the workgroup, everyone but you, or a named individual. Use Where to specify the rows and columns you want to monitor.

When someone makes a change, Excel indicates the change by placing a small purple triangle in the upper-left corner of the changed cell. Excel records cell changes in automatically generated cell comments. When Highlight Changes is activated, you can view these comments by moving your mouse pointer over the cells.

You can use the Accept or Reject Changes dialog box to review every change made to a worksheet and either accept or reject the change.

Before you share a workbook, enter and format your data because there are many features you cannot change in a shared workbook.

Track Changes

1 Click the Review tab.

2 Click Track Changes.

A menu appears.

3 Click Highlight Changes.

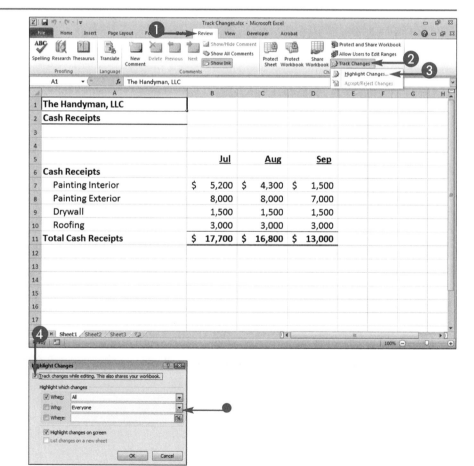

The Highlight Changes dialog box appears.

4 Click the Track changes while editing option (☐ changes to ✔). This also shares the workbook.

● The When, Who, and Where fields become available.

5 Click the When option and then click the down arrow (⏷) to select when to track changes.

6 Click the Who option and then click the ⏷ to select whose changes to track.

7 Click the Where option and then enter the cell ranges you want to monitor in the field.

8 Click the Highlight changes on screen option to insert a purple flag in edited cells (☐ changes to ☑).

9 Click OK.

A message informs you that Excel will save your workbook.

● Purple flags appear in edited cells.

● To view a cell's comment, position your mouse cursor over the cell.

Note: *For more about comments, see the previous section, "Add Comments to Your Worksheet."*

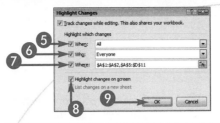
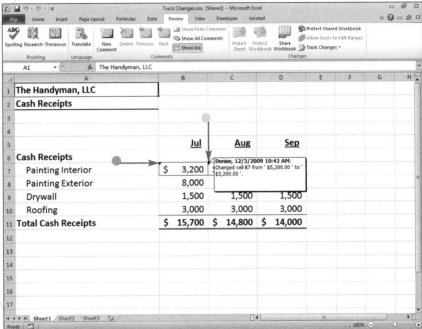

Extra

When you share a workbook, you cannot modify the following: merged cells, conditional formats, data validations, charts, pictures, objects, hyperlinks, scenarios, outlines, subtotals, data tables, PivotTable reports, workbook and worksheet protection, and macros.

You can use the Accept or Reject Changes dialog box to review every change made to a worksheet and either accept or reject the change. To Access the Accept or Reject Changes dialog box, click the Review tab. Click Track Changes in the Changes group. A menu appears. Click Accept/Reject Changes. The Select Changes to Accept or Reject dialog box appears. Enter the criteria for the changes you want to review in the When, Who, and Where fields and then click OK. The Accept or Reject changes dialog box appears.

To view all worksheet changes after you or others make edits, open the Highlight Changes dialog box and click the List Changes on a New Sheet option (☐ changes to ☑). In the Who field, click Everyone. Click to deselect the When and Where fields (☑ changes to ☐). Click OK. Excel creates a new worksheet called History that shows each change, the type of change, the values changed, the person who made the change, and so on. You can sort and filter the worksheet.

Protect Your Worksheet

If you share your worksheets with others, you can lock them so others can view and print them but cannot make changes to the areas you do not allow them to change. Even if you do not share your worksheets, you may want to lock certain areas so you do not inadvertently make changes. Locking your worksheet enables you to allow users to make certain types of changes while disallowing others. You can choose which changes users can make. For example, you can allow users to make changes to formats; insert or delete columns, rows, or hyperlinks; sort; filter; use PivotTables; and/or edit objects or scenarios.

By default, when you lock a worksheet, Excel locks every cell in the worksheet and the formulas are visible to anyone who uses the worksheet. Prior to locking a

worksheet, you can choose to leave specific cells unlocked and hide the formulas in specific cells. For example, you can lock every area except the current month. That way, users can make updates to the current month, but they cannot change previous months.

To protect your worksheet, you can enter a password in the Protect Sheet dialog box. If you add a password, only users who know the password can unlock the sheet. You should make your password strong by including upper- and lowercase letters, numbers, and symbols. Adding a password is optional. Keep a list of your worksheet passwords in a safe place, because you cannot recover a worksheet password. If you lose or forget your password, you can no longer access the locked areas of your worksheet.

Protect Your Worksheet

① Select the cells you want to remain unlocked or whose formulas you want to hide.

② Click the Home tab.

③ Click Format.

A menu appears.

④ Click Format Cells.

The Format Cells dialog box appears.

⑤ Click the Protection tab.

By default, Locked is selected.

⑥ Click Locked to lock (☑) or unlock (☐) the selected cells.

By default, Hidden is unselected.

⑦ Click Hidden to hide selected formulas (☑) or deselect (☐) to view selected formulas.

⑧ Click OK.

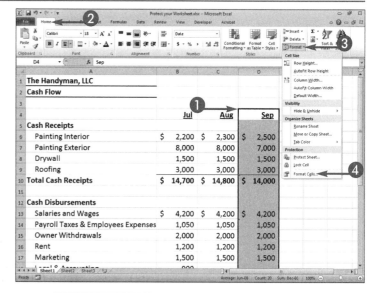

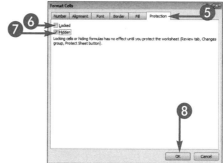

⑨ Click Format.

A menu appears.

⑩ Click Protect Sheet.

The Protect Sheet dialog box appears.

⑪ Enter a password if you want to password-protect your worksheet.

⑫ Click options to select the ones you want to allow users to perform (☐ changes to ✔).

⑬ Click OK.

The Confirm Password dialog box appears.

⑭ Retype your password.

⑮ Click OK.

Excel locks your worksheet.

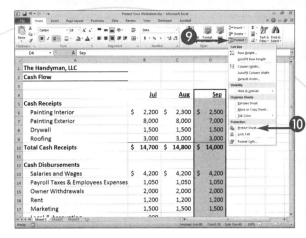

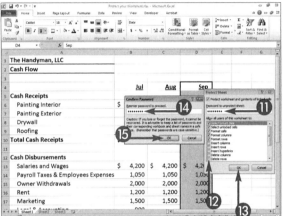

Apply It

You can protect a workbook from unwanted changes. Click the Review tab, click Protect Workbook. The Protect Structure and Windows dialog box appears. Select Structure (☐ changes to ✔) to protect your workbook from the moving, addition, and deletion of worksheets. Select Windows (☐ changes to ✔) to protect your workbook from changes in the size and position of windows. Optionally, require a password to remove these protections.

You can use the Allow Users to Edit Ranges dialog box to password-protect specific ranges in your worksheet. To password-protect a range, select the range you want to password-protect, click the Review tab, and then click Allow Users to Edit Ranges in the Changes group. The Allow Users to Edit Ranges dialog box appears. Click New. The New Range dialog box appears. In the Title field, name the range; in the Range password field, assign a password; then click OK. The Confirm Password dialog box appears. Retype your password, click OK, click Apply, and then click OK again. Your sheet must be protected and the range must be locked for this feature to work.

Save Your Workbook as a Template

Templates are special-purpose workbooks you can use to create new worksheets. They can contain formats, styles, and specific content such as images, and column heads you want to reuse in other worksheets. Templates save you the work of re-creating workbooks for recurring purposes such as filling out invoices and preparing monthly reports.

You create a template by designing a generic workbook that contains the worksheet layouts you want. You can create custom styles, number formats, macros, and formulas and include them in your template. For example, if you regularly use Excel to create and issue invoices, you can create an automatically calculating invoice that includes your logo and other basic information.

Your custom template includes all the changes you have made to your workbook, including formats, formulas, and

such changes as opening multiple windows or deleting tabs. Saving formulas with your template causes your worksheet to calculate automatically. Saving formats saves you from having to re-create them.

When you work with a template, you edit a copy — not the original — so you retain the original template to use when structuring other workbooks. Excel 2010 workbooks ordinarily have an .xlsx file extension. Saving an Excel workbook as a template creates a file with an .xltx extension.

Excel comes with ready-made templates that serve basic business purposes such as invoicing. You can use the Available Templates dialog box to access these templates. To access the Available Templates dialog box, click the File tab and then click New. You can also use the Available Templates dialog box to access Office.com, which has several categories of templates that you can download.

Save Your Workbook as a Template

① Click the File tab.

A menu appears.

② Click Save As.

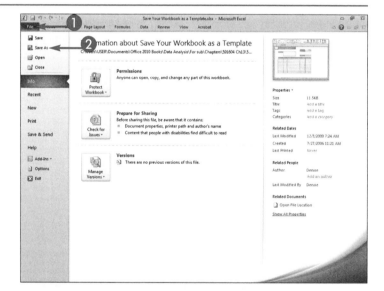

The Save As dialog box appears.

③ Type a name for your template.

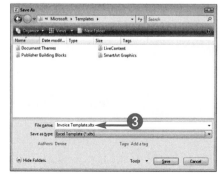

4 Click the ▼ and then select Excel Template (*.xltx).

● The save in folder changes to Templates.

5 Click Save.

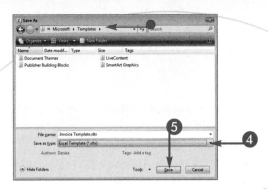

● Excel creates the template.

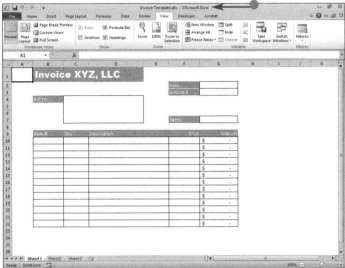

Choose a Format When Saving a Workbook

After you create a worksheet, you may want to share it with others. The file format you choose when you save your file is important. The default format for Office 2010 is Excel Workbook (*.xlsx). This file format was introduced in Office 2007. The smaller files it creates are easily accessible in other software programs because they are in Extensible Markup Language (XML) format, which is a data-exchange standard.

Versions prior to Excel 2007 did not use XML as the default format. These files have an .xls extension. If you want to share your documents with people who use Excel 97–2003, you can save your file as an Excel 97–2003 workbook (*.xls). Features that are not supported in earlier versions of Excel are lost when you save your file as an Excel 97–2003 workbook.

If you have a computer with Excel 97–2003 installed, you can go to the Office Update Web site and download the

Microsoft Office Compatibility Pack for Excel. After you install the Compatibility Pack, you can open Excel Workbook *.xlsx files in Excel 97–2003. Excel Workbook *.xlsx formatting and other features may not display in the earlier version, but they are still available when you open the file again in Excel 2010.

If you want to see the XML layout for an Excel 2010 file, change the file extension on the file to .zip and then double-click the file. The file opens and several folders and files appear. Double-click the files to open and view them.

You can also save your worksheet in other file formats, including Web Page formats (*.htm; *.html) and several text-based formats, such as Text (MS-DOS) (*.txt), Text (Macintosh) (*.txt), and CSV (comma-delimited). These formats save the worksheet as text, which can be read by other applications, or in Hypertext Markup Language (HTML), which can be read by browsers.

Choose a Format When Saving a Workbook

1 Click the File tab.

A menu appears.

2 Click Save As.

The Save As dialog box appears.

3 Locate the folder where you want to save your file.

4 Type a filename.

5 Click the ▾ and then select a file type.

6 Click Save.

Excel may warn you about incompatibilities.

Excel saves your worksheet in the format you specify.

- This example shows the file saved in.CSV format.

- This example shows the file saved for in.html format (for the Web).

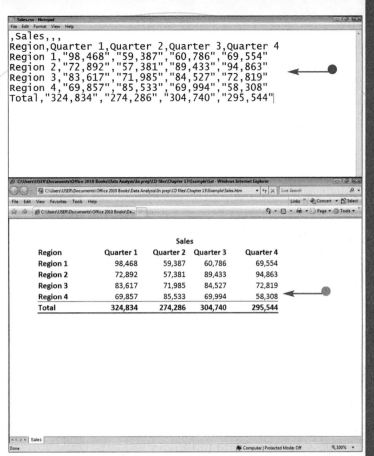

Extra

To save your workbook as an .xlsx file, click the File tab and then click Save. The Save As dialog box appears. In the Save In field, locate the folder in which you want to save your file, type a filename in the Filename field, and then click Save.

Before you distribute a document to others, you may want to save it in a *fixed format* — one that others cannot easily modify. For example, say you create an invoice you want to e-mail to a client, but you do not want to e-mail an Excel workbook. In cases such as this, you should save the file as a PDF (Portable Document Format) or XPS (XML Paper Specification). When you save files as PDF or XPS files, they retain the formatting you have applied and others cannot easily modify your files.

Print Your Workbook

The most common way to share a workbook with others is to print the worksheets and distribute paper copies. Excel has several features to help you format and print your worksheets. You can select the worksheet's margin size, orientation, paper size, print area, page breaks, and much more. If you want to see a live view of how print settings affect your report, use Page Layout view.

You can print part of your worksheet or your entire worksheet. If you want to print part of your worksheet, you can use the Set Print Area option on the Page Layout tab to tell Excel the area you want to print.

On the Page Layout tab, use the Size option to tell Excel the size of your paper. When you click Size, the most commonly used paper sizes appear on the menu. If you

do not see the paper size you are using, click More Paper Sizes and select a size from the Page tab of the Page Setup dialog box. While in the Page Setup dialog box, you can select the orientation of your worksheet: Landscape or Portrait. Selecting Portrait makes the shortest edges of your paper the top and bottom and the longest edges of your paper the sides. Selecting Landscape makes the longest edges of your paper the top and bottom and the shortest edges of your paper the sides.

If at any time during the process of setting up your document for printing, you want to see a preview of how your printed document will look, you can click the Print Preview button, which is located on every tab in the Page Setup dialog box.

Print Your Workbook

Set the Print Area

1. Select the area you want to print.

2. Click the Page Layout tab.

3. Click Print Area.

    A menu appears.

4. Click Set Print Area.

    Excel sets the print area.

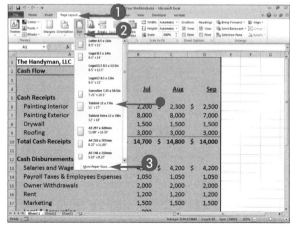

Set the Orientation and Page Size

1. Click the Page Layout tab.

2. Click Size.

3. Click More Paper Sizes.

● Alternatively, select a paper size from the menu.

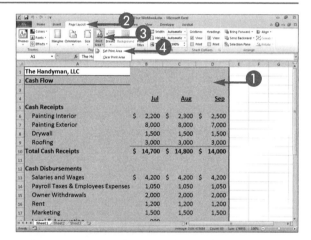

The Page Setup dialog box appears.

④ Click the ⏷ and select a paper size.

⑤ Click an option to select an orientation (◎ changes to ◉).

● Alternatively, click the Page Orientation button and select an orientation.

◉ Click Print Preview to see a preview of your document.

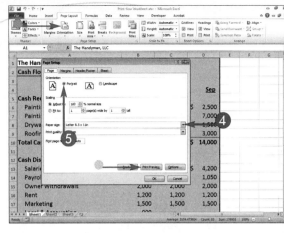

Set the Margins

① Click the Margins tab.

● Alternatively, click the Margins button and then set the margins.

② Type your margin sizes, including the area used for headers and footers.

③ Click a Center on page option if you want to center the print range horizontally and/or vertically (▢ changes to ✔).

④ Click OK.

The Page Setup dialog box closes.

Excel sets the margins.

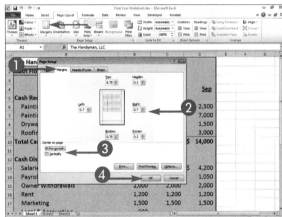

Extra

Clicking the launcher in the Page Setup, Scale to Fit, or Sheet Options group on the Page Layout tab opens the Page Setup dialog box. Every page of the Page Setup Dialog box has a Print Preview button. If you want to see a preview of how your document will look when you print it, click the Print Preview button. You can use the buttons below your document to scroll through your document. If you want to view the margins, select the Show Margins button (▣) in the lower-right corner. To zoom in and out, click the Zoom button (▦).

Click Page Setup, which is located under the print options, to open the Page Setup dialog box. Use the Page Setup dialog box to adjust your settings. When you are ready to print, click the Print button.

On the Ribbon, you can click Breaks in the Page Setup group of the Page Layout tab to specify where a new page is to begin in your printed copy. Select where you want to place the break. Click the Breaks button and then click Insert Page Break. Excel inserts a page break above and to the left of your selection.

continued ➡

Print Your Workbook (continued)

Margins define the amount of white space that surrounds your document. You can apply Excel's predefined margins by selecting them from the Margins menu, or you can open the Page Setup dialog box to define your margins. By default, Excel places your data in the upper-right corner of the page. The Margins tab in the Page Setup dialog box has options you can use to center your worksheet horizontally and/or vertically.

A *header* is text that prints across the top of every page of your worksheet. A *footer* is text that prints across the bottom of every page of your worksheet. You can set the amount of margin space Excel reserves for headers and footers on the Margins tab.

When you click in the header or footer area while in Page Layout view, the Header and Footer tools become

available. You can use the Design tab to tell Excel what data you want to include in your header and/or footer. The Header and Footer options provide you with a list of predefined headers and footers. In the Header & Footer Elements group, you can select the options you want to place in your header or footer.

If your data does not fit on the number of pages you want, you can scale your data. You can use a percentage to make your data larger or smaller. For example, setting the scale to 110 makes your data 10 percent larger than its normal size. Setting the scale to 90 makes your data 90 percent of its normal size. You can also scale your data by selecting the number of pages on which you want your data to fit. If you choose Automatic, Excel determines the amount of data to put on each page.

Print Your Workbook *(continued)*

Create a Header or Footer

1. Click the View tab.

2. Click Page Layout.

   Excel changes to layout view.

   ● Click Normal to return to normal view.

3. Click the left, right, or center of the header area in Page Layout view.

   The left area places information on the left.

   The center area places information in the center.

   The right area places information on the right.

   ● The Header & Footer tools become available.

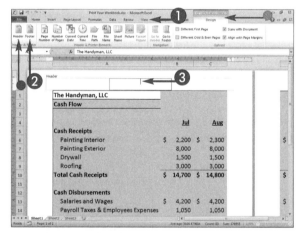

4. Click the Design tab.

5. Click an option in the Header & Footer Elements group.

   ● Excel places the option in the area you selected.

   This example adds a page number in the center.

   ● Click Header or Footer to use a predefined header or footer.

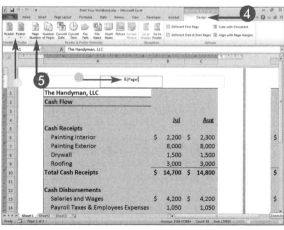

Scale to Fit

1. Click a cell in your data area.

2. Click the Page Layout tab.

3. Click the ⏷ and select the number of pages wide you want your document to be.

4. Click the ⏷ and select the number of pages long you want your document to be.

   Excel scales your document.

● Alternatively, click select a scale option to scale your document.

Print

1. Press Ctrl+P.

   The Print dialog box appears.

2. Click to tell Excel what you want to print.

● The Print Preview.

   Excel prints your worksheet.

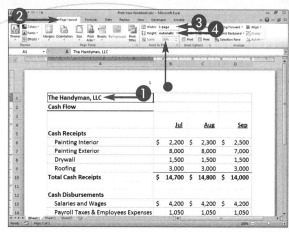

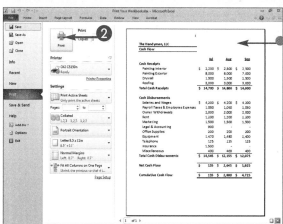

Extra

If you have many rows of data, you may want the column headings to print at the top of each page of your printed worksheet. If you have many columns of data, you may want the row labels to print on the left side of each page of your printed worksheet. To print column headings and row labels, click the Page Layout tab and click the launcher in the Sheet Options group. The Page Setup dialog box opens to the Sheet tab. In the Rows to Repeat at Top field, click and drag to select, or type the range of, the rows you want to appear at the top of each page. In the Columns to Repeat at Left field, click and drag to select, or type the range of, the columns you want to appear on the left and then click OK.

Gridlines separate the columns and rows in your data. To see the gridlines in your printed document, select the Print check box under Gridlines in the Sheet Options group on the Page Layout tab. To see gridlines on-screen, select the View check box under Gridlines in the Sheet Options group on the Page Layout tab.

Print Multiple Areas of Your Worksheet

You can print noncontiguous areas of your worksheet, thereby limiting your printing to the information that is of relevance. This feature involves little more than selecting the cells you want to print.

There are many reasons why you may want to print noncontiguous areas of your worksheet. For example, if you have sales data for several products, each in a column, you can select and print only the columns in which you are interested. You select noncontiguous areas of the worksheet by pressing and holding Ctrl as you click and drag. After you select areas, you set them as the print area. Print areas stay in effect until you clear them. You can add to the print area by selecting a range, clicking Page Layout, and then clicking Print Area; or by clicking Page Layout and then clicking Add to Print Area. To clear

the print area, click Page Layout, click Print Area, and then click Clear Print Area.

Excel places the ranges you select in the Print Area field in the Page Setup dialog box. A comma follows each range. Use the same format if you want to enter your print ranges manually into the Print Area field.

When printing a worksheet, you may have column headings or row labels you want to print with each selection. You can specify the rows you want to repeat at the top or the columns you want to repeat down the left side of every page you print by entering the ranges in the Rows to Repeat at Top and Columns to Repeat at Left fields in the Page Setup dialog box.

When you print a worksheet with multiple selected areas, each area prints on its own page.

Print Multiple Areas of Your Worksheet

① Press and hold the Ctrl key as you click and drag to select each area you want to print.

② Click the Page Layout tab.

③ Click Print Area.

④ Click Set Print Area.

Excel sets the print area.

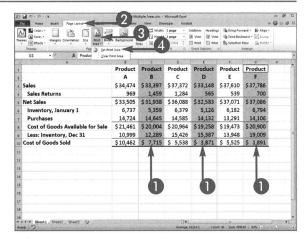

⑤ Click Print Titles.

The Page Setup dialog box appears.

⑥ Click the Sheet tab.

⑦ Click and drag the columns or rows you want to repeat or type the range.

⑧ Click Print Preview.

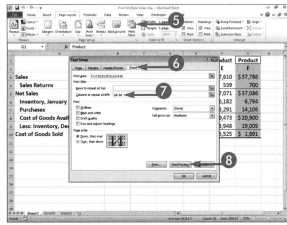

- The Print Preview window shows the first page of the printout containing an area you selected in Step 1.

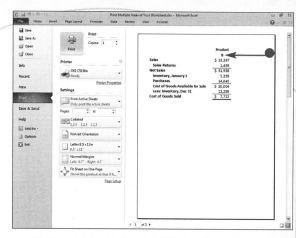

⑨ Click the Previous Page (◀) and Next Page (▶) buttons to view previous and subsequent pages.

- The Print Preview window shows the next page of the printout, which contains an area you selected in Step 1.

⑩ Click Print when you are satisfied with the layout.

Excel prints the selected areas.

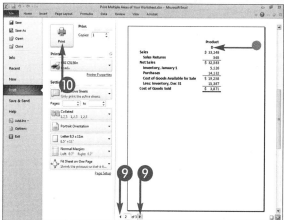

Extra

To open the Page Setup dialog box, click the launcher in the Page Setup group. You can use the Header/Footer tab in the Page Setup dialog box to add page numbers as well as a header or footer. Click Custom Header or Custom Footer to add dates and page numbers to each page.

You can access print options such as number of copies to print, printer to use, sheets and area to print by clicking the File tab and then clicking Print on the menu that appears.

You can print row numbers and column letters on every page. Click the launcher in the Page Setup group on the Page Layout tab to open the Page Setup dialog box. On the Sheet tab, click Row and column headings (☐ changes to ✔) before printing your worksheet. Alternatively, click the Page Layout tab on the Ribbon and then click the Print check box under Headings (☐ changes to ✔) in the Sheet Options group.

Introducing Macros

You can use macros to automate many of the tasks you perform in Excel. For example, if you frequently format your data in a particular way, you can use Excel's macro recorder to record the steps you use to format your data. You can then play back the recorded steps whenever you want to apply your format. Most of the commands you can execute in Excel, you can also record and play back.

The commands you use to create and execute macros are located on the Developer tab. By default, the Developer tab does not display in Excel. To display it, you must choose Developer in the Customize the Ribbon pane in the Excel Options dialog box.

You begin recording macros by clicking Record Macro on the Developer tab or by clicking the Record Macro button

on the status bar. Both options open the Record Macro dialog box. For detailed instructions on how to use the Record Macro dialog box, see the section "Record a Macro."

When you record a macro, you can record it using an absolute reference or a relative reference. If you record using an absolute reference, when Excel plays back your macro, it plays back the exact cells you clicked when you recorded the macro. If you record using a relative reference, Excel plays back the relative location of the cells you used when you recorded your macro. Click Use Relative References on the Developer tab to record using a relative reference. To learn more about absolute and relative references, see the section "Record a Macro."

When you save a workbook that has macros, you must save it as a macro-enabled workbook. Excel gives macro-enabled workbooks an .xlsm extension.

Introducing Macros

Show the Developer Tab

① Click the File tab.

A menu appears.

② Click Options.

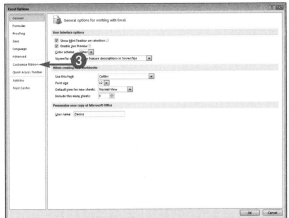

The Excel Options dialog box appears.

③ Click Customize Ribbon.

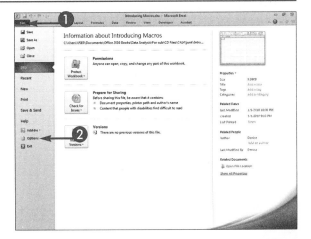

The Customize the Ribbon pane appears.

④ Click the down arrow (▾) and then select Main Tabs.

⑤ Click Developer (☐ changes to ☑).

⑥ Click OK.

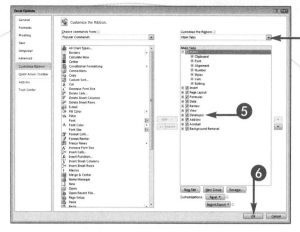

● The Developer tab appears on the Ribbon.

● Click Record Macro to record a macro.

● Click Use Relative References to record with a relative reference.

● Click Macro Security to change macro security.

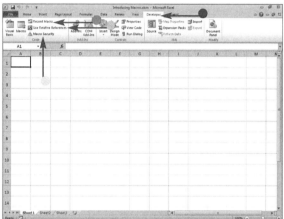

Extra

Because of problems with macro viruses, by default Excel disables all macros when you open a workbook. You can read the file, but you cannot execute the macros. You can click Macro Security on the Developer tab to change the default setting or you can click the Enable Content button that appears when you open the workbook to enable the macros. To learn more about macro security, see the sections "Set Macro Security," "Create a Digital Signature," and "Assign a Digital Signature to a Macro" in this chapter.

To save a workbook that has macros, click the Office button. A menu appears. Click Save As. The Save As dialog box appears. Locate the proper folder. Type a filename in the Filename field. Select Excel Macro-Enabled Workbook in the Save as type field. Click Save. Excel saves your workbook as a macro-enabled workbook and gives the workbook an .xlsm extension.

If you have programming experience or aptitude, you can edit Excel macros by using Visual Basic Editor, available by clicking Visual Basic on the Developer tab.

Set Macro Security

B ecause of increasing problems with computer viruses, specifically macro viruses, the default Excel macro security setting disables all macros when you open a workbook and enables you to decide on a case-by-case basis whether you want to enable them. This is true whether you created the macros or someone else created them. You can change the Excel macro security setting by selecting one of four options.

The Disable all macros without notification option disables all macros. This option does not provide you with any security alerts to let you know macros exist.

The Disable all macros with notification option is the default setting. It notifies you if macros are present so you can enable them on a case-by-case basis.

The Disable all macros except digitally signed macros option disables all macros except those digitally signed by a trusted publisher. If the publisher has digitally signed

the macro but you have not opted to trust the publisher, you can enable the macro or trust the publisher. See the Extra section in the section "Assign a Digital Signature to a Macro" to learn how to trust a publisher.

The Enable all macros (not recommended; potentially dangerous code can run) option enables you to run all macros. Because potentially dangerous code can run, Microsoft does not recommend this option. Changes you make to macro security in Excel do not change the macro security in other Office programs.

Macro creators use digital signatures to verify the safety of the macros they create. You can create a digital signature by using the Microsoft SelfCert.exe tool or you can obtain a digital certificate from a commercial certification authority. For more information on the Microsoft SelfCert.exe tool, see the next section, "Create a Digital Signature."

Set Macro Security

① Click the Developer tab.

Note: *See the section "Introducing Macros" to learn how to display the Developer tab.*

② Click Macro Security in the Code group.

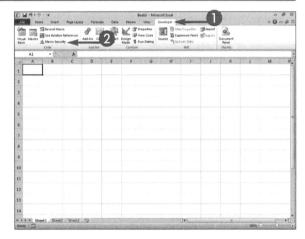

The Trust Center dialog box appears.

③ Click a macro security setting (⊙ changes to ◉).

④ Click OK.

Excel changes your macro security setting.

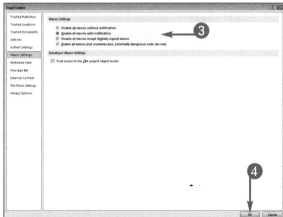

Create a Digital Signature

I
f you create a workbook that contains macros, you should consider using a digital signature. A digital signature provides assurance that no one has altered the macros. You can create a personal digital signature by using the Microsoft SelfCert.exe tool. Digital signatures created with the SelfCert.exe tool only work on the computer on which the digital signature was created.

If you plan to distribute your workbook to others, you should consider acquiring a commercial digital signature file. When you use a commercial digital signature, the digital ID attaches to the macro and remains with it; if anyone alters the macro, Excel notifies the user that macro should not be trusted. The most common provider of commercial digital certification is VeriSign, Inc.

Extra

To obtain a commercial certification, you must submit an application and pay a fee. You can find out more at www.verisign.com.

To view the certificates in your Personal Certificate store, open Windows Internet Explorer. On the Internet Explorer menu, click Tools and then click Internet Options. The Internet Options dialog box appears. Click the Content tab. Click the Certificates button. The Certificates dialog box appears. Click the Personal tab. All of your personal certificates appear.

Create a Digital Signature

1. Click the Start button.
2. Click All Programs.
3. Click Microsoft Office.
4. Click Microsoft Office Tools.
5. Click Digital Certificate for VBA Projects.

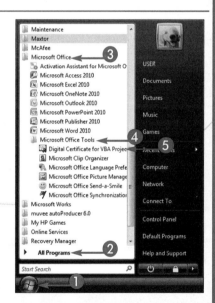

The Create Digital Certificate dialog box appears.

6. Type the name you want to give your certificate.
7. Click OK.

Excel creates a Personal Digital Certificate.

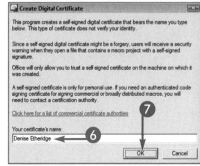

Record a Macro

A macro enables you to automate common tasks. You can use a macro to record any series of commands you can execute in Excel. For example, if you frequently apply a certain format to your worksheet, you can record the steps for creating the format and then play them back each time you want to apply the format.

Clicking the Macro Recorder button opens the Record Macro dialog box in which you can name your macro, assign your macro to a shortcut key, and tell Excel where you want to store your macro. You can name your macro anything you want; however, the name must start with a letter; only contain letters, numbers, and underscores; and not contain any spaces. You can assign any upper- or lowercase letter to act as the shortcut key.

In the Record Macro dialog box, the Store Macro In field tells Excel where to store your macro. You can choose to store your macro in the Personal Macro Workbook, a New Workbook, or This Workbook. Use the Personal Macro Workbook option if you want to make your macro available to all Excel files. After you have stored at least one macro in the Personal Macro Workbook, the workbook opens whenever you open an Excel file. Use the New Workbook option if you have specialized macros that you want to use with multiple files. If you store your macro in a New Workbook, you can use the macros whenever that workbook is open. Use the This Workbook option if you want your macro to be in the workbook in which you are currently working.

Record a Macro

1 Click the Developer tab.

Note: See the section "Introducing Macros" to learn how to display the Developer tab.

- Alternatively, click the Record Macro button (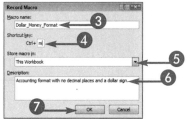) on the status bar and skip Step 2.

2 Click Record Macro.

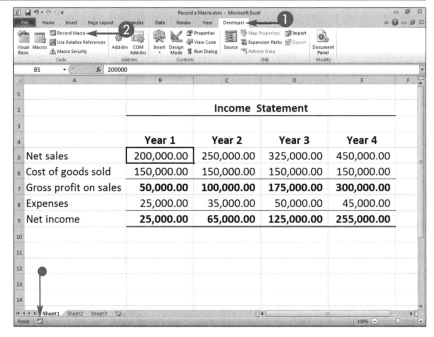

The Record Macro dialog box appears.

3 Type the name you want to give your macro.

4 Type the shortcut key you want to assign to your macro.

Press Shift as you type to assign an uppercase key.

5 Click the ▼ and then select the workbook in which you want to store your macro.

6 Type a description of your macro.

7 Click OK.

⑧ Perform the steps you want to record.

Note: *This example changes the number format using the following steps. Click the Home tab. Click the Number Group launcher. Click Accounting. Set Decimal Place to 0. Select $ as Symbol. Click OK.*

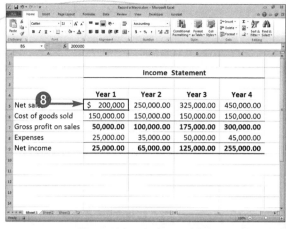

⑨ Click the Developer tab.

● Alternatively, click the Stop Recording button (■) on the status bar and skip Step 10.

⑩ Click Stop Recording.

Excel stops recording your macro.

Your macro is ready for you to use.

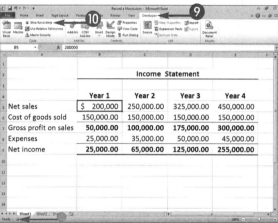

Extra

A macro you create in Excel can have a relative, an absolute, or a mixed reference. If you use a relative reference, Excel performs the macro based on a relative location. For example, suppose you move up two cells from cell A3 to cell A1 when creating your macro. When you run your macro, if you are in cell C3, Excel will move up two cells from cell C3 to cell C1. If you use an absolute reference, however, Excel performs the macro based on the exact cell addresses. For example, suppose again that you move up two cells from cell A3 to A1. When you run your macro, if you are in cell C3, Excel moves from there to the cells you used when you recorded your macro. That is, Excel moves from cell A3 to cell A1.

By default, Excel creates macros with an absolute reference. To create a macro with a relative reference, click Use Relative References in the Code group on the Developer tab to toggle the relative reference option on. To create a macro with both a relative and an absolute reference — a mixed reference — toggle the Use Relative References button on and off as needed as you create your macro.

Assign a Digital Signature to a Macro

A digital signature provides assurance that a workbook file that contains macros is valid and no one has altered the macros. There are two types of digital signatures: personal digital signatures and commercial digital signatures. You can create a personal digital signature by using the Microsoft SelfCert.exe tool, or you can purchase a digital signature. Refer to the section "Create a Digital Signature" to learn how to create digital signatures. After you create a digital signature, you must attach it to your workbook. Attaching a digital signature is similar to sealing an envelope. If an envelope arrives sealed, you have some level of assurance that no one has tampered with its contents.

Use the Digital Signature dialog box to attach a digital signature. Visual Basic Editor (VBE) is a separate Excel module that you can use to edit your macros. Access the Digital Signature dialog box by opening the VBE. The Digital Signature dialog box lists valid certificates. You can use the Digital Signature dialog box to view certificates and to select the one you want to use.

Unless you have on your computer a valid digital signature certificate for the signature used to sign a macro, Excel removes the digital signature when you modify a macro and you must reattach it. If you are not sure if a workbook has a digital signature, you can check the signature by reviewing the Digital Signature dialog box. If a workbook has a digital signature, the name of the signature appears in the Certificate Name field. If you click the Remove button in the Digital Signature dialog box, Excel removes the digital signature.

Assign a Digital Signature to a Macro

① Click the Developer tab.

Note: *See the section "Introducing Macros" to learn how to display the Developer tab.*

② Click Visual Basic in the Code group.

Visual Basic Editor appears.

③ Click Tools → Digital Signature.

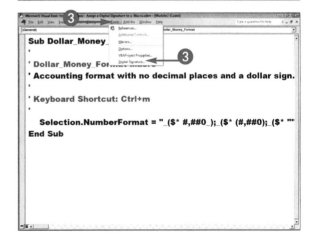

The Digital Signature dialog box appears.

④ Click Choose.

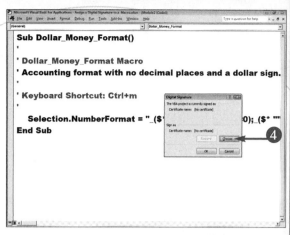

The Select Certificate dialog box appears.

Note: *See the section "Create a Digital Signature" to learn how to create a digital signature.*

⑤ Click the signature you want to apply.

⑥ Click OK to close the Select Certificate dialog box.

⑦ Click OK to close the Digital Signature dialog box.

Excel attaches the digital signature to your workbook.

Note: *To return to Excel, press Alt+Q.*

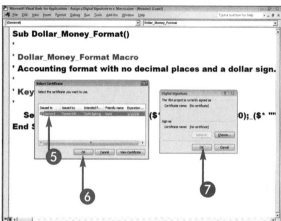

Extra

If you have Macro Security enabled, Excel displays the Trust Bar below the Ribbon when you open a workbook containing a signed macro. You can modify the workbook, but you cannot use the macros. If you trust that the document is safe, you can click the Enable Content button on the Trust Bar to enable the macros in the workbook. The workbook then becomes a trusted document and you will not need to enable the workbook again.

You can use the Microsoft Office Security Options dialog box to select the security option you want. On the Trust Bar, click Macros have been disabled. Security warning options appear. Click the Enable Content button. A menu appears. Click Advanced Options. The Microsoft Office Security Options dialog box appears. Click, Help protect me from unknown content (Recommended), to disable the macros; click, Enable the content for this session, to enable the macros for one session; or click, Trust all documents from this publisher, to add the macro publisher to the Trusted Publisher list. Excel does not display a warning when you open workbooks with macros if the publisher is on the Trusted Publisher list.

Run a Macro

Macros enable you to quickly perform tasks that would normally take multiple steps. When you run a macro, Excel replays the steps you recorded when you created the macro. You can run any macro located in any workbook as long as the workbook in which the macro is located is open. To run a macro, you can press the shortcut key you assigned when you created the macro or you can select the macro from the Macro dialog box.

When you create a macro, you can choose to store it in one of three locations: the current workbook, a new workbook, or the Personal Macro Workbook. By default, the Macro dialog box lists all the macros in open workbooks. If a macro is stored in the Personal Macro Workbook, the macro opens in a hidden file each time

you open a file. By default, the files in the Personal Macro Workbook always appear in the Macro dialog box.

You can use the Macros in field to limit the number of macros listed in the Macro dialog box. To see the macros in any open workbook, including the Personal Macro Workbook, select the All Open Workbooks from the macros in drop-down list. To see the macros from a specific workbook, select the name of the workbook from the Macros in drop-down list. To see global macros stored in the Personal Macro Workbook, select the Personal.xlsb from the Macros in drop-down list.

To run macros from another workbook, the macros must be from a signed source or you must enable the macros. You can set the security setting for macros. See the section "Set Macro Security" to learn more about macro security.

Run a Macro

① Select the cells where you want to apply your macro.

② Click the Developer tab.

Note: *See the task "Introducing Macros" to learn how to display the Developer tab.*

③ Click Macros.

Alternatively, press Alt+F8.

The Macro dialog box appears.

④ If your macro does not appear in the Macro dialog box, click the ▾ and then select the workbook that contains your macro.

⑤ Click the name of the macro you want to run.

⑥ Click Run.

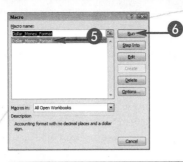

● Excel runs the macro.

You can also run your macro by pressing the shortcut key you assigned when you created your macro.

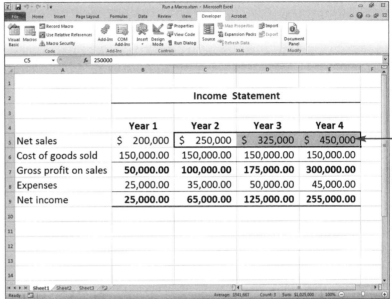

Extra

Excel differentiates between macros listed in the Macro dialog box by placing the name of the workbook that contains the macros in front of the macro name. For example, Excel lists a macro named Sum_Expenses in the Personal Macro Workbook as PERSONAL. XLSB!Sum_Expenses. If the macro Sum_Cells exists in both the Budget.xlsm and Expenses.xlsm workbooks, Excel treats them as two different macros. The Macro dialog box lists them as Budget.xlsm!Sum_Cells and Expenses.xlsm!Sum_Cells.

Unless you have your macro settings set to enable all macros, Excel checks all documents you open for macros. See the section "Set Macro Security" for more information. If you have files that you do not want Excel to check, you can store them in a trusted location. Click the Developer tab. Click Macro Security in the Code group. The Trust Center appears. Click Trusted Locations. The Trust Location pane appears. Click Add New Location. The Microsoft Office Trusted Location dialog box appears. Enter the path to the trusted location. Click OK.

Create and Launch a Keyboard Shortcut

A keyboard shortcut is a combination of keys you press to execute a command. You can use a keyboard shortcut to launch an Excel macro command. You can assign an upper- or lowercase key to a macro when you create it or assign one later by using the Macro Options dialog box. You execute a macro keyboard shortcut by pressing the Ctrl key along with that upper- or lowercase key. Refer to the task "Record a Macro" to learn how to create a macro.

Keyboard shortcuts are case sensitive. For example, Excel interprets a lowercase *m* and an uppercase *M* as two different keys. To execute a macro you have assigned to a lowercase letter, press Ctrl plus the letter; for example, Ctrl+m. To execute a macro you have assigned to an uppercase letter, press the Ctrl key and the Shift key plus the letter; for example, Ctrl+Shift+M.

If you give the same keyboard shortcut to macros in two different workbooks, you may execute the wrong macro if you use the shortcut while you have both workbooks open. Excel cannot discern from which workbook you want the macro. You can use the Macro Options dialog box to reassign one of the conflicting macros to a new key.

You should also be careful not to assign the macro to a keyboard shortcut that Excel uses. If you do, Excel will execute your macro instead of the command it created. For example, by default, Ctrl+o opens the Open dialog box. If you assign *o* to a macro, your macro will override Excel's assignment.

Create and Launch a Keyboard Shortcut

Create a Keyboard Shortcut

1. Click the Developer tab.

2. Click Macros.

   The Macro dialog box appears.

3. Click the desired macro.

4. Click the Options button.

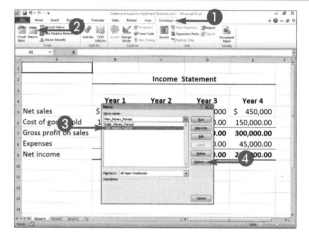

   The Macro Options dialog box appears.

5. Type the desired shortcut key.

   Press Shift as you type to assign an uppercase key.

6. Type a description.

7. Click OK to close the Macro Options dialog box.

8. Click Close to close the Macro dialog box.

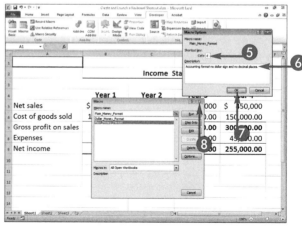

Launch a Keyboard Shortcut

① Select the cells where you want the macro to execute.

② Press Ctrl and the shortcut key.

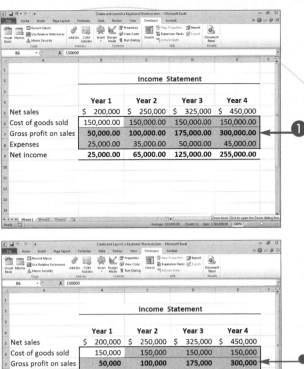

● The macro executes.

③ Repeat Steps 1 and 2 to execute the macro again.

Note: *In this example, the macro removes the decimal places.*

Extra

If you do not use a macro shortcut frequently, it is easy to forget the keyboard shortcut you assigned to your macro. If you forget your keyboard shortcut, you can view it in the Macro Options dialog box.

You can execute a macro by assigning the macro to a picture, clip art, shape, or smart art. For example, if you want to assign a macro to a picture, you start by inserting the picture into your worksheet by clicking the Insert tab and then clicking Picture. The Insert Picture dialog box appears. In the Look In field, select the folder in which you stored the picture you want to insert. The pictures in that folder appear. Click the picture you want to insert and then click the Insert button. The picture appears in the worksheet. Click and drag the picture to place it where you want it and then right-click the picture twice. A menu appears. Click Assign Macro. The Assign Macro dialog box appears. Click the macro you want to assign to the picture and then click OK. Excel assigns the macro to the picture. Click the picture when you want to execute the macro.

Assign a Macro to the Quick Access Toolbar

You can assign a macro to the Excel Quick Access Toolbar. You can execute macros assigned to the Quick Access Toolbar using a shortcut key or the Macro dialog box; however, using the Quick Access Toolbar means you can access the macros by simply clicking the appropriate button.

When you add a button to the Quick Access Toolbar, you can specify whether it should appear on the toolbar of all Excel workbooks or only on the Quick Access Toolbar in the workbook you specify. By default, the button will appear in all workbooks. If you have placed your macro in the Personal Macro Workbook, you will probably want your macro button to appear in all workbooks because the macro will be available to all workbooks. If your macro will only be available to a single workbook, your

macro button should only appear on the Quick Access Toolbar for that workbook.

You use the Customize the Quick Access Toolbar page of the Excel Options dialog box to add a macro button to the Quick Access Toolbar. You can use the Modify button to specify the button you want to use to represent your macro. You can specify where on the Quick Access Toolbar your button appears and whether the Quick Access Toolbar appears above or below the Ribbon. You can click the Reset button to return the Quick Access Toolbar to its default state.

Deleting a macro does not remove the macro button from the Quick Access Toolbar. When you press the button for a deleted macro, you receive an error message. Use the Remove button on the Customize the Quick Access Toolbar page of the Excel Options dialog box to remove a macro button.

Assign a Macro to the Quick Access Toolbar

① Click the Customize Quick Access Toolbar button and then select More Commands.

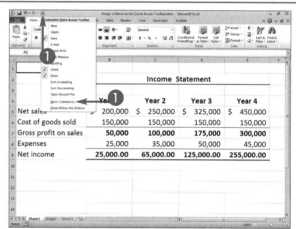

The Excel Options dialog box appears.

② Click the Choose commands from ⏷ and then select Macros.

③ Click the Customize Quick Access Toolbar ⏷ and then select the workbook in which the button should appear.

④ Click the macro you want to assign to the Quick Access Toolbar.

⑤ Click Add.

● The macro appears in the box on the right.

⑥ Click Modify.

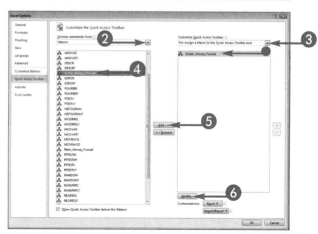

The Modify Button dialog box appears.

7 Click the button you want to use to represent your macro.

8 Click OK to close the Modify Button dialog box.

9 Click OK to close the Excel Options dialog box.

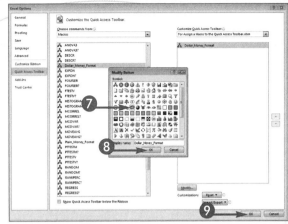

● The button appears on the Quick Access Toolbar.

10 Click the button to execute your macro.

Excel executes the macro.

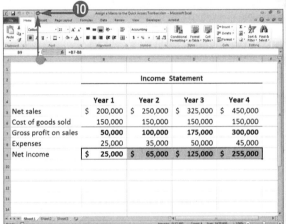

Extra

You can also assign a macro to a custom Ribbon tab. Right-click the Microsoft Office Ribbon. A menu appears. Click Customize the Ribbon. The Excel Options dialog box appears with the Customize the Ribbon pane selected. Click the down arrow next to the Choose commands from field and then select Macros. Click the down arrow next to the Customize the Ribbon field and then select Main Tabs. Click the New Tab button. Excel creates a new tab and a new group. Click New Tab (Custom) and then click Rename. The Rename dialog box appears. Type the name you want to give the tab. Click New Group (Custom) and then click Rename. The Rename dialog box appears. Type the name you want to give the group. Click the macro you want to add to the custom Tab and then click the Add button. Excel places the macro in the Main tabs box. Click Rename. The Rename dialog box appears. Click the symbol you want to use to represent the macro. Click OK to close the Rename dialog box. Click OK to close the Excel Options dialog box. The macro appears on the new tab you created.

Delete a Macro

You can delete macros you no longer need by clicking the Delete button in the Macro dialog box. Because the Macro dialog box only displays macros in open workbooks, the workbook that contains the macro must be open before you can delete the macro.

The Personal Macro Workbook stores macros you want to make available to all workbooks. Excel creates the Personal Macro Workbook when you choose to store your first macro in it. After Excel creates the Personal Macro Workbook, the workbook opens as a hidden file every time you open Excel. To learn more about storing macros in the Personal Macro Workbook, see the section "Record a Macro."

If your macro is in a hidden workbook such as the Personal Macro Workbook, you must unhide the workbook before you can delete the macro. If you try to delete a macro from the Personal Macro Workbook prior to unhiding it, Excel displays the following message: "Cannot edit a macro on a hidden workbook, Unhide the workbook using the Unhide command." You unhide the Personal Macro Workbook and other hidden workbooks by executing the Unhide command on the View tab.

If you unhide the Personal Macro Workbook, make sure you hide it again using the Hide command on the View tab after you delete the macros. Hiding the workbook prevents you from making inadvertent changes to it.

You cannot undo the deletion process. If you delete a macro by mistake, you can close the workbook without saving. Of course, if you close without saving, you will lose all the work you have done since saving. Your only other alternative is to re-create the macro.

Delete a Macro

Unhide a Workbook

1 Click the View tab.

2 Click Unhide.

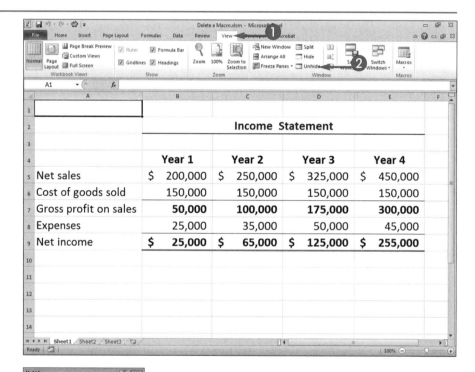

The Unhide dialog box appears.

3 Click the workbook you want to unhide.

4 Click OK.

Excel unhides the workbook.

Delete a Macro

1. Click the Developer tab.

2. Click Macros.

   The Macro dialog box appears.

3. Click the macro you want to delete.

4. Click Delete.

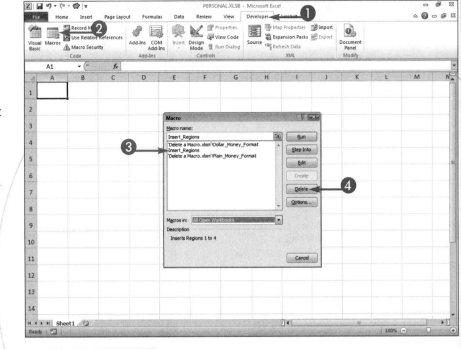

A message box appears, asking you to confirm you want to delete the macro.

5. Click Yes.

   Excel deletes the macro.

Extra

There are two ways to create a macro. One way is to use the macro recorder to record the steps needed to perform the action. The other way is to create the steps by typing the Visual Basic for Applications (VBA) code into the Code window of the Visual Basic Editor (VBE). When you use the macro recorder, Excel automatically creates the VBA code for you. You can use the VBE to edit macros you have created with the macro recorder. Often, it is convenient to use a combination of the two methods to create your VBA code: You record part of the VBA code and then you use the VBE to augment or modify your code.

To activate the VBE, you can press Alt+F11 while in Excel or click the Visual Basic button on the Developer tab. If you create your macros using the macro recorder, Excel defines each macro you create as a procedure and stores each procedure in a module. The VBE lists modules in the Project Explorer under the workbook in which they are located. If you are interested in learning more about VBA, refer to *Excel Programming: Your Visual Blueprint for Creating Interactive Spreadsheets, 3rd Edition (Wiley, 2010)*.

Place a Screenshot in Your Worksheet

A *screenshot* is a picture of a computer screen. You can use Excel's screenshot option whenever you want to illustrate a worksheet by adding a picture of a computer screen. For example, you may want to include a screenshot of a Web page or a screenshot of a software application window in your worksheet.

You can take a screenshot of any open window; however, the window must be maximized. The shot can be of the entire window or a portion of the window. A screenshot of a portion of a window is called a *clipping*. If you only want a portion of a window, the window you want the clipping of should be the only window maximized.

When you click a screenshot, the Picture tools appear and, just as you can with any other picture, you can

adjust the brightness and contrast, apply artistic effects, compress the picture, change the picture, reset the picture, apply a style, insert the picture in a layout, resize the picture, or perform any other picture task. This chapter teaches you how to perform these picture tasks.

In Excel 2010 and Excel 2007, when you open a workbook that was created in Excel 2003 or earlier, you are working in compatibility mode. When you are in compatibility mode, the words "Compatibility Mode" appear on the title bar. You cannot use the screenshot option in compatibility mode. To enable the screenshot option, save your workbook as an Excel 2010 worksheet with an .xlsx extension.

Place a Screenshot in Your Worksheet

Take a Screenshot

1 Click the Insert tab.

2 Click Screenshot.

The windows you can take screenshots of appear.

3 Click the window for which you want a screenshot.

● A screenshot of the window appears in your worksheet.

Take a Screenshot of a Portion of a Window

1 Make sure the window you want a screen shot of is the only window maximized.

2 Click the Insert tab.

3 Click Screenshot.

A menu appears.

4 Click Screen Clipping.

Excel moves to the maximized window and the mouse pointer becomes a crosshair.

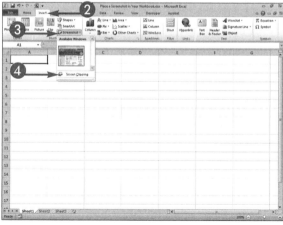

292

⑤ Click and drag to select the portion of the window you want.

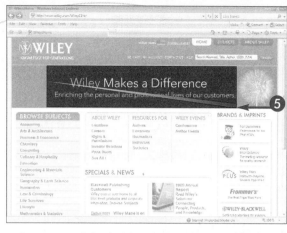

● When you release the mouse, the portion of the window you selected appears in your worksheet.

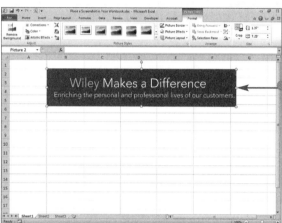

Extra

You can use the screenshot feature on maximized windows. A window is *maximized* when it fills your entire computer screen. A window is *minimized* when it appears on the taskbar, but cannot otherwise be seen. To open a minimized window, click the windows name on the taskbar. To maximize the window, click the Maximize button (▣) in the upper-right corner of the window. To minimize a window, click the Minimize button (▭) in the upper-right corner of the window.

In Windows, you can take a picture of your computer screen at any time by pressing the Print Screen key. Pressing the Print Screen key places a copy of the screen on the clipboard. Once the screen is on the clipboard, you can paste it into Excel by clicking the Paste button on the Home tab or by pressing Ctrl+V. The screen arrives in Excel as a picture and when you click the picture, the Picture tools appear.

Insert Clip Art into Your Worksheet

Y ou can use clip art to illustrate your worksheet. Clip art comes with Microsoft Office. You access it through the Clip Art pane. You probably think of clip art as illustrations, but you can access illustrations, video, audio, and photographs by using the Clip Art pane.

You tell Excel what you are looking for by typing a word or phrase in the Search for field and then selecting the types of media you want. If you are connected to the Web, you can include Office.com media in your search.

After you have inserted a clip art illustration or a photograph in your worksheet, you can move and resize it. You can also apply any of the Picture tools.

Apply It

When you right-click an object in the clip art pane, a menu appears. Click Preview/Properties to open the Preview/Properties dialog box. The Preview/Properties dialog box provides you with information on the properties of the object such as the file type, size, and orientation. You can use the Preview/Properties dialog box page through all of the objects in the Clip Art pane.

Insert Clip Art into Your Worksheet

① Click the Insert tab.

② Click Clip Art.

The Clip Art pane appears.

③ Type what you a searching for in the Search for field.

④ Click the 🔽 and then select the media types you want.

⑤ Click Include Office.com if you want to search Office.com (changes to ✔).

⑥ Click Go.

Excel retrieves the clip art.

⑦ Double-click the clip art you want.

Excel places the clip art in your worksheet.

● Click the Close button (⊠) to close the Clip Art pane.

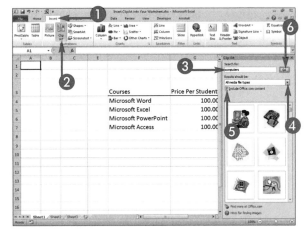

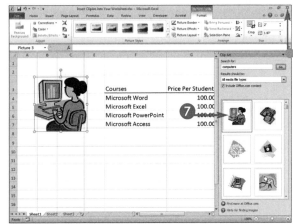

Crop a Clip Art Illustration or a Photograph

I f a picture is too large or contains extraneous information around the edges, you can crop the picture to make it smaller or to remove the extraneous information. You can crop clip art illustrations and photographs, but you cannot crop shapes, text boxes, Smart Art graphics or WordArt.

The crop tool places crop markers on the sides and corners of a picture. You can drag the markers to indicate the portion of the picture you want to keep. Excel will darken the portion of the picture it will remove when you press the Crop button.

You compress pictures to make the file size smaller. When you compress a picture, you can further reduce the file size by telling Excel to delete the cropped areas of the picture. See the section, "Compress a Picture" to learn more.

Extra

You can also crop to a shape. For example, you can crop a picture so that it appears in the shape of an arrow. To crop to a shape, place your crop marks where you want them. Click the down arrow (⏷) under crop. A menu appears. Select Crop to Shape. A submenu appears. Click th shape you want. Excel crops the picture to the shape you selected.

Crop a Clip Art Illustration or a Photograph

1 Click the picture.

The Picture tools appear.

2 Click the Format tab.

3 Click Crop.

4 Drag the crop markers to indicate the portion of the picture you want to keep.

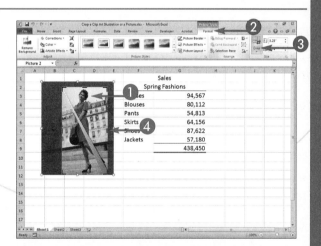

5 Click Crop.

Excel crops the picture.

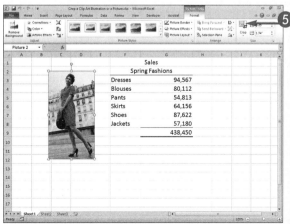

Insert a Picture into Your Worksheet

Pictures, like screenshots and clipart, can illustrate your point, emphasize your message, and enhance your worksheet. You can include pictures from your personal collections of digital drawings, digital photographs, or scanned photographs in your worksheet. For example, a real estate sales office can include in a worksheet pictures of all the homes available for sale.

Adding a picture is easy. Just locate the picture and insert it. Once a picture is inserted, you can modify it by using any of the Picture tools. For example, you can adjust the brightness and contrast or you can use a style to add a border, reflection, and/or shadow to a picture.

Apply It

It is easy to include photographs found on the Web in your Excel worksheet. Just right-click the photograph and then click Copy on the menu that appears. Move to your worksheet, click the upper-left corner of the location where you want to paste the picture, right-click, and then click Paste. The picture appears in your worksheet.

Insert a Picture into Your Worksheet

① Click the Insert tab.

② Click Picture.

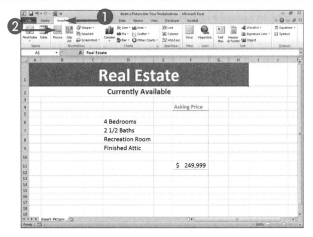

The Insert picture dialog box appears.

③ Locate the folder that contains the picture you want.

④ Click the picture.

⑤ Click the Insert button.

● The picture appears in your worksheet.

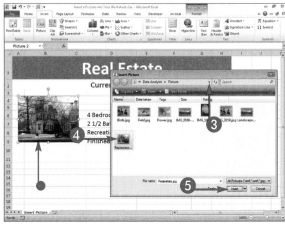

Recolor a Picture

*S**aturation* is a measure of the intensity of color. In Excel, Saturation levels range from 0 to 400% with 400% creating the most vivid colors. If your image is dull or washed out, you may want to increase the saturation. If the colors in your image are too bright, you may want to decrease the saturation.

Color tone refers to temperature of an image. In Excel, temperature values range from 1,500 to 11,500. Warmer images have more red tones. You can use Excel's Color option to make your pictures warmer.

You can recolor your pictures by using Excel's Recolor option. You change an image to gray scale, sepia, or black and white, or you can use the Recolor option to add a color cast to your picture.

Apply It

When you click the Color button, Excel provides you with preset values for color saturation and color tone. If you want to manually set theses values, you can. Click the picture. The Picture tools appear. Click the Format tab and then click Color in the Adjust group. A menu appears. Click Picture Color Options. The Format Picture dialog box appears. You can use the sliders to adjust the Saturation or Temperature.

Recolor a Picture

① Click the screenshot, photograph, or clip art.

The Picture tools appear.

② Click the Format tab.

③ Click Color.

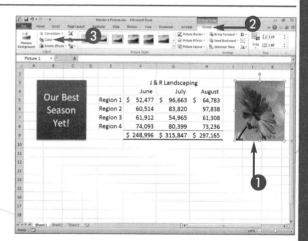

The Color Saturation, Color Tone, and Recolor options appear.

④ Click the option you want.

Excel applies the option to your image.

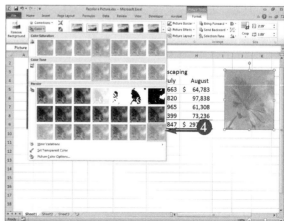

Adjust the Sharpness, Brightness, and Contrast

*S*harpness is a measure of how clearly you can see the details in an image, *brightness* is a measure of how light or dark an image is, and *contrast* is a measure of the difference between the darkest and the lightest areas of an image. Pictures that are blurred are soft and have a low level of sharpness, pictures that are dark have a low level of brightness, and pictures that have little detail may have too much or too little contrast. In Excel, you can adjust the sharpness, brightness, and contrast of pictures.

Sharpness, brightness, and contrast are measured by values that range from –100% to +100%. To increase the sharpness, set the sharpness value higher. Conversely, to decrease the sharpness or make an image softer, set the sharpness value lower. To lighten an image, set the

brightness value higher. Conversely to darken an image, set the brightness value lower. Contrast works in a similar fashion. To reduce contrast, lower the contrast value; to increase contrast, increase the contrast value.

In Excel, the Sharpen and Soften and Brightness and Contrast options display a preview of the selected image at various preset levels. Sharpen and Soften display five sharpness values: Soften 50%, Soften 25%, Sharpen 0%, Sharpen 25%, and Sharpen 50%. Brightness and Contrast display 25 brightness and contrast levels with preset values ranging from Brightness –40 Contrast –40 to Brightness +40 Contrast +40. As you position your mouse pointer over each option, you can see the effect the selection will have on your picture.

Adjust the Sharpness, Brightness, and Contrast

Adjust the Sharpness

1 Click the screenshot, photograph, or clip art.

The Picture tools appear.

2 Click the Format tab.

3 Click Corrections.

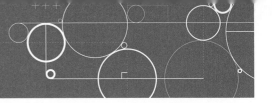
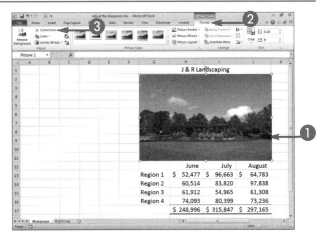

The Sharpen and Soften options appear.

4 Click the option you want.

Excel applies the option to your image.

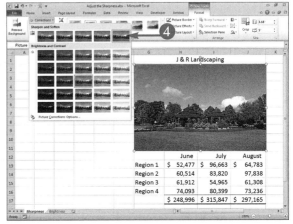

Adjust the Brightness and Contrast

① Click the screenshot, picture or clip art.

The Picture tools appear.

② Click the Format tab.

③ Click Corrections.

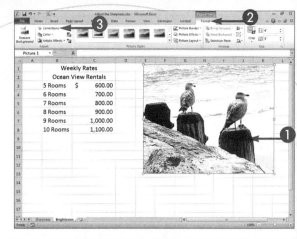

The Brightness and Contrast options appear.

④ Click the option you want.

Excel applies the option to your image.

Apply It

When you click the Corrections button, Excel provides you with preset values for sharpness and brightness and contrast. If you want to manually set theses values, you can. Click the screenshot, picture, or clip art. The Picture tools appear. Click the Format tab and then click Corrections in the Adjust group. A menu appears. Click Picture Corrections Options at the bottom of the menu. The Format Picture dialog box appears with the Picture Corrections pane selected. You can use the Soften and Sharpen, Brightness, and Contrast sliders to incrementally adjust each of these values. When using the Format Picture dialog box, you can apply the full range of values, from –100% to +100%, and can adjust each of the options separately.

To set the image back to the state it was in before you made any adjustments, click the Reset button. To apply one of the preset values, click the down arrow ( ) in the Sharpen and Soften presets area or click the down arrow ( ) in the Brightness and Contrast presets area and then select the preset you want. Click Close when you have completed your adjustments.

Compress a Picture

Images, such as photographs, can be extremely large files and, as a result, you can dramatically increase an Excel workbook's overall file size. Large files take up a lot of space on your hard drive and if you e-mail them to someone else, they can take a long time to download. You can reduce the size of an image by compressing the image, reducing the resolution, and/or discarding cropped portions of the image. Compressing the image reduces the file size with no loss of quality. You can compress individual images or all the images in a workbook.

Digital photographs are made up of small dots called *pixels*. Each pixel represents a color and putting all the pixels together creates the photograph. *Resolution* refers to the number of pixels per inch. Images with more pixels

per inch — higher resolution — show more detail. Reducing an image's resolution reduces the file size. It may also reduce the quality of the image. The Compress pictures dialog box provides you with several options for reducing resolution. Generally speaking, you want to lowest pixel per inch (ppi) that will give you a satisfactory quality. Excel provides some guidelines: for workbooks that will be printed, choose the Print option; for workbooks that will be primarily viewed on-screen, use the Screen option; and for workbooks that will be e-mailed, use the E-mail option. If you do not want to change the resolution, choose Use Document Resolution.

In Excel, when you crop an image, you hide portions of the image from view. Discarding the hidden portions reduces the size of the file.

Compress a Picture

① Click the photograph or screenshot.

The Picture tools appear.

② Click the Format tab.

③ Click Compress Pictures (icon).

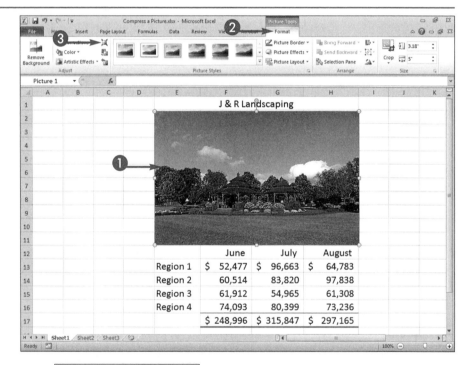

The Compress Pictures dialog box appears.

④ Click the Apply only to this picture option to compress only the selected picture (☐ changes to ✔).

⑤ Click the Delete cropped areas of the picture option to delete cropped areas (☐ changes to ✔).

6 Click a Target output selection to reduce the resolution (⊙ changes to ◉).

7 Click OK.

Excel applies the options you selected to your image.

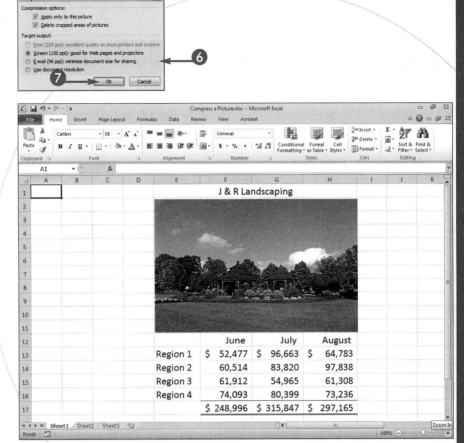

Add a Border

You can make a picture more attractive by adding a border. You can choose the color of the border from Theme Colors, Standard Colors, or the Microsoft Color Box. Theme Colors are sets of colors for use throughout a document. If you choose a Theme Color, and later change the theme, the color of your border changes to the appropriate color for the new theme.

Standard colors are popular colors that are often used. On the Picture Border menu, the More Outline Colors option opens the Microsoft Color Box. The Microsoft Color Box enables you to choose virtually any color. If you use a standard color or a color from the Microsoft Color Box, the color of your border will not change when you change the theme.

Apply It

The weight you assign the border determines how wide the border is. Weight values are measured in points (pt). The higher the point value, the wider the border. To set the width of a border, click the picture, click the Format tab, click Picture Border, click Weight. A menu appears. Click the weight you want.

Add a Border

1 Click the screenshot, photograph, or clip art.

The Picture tools appear.

2 Click the Format tab.

3 Click Picture Border.

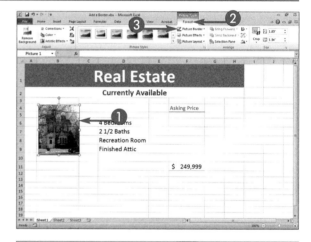

A menu appears.

4 Click the border color you want.

● Excel creates a border around your image using the color you selected.

Add a
Picture Effect

You can enhance the pictures in your Excel worksheets by adding the effects such as Shadow, Reflection, Glow, Soft Edges, Bevel, 3-D Rotation, and Preset.

- Shadow effects apply a drop-shadow or inner shadow to the picture. A drop-shadow creates the illusion that the picture is above the worksheet and a shadow is being cast behind it. An inner shadow creates a shadow inside the picture.

- Reflection effects create a transparent mirror image of the picture. You can choose how close the reflection is to the original picture and how large the reflection is.

- Glow effects create a transparent border around the picture. You can choose the color and size of the border.

- Soft Edges effects feather the edges of the picture so that the edges gradually become transparent. The picture seems to fade into the worksheet.

- Bevel effects give the picture a three-dimensional look by making the edges appear to be beveled. You can choose from several bevel styles.

- 3-D Rotation effects rotate the picture so that the picture appears to be three-dimensional. You can choose the rotation angle.

- Preset effects combine the Shadow, Reflection, Glow, Soft Edges, Bevel, and 3-D Rotation effects to create a variety of interesting results.

Picture effects can be applied to screenshots, clip art, photographs, and shapes. Some effects can also be applied to WordArt. You can even apply multiple picture effects to the same picture. To remove each picture effect, click the No option at the top of the effect's menu.

Add A Picture Effect

1. Click the picture.

   The Picture tools appear.

2. Click the Format tab.

3. Click Picture Effects.

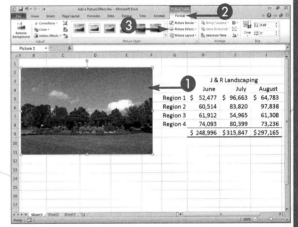

A menu appears.

4. Click the type of picture effect you want to apply.

   A gallery appears.

5. Click a picture effect.

   Excel applies the Picture Effect.

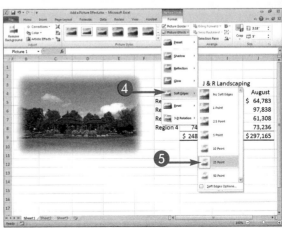

Apply a Picture Style

You can create a frame for a picture by adding a border. See the section, "Add a Border" in this chapter to learn more about borders. You can further enhance your picture by adding picture effects such as shadows, reflections, glows, soft edges, bevels, 3-D rotations, or presets. See the section, "Add a Picture Effect" in this chapter to learn more about picture effects. All these elements can be combined in a myriad of ways to create a myriad of effects. This can be fun, but also time-consuming. You can save time by using a Picture Style. Excel has combined a number of borders and picture effects and placed them in the Style gallery so that you can apply them with just a few clicks.

Apply a Picture Style

1 Click the picture.

The Picture tools appear.

2 Click the Format tab.

3 Click the More button (▾).

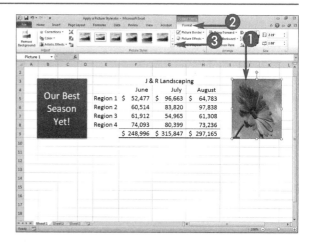

A gallery of styles appears.

4 Click the style you want to apply.

Excel applies the style.

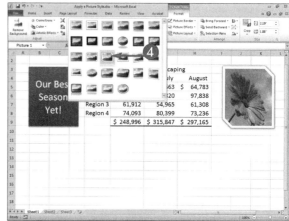

Add an Artistic Effect

By adding an artistic effect, you can make a photograph appear to be a painting, a drawing, or an interesting piece of art. Applying an artistic effect is not complicated. After you choose the Artistic Effects option on the Format tab, you hover your mouse pointer over the items in the gallery; Excel displays the name of the effect and provides you with a live preview of how your picture will appear if you click the effect to choose it. There are many effects from which to choose. None is the first option. Choose None if want to remove an effect.

The Marker, Paint Strokes, and Watercolor Sponge effects each cause the picture to appear to have been painted by using a particular medium: the Marker effect, by using a marker; the Paint Strokes effect,

by using a brush; and the Watercolor Sponge effect, by using watercolors with a sponge. The Texturizer and Cement effects add texture and cause your picture to appear to be painted on canvass.

The Pencil Grayscale, Grayscale Sketch, Line Drawing, and Chalk Sketch effects cause your picture to appear to be a drawing. The Pencil Grayscale effect changes your picture into a grayscale image and causes it to appear to be drawn in pencil. The Chalk Sketch effect changes your picture into a grayscale image and causes it to appear to be drawn in chalk. The Line Drawing effect causes your picture to appear to be drawn in colored pencils, and the Pastels Smooth effect causes your picture to appear to be drawn using pastels. Film Grain adds grain to your picture and Plastic Wrap causes your picture to appear to be molded from plastic.

Add an Artistic effect

① Click the picture.

The Picture tools appear.

② Click the Format tab.

③ Click Artistic Effects.

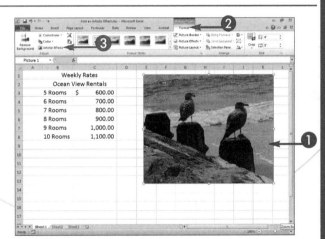

A gallery of artistic effects appears.

④ Click the artistic effect you want to apply.

Excel applies the artistic effect.

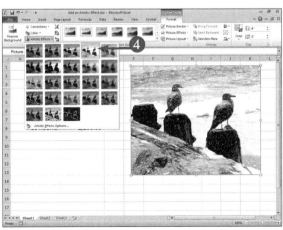

Remove a Background

You can use Excel to remove a background from a picture. This option is useful when you like the person or object in the picture but you do not like the setting. The Background Removal tool works best when there is a clear color contrast between the object you want to keep and the background.

When you click the Background Removal button, Excel makes its best guess at what you want to remove. It places a rectangular bounding box around the rectangular area of the picture that it will include in the final picture. It covers the parts of the picture it will remove with a transparent purple film. You can click and drag the handles on the bounding box to increase or decrease the area of the picture that will be included in the final picture.

To keep parts of a picture that Excel wants to remove, use the Mark Areas to Keep button. Excel places a plus sign on the part of the picture you want to keep and keeps that portion of the picture. To remove parts of a picture that Excel wants to keep, use the Mark Areas to Remove button. Excel places a minus sign on the part of the picture you want to remove and removes that portion of the picture. If you change your mind about a portion of a picture that is marked to be kept or removed, use the Delete Mark button. When you close the Background Removal tool, Excel makes the area it removes transparent.

Remove a Background

① Click the picture.

The Picture tools appear.

② Click the Format tab.

③ Click Background Removal.

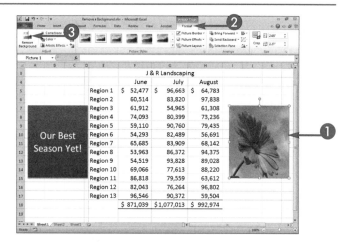

The Background Removal tab appears.

● Your picture appears with a bounding box.

● A purple film covers the area to be removed.

④ Click and drag the handles to adjust the size of the bounding box.

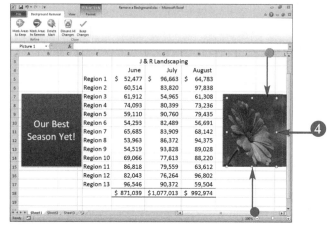

5 Click Mark Areas to Keep and then click the picture to include areas Excel wants to remove.

6 Click Mark Areas to Remove and then click the picture to remove areas Excel wants to include.

7 Click Keep Changes.

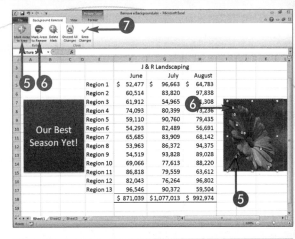

Excel removes the background and replaces it with a transparent area.

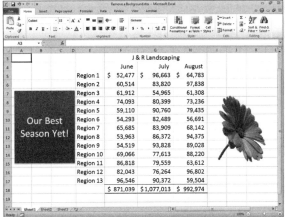

Apply It

After you remove a background, you can add a new one. Click the picture. Click Format and then click the launcher in the Picture Styles group. The Format Picture dialog box appears. Click Fill. The Fill options appear.

- To add a solid color fill, click the Solid Color radio button (⊙ changes to ⊙). Click the Color drop-down list and then click a color. Use the slider to adjust the transparency. Click Close. Excel adds a solid color background to your picture.

- To add a gradient fill, click the Gradient fill radio button (⊙ changes to ⊙). To use a preset fill, click the Preset Colors drop-down list and then click a preset gradient. Click the Type drop-down list and then click a gradient option. Click the Direction drop-down list and then click a direction option. Click Close. Excel adds a gradient background to your picture.

- To add a pattern fill, click the Pattern fill radio button (⊙ changes to ⊙). Click a pattern option. Click the Foreground Color drop-down list and then click a foreground color option. Click the Background Color drop-down list and then click a background color option. Click Close. Excel adds a pattern fill to your picture.

Insert a Text Box

A *text box* is a graphic that displays text. You draw the text box and then you type the text. You can add any amount of text to a text box; your text will automatically wrap when it reaches the width of the box. If you want your text box to be a perfect square, press and hold the Shift key as you click and drag to create the box. If you want it to align with the cell grid, press and hold the Alt key as you click and drag.

You can use a text box to create logos, add text to graphics, or annotate your worksheet. Additionally, you can apply a *style*, which is a set of formats, to a text box.

Apply It

You can use WordArt to create a text box that has a decorative text style. Click the Insert tab. Click WordArt. A gallery of WordArt styles appears. Click the WordArt style you want. A text box appears with text. Delete the text that appears and type your own text. You can modify WordArt text by using any of the options on the Format tab.

Insert a Text Box

1. Click the Insert tab.

2. Click Text Box.

3. Click and drag to create a text box.

- The Drawing tools appear.

4. Type your text.

5. Click the Format tab.

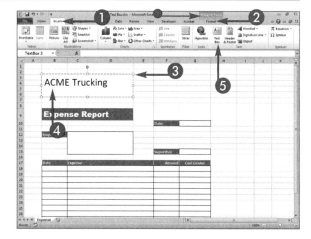

6. Click the More button (⬇) in the WordArt Styles group.

A gallery of choices appears.

7. Click a style.

- Excel applies the style.

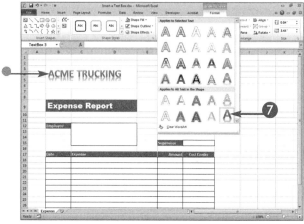

Format a Text Box

ou can add text effects to a text box. You simply select the text and then apply the effect. You can create text with shadows, reflections, glows, bevels, 3-D rotations, and transforms. Shadows give the illusion that a light is being cast on the text. Reflections create a transparent mirror image. Glows create a transparent border around the text. Bevels give the text a 3-D look. 3-D rotations rotate the text so it appears three-dimensional. Transforms warp or place the text on a path. For each option, you can choose from several subgroups and you can apply multiple effects. You can combine text effects with styles and other formatting options.

Apply It

A *fill* is a background color. Click the Fill button on the Format tab to add a fill to a text box. The fill can be a theme color; a standard color; any other color; a picture; a gradient; or a texture.

Click the Text Outline button to add or change a text outline. You can set the color, weight, or style of an outline.

Format a Text Box

① Select the text.

② Click the Format tab.

③ Click the Text Effects button.

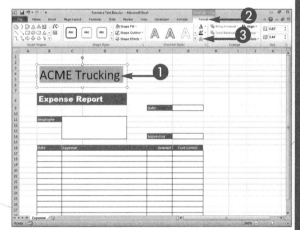

A menu appears.

④ Click a category.

⑤ Click a text effect.

● Excel applies the effect.

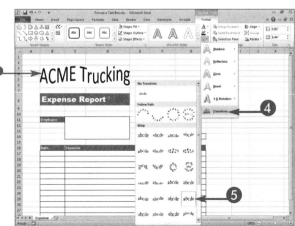

Insert a Shape

S hapes have a variety of purposes. For example, arrows point out relationships between data, and flowchart elements convey the structure of data. Excel provides a variety of shapes, including lines, rectangles, arrows, flowchart elements, stars, banners, and callouts — all of which you can use in your worksheet.

To create a shape you simply select a shape from the Shapes gallery and then click and drag to add the shape to your worksheet. Press and hold the Shift key while you click and drag if you want the shape to maintain its original proportions. Press and hold the Alt key as you click and drag if you want the shape to align with the table grid. A *style* is a predefined set of formats. You can apply a style to a shape.

Apply It

You can use Paste Special to copy and paste shapes. Select the shape. Click the Home tab. Click the Copy button (🖼). Click the down arrow under Paste. A menu appears. Click Paste Special. The Paste Special Dialog box appears. In the As box, click Microsoft Office Drawing Object and then click OK. A copy of the shape appears in the worksheet.

Insert a Shape

1 Click the Insert tab.

2 Click Shapes.

   A gallery of shapes appears.

3 Click a shape.

4 Click and drag to draw the shape.

● Excel creates the shape.

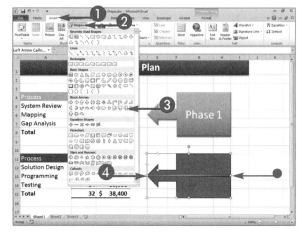

5 Click the Format tab.

6 Click the More button (▾) in the Shape Styles group.

   A gallery of styles appears.

7 Click a style.

● Excel applies the style.

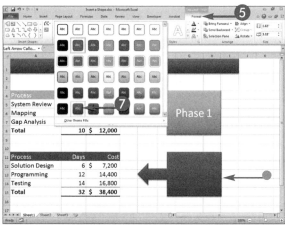

Add Text to a Shape

You can add text to a shape. You simply click the text button, click the shape, and then type the text. You can add any amount of text. Your text automatically wraps when it reaches the width of the box. When adding text, you can move to a new line at any time by pressing the Enter key.

By default, Excel centers text and uses a default font, font color, and size. You can use most of the options on the Home tab in the Font and Alignment groups to format the text. For example, you can change the alignment, change the font, change the font size, and change the font color, apply bold, italics, underlines, and more. To learn more about formatting text, see Chapter 2.

Apply It

You can apply WordArt styles and text effects to the text in shapes. To add a WordArt style, select the text. Click the Format tab. Click the More button in the WordArt Styles gallery. Click a style. Excel applies the style. To add a text effect, select the text. Click the Text Effects button. A menu appears. Click a category. A submenu appears. Click a text effect.

Add Text to a Shape

1. Click the shape to select it.

● The Drawing tools appear.

2. Click the Format tab.

3. Click Text Box.

4. Click the shape.

   You can now add text to the shape.

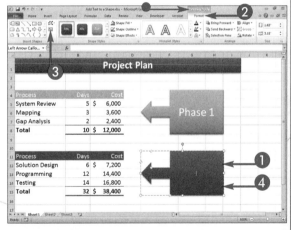

5. Type your text.

   Excel adds your text.

6. Click the Home tab.

● You can use most of these options to format your text.

Note: *See Chapter 2 to learn more about formatting.*

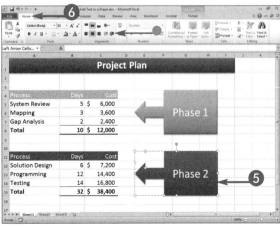

Change the Size of an Object

You click a graphic object to select it. When you select a graphic object, handles appear on its top, bottom, sides, and corners. Square handles appear on the top, bottom and sides. Round handles appear on the corners. You can use these handle to resize the graphic. Drag the top or bottom handles to resize the graphic object vertically. Drag the side handles to resize the graphic object horizontally. Drag a corner handle to change the overall size of the graphic.

To select more than one graphic object, press and hold the Ctrl key as you select each object. If you have more than one object selected, when you resize one object, Excel resizes all the other selected objects.

Change the Size of an Object

1. Click the object to select it.

   Handles appear.

2. Drag the handles to resize the object.

   - Drag a side handle to change the width.

   - Drag a top or bottom handle to change the height.

   - Drag a corner handle to change the overall size.

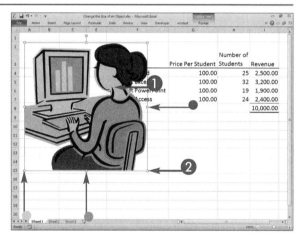

   - Excel changes the size of the object.

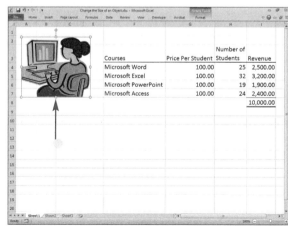

Rotate
an Object

Y ou can rotate any graphic object. For example, if you create a shape that points right and you want it to point left, you can rotate the shape so that it points left. When you select a graphic object, a rotation handle appears. To rotate the object, drag the rotation handle. If you want to constrain the rotation to intervals of 15 degrees, press and hold the Shift key as you drag.

You can use the Ribbon to rotate shapes 90 degrees left or 90 degrees right or to flip them vertically or horizontally. For example, if you have an arrow that is pointing to the right, you can select Flip Horizontal from the Rotate menu on the Format tab to flip it so it points left.

Extra

You can specify the exact number of degrees you want to rotate a graphic object. Select the object. The Drawing tools appear. Click the Format tab. Click Rotate in the Arrange group. A menu appears. Click More Rotation Options. The Format Shape dialog box appears. Enter the number of degrees you want to rotate the object in the Rotation field. Click Close. Excel rotates the object.

Rotate an Object

① Click an object to select it.

● The Drawing tools appear.

● Click and drag the rotation handle to rotate.

② Click the Format tab.

③ Click Rotate.

A menu appears.

④ Click an option.

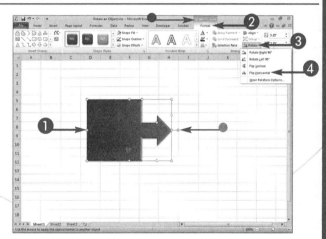

● Excel rotates the object.

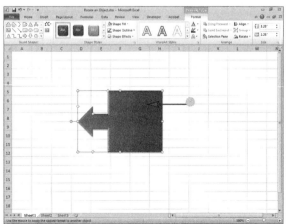

Change the Stacking Order

W hen you place a shape, text box, photograph, clip art, or any other type of graphic in your Excel worksheet, Excel stacks it. When graphics overlap, graphics that are higher in the stack appear to be on top of graphics that are lower in the stack. This can cause problems. For example, the text you want to place on a picture could actually appear behind the picture. Fortunately, you can change the stacking order. You can use the Selection and Visibility pane to choose the exact stack order to display your graphics.

Excel names each graphic as you create or add it to your worksheet. When you open the Selection and Visibility pane, these names display. You can change the Excel-generated names to names that are more meaningful.

Extra

You can use the Bring to Front and Send to Back options on the Format tab in the Arrange group to change the stacking order of your graphics. Send to Back sends your graphic to the bottom of the stack. Send Back moves it down one level. Bring to Front brings your graphic to the top of the stack. Bring Forward brings it up one level.

Change the Stacking Order

① Click the graphic.

● The Drawing tools appear.

② Click the Format tab.

③ Click Selection Pane.

● The Selection and Visibility pane appears.

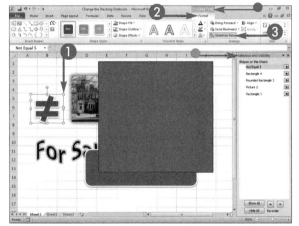

④ Double-click a name and type to change the name.

⑤ Click the up arrow (▲) to move the graphic up.

⑥ Click the down arrow (▼) to move the graphic down.

⑦ Click 👁 to hide a graphic.

⑧ Click the Close button ✕ to close pane.

● Excel rearranges the graphics.

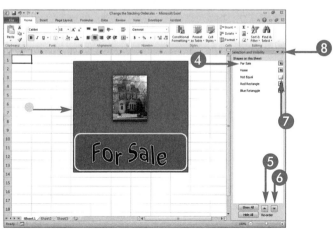

Group Objects

You can create a series of graphics that illustrate a single point. For example, you can create a set of graphics that show a house for sale. You may want to work with these graphics as a group. You can group graphics so that when you select one graphic, every graphic in the group is selected. You can move and resize grouped objects as if they were one object. You cannot edit, format, move, or size objects in a group individually until they are ungrouped. For example, if you apply an All Text in the Shape WordArt style to one object in the group, Excel applies it to all the objects in the group.

Extra

If you need to make changes to individual objects in a group, you must ungroup the objects. Select the grouped objects. The Drawing tools appear. Click the Format tab. Click Group. A menu appears. Click Ungroup. Excel ungroups the objects. Make your changes. Click the Format tab. Click Group. A menu appears. Click Regroup. Excel regroups the objects.

Group Objects

1. Press and hold the Ctrl key and then click to select each graphic you want to include.

● The Drawing and Picture tools appear.

2. Click the Format tab.

3. Click the Group button.

   A menu appears.

4. Click Group.

● Excel groups the objects.

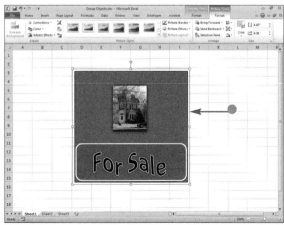

Align
Objects

When you place graphic objects in a worksheet, you may want them to line up perfectly with one another. For example, you may want shapes you draw to be perfectly aligned. You can use Excel's alignment options to align objects left, center, right, top, middle, or bottom. When you align objects left, the left edges of all the objects are flush. When you align objects center, the vertical center of all the objects is uniform. When you align objects right, the right edges of all the objects are flush. When you align objects top, the top edges of all the objects are flush. When you align objects middle, the horizontal center of all the objects is uniform. And when you align objects bottom, the bottom edges of all the objects are flush.

Extra

To move a graphic object, click the object and then drag. An easy way to make a copy of a graphic is to press and hold the Ctrl key, click the graphic, and then drag.

If you choose Snap to Grid or Snap to Objects from the Alignment menu on the Format tab, objects will automatically snap to the worksheet grid or to other objects when you draw them.

Align Objects

1 Press and hold the Ctrl key and then click to select each graphic you want to align.

● The Drawing tools appear.

2 Click the Format tab.

3 Click the Align button.

A menu appears.

4 Click an align option.

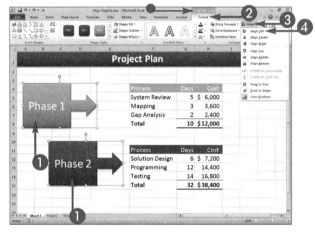

● Excel aligns the objects.

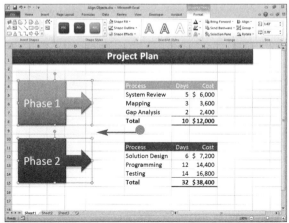

316

Insert a Symbol

I n Excel, you are not restricted to the standard numbers, letters, and punctuation marks on your keyboard. You can also select from hundreds of symbols, such as foreign letters, and currency characters, such as the Euro (€). Each font has a different set of symbols.

Symbols serve many uses in Excel. Many financial applications call for currency symbols. Symbols are useful in column and row heads as part of the text describing column or row content. For example, Net Sales in €.

Using a symbol in the same cell with a value such as a number, date, or time usually prevents the

value from being used in a formula. If you need to use a special character in a cell that is referenced by a formula, use a number format.

Extra

A smaller set of standard characters, called *special characters*, is always available; they include dashes, hyphens, and quotation marks. To access special characters, click the Insert tab. Click Symbol (Ω) in the Symbol group. The symbol dialog box appears. Click the Special Characters field. Click the character you want. Click Insert. Excel places the character in the current cell. Click Close. The Symbol dialog box closes.

Insert a Symbol

1 Click the cell where you want to insert a symbol.

2 Click the Insert tab.

3 Click Symbol.

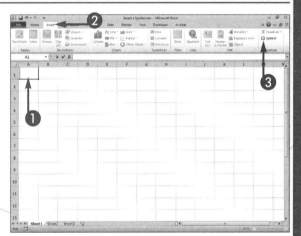

The Symbol dialog box appears.

4 Click the down arrow (▼) and then select a font.

5 Click a symbol.

6 Click Insert.

● Excel inserts the symbol.

7 Click Close.

The Symbol dialog box closes.

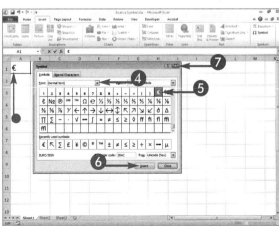

Using SmartArt Graphics

SmartArt graphics are predesigned layouts that you can use to illustrate your ideas. Presenting ideas as a graphic makes them easier to understand. For example, you can use a SmartArt graphic to create an organization chart. Excel provides the layout. All you have to do is enter the proper information.

There are seven categories of SmartArt graphics: List, Process, Cycle, Hierarchy, Relationship, Matrix, and Pyramid. Each category has several layouts. Before you choose a graphic, consider carefully which category will best illustrate your ideas. Use the List category to show steps in a task, the sequence of events, or groups of related ideas; the Workflow category to show the progression of tasks or the sequence of events over time;

the Cycle category to show the cycle of events or the stages of a project; the Hierarchy category to show hierarchical relationships; the Relationship category to show how ideas compare and contrast; the Matrix category to show how parts relate to the whole; and the Pyramid category to show the proportional relationship of parts to the whole.

After you select a graphic, Excel places it in your worksheet. You can then type your information into the text box on the shapes or you can open the Text pane and type your information there. Excel adjusts the size of the font to fit the box. Your text will automatically wrap when it reaches the end of the box. If at any time you want to start a new line of text, press the Enter key.

Using SmartArt Graphics

① Click the Insert tab.

② Click SmartArt.

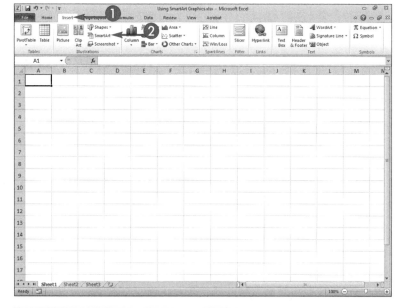

The Choose a SmartArt Graphic dialog box appears.

③ Click a category.

④ Click a layout.

⑤ Click OK.

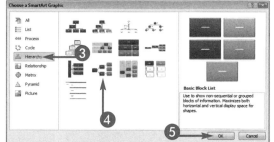

The SmartArt graphic appears in your worksheet.

6 Click the expand/collapse button to open the Text pane.

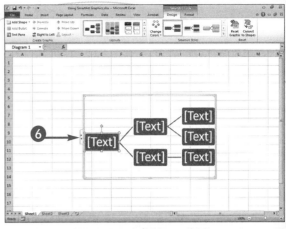

7 Click the box where you want to enter text.

8 Type the text.

9 Repeat Steps 7 and 8 until you have completed your illustration.

10 Click the Close button (⊠) to close the Text pane.

Excel creates your SmartArt graphic.

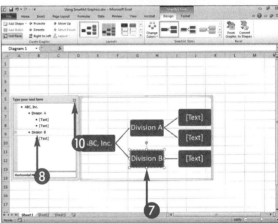

Extra

You can type text directly on a SmartArt graphic. Simply click the word Text and begin typing. When you are finished typing, click the next shape or click outside the SmartArt graphic. While Excel does not limit the amount of text you can type, most SmartArt layouts are best suited for illustrations that only require a small amount of text.

You can delete a SmartArt graphic. Click the border to select the graphic. Press the Delete key. Excel deletes the graphic.

When you select a SmartArt graphic, a border surrounds it. The border has dots on the sides and corners. Click and drag the dots on the top or bottom to change the height of your SmartArt graphic. Click and drag the dots on a side to change the width of your SmartArt graphic. Click and drag the dots on a corner to change the overall size of your SmartArt graphic. You can also change the size of your SmartArt graphic by doing the following: Select your SmartArt graphic. Click the Format tab. Click the Format button. Click Size. A size box appears. Enter a size for your SmartArt graphic or use the spinners to adjust the size.

Modify a SmartArt Graphic

Each SmartArt graphic has a default number of shapes included. This number depends on the layout. You can use the Add Shape menu to add additional shapes to most layouts. For example, if you are creating an organization chart for your company and you have two regions at the third level, but the SmartArt layout you have chosen only has one shape at that level, you can add an additional shape.

The Add Shape menu has four options: Add Shape After, Add Shape Before, Add Shape Above, and Add Shape Below. Add Shape After creates a new shape on the same level after the selected shape. Add Shape Before creates a new shape on the same level before the selected shape. Add Shape Above creates a new shape on the level above the selected shape. Add Shape Below creates a new shape on the level below the selected shape. You can use the Promote and Demote options in the Create Graphic group to move shapes up and down the levels. Promote moves a shape up a level. Demote moves a shape down a level. You can use Reorder Up and Reorder Down to move shapes up and down a stack. Reorder Up moves a shape up. Reorder Down moves a shape down.

As you add shapes, Excel adjusts the size of the other shapes in the graphic, thereby keeping the size of all the shapes in proportion. When you add a new shape to a SmartArt graphic, you cannot immediately add text to it unless you use the Text pane, or right-click and then select Edit Text from the context menu.

Modify a SmartArt Graphic

Add a Shape

1 Click a shape.

The SmartArt tools appear.

2 Click the Design tab.

3 Click the ▼ next to Add Shape.

The Add Shape menu appears.

4 Click an option.

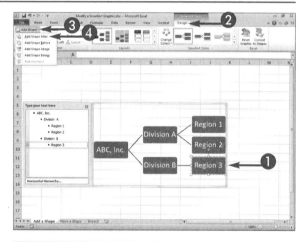

Excel adds a shape.

● You can right-click and then select Edit Text from the context menu to add text.

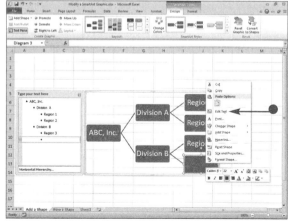

Move a Shape

1 Click a shape.

SmartArt tools appear.

2 Click the Design tab.

3 Click Move Down to move down the stack.

Alternatively, click Move Up to move up the stack; Promote, to move up a level; and Demote to move down a level.

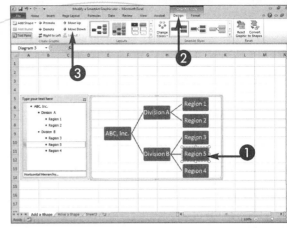

● Excel moves the shape.

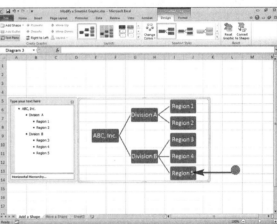

Extra

You can use the Text pane to create new shapes in a SmartArt graphic. When typing your text into the Text pane, press Enter after you complete your entry to create a new shape below the current shape. Press Enter at the beginning of a text entry to create a new shape above the current shape.

To open the Text pane, click the graphic. The Drawing tools appear. Click the Design tab. Click the Text Pane button in the Create Graphic group. Excel opens the Text pane. Click the Text Pane button in the Create Graphic group again to close the Text pane.

To delete a shape, click the border of the shape and then press the Delete key.

You can flip a SmartArt graphic horizontally. Click the border of the SmartArt graphic. The Drawing tools appear. Click the Design tab. Click Right to Left in the Create Graphic group.

SmartArt graphics appear in the default color. You can change the color. Click the border of the SmartArt graphic. The Drawing tools appear. Click the Design tab. Click Change Colors in the SmartArt Styles group. A gallery of colors appears. Click a color.

Apply a SmartArt Style

A *style* is a collection of formats. The formatting can consist of a fill, an outline, colors, fonts, and shape effects such as bevels, shadows, 3-D rotations, and much more. You could apply each of these formats individually to the objects in a SmartArt graphic, but by using a style, you can complete the process in just a few clicks.

One of the reasons you may want to change the style applied to a SmartArt graphic is to give your documents a consistent look and feel. You can, for example, apply the same style to all your graphics. Changing the style can dramatically change the look of a SmartArt graphic but it does not affect your SmartArt graphic content.

Extra

You can use the options on the Format tab to apply formats to the elements in a SmartArt graphic. For example, you can apply shape effects to the shapes and WordArt styles to the text. To undo a SmartArt style, shape effect, or WordArt style, click the Design tab and then click Reset Graphic.

Apply a SmartArt Style

1 Click the SmartArt graphic to select it.

The SmartArt tools appear.

2 Click the Design tab.

3 Click the More button ($\boxed{\cdot}$) in the SmartArt Styles group.

A gallery of styles appears.

4 Click a style.

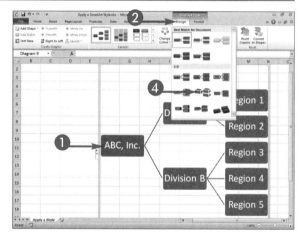

Excel applies the style.

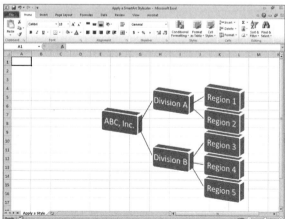

Apply a SmartArt Layout

Excel divides SmartArt graphics into categories. Within each category there are several layouts from which you can choose. If after choosing a layout, you want to change to another layout, you can. Excel automatically transfers the data from your current layout to the new layout. For example, if you have created a horizontal organization chart but your manager prefers a vertical organization chart, you can make the change simply by changing the layout.

By default, the Layouts gallery displays layouts in the same category as your current layout. However, you can select a layout from another category. For example, if your current layout is from the Hierarchy category, you switch to the List category and then select a layout from there.

Apply It

If you want to change your layout from a layout in one category to a layout in another category, click your SmartArt graphic to select it. Click the Design tab. Click the More button (☑) in the Layouts group. Click More Layouts. The Choose a SmartArt Graphic dialog box appears. Click a category and then click a layout. Excel changes the layout applied to your SmartArt graphic.

Apply a SmartArt Layout

① Click the SmartArt graphic to select it.

The SmartArt tools appear.

② Click the Design tab.

③ Click the More button (☑) in the Layouts group.

A gallery of layouts appears.

④ Click a layout.

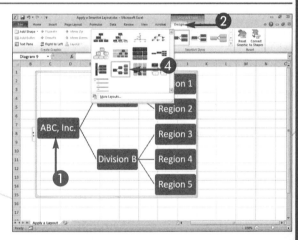

Excel applies the layout.

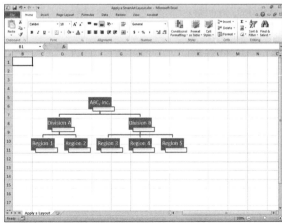

Add a Form Control to a Worksheet

You can add controls to a worksheet to make it easier to enter data into a cell. Form controls can aid users who are not familiar with Excel and can increase the accuracy of data entry by limiting the options a user has. For example, you can add check boxes to your worksheet so your worksheet looks like a paper form. You can also add a combo box from which users can select an entry.

Excel provides nine controls you can add to a worksheet. You add controls by selecting the control you want from the Form Controls menu. After you add a control, you can adjust its size by dragging the side or corner handles. When you add a control or when you right-click a control

twice and then click the control, you are in design mode. In design mode, you can modify the properties and size of the control, but you cannot test its functionality.

When you place a control on a worksheet, it sits on top of the worksheet. You can size it so it appears to be located in a cell, but controls are separate from cells. You can place controls anywhere on the worksheet. A control can cover any portion of a cell or range of cells.

After you add a control to a worksheet, you can assign it values. See the next section, "Assign Values to a Form Control," to learn how. Form control options are located on the Developer tab. See Chapter 14 to learn how to display the Developer tab.

Add a Form Control to a Worksheet

① Click the Developer tab.

Note: *See Chapter 14 to learn how to display the Developer tab.*

② Click Insert.

The Form Controls menu appears.

③ Click a control group to select it.

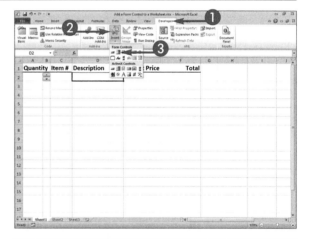

④ Click and drag the mouse pointer to create the control.

⑤ Click and drag the handles on the sides and corners to adjust the size.

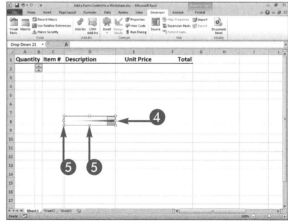

6 Place your mouse pointer on the control. When the mouse pointer turns into a four-sided arrow, drag the control to change the location.

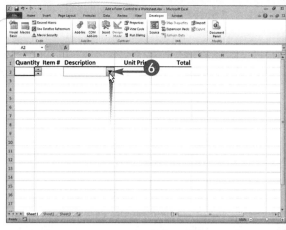

7 Right-click the control twice and then click it to place it in design mode.

To cancel design mode, click any cell in the worksheet.

To remove a control, place it in design mode and then press the Delete key.

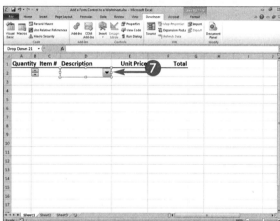

Extra

You can add the controls listed in the following table to your worksheets.

CONTROL	CONTROL NAME	DESCRIPTION
	Button	Runs an associated macro when clicked.
	List box	Displays a list of items for selection.
	Check box	Selects or deselects an option.
	Spinner	Scrolls up and down through a list of numeric values.
	Combo box	A menu that displays a list of items.
	Radio button	Selects one of a group of items.
	Group box	Places related controls together.
	Label	Provides information about an associated control.
	Scroll bar	Increases or decrease a value when the user clicks the arrows or drags the bar.

Assign Values to a Form Control

fter you add a control to a form, you can assign values to it. For example, if your worksheet contains a list box, you can assign the list of values that will appear when users access the list box. Some controls enable you to define a range of valid numeric values for the control. For example, if you use a spinner, you define the starting value and the maximum value for the control. For combo boxes and list boxes, you can place the options associated with the control in a range of cells. For example, if you use a combo box, you tell Excel the list of values used by the control by entering the range of cells containing the values. The values can be located on another worksheet, or even in another workbook as long as Excel can access the workbook when users view the worksheet that contains the control.

You can link a cell to a control. If you link a cell to a control, whatever value users select when using the control becomes the value in the linked cell. If you use a combo box control or list box control, the value in the linked cell is a number that represents the user's selection. Excel assigns the number based on the position of the selected value in your list. If the list is Computer, Monitor, Keyboard, and the user selects Monitor, the linked cell receives the value 2, because Monitor is second in the list.

With a control, such as a check box, you can tell Excel whether you want the option initially selected or unselected. Both options — selected and unselected — have an associated value.

Assign Values to a Form Control

1 Right-click the control twice.

A menu appears.

2 Click Format Control.

The Format Object dialog box appears.

3 Click the Control tab.

The available fields depend on the control type. This example uses a combo box.

4 Click and drag to select the range that lists the valid values, or type the range.

5 Click a cell to assign a linked cell.

The value associated with your selection appears in the linked cell.

6 Enter the number of items in your list.

7 Click OK.

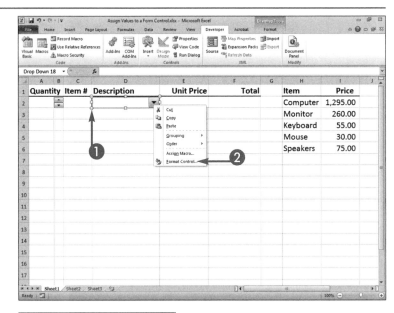

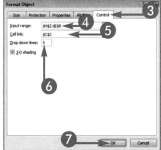

8 Click the down arrow (▾) and then select the desired control value.

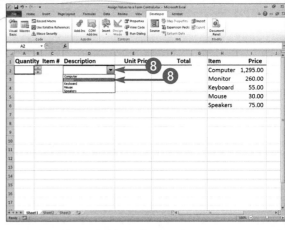

● Excel places a numeric value representing the control selection in the linked cell.

● Excel displays the value in the control.

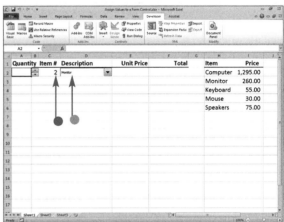

Apply It

When working with a value selected from a list box or combo box control, you may want to use the value in the linked cell to set the value of another cell. For example, assume you have the following Excel list in cells H2:I4:

```
Computer    $1295
Monitor     $995
Keyboard    $55
```

You can use the INDEX function to determine the price based on the equipment selection. For example, if the user selects Monitor from the control, Excel places a value of 2 in the linked cell. If you want users to find the cost of the selection, you type a formula similar to the following, assuming that C2 is the linked cell:

```
=INDEX($H$2:$I$4,C2,2)
```

When the user selects Monitor, the INDEX function returns $995.The INDEX function actually creates an array of the Excel list and uses the control selection to determine which element in the array to return. The function uses three arguments: Array, Row_num, and Column_num. See Chapter 5 to learn more about the INDEX function.

Add a Macro to a Form Control

You can use macros to automate the tasks you perform in Excel. See Chapter 14 to learn more about macros. You can assign a macro to any form control on a worksheet. For example, if a user clicks a radio button control, you can have Excel add a postage amount to an invoice.

You can create one macro for each control on a worksheet. You create a macro either by recording a series of keystrokes or by writing a Visual Basic for Applications (VBA) procedure. This book does not cover writing procedures. When you select the Assign Macro menu option, Excel automatically creates a new macro name by using the name of the control followed by an underscore and an event name, such as _Click. Excel assigns the control name to the control when you add it

to a worksheet. For example, the first `OptionButton` control that you add to a worksheet is named `OptionButton1`. If you create a macro for the option button, Excel gives the macro the name `OptionButton1_Click`. Every time you add a new control, Excel gives the control a unique name by adding a sequential number to `OptionButton`; for example, `OptionButton2_Click`, `Option Button3_Click`, and so on.

The portion of the macro name following the underscore character corresponds to an action, commonly referred to as an *event*. For example, with an `OptionButton` control, the user clicks the radio button to select the option, so the event is `Click`. If you create a macro for a combo box control, Excel assigns `Change` as the name of the event because you want to execute the macro when the value of the control changes.

Add a Macro to a Form Control

1. Right-click your control twice.

   A menu appears.

2. Click Assign Macro.

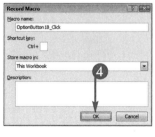

The Assign Macro dialog box appears.

- Excel assigns a default macro name for the selected control.

3. Click Record.

   The Record Macro dialog box appears.

4. Click OK.

5. Record your macro.

Note: *See Chapter 14 to learn how to record a macro.*

6 Click the control with the assigned macro.

- Excel executes the associated macro.

- In the example, Excel assigns postage to the invoice.

Extra

It is a good idea to create and test your macro before you assign it to a control. To assign a macro you have already created to a control, click the Developer tab. Click Insert in the Controls group. Click the control you want to add. Click and drag to create the control. The Assign Macro dialog box appears. Click the name of the macro you want to add and then click OK. Excel adds the macro to the control.

If you no longer want a macro to be assigned to a control, right-click the control and then click the Assign Macro option. In the Assign Macro dialog box, clear the macro name from the Macro Name field and then click OK. Excel removes the macro assignment from the control, but the macro remains as part of the workbook. To remove the macro from the workbook, click the View tab. Click Macros in the Macros group. Click View Macros. The Macro dialog box appears. Select the macro you want to delete and then click Delete.

Customize the Quick Access Toolbar

The Quick Access Toolbar enables you to access commands with a single click. By default, Save, Undo, and Redo appear on the toolbar. You can use the Customize the Quick Access Toolbar pane to add more commands.

In the Customize the Quick Access Toolbar pane, you use the Choose commands from drop-down list to select the category from which you want to choose commands. Excel divides commands into the following categories to make it easier for you to find the commands you want: Popular Commands, Commands Not in the Ribbon, All Commands, and Macros. You should review the commands listed under Commands Not in the Ribbon. This is particularly true if you find that you have to

perform a large number of steps to get to the command you want. A number of commands that are found on panes or listed in menus can be found under Commands Not in the Ribbon. Select the macros option to add macros to the toolbar. See Chapter 14 for detailed instructions on how to add a macro to the Quick Access Toolbar.

You can use the Customize Quick Access Toolbar drop-down list to specify whether the command should appear on the toolbar of all Excel workbooks or only on the toolbar in the Workbook you specify. By default, the buttons will appear in all workbooks.

Some sections in Chapter 11 and Chapter 12 require that you add commands either to the Quick Access Toolbar or to the Ribbon.

Customize the Quick Access Toolbar

① Click the Quick Access Toolbar button.

A menu appears.

② Click More Commands.

The Customize the Quick Access Toolbar pane appears.

③ Click the Choose command from ▼ and then select a category.

④ Click the Customize Quick Access Toolbar ▼ and then select the workbook in which you want the commands to appear.

⑤ Click the command you want.

⑥ Click Add.

● Excel adds the command.

You can repeat Steps 5 and 6 to add additional commands.

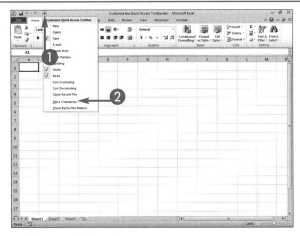

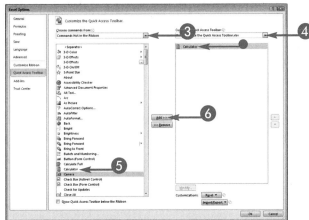

7️⃣ Click the Move Up button (▲) to move commands up.

8️⃣ Click the Move Down button (▼) to move commands down.

9️⃣ Click a command and then click Remove to remove it.

🔟 Click OK.

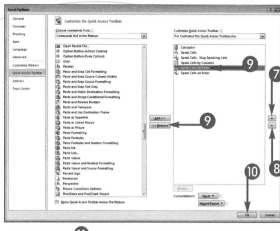

Excel places the commands on the Quick Access Toolbar.

1️⃣1️⃣ Click a command to execute it.

Excel executes the command.

● In this example, Excel opens the calculator.

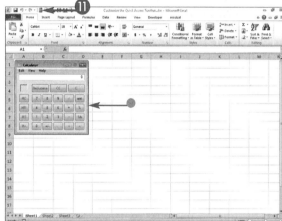

Extra

When you click the Quick Access Toolbar button, a menu appears. The menu has several popular Excel commands on it. Click a command to add it to the Quick Access Toolbar. Try each of these commands. You will be surprised at how quickly they get you to where you want to go.

When you right-click any button on the Ribbon, a menu appears. Choose the Add to Quick Access Toolbar option to add the button to the Quick Access Toolbar. The Quick Access Toolbar can appear above or below the Ribbon. Click Show Quick Access Toolbar Below the Ribbon to move the Quick Access Toolbar below the Ribbon.

You can export and import customizations to the Quick Access Toolbar and the Ribbon. To export your customizations, click the Quick Access Toolbar button, and then click More Commands. The Customize the Quick Access Toolbar pane appears. Click Import/Export. The Import/ Export menu appears. Click Export all customizations. Excel creates a file named Cutomizations.exportedUI and opens the File Save dialog box. Save the file. To Import customizations choose Import Customization File from the Import/Export menu.

Customize the Ribbon

To make the commands that you use most frequently readily available to you, you can place them in the Ribbon on a custom tab and the tab can be divided into groups. You can add a new tab and name it Speak, and then put all the commands in a group called Speak Commands.

You can also add command groups and commands to existing tabs. For example, if you frequently use the Format Cells dialog box, you can add it to the Home tab next to the Styles group. You can rename tabs and groups. For example, if you do not like the name Home tab, you can change the name to Basic Commands or some other name. You can also choose which tabs display and the order in which they display. For example, if you never use the Review tab, you can remove it from view. If you frequently use the Formulas tab, you can have it display first.

You can select a command category from the Choose command from drop-down list. Excel divides commands into the following categories to make it easier for you to find the commands you want: Popular Commands, Commands Not in the Ribbon, All Commands, Macros, Office Menu, All Tabs, Main Tabs, Tool Tabs, and Custom Tabs and Groups. Main Tabs are the tabs that you see when you use Excel without any customizations. Tool tabs are the context-sensitive tabs that appear when you work on objects such as charts or PivotTables.

Customize the Ribbon

Open the Customize the Ribbon Pane

1 Right-click any button in the Ribbon.

A menu appears.

2 Click Customize the Ribbon.

● The Customize the Ribbon pane appears.

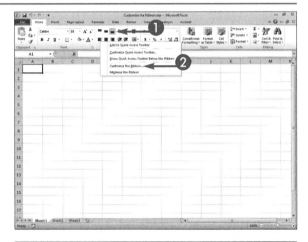

Choose the Tabs to Display

1 Open the Customize the Ribbon pane.

2 Click the ⏷ and then select the type of tab you want to customize.

3 Click to select or deselect the tabs you want to display (▢ changes to ☑ or ☑ changes to ▢).

4 Click OK.

● Only the selected tabs appear.

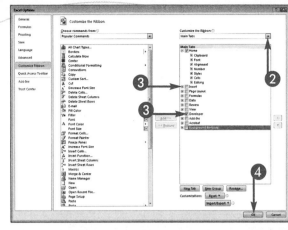

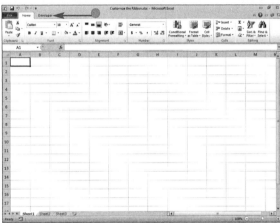

Apply It

Tabs, groups, and commands display in the order they appear in the Customize the Ribbon pane. To change the order, open the Customize the Ribbon pane. Click a tab, group, or command and then use the Move Up (▲) or Move Down (▼) buttons to change the location. Move Up moves the tab, group, or command up and Move Down moves the tab, group, or command down.

If you no longer want a tab, group, or command, you can remove it. Open the Customize the Ribbon pane. Click the tab, group, or command you want to remove and then click the Remove button. Excel removes the tab, group, or command.

You can restore the Excel Ribbon back to the way it was before you made any customizations. To remove all customizations, click the Reset button. A menu appears. Click Reset all customizations. A prompt appears. Click Yes. Note the Quick Access Toolbar customizations are also removed. To restore a specific tab, click the tab. Click the Reset button. A menu appears. Click Reset only selected Ribbon tab. Excel restores the tab.

continued →

Customize the Ribbon (continued)

I t is a good idea to review the commands listed in the Choose commands from drop-list under Commands Not in the Ribbon. This is particularly true if you find that you have to perform a large number of steps to get to the command you want. A number of the commands that are found on panes or listed in menus can be found under Commands Not in the Ribbon. You can use the Macros option in the Choose commands from drop-list to add Macros to the Ribbon. Once you select a category, the options in that category appear in the box below the Choose commands from field.

You can use the Customize the Ribbon drop-down list to tell Excel the type of tab you want to modify. Choose from All Tabs, Main Tabs, or Tool Tabs. Once you choose a tab type, the options appear in the box below the

Customize the Ribbon field. A check box appears next to each tab listed. Only the selected tabs appear in the Ribbon. For a number of tasks in this book, you need to display the Developer tab, which is unselected by default and does not display. The Developer tab can be found under Main Tabs. To display the Developer tab, make sure the Developer tab check box is selected.

You can click the New Tab button to add a new tab. You can click the New Group button to add a new group. When you click the New Tab button or the New Group button, Excel usually places the new tab or group under the highlighted tab or group. Tabs and groups appear in the order listed on the Customize the Ribbon pane. You can use the Rename button to rename any tab or group.

Customize the Ribbon *(continued)*

Add a Custom Tab

① Open the Customize the Ribbon pane.

② Click the Choose commands from ▾ and then select the category of commands from which you want to choose.

③ Click the Customize the Ribbon ▾ and then select the type of tab you want to customize.

④ Click New Tab.

● A new tab appears.

⑤ Click New Group.

● A new group appears.

⑥ Click a command.

⑦ Click Add.

Repeat Steps 6 and 7 for every command you want to add.

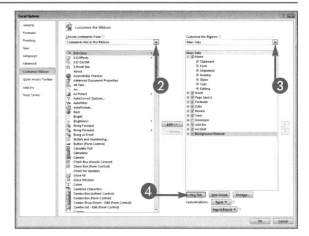

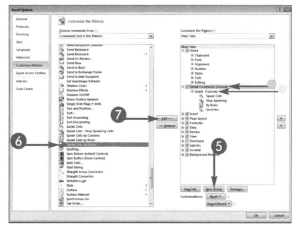

- Excel adds the command to the new group.

⑧ Click a tab or group name.

⑨ Click the Rename button.

The Rename dialog box appears.

⑩ Type a new name.

⑪ Click OK to close the rename box.

Excel renames the tab or group.

You can repeat Steps 7 to 9 for every tab and group you want to rename.

⑫ Click OK to close the Customize the Ribbon pane.

- Excel adds the Custom tab and Commands to the Ribbon.

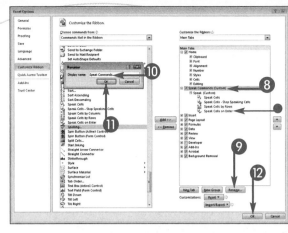

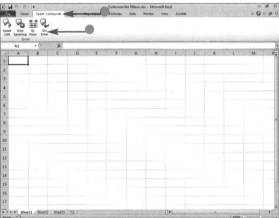

Apply It

To add a new group to a standard Excel tab, follow these steps: Open the Customize the Ribbon pane. Click the down arrow next to the Choose commands from field and then choose the category from which you want to choose commands. Click the down arrow next to the Customize the Ribbon field and then choose the type of Ribbon you want to customize. Click the tab to which you want to add the new group. Click New Group. Excel adds the new group. Click Rename. The Rename Dialog box appears. Type the name you want to give the new group and then click OK. Excel renames the group.

Click the command you want to add. Click the Add button. Excel adds the command. Repeat the process to add additional commands. Groups display in the order they appear in the Customize the Ribbon pane. Click the new group's name. Click the Move Up button (▲) to move the group up. Click the Move Down button (▼) to move the group down. Click OK. The group and the commands appear on the Ribbon on the tab you selected.

Using Excel Keyboard Shortcuts

You can execute Ribbon commands without taking your hands off the keyboard. This enables you to work quickly. This is particularly true if you are an excellent typist. The process is simple. You press the Alt key. Excel displays KeyTips — letters or numbers you can press to display more KeyTips or to execute a command. If a menu or dialog box appears after you press a KeyTip, use the arrow keys to move to your selection. Press the Enter key or the spacebar to make your selection.

For example, you can activate KeyTips to change the color of your type by clicking the keys shown in the KeyTip and then using the arrow keys to select the color you want. To cancel a KeyTips session, press F10.

In Excel 2003, you can execute menu and toolbar commands by pressing the Alt key. Excel 2007 and Excel 2010 do not use menus and toolbars, but if you have memorized those commands, you can use them. As you execute Excel 2003 commands, Excel displays a message. For example, pressing Alt+E+A+A clears a cell. As you execute the command, Excel displays the message, Office 2003: ALT, E, A, A.

General Program Shortcuts

SHORTCUT	RESULT
Ctrl+N	Creates a new workbook.
Ctrl+O	Opens the Open dialog box.
Ctrl+F12	Opens the Open dialog box (same as Ctrl+O).
Ctrl+S	Saves a workbook. (The Save As dialog box opens if you have not previously saved the workbook.)
Shift+F12	Saves a workbook (same as Ctrl+S).
F12	Opens the Save As dialog box.
Ctrl+W	Closes the active workbook; if it is the only workbook open, it also closes Excel.
Alt+F4	Closes the active workbook (same as Ctrl+W).
F1	Opens Excel Help.
F7	Runs the spell checker.
F10	Turns KeyTips on and off.
Shift+F10	Opens a context menu containing options related to the current worksheet selection. This is the same as clicking the right mouse button.
F9	Calculates all worksheets in all open workbooks.
Ctrl+F9	Minimizes the workbook.
Ctrl+F10	Restores or maximizes the workbook.
Ctrl+P	Opens the Print dialog box.
Ctrl+Shift+F12	Opens the Print dialog box (same as Ctrl+P).
Alt+F8	Opens the Macro dialog box.
Alt+F11	Opens Visual Basic for Applications.

Data Entry Shortcut

SHORTCUT	RESULT
Enter	Completes the cell entry and moves to the next cell.
Alt+Enter	Starts a new line within the same cell.
Shift+Enter	Completes the cell entry and moves up to the cell above.
Tab	Completes the cell entry and moves to the next cell on the right.
Shift+Tab	Completes the cell entry and moves to the next cell on the left.
Esc	Cancels the cell entry and restores original cell contents.
Ctrl+D	Fills the active cell with the contents of the cell above it.
Ctrl+R	Fills the active cell with the contents of the cell to the left of it.
Ctrl+F3	Displays the Name Manager dialog box.
Ctrl+K	Displays the Insert Hyperlink dialog box.
F2	Gives you the ability to edit the active cell by placing the insertion point at the end of the cell contents and in the formula bar.

Editing Shortcuts

SHORTCUT	RESULT
Ctrl+C	Copies the selection to the Office Clipboard.
Ctrl+X	Cuts the selection and places it on the Office Clipboard.
Ctrl+V	Pastes the information on the Office Clipboard.
Backspace	Deletes entire contents of a cell, or deletes the character on the left of the insertion point if you are editing the cell contents.
Delete	Deletes entire contents of a cell, or deletes the character on the right of the insertion point if you are editing the cell contents.
Ctrl+Delete	Deletes text from the insertion point to the end of the cell contents.
Ctrl+Z	Undoes an action.
Ctrl+Y	Repeats an action (Redo).
F4	Repeats an action (same as Ctrl+Y).
Ctrl+-	Opens the Delete dialog box.
Ctrl+Shift++	Opens the Insert dialog box.

continued ➡

Formula Shortcuts

SHORTCUT	RESULT
Alt+Shift+Right Arrow	Displays the Group dialog box.
Alt+Shift+Left Arrow	Displays the Ungroup dialog box.
Ctrl+9	Hides the selected rows.
Ctrl+Shift+(	Unhides the hidden rows within the range selection.
Ctrl+0	Hides the selected columns.
Ctrl+Shift+Enter	Enters a formula as an array.
Ctrl+Shift+A	Inserts the argument names in parentheses for the specified function name.
F3	Opens the Paste Name dialog box when you have range names defined.
Shift+F3	Opens the Function Arguments dialog box.
=	Starts a formula.
Alt+=	Inserts the AutoSum formula.
Ctrl+;	Enters the current date.
Ctrl+Shift+:	Enters the current time.
Ctrl+Shift+"	Copies the value in the cell above the active cell.
Ctrl+`	Alternates between displaying the value of the cell and the cell formula.

Formatting Shortcuts

SHORTCUT	RESULT
Alt+'	Opens the Style dialog box.
Ctrl+1	Opens the Format Cells dialog box.
Ctrl+B	Applies or removes bold formatting.
Ctrl+I	Applies or removes italic formatting.
Ctrl+U	Applies or removes underlining.
Ctrl+5	Applies or removes strikethrough formatting.
Ctrl+Shift+~	Applies the General number format.
Ctrl+Shift+$	Applies the Currency format with two decimal places and negative numbers in parentheses.
Ctrl+Shift+^	Applies the Exponential format with two decimal places.
Ctrl+Shift+#	Applies the Date format with dates formatted as dd-mm-yy.
Ctrl+Shift+@	Applies the Time format with hour, minute, and AM or PM.
Ctrl+Shift+!	Applies the Number format with two decimal places, a thousands separator, and minus sign for negative numbers.
Ctrl+Shift+%	Applies the Percent format.
Ctrl+Shift+&	Applies outside borders.
Ctrl+Shift+_	Removes outside borders.

continued ➡

Selection Shortcuts

SHORTCUT	RESULT
Shift+Right Arrow	Expands the selection one cell to the right.
Shift+Left Arrow	Expands the selection one cell to the left.
Shift+Up Arrow	Expands the selection up one cell.
Shift+Down Arrow	Expands the selection down one cell.
Ctrl+Shift+·	Selects the current region, or cells containing values, around the active cell.
Ctrl+Shift+Right Arrow	Expands the selection right to the next nonblank cell in the row.
Ctrl+Shift+Left Arrow	Expands the selection left to the next nonblank cell in the row.
Ctrl+Shift+Up Arrow	Expands the selection up to the next nonblank cell in the column.
Ctrl+Shift+Down Arrow	Expands the selection down to the last nonblank cell in the column.
Shift+Home	Expands the selection to the beginning of the row.
Ctrl+Shift+Home	Expands the selection to the beginning of the worksheet.
Ctrl+Shift+End	Expands the selection to the end of the active area of the worksheet.
Ctrl+Spacebar	Selects the entire column.
Shift+Spacebar	Selects the entire row.
Ctrl+A	Selects the entire worksheet.
Shift+Page Down	Expands the selection down one screen.
Shift+Page Up	Expands the selection up one screen.
Ctrl+Shift+Spacebar	If an object is selected, selects all objects.
Ctrl+6	Alternates between hiding objects, displaying objects, and displaying object placeholders.
Shift+F8	Adds another range of cells to the selection.

Worksheet Navigation Shortcuts

SHORTCUT	RESULT
Up Arrow	Moves the active cell up one row.
Down Arrow	Moves the active cell down one row.
Left Arrow	Moves the active cell left one column.
Right Arrow	Moves the active cell right one column.
Home	Moves to the beginning of the current row.
Ctrl+Home	Moves to the beginning of the worksheet (typically cell A1).
Ctrl+End	Moves to the last cell in the worksheet (the cell at the intersection of the last used row and column in the worksheet).
Page Up	Scrolls up one screen.
Page Down	Scrolls down one screen.
Alt+Page Up	Scrolls right one screen.
Alt+Page Down	Scrolls left one screen.
Ctrl+Page Up	Moves to the previous worksheet in the workbook.
Ctrl+Page Down	Moves to the next worksheet in the workbook.
Ctrl+F6	Switches to the next open workbook.
Ctrl+Shift+F6	Switches back to the previously viewed open workbook.
F6	Moves the focus from the status bar to the Ribbon to the worksheet, and if the worksheet is split from pane pane.
F5	Opens the Go To dialog box.
Shift+F5	Opens the Find and Replace dialog box.
Shift+F4	Repeats the last Find command.
Tab	Moves between the unlocked cells of a protected worksheet.
Ctrl+.	Moves clockwise to the next corner of the selected range of cells.

INDEX

/ (division) operator, 58
- (minus sign) operator, 58
< > (unequal) operator, 58
+ (addition) operator, 58
& (ampersand), joining text and, 240
' (apostrophe), 25
= (equal) operator, 58
= (equal sign), 58
error, 79
^ (exponent) operator, 58
> (greater than) operator, 58
< (less than) operator, 58
<= (less than or equal) operator, 58
* (multiplication) operator, 58
% (percent) operator, 58
& (text concatenation) operator, 59
3-D charts, 194
3-D option for charts, 188
1900 date system, 20

A

absolute cell addresses, 67, 281
Access databases, 224–229
active cell, 12, 13
add-ins, 129–131
Advanced Filter, 150–151
advanced filtering techniques, 152–153
alignment
    font, 29
    indents, 33
    objects, 316
Analysis Toolpak, 129
annuities, 96–97, 98–99
apostrophe ('), 25
area charts, 194
arithmetic operators, 58
Array form, 93
array formulas, 62–63
array functions, 84
arrays, description, 116
artistic effects, 305
Auto Outline, 160–161
AutoComplete, 61
AutoFill, 238–239
AutoFit Row Height feature, 35
AutoSum, 64
averages
    calculating, 116
    conditional, 117
    moving averages, 132
axes on charts, 191–192

B

background color, adding, 30
background in photos, removing, 306–307
Backstage view, 7
bar charts, 194
borders
    active cell, 12
    color, 27
    erasing, 27
    gridlines and, 57
    line location, 26
    lines, 26
    one side of cell, 27
    photographs, 302
    styles, 26
brightness, 298–299
buttons
    AutoFilter, 143
    Border, 26
    Bottom Align, 33
    Center, 33
    Clear, 39
    controls, 325
    Copy, 40
    Cut, 41
    Decrease Decimal, 17
    Decrease Font Size, 29
    Delete, 141
    Error, 13
    Error Checking, 77
    Error Indicator, 25
    Evaluate Formula, 76
    Fill Color, 30
    Find & Select, 48
    Find All, 48
    Find Next, 48
    Form, 140
    Increase Decimal, 17
    Increase Font Size, 29
    Insert Function, 68, 80, 82, 96
    Insert Worksheet, 47
    Merge & Center, 36
    Middle Align, 33
    New, 140
    Paste, 40, 41
    Paste All, 44
    Percent Style, 22
    Rename Sheet, 50
    Replace All, 48
    Restore, 141
    Top Align, 33
    Wrap Text, 35

INDEX

E

INDEX

G

H

INDEX

INDEX

INDEX

X

Y

Z

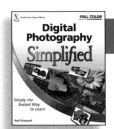

...all designed for visual learners—just like you!

Master VISUALLY®

Your complete visual reference. Two-color interior.

- 3ds Max
- Creating Web Pages
- Dreamweaver and Flash
- Excel
- Excel VBA Programming
- iPod and iTunes
- Mac OS
- Office
- Optimizing PC Performance
- Photoshop Elements
- QuickBooks
- Quicken
- Windows
- Windows Mobile
- Windows Server

Visual Blueprint™

Where to go for professional-level programming instruction. Two-color interior.

- Ajax
- ASP.NET 2.0
- Excel Data Analysis
- Excel Pivot Tables
- Excel Programming
- HTML
- JavaScript
- Mambo
- PHP & MySQL
- SEO
- Ubuntu Linux
- Vista Sidebar
- Visual Basic
- XML

Visual Encyclopedia™

Your A to Z reference of tools and techniques. Full color.

- Dreamweaver
- Excel
- Mac OS
- Photoshop
- Windows

Visual Quick Tips

Shortcuts, tricks, and techniques for getting more done in less time. Full color.

- Crochet
- Digital Photography
- Excel
- Internet
- iPod & iTunes
- Knitting
- Mac OS
- MySpace
- Office
- PowerPoint
- Windows
- Wireless Networking

Visual
An Imprint of ®WILEY
Now you know.